Festivals and the City

The Contested Geographies
of Urban Events

Edited by
Andrew Smith, Guy Osborn
and Bernadette Quinn

Festivals and the City

The Contested Geographies
of Urban Events

Edited by
Andrew Smith, Guy Osborn
and Bernadette Quinn

University of Westminster Press
www.uwestminsterpress.co.uk

Published by
University of Westminster Press
115 New Cavendish Street
London W1W 6UW
www.uwestminsterpress.co.uk

First published 2022
Cover: Diana Jarvis
Front cover image: © Andy Hughes/Fanatic

Print and digital versions typeset by Siliconchips Services Ltd.

ISBN (Hardback): 978-1-915445-01-8
ISBN (Paperback): 978-1-914386-44-2
ISBN (PDF): 978-1-914386-45-9
ISBN (EPUB): 978-1-914386-46-6
ISBN (Mobi): 978-1-914386-47-3

DOI: https://doi.org/10.16997/book64

The full text of this book has been peer-reviewed to ensure
high academic standards. For full review policies,
see: http://www.uwestminsterpress.co.uk/site/publish.

To read the free, open access version of this book online,
visit https://www.uwestminsterpress.co.uk/site/books
/10.16997/book64 or scan this QR code with your
mobile device:

Contents

List of Tables

List of Figures

Preface

This book explores the concept of urban festivity, with a particular focus on how festivals and events affect city spaces and the communities that use them. The book emanates from the research project, 'Festivals, Events and Inclusive Urban Public Spaces in Europe' (FESTSPACE) which was funded via the Humanities in the European Research Area (HERA) programme 'Public Spaces: Culture and Integration in Europe'. This programme aimed to '... mobilise the wide range of multi-disciplinary perspectives necessary to [advance] the understanding of relationships between 'public space' culture and other phenomena, such as, European integration' (HERA 2019). The FESTSPACE project addressed this theme through the lens of how festivals and events affect public spaces, focusing on how interactions between people from different cultural, ethnic, socio-economic and other backgrounds might be fostered and the extent to which '... diversity is embedded in the conception, organisation and delivery of festivals and events and the wider effects of this involvement' (FESTSPACE 2019).

FESTSPACE is a collaborative project involving five European institutions: the University of the West of Scotland, University of Westminster, Technological University Dublin, Universitat Oberta de Catalunya and the University of Gothenburg. Alongside contributions from authors based at four of these institutions, this book features chapters written by a range of authors based at other universities. These authors were engaged via themed sessions convened for the 2020 RGS-IBG Annual Conference entitled *Festivals and the City:*

The Festivalisation of Public Space. A call for papers was issued in early 2020 and this attracted a large number of abstracts. The conference was ultimately postponed due to the pandemic, so an online symposium was convened in September 2020 instead. This was organised by the FESTSPACE team and sponsored by the Geographies of Leisure and Tourism Research Group, a Royal Geographical Society research group. All but one of the chapters that feature here were either produced as part of the FESTSPACE project or presented at the *Festivals and the City* Symposium.

Given the timeframe of the FESTSPACE project (2019–2022), and the Festivals and the City symposium, related research was affected by the impact of the Covid-19 pandemic which brought the roles played by public spaces, events and festivals into sharp relief. Indeed, Covid-19-related cancellations in 2020 and, to a lesser extent in 2021, served to emphasise how important festivals are to the economic, social and cultural functioning of contemporary cities. Cancelling or postponing festivals deprived some citizens of their chance to earn an income, whilst for others the absence of festivals impoverished their social and cultural lives. Some city dwellers were relieved that the disruption caused by festivals was temporarily absent, but many others were left feeling bereft that an attractive part of urban living and a key aspect of their city's identity had been taken away. The pause in festivals and events and the experimental reconfiguration of festivity in this period provided a rare chance to reflect on their significance for contemporary cities, and an opportunity to think about how programmes of festivals and events might be realigned to ensure they prioritise the needs of citizens. Organised gatherings of people were discouraged in the era of Covid-19, but as the various waves of the pandemic subsided, festivals and other events were important ways of encouraging people back into European city centres. This suggests that the Coronavirus pandemic merely interrupted, rather than ended, the growing significance of urban festivals in the first two decades of the twenty-first century.

References

FESTSPACE. 2019. Festivals, Events and Inclusive Urban Spaces in Europe. Available at: https://heranet.info/projects/public-spaces-culture-and-integration -in-europe/festivals-events-and-inclusive-urban-public-spaces-in-europe/ (accessed 12 January 2022).

HERA. 2019. Public Spaces: Culture and integration in Europe 2019–2022. Available at: https://heranet.info/projects/public-spaces-culture-and-inte gration-in-europe/ (accessed 12 January 2022).

CHAPTER I

Introduction: Festivalisation as a Contested Urban Strategy

Andrew Smith, Guy Osborn and Bernadette Quinn

Festivals are important features of contemporary cities that can be understood as celebrations or attractions, but also as agents of urban change. City festivals are associated with a range of intended and unintended outcomes for host places: from community building to commercialisation. Festivals can create visual spectacles, but also distinct soundscapes and atmospheres. They occupy urban spaces, but are also inherently linked to time, allowing for fascinating spatial and temporal analyses of their effects. As such festivals and festivalisation can help illuminate a range of issues relevant to urban studies and urban geography. Festivals have long been understood as distinct time-spaces, defined by their contrast to the everyday. However, it is increasingly clear that festivals are better understood as phenomena linked to the quotidian workings of the city: with urban districts redeveloped as festive places, and festivals appropriated as an urban *strategy*.

The key themes addressed by this book are the contested geographies of festival spaces and places and the role of festivals in the quest for more inclusive cities. Festivals and events are often used by municipal authorities to break down symbolic barriers that restrict who uses public spaces and what those spaces are used for. However, the rise of commercial festivals and ticketed

How to cite this book chapter:
Smith, A., Osborn, G. and Quinn, B. 2022. Introduction: Festivalisation as a Contested Urban Strategy. In: Smith, A., Osborn, G. and Quinn, B. (Eds.) *Festivals and the City: The Contested Geographies of Urban Events*. London: University of Westminster Press. Pp. 1–15. London: University of Westminster Press. DOI: https://doi.org/10.16997/book64.a. License: CC-BY-NC-ND 4.0

events means that they are also responsible for imposing physical and financial obstacles that reduce the accessibility of city parks, streets and squares. Even free festivals can be exclusive, with atmospheres and pressures to consume deterring some groups. Festival sites provide good examples of how urban spaces are de- and re-territorialised and tend to be highly contested. Alongside addressing the contested effects of urban festivals on the character and inclusivity of public spaces, the book addresses more general themes including the role of festivals in culture-led regeneration. Several chapters analyse festivals and events as economic development tools, and the book also covers contested representations of festival cities and the ways related images and stories are used in place marketing.

The use and management of urban places and public spaces varies in different parts of the world, and this book focuses deliberately on Western European cities. This is a particularly interesting context given the socio-cultural issues associated with high levels of in-migration and concerns over the commercialisation and privatisation of public spaces. Festivals and events are linked to these issues in complex ways – they can contribute to urban commercialisation, but are also commonly used as policy responses to achieve more inclusive cities (Quinn et al. 2021). The geographical focus of the book also means we can assess whether positive accounts of festivals and festivalisation in North American cities – for example in recent books by Wynn (2015) and Delgado (2016) – reflect experiences in Western Europe.

A range of cases from across Western Europe are used to explore these issues, including chapters on some of Europe's most significant and contested festival cities: Venice, Edinburgh, London and Barcelona. The book also covers a wide range of festivals including those dedicated to music and the arts, but also events celebrating particular histories, identities and pastimes. Chapters address multiple festival genres: from the Venice Biennale and Dublin Festival of History to music festivals in Rotterdam and craft beer festivals in Manchester. Festivals are central to various international schemes such as the European Capitals of Culture programme, but also the UNESCO Creative Cities initiative which nominates cities of literature, film and music. Several of the cases featured in this book have been awarded one of these titles.

The diverse and innovative qualities of the book are also enhanced by the range of urban spaces covered: obvious examples of public spaces are addressed such as parks, streets, squares and piazzas, but the book includes chapters on indoor public spaces (e.g. city libraries) and blue spaces (canals) too. This reflects our interpretation of public spaces as socio-material entities: they are produced informally through their use – including for festivals and events – as well as through their formal designation, design and management.

The book examines these issues through multiple chapters arranged into 4 sections. Several contributions analyse how festivals and events affect urban public spaces (section 1), in particular their effects on their inclusivity (section 2). The book also examines the ways that festivals influence representations of space via their communication of visual images and narratives (section 3). To counter the focus on major European cities (Barcelona, Manchester, Glasgow, Rotterdam) and national capitals (London, Dublin, Edinburgh) in the first three sections, the final section of the book analyses the significance of festivals for, and impact on, smaller towns and cities. This final section examines the economic development rationale underpinning many city festivals and explores how this influences their social and cultural value. The book concludes with a summary of core themes, but also some forward looking analysis that examines how urban festivals may develop in the future.

To provide a foundation for the chapters and case studies that follow, some key trends, ideas and processes are introduced below. These include shifting definitions of what we mean by city festivals; the contemporary role of festivals and events in urban strategies and place-making; and finally, the notion of festivalisation, a trend which highlights the contested nature of urban festivals.

A Movable Feast: The Shifting Meaning of Festivals

The contemporary notion of a *festival* is increasingly ubiquitous and hard to define. The positive connotations associated with the term mean it has been adopted by a wide variety of organisations to refer to a wide variety of events. The word festival derives from 'feasts' and in English it was first used as an adjective, and then a noun, to refer to religious celebrations or seasonal rituals (Rönstrom 2016). This term was subsequently adopted to describe extended arts events, both in the world of high arts (e.g. opera, theatre, dance) and, later, in popular culture – for example in the fields of rock music and comedy. In this latter phase, festivals became associated with experimentation and counter-culture(s) that challenged the status quo. In the contemporary era, the term has been 'mainstreamed' and festivals now include a wide range of pop concerts and industry-oriented events – for example, film festivals. Festivals dedicated to consumption are now common too. Examples include those dedicated to food and beer which, in line with the etymology outlined above, are perhaps more accurately described as eating and drinking festivals. The notion of using festivals to generate footfall for local businesses has also spawned a series of consumer-oriented festivals, such the Dubai Shopping Festival (Peter and Anandkumar 2014) and the Glasgow Style Mile Shopping Festival (Smith et al. 2021). Some sports events also use the term to highlight their extended length and cultural significance. The Cheltenham Festival – 28 horse races staged over 4 days every March – is perhaps the most famous example (Oakley 2014).

One of the defining features of urban festivals is their extended duration – they are usually programmed over multiple days, or even several weeks. This means there are similarities between a festival and a 'season' of events. Organising and theming events in this way is an established practice but, in the contemporary era, turning a set of disparate events into a coherent festival has become an event portfolio management strategy (Antchak, Ziakas and Getz 2019). Festivals are formed by linking together a series of events that share a common theme or happen at a particular time of year: for example, winter festivals (Foley and McPherson 2007). Just to add to confusion over what a contemporary urban festival is, festival branding is also used to infuse dull sounding meetings, conferences and exhibitions with a festive flavour. Academics are culpable here: there is, after all, a Festival of Social Science, and several London Universities (including the University of Westminster) have launched Graduate School festivals. In short, the ubiquitous use of the term has caused confusion and ambiguity regarding what a festival actually is. This trend, plus the high turnover of festivals, means working out how many festivals are staged in a particular city has become nearly impossible.

One consequence of the broadening use of the term festival outlined above is to blur the distinction between festivals and events. According to Rönstrom (2016), the renaming of events as festivals is a key dimension of the ongoing process of festivalisation. In conventional usage, a festival involves multiple, festive, events staged across several days, united by a shared theme and location. However, the extended use of the term festival to describe one-day events, plus the introduction of festival elements to make mundane events more interesting, has further blurred the differentiation. This is highlighted by some of the chapters featured here where the term festivals and events are used interchangeably (e.g. Chapter 2 and Chapter 5) and, indeed, the title of this book!

Festivals and Urban Strategy

There is an established and large body of literature that examines festivals and festivity, with some of the most influential work produced by sociologists (Durkheim 1976 [1912]), anthropologists (Turner 1978) and folklorists (Falassi 1987). Many festival ideas and theories are derived from sociological analysis of religion, and authors such as Ehenrieich (2007) have applied key ideas (e.g. Durkheim's notion of collective effervescence) from this body of work to explain the popularity of contemporary (secular) festivals. There is also some very interesting historical work on the festivals of the medieval city which highlights how festivity shaped urban buildings and districts (Browne, Frost and Lucas 2019). Festivities not only helped to shape the design of places like Venice, they allowed these cities to impose political dominance over their rivals (Delanty, Giorgi and Sassatelli 2011).

Perhaps because of the links with marginality and liminality, festivals were traditionally regarded by academics as ex-urban phenomena that existed beyond the confines of the modern city. In recent years, there has been more focus on city festivals and their urban geographies. This attention corresponds to the re-emergence of urban festivity in the late modern era (Richards and Palmer 2010), and the rise of festival genres that are intrinsically urban: for example, film festivals and art biennales. A new focus on city festivals is also a response to the *urbanisation* of festivals that were previously associated with rural or peripheral sites: for example, music festivals and food festivals (Smith 2016).

Understanding the role of festivals play in shaping cities has been advanced via a series of recent books, including Gold and Gold's (2020) work on the historical evolution of *Festival Cities*, Wynn's (2015) book *Music/City* which analyses urban music festivals in the US, and Richards and Palmer's (2010) influential text *Eventful Cities* which has a strong focus on European cultural festivals. Academic analyses of festivals now tend to be genuinely multi- or interdisciplinary with important contributions from theatre, media, tourism, marketing, and music academics supplementing work produced by researchers working in the fields of sociology, cultural studies and anthropology. The coherence of the literature on festivals has also been advanced by the emergence of a discernible field of work dedicated to festival or festive studies (Fournier 2019), and by the critical turn in event studies (Robertson et al. 2018).

In terms of the urban geographies of festivals, influential texts include Bernadette Quinn's (2005) paper in *Urban Studies* which focused on the relationship between arts festivals and the city. A subsequent paper by Gordon Waitt published in *Geography Compass* in 2008 reinforced the idea that festivals were important urban phenomena that needed to be analysed critically, taking into account the 'powerful globalising and neoliberalising tendencies' (Waitt 2008, 515). More recently Finkel and Platt (2020), writing in the same journal, analysed the urban geography of festivals, highlighting the ways that festivals are used in various policy fields; particularly in urban regeneration, place marketing and in efforts to achieve community cohesion. These papers have been influential in communicating the idea that festivals are now 'go-to' options for municipal authorities seeking to address a wide range of urban problems (Richards and Palmer 2010). For example, Richards and Palmer (2010) define an eventful city as one that purposefully uses festivals and events to support long-term policy agendas; and Wynn (2015) suggests festivals represent a 'serious cultural strategy'.

This notion of the festival as an urban 'strategy' is criticised by some authors for constituting a rather superficial and insubstantial response to deeper rooted issues. For example, Quinn (2005) notes that festivals are seen by some cities as a 'quick fix' solution to their image problems. Using de Certeau's terminology, the rise of festival cities is a good example of the 'concept city' that simplifies the multiplicities of city life to convey an appealing unified impression (Jamieson 2004). Others are even more critical, arguing that festivals represent an attempt by some cities to 'cover up' urban problems, hiding inequities behind a 'carnival mask' (Harvey 1989). Critical commentators also worry that using festivals as urban strategies compromises the integrity of festivals, prioritising their instrumental value over their wider social and cultural significance. The established (socio-cultural) and the emerging (strategic) functions of festivals are often seen as incompatible. As Finkel and Platt (2020, 2) contend: 'contemporary festivals now often exhibit complex and uneasy tensions between the socio-economic strategies of commercialised neoliberal cities and the cultural needs of diverse communities to gather and celebrate'. This is why some authors reject the reconfiguration of festivals as urban strategies. For example, Reece (2020, 109) asserts that, whilst festivals can be used strategically, 'a festival is not a strategy'.

Whilst some stakeholders may try to protect the integrity of arts and cultural festivals from their reconfiguration as urban policy tools, we should recognise that policy oriented festivals can still have very positive social and cultural effects. And we cannot ignore the fact that some festivals were established to strategically assist urban areas. In other words, they have always been strategic interventions rather than artistic, social or cultural phenomena. Film festivals are a good example: many of these events were established for economic reasons: for example, the Cannes Film Festival (est. 1946) was launched to prolong the tourist season. The Brighton Festival (est. 1967) was created for similar reasons. The re-establishment of the Venice Carnival in 1979, following a long hiatus, was also a deliberate attempt to address some of the issues the city was facing at that time, including the lack of provision for young people (Davis and Marvin 2004). These festivities have not been appropriated as urban policy tools: they have always been staged with wider objectives in mind.

The Geographies of Urban Festivals

Whilst most analyses of festivals tend to focus on their temporal dimensions and the way they create 'time out of time' (Falassi 1987), there is less attention to their geographies. This is a major oversight as city festivals tend to be unevenly distributed and skewed towards central sites (see, for example, Chapter 3 in this volume), something that adds to the contested status of festivals (see Chapter 11). Some recent texts have attempted to summarise the geographical distribution of urban festivals. Several texts highlight the disparity between cities – why some cities seem to be more festive than others – whilst others examine the internal geographies of festival provision. For example, Wynn (2015) has developed a conceptualisation of music festivals that explains how they tend to occupy contemporary (US) cities. He identifies 3 key common configurations – the citadel, core, and confetti patterns – which help us to understand the density, turbulence and porosity of urban festivals and the significance of these critical characteristics (Wynn 2015). In a similar vein, Smith et al. (2021) have analysed the different ways that urban public spaces are occupied by festivals and events: these authors identify nine different event types according to their accessibility (free, sometimes free, paid entry) and mobility (mobile audience, semi-mobile audience, static audience). The notion of mobile festivals is also the subject of Marin's (2001) work on perambulatory festivals – parades, processions and corteges. Marin's work is also inherently geographical as he highlights the significance of the routes selected, particularly the beginning and end points, but also the direction taken.

Any attempt to analyse the geography of urban festivity has to tackle the complex and highly significant relationship between festival and place. Duffy (2014, 229) suggests that the transformative capacity of festivals 'arises out of affective relations facilitated by the festival between people and place'. Reece (2020, 108) adopts a similar perspective and suggests that creating and presenting art during festivals 'gives people and communities a shared experience and a connection to place'. For Richards and Palmer (2010, 72) this is something created by festivals' open structure which 'encourages a more playful relationship between people, places and meaning'. Places can give festivals their meaning and identity, but the relationship is reciprocal: festivals can help to shape the meanings attached to places (Van Aalst and Van Melik 2012).

In many cases, city festivals are not merely festivals *in a place*, but festivals *of a place*: the host location is as important to the meaning of the occasion as the artforms on display. It is inconceivable that these latter examples could move to another city: they are *hallmark* events that are indelibly associated with their host city. Even when the focus is very much on the artform on display, rather than the venue, festivals 'seem to take on something of the character and aspects of the area in which they are situated' (Mitchell 1950, 7). To enhance their placefulness, festivals often occupy public spaces such as prominent parks, streets and squares in city centres (Smith 2016). This is a long established tradition. Quinn (2005) notes that the pioneering Avignon festival (est. 1947) envisaged that residents, organisers and artists would interact with each other and *with their place*. This trend has intensified in the contemporary era: for example the creative director of the Pop Montreal music festival has said 'we try to really be part of the city and make the city kind of the landscape where the festival happens' (cited in Wynn 2015, 18). Cities are keen to ensure that urban festivals are visibly located in recognisable places, to encourage place enriched festival experiences, but also to achieve various place marketing benefits.

Richards and Palmer (2010) see festivals and events as ideal vehicles to counter placelessness. However, the serial reproduction of successful festival genres and the globalisation of festival brands mean that some festivals now contribute to, rather than resolve, the problem of homogeneous and generic urbanism (Quinn 2005). Using a new type of arts festival – light art festivals – to generate off-season tourism, public art and after dark attractions is perhaps the latest example of a festival strategy that has proliferated globally (Giordano and Ong 2017). MacLeod (2006, 229) notes the emergence of festivals that are 'global in appeal, ungrounded in local identity'. This is a useful reminder that the relationship between place and festival is not always as strong as we might assume. As Van Aalst and Van Melik (2012) argue, festivals differ in their degree of place dependency, and the importance of place for festivals may be becoming weaker. Festival organisers often aim to create immersive experiences, consciously separated from quotidian urban experience, and the destination sought and experienced by attendees is often the festival space not the city place (Van Aalst and Van Melik 2012). We know much about what festivals do for places, but we need to better understand how places contribute to festivals and festival experiences. McClinchey and Carmichael (2010) note that more research is needed to examine the relationship between festivals and place, particularly the role of place perceptions and the ways these connect to experiences.

Festivals and City Making

There is a substantial amount of literature on the ways that one-off mega-events, including cultural events like the European Capital of Culture event and World Expos, are used in urban development and regeneration (Smith 2012). However, the relationship between *festivals* and urban development is less well understood. Festivals have long been associated with urban revitalisation – making cities more alive – but are less frequently linked to urban regeneration strategies. There are obvious reasons for this – regular festivals and smaller events do not require the construction of purpose-built arenas and new infrastructure in the same ways that sports mega-events seem to. However, festivals and urban regeneration *are* linked, both in obvious, material ways (new venues and physical facilities have been developed to stage festivals) but also more subtly. As urban regeneration is, ultimately, about instigating social and economic change as much as physical transformation, festivals can be used as catalysts for a softer, more people-oriented approach. As criticisms of top-down physical regeneration intensify because of related gentrification and reliance on trickle down effects, socio-economic development is arguably the most important and most justifiable form of urban change – particularly when it builds on what already exists. This highlights the potential of festivals to be catalysts for, or agents of, urban regeneration.

Jonathan Wynn has emerged in recent years as one of the key exponents of festival-led urban development. Wynn (2015, 228) argues that we now have seen the failings of high stake cultural projects such as those driven by sporting arenas, museums or entertainment districts, and suggests a festival-led strategy 'can more fluidly respond to the changing needs of the city, its residents and the audience'. He is not suggesting a radical alternative to neoliberal approaches which aim to reinvent cities as sites of consumption: Wynn suggests this objective can be achieved using temporary and flexible festivals rather than more permanent, concrete culture. In his view festivals not only provide experiences, they are 'effective tools for branding and promotion in the post-industrial, experience focused economy' (Wynn 2015, 43), and have the added bonus of bolstering not-for-profit organisations. This latter point is supported by Davies'

(2015) observation that we tend to underestimate the role of festivals in developing community leadership – a key factor in achieving positive urban change.

Wynn's notion that festivals could lead urban development in cities suffering from structural decline seems perhaps a little simplistic and optimistic, but his thesis is more convincing when viewed in conjunction with other ideas. In recent years, festivals have been increasingly understood as 'field-configuring events' (Lampel and Meyer 2008). This term was traditionally reserved for conferences, fairs and trade shows that bring key people and ideas together; forming the basis for new industrial clusters. But now various cultural festivals – from electronic music festivals (Colombo and Richards 2017) to light art festivals (Freire-Gibb and Lorentzen 2011) – are used to forge relationships with creative professionals, and to use the regular (albeit temporary) presence of those involved in the production of festivals to bolster local creative industries. Festivals involve the transfer of knowledge between cities via networks of festival professionals (Jarman 2021). And, as Comunian (2017) reminds us, festivals are also opportunities for artists to interact and learn from each other, and provide chances for local creatives to learn directly from the temporary influx of professionals from around the world. This means festivals can be used to nurture the development of creative industries. There are some fascinating cases where urban festivals have been used as the basis for more permanent creative clusters. One of the best examples is Roskilde in Denmark which has used its world famous rock festival (est. 1971) to develop Musicon Valley – a new district which hosts education and research organisations, a museum and small creative firms (Hjalager 2009). The project is described as both an 'offspring of a festival, which rebuilds itself from nothing every year, and of a historical city with a global heritage and proud traditions' (Musicon 2021). Other examples include a cluster of small businesses (and a museum) on the outskirts of Valencia which designs and produces the figures used in the city's hallmark festival *Las Fallas* (Richards and Palmer 2010).

The idea of field configuring events highlights that the economic value of festivals to cities lies in their production and their potential to boost creative enterprises, not just their potential to generate tourism, consumption and attractive images. And the *making* of city festivals is not merely something that can assist economic and cultural development, it can also assist social development too. The acts of planning, organising and making city festivals provide opportunities to get people involved – building connections, skills and confidence amongst host communities (Edensor 2018). If those involved are from a range of diverse social groups, or from disadvantaged backgrounds, there is great potential to assist community cohesion and marginalised people (Mair and Smith 2021). There are now a series of organisations that specialise in using the processes associated with festival making to build community development and assist disadvantaged groups. These include Handmade Parade, an organisation based in Hebden Bridge, West Yorkshire that works across various UK towns and cities to help local people put on festival parades for themselves. By organising workshops prior to events, and by taking those workshops to marginalised groups (carers, refugees, people with disabilities), Handmade Parade not only guarantee local involvement in festivities, they engineer positive social legacies from the making of the festival. This approach chimes with Reece's view that 'festivals are not audience engagement strategies. They are a critical act of community building' (Reece 2020, 105).

We started this section by arguing that one of the benefits of using festivals in urban policy is that it doesn't involve expensive, risky or exclusive physical transformations. However, in some instances, festivals have instigated physical changes to cities, something illustrated well by Gold and Gold's chapter on the Venice Biennale that features in this book (Chapter 9). Film festivals also provide good examples. Several cities have built a dedicated cinema to provide the key venue for their festival, including Rome which built a special cinema designed by Renzo Piano to launch a new festival in 2006. The critically acclaimed Tribeca Festival in New York (est. 2002) also has its own purpose built cinema, a structure which has assisted its founding mission: to assist the cultural revitalisation of Lower Manhattan in the wake of the 9/11 terrorist attacks (Wong 2011). In 2020 plans were announced to build a new Filmhouse for the Edinburgh International Film Festival which aimed to enhance the programme and the prominence of this event. Controversially, the new building is to be constructed in a public space which, in typically dismissive fashion, the developers argue is a deserted site that needs bringing to life (Murphy 2020). This depiction is somewhat ironic given the name of the public space earmarked to host the venue – Festival Square. The issue of exclusive festivals 'occupying' urban public spaces generates controversy, but the development of Edinburgh's Festival Square seems to be an even more extreme example of the ways that festivals can occupy, commodify and privatise public spaces. Giving a festival a permanent home with year round programming also seems to contradict some of the defining features of a festival. As Reece (2020, 108) notes 'a festival doesn't have to be an ephemeral thing that appears and disappears. Yet, critically it is not an institution or a venue'.

The significance of festivals to place-making in contemporary cities has been reinforced by the introduction or rebranding of sites, spaces and buildings as festival facilities. The most obvious examples are festival marketplaces which were initiated in the US by James Rouse and replicated across the world (Cudny 2016). There are also festival 'quarters' in various cities, such as Montreal, and individual festival buildings – most famously the Royal Festival Hall in London which was developed for the 1951 Festival of Britain. The history of sites as venues for notable festivals is sometimes inscribed into the names of contemporary facilities too. A good example is Festival Park in Stoke on Trent – a retail park built on the site of the 1986 Garden Festival. Festival branding is now being extended to settings with seemingly few links to urban festivity: for example, a redeveloped part of Poplar in East London has been renamed New Festival Quarter. At a wider spatial scale, entire districts are now promoted as Festival Boroughs – for example Tower Hamlets in east London (Koutrolikou 2012) – or Festival Cities. The most famous example of the latter is Edinburgh – a case discussed at length by Louise Todd in Chapter 11. Using festival branding to provide positive place identities and city images is a key way that festivals contribute to urban place-making, and this is addressed by several chapters that feature in this book, particularly in the third section which is dedicated to city narratives.

Urban Festivalisation: Festival Spaces as Contested Sites

Over the past two decades, various commentators have not only examined the roles played by festivals in cities, they have identified a process of urban festivalisation. This term is used by different authors to refer to various trends, so it is worth providing some clarity here as to what festivalisation means. At its most basic level, festivalisation involves an increase in the number of festivals and events that are staged in cities in general, and in public spaces in particular (Smith 2016). The rise of the experience economy and increased demand for events has driven this trend, but it is also due to the ways municipal authorities have enthusiastically adopted festivals and events as urban policy tools (Richards and Palmer 2010). At a more complex level, festivalisation involves the repackaging of culture as a festival – mainly to expand audiences and to increase the instrumental value of various art forms (Ronström 2016). This happens at the mega-event scale – for example, the festivalisation of national culture during the Olympic Games (Roche 2011), but it is now a feature of more mundane, everyday leisure too. A good example is the re-presentation of multiple cinema screenings as a film 'festival' (Négrier 2015).

This book is particularly interested in the festivalisation of urban public spaces, and so it is useful to apply the different interpretations of festivalisation to this specific context. Inevitably, an expansion in the number of city festivals means an expansion in the number of festivals staged in public spaces (Smith 2016). But the increased use of public spaces as venues is a deliberate rather than accidental trend with municipal authorities keen to animate and promote prominent parks, squares and streets, and to use festive spaces as sites to nurture communitas. This is reaffirmed by Wynn's (2015, 12) statement: 'I see festivalisation as not just the general rise of festivals but an ongoing organisational process wherein short-term events are used to develop, reinforce and exploit an array of communal goals'. Other uses of the term also highlight interesting trends. Festivalisation is used by some authors in a more narrowly defined way to refer to the tendency for city festivals to 'spill out' beyond their temporal and spatial boundaries (Duffy 2014). Following this interpretation, a city is festivalised when festivals are no longer confined to specific venues or specific time periods. This is why some authors, such as Richards and Palmer (2010), use the term festivalisation to refer to the ways the city has entered an almost permanent state of festivity.

Festivalisation is not merely a descriptive term that refers to recognised processes of change, it is also a loaded and pejorative concept that tends to be used by academics to connote problematic effects (Getz 2010). Indeed, festivalisation has become associated with neoliberalisation and the associated commercialisation, privatisation and securitisation of urban public spaces (Smith 2016). In this sense, the term helps us to understand why urban festival spaces are often regarded as exclusionary or contested sites – a key issue covered by various chapters in this book. However, some authors adopt a more positive perspective, including Wynn (2015) who argues that festivalisation is a cultural policy that combines cultural activity and place-making; and Newbold and Jordan (2015, xiv) who feel that festivalisation 'has become a key element in the endeavours of local governments to act out community cohesion policies and give cultural voices and diversity a platform'. This latter view is also reflected in Chalcraft and Magaudda's (2011, 175) nuanced take on festivalisation that recognises it is about city branding, but that festive space can also be 'democratic space where the performance of culture requires the interaction of artists, audience and locality'.

The festivalisation of urban public spaces is one of the key themes addressed in the first section of this book. This section includes four chapters, each written by one of the FESTSPACE project teams about their case study city (2019). These chapters are all dedicated to different types of public spaces: squares, streets, parks, plus indoor public spaces. Chapter 2 addresses the festivalisation of London's parks; Chapter 3 focuses on the types and locations of festivals and events that are staged in Barcelona (particularly in the city's streets); and Chapter 4 addresses the ways a prominent square in Glasgow is used and designed as a venue for events. The final chapter in Part 1 examines a different type of public space: libraries (in Dublin). These spaces have also been transformed into venues for festivals and events.

References

Antchak, Vladimir, Vassilios Ziakas and Donald Getz. 2019. *Event Portfolio Management: Theory and Methods for Event Management and Tourism*. Oxford: Goodfellow Publishers.

Browne, Jemma, Christian Frost and Ray Lucas (Eds.) 2019. *Architecture, Festival and the City*. Abingdon: Routledge.

Chalcraft, Jasper and Paolo Magaudda. 2011. Space in the Place. In Gerard Delanty, Liana Giorgi and Monica Sassatelli (Eds.) *Festivals and the Cultural Public Sphere*, pp. 173–189. Abingdon: Routledge.

Colombo, Alba and Greg Richards. 2017. Eventful Cities as Global Innovation Catalysts: The Sónar Festival Network. *Event Management*, 21(5), 621–634.

Comunian, Roberta. 2017. Temporary Clusters and Communities of Practice in the Creative Economy: Festivals as Temporary Knowledge Networks. *Space and Culture*, 20(3), 329–343.

Cudny, Waldemar. 2016. Manufaktura in Łódź, Poland: An Example of a Festival Marketplace. *Norsk Geografisk Tidsskrift-Norwegian Journal of Geography*, 70(5), 276–291.

Davies, Amanda. 2015. Life After a Festival: Local Leadership and the Lasting Legacy of Festivals. *Event Management*, 19(4), 433–444.

Davis, Robert C. and Garry R. Marvin. 2004. *Venice, the Tourist Maze: A Cultural Critique of the World's Most Touristed City*. Berkeley, CA: University of California Press.

Delanty, Gerard, Liana Giorgi and Monica Sassatelli. 2011. Urban Festivals and the Cultural Public Sphere: Cosmopolitanism Between Ethics and Aesthetics. In Gerard Delanty, Liana Giorgi and Monica Sassatelli (Eds.) *Festivals and the Cultural Public Sphere*, pp. 24–40. Abingdon: Routledge.

Delgado, Melvin. 2016. *Celebrating Urban Community Life: Fairs, Festivals, Parades, and Community Practice*. Toronto: University of Toronto Press.

Duffy, Michelle. 2014. The Emotional Ecologies of Festivals. In Jody Taylor and Andy Bennett (Eds.) *The Festivalization of Culture*, pp. 229–250. Farnham: Ashgate.

Durkheim, Émile. 1976 [1912]. *The Elementary Forms of Religious Life*. London: George Allen and Unwin.

Edensor, Tim. 2018. Moonraking in Slaithwaite: Making Lanterns, Making Place. In Laura Price and Harriet Hawkins (Eds.) *Geographies of Making, Craft and Creativity*, pp. 44–59. Abingdon: Routledge.

Ehrenreich, Barbara. 2007. *Dancing in the Streets: A History of Collective Joy*. London: Granta.

Falassi, Alessandro. 1987. *Time Out Of Time: Essays on the Festival*. Alburqurque, NM: University of New Mexico Press.

FESTSPACE. 2019. Festivals, Events and Inclusive Urban Spaces in Europe. Available at: https://heranet.info/projects/public-spaces-culture-and-inte gration-in-europe/festivals-events-and-inclusive-urban-public-spaces-in -europe (accessed 12 January 2022).

Finkel, Rebecca and Louise Platt. 2020. Cultural Festivals and the City. *Geography Compass* 14(9), e12498, 1–12. https://doi.org/10.1111/gec3.12498

Foley, Malcolm and Gayle McPherson. 2007. Glasgow's Winter Festival: Can Cultural Leadership Serve the Common Good? *Managing Leisure*, 12(2–3), 143–156.

Fournier, Laurent Sébastien. 2019. Traditional Festivals: From European Ethnology to Festive Studies. *Journal of Festive Studies*, 1(1), 11–26.

Freire-Gibb, Lucio Carlos and Anne Lorentzen. 2011. A Platform for Local Entrepreneurship: The Case of the Lighting Festival of Frederikshavn. *Local Economy*, 26(3), 157–169.

Getz, Donald. 2010. The Nature and Scope of Festival Studies in *International Journal of Event Management Research*, 5(1), 1–47.

Giordano, Emanuele and Chin-Ee Ong. 2017. Light Festivals, Policy Mobilities and Urban Tourism. *Tourism Geographies*, 19(5), 699–716.

Gold, John R. and Margaret M. Gold. 2020. *Festival Cities: Culture, Planning and Urban Life*. Abingdon: Routledge.

Harvey, David. 1989. *The Condition of Postmodernity: An Enquiry into the Origins of Cultural Change*. Oxford: Blackwell.

Hjalager, Anne-Mette. 2009. Cultural Tourism Innovation Systems– The Roskilde Festival. *Scandinavian Journal of Hospitality and Tourism*, 9(2–3), 266–287.

Jamieson, Kirstie. 2004. Edinburgh: The Festival Gaze and its Boundaries. *Space and Culture*, 7(1), 64–75.

Jarman, David. 2021. Festival to Festival: Networked Relationships between Fringe Festivals. *Event Management*, 25(1), 99–113.

Koutrolikou, Penny-Panagiota. 2012. Spatialities of Ethnocultural Relations in Multicultural East London: Discourses of Interaction and Social Mix. *Urban Studies*, 49(10), 2049–2066.

Lampel, Joseph and Alan Meyer. 2008. Field-Configuring Events as Structuring Mechanisms: How Conferences, Ceremonies, and Trade Shows Constitute New Technologies, Industries, and Markets. *Journal of Management Studies*, 45(6), 1025–1035.

MacLeod, Nicola E. 2006. The Placeless Festival: Identity and Place in the Post-Modern Festival. In David Picard and Mike Robinson (Eds.) *Festivals, Tourism and Social Change: Remaking Worlds*, pp. 222–237. Clevedon: Channel View Publications.

Mair, Judith and Andrew Smith. 2021. Events and Sustainability: Why Making Events More Sustainable is Not Enough. *Journal of Sustainable Tourism*, 29(11/12), 1739–1755.

Marin, Louis. 2001. *On Representation*. Stanford, CA: Stanford University Press.

McClinchey, Kelley A. and Barbara A. Carmichael. 2010. The Role and Meaning of Place in Cultural Festival Visitor Experiences. In Michael Morgan, Peter Lugosi and J.R. Brent Ritchie (Eds.) *The Tourism and Leisure Experience*, pp. 59–78. Bristol: Channel View Publications.

Mitchell, Donald. 1950. British Festivals: Some Comments on their Customs. *Tempo* 16, 6–11.

Murphy, Richard. 2020. New FilmHouse, Edinburgh, 2020. Available at: https://www.richardmurphyarchitects.com/New-Filmhouse-Edinburgh

Musicon. 2021. About Musicon. Available at: https://www.musicon.dk/da-dk/about-musicon

Négrier, Emmanuel. 2015. Festivalisation: Patterns and Limits. In Chris Newbold, Christopher Maughan, Jennie Jordan and Franco Bianchini. (Eds.) *Focus on Festivals*, pp.18–27. Oxford: Goodfellow Publishers.

Newbold, Chris and Jennie Jordan (Eds.) 2016. *Focus on World Festivals: Contemporary Case Studies and Perspectives*. Oxford: Goodfellow Publishers.

Oakley, Robin. 2014. *The Cheltenham Festival: A Centenary History*. London: Aurum.

Peter, Sangeeta and Victor Anandkumar. 2014. Dubai Shopping Festival: Tourists' Nationality and Travel Motives. *International Journal of Event and Festival Management*, 5(2), 116–131.

Quinn, Bernadette, Alba Colombo, Kristina Lindström, David McGillivray and Andrew Smith. 2021. Festivals, Public Space and Cultural Inclusion: Public Policy Insights. *Journal of Sustainable Tourism*, 29(11–12), 1875–1893.

Quinn, Bernadette. 2005. Arts Festivals and the City. *Urban Studies*, 42(5–6), 927–943.

Reece, Anna. 2020. The Role of Festival Making. In Jade Lillie, Kate Larsen, Cara Kirkwood and Jax Jacki Brown (Eds.) *The Relationship is the Project: Working with Communities*, pp. 103–109. Melbourne: Brow Books.

Richards, Greg and Robert Palmer. 2010. *Eventful Cities: Cultural Management and Urban Revitalisation*. Oxford: Butterworth-Heinemann.

Robertson, Martin, Faith Ong, Leonie Lockstone-Binney and Jane Ali-Knight. 2018. Critical Event Studies: Issues and Perspectives. *Event Management*, 22(6), 865–874.

Roche, Maurice. 2011. Festivalisation, Cosmopolitanism and European Culture. In Gerard Delanty, Liana Giorgi and Monica Sassatelli (Eds.) *Festivals and the Cultural Public Sphere*, pp. 124–141. Abingdon: Routledge.

Ronström, Owe. 2016. Four Facets of Festivalisation. *Puls – Journal for Ethnomusicology and Ethnochoreology*, 1(1), 67–83.

Smith, Andrew. 2012. *Events and Urban Regeneration: The Strategic Use of Events to Revitalise Cities*. Abingdon: Routledge.

Smith, Andrew. 2016. *Events in the City: Using Public Spaces as Event Venues*. Abingdon: Routledge.

Smith, Andrew, Goran Vodicka, Alba Colombo, Kristina N. Lindstrom, David McGillivray and Bernadette Quinn. 2021. Staging City Events in Public Spaces: An Urban Design Perspective. *International Journal of Event and Festival Management*, 12(2), 224–239

Turner, Victor. 1978. In and Out of Time: Festivals, Liminality, and Communitas. *Festival of American Folklife*, 7–8.

Van Aalst, Irina and Rianne Van Melik. 2012. City Festivals and Urban Development: Does Place Matter? *European Urban and Regional Studies*, 19(2), 195–206.

Waitt, Gordon. 2008. Urban Festivals: Geographies of Hype, Helplessness and Hope. *Geography Compass*, 2(2), 513–537.

Wong, Cindy Hing-Yuk. 2011. *Film Festivals: Culture, People and Power on the Global Screen*. New Brunswick, NJ: Rutgers University Press.

Wynn, Jonathan R. 2015. *Music/City: American Festivals and Placemaking in Austin, Nashville and Newport*. Chicago, IL: University of Chicago Press.

PART I

Festivals and Urban Public Space

CHAPTER 2

The Festivalisation of London's Parks: The Friends' Perspective

Andrew Smith, Guy Osborn and Goran Vodicka

Introduction

Public parks are deemed to be pivotal spaces in the drive to make our cities more liveable, more equitable and, ultimately, more sustainable. This ambitious agenda highlights one of the biggest challenges facing those tasked with managing parks: they are now asked to serve an increasing number of functions: as places to escape, socialise, play and relax, but also as 'green infrastructure' or 'ecological services' that absorb CO_2, cool our cities and provide habitats for wildlife. Parks are also viewed as assets that can be hired out, add value to real estate, or attract tourists. These varied functions are not always compatible, creating tensions and conflicts over what and who city parks are for.

Contested uses and debates over whether parks should be more focused on environments or entertainments are perhaps most obviously illustrated in disputes over park festivals and events (Smith 2018). In recent years, reflecting wider processes witnessed in other types of urban space, there has been a 'festivalisation' of some city parks, with festivals and events used to populate, animate, promote and subsidise green spaces (Smith 2016). Parks have long

How to cite this book chapter:
Smith, A., Osborn, G. and Vodicka, G. 2022. The Festivalisation of London's Parks: The Friends' Perspective. In: Smith, A., Osborn, G. and Quinn, B. (Eds.) *Festivals and the City: The Contested Geographies of Urban Events*. London: University of Westminster Press. Pp. 19–37. London: University of Westminster Press. DOI: https://doi.org/10.16997/book64.b. License: CC-BY-NC-ND 4.0

been 'eventful' (Richards and Palmer 2010), but there are signs that the number and range of events staged has grown (London Assembly 2017), partly due to the increased demand for experiences, but also because events have become key tools to help achieve various public policies. As Wynn (2015: 12) notes in his definition of festivalisation, festivals and events are now used to 'develop, reinforce, and exploit an array of communal goals'.

This chapter examines park festivalisation with particular reference to one particular city, London, and one set of stakeholders, Friends of Parks groups (hereafter Friends groups). London is well known for its green spaces and, during the Victorian era, the city played an influential role in the development of public parks (Elborough 2015). In 2019 London became the world's first National Park City, a title partly justified by the large proportion of the city designated as green space. London has approximately 3,000 parks and, over the past 35 years, Friends groups have formed to help protect and maintain them. There are now estimated to be over 600 groups representing parks and green spaces in London (LFGN 2021). Many of these were established to respond to various threats facing public parks, particularly reductions in local authority budgets. Alternative funding sources – such as grants awarded by the Heritage Lottery Fund – encouraged groups to be established as community involvement was a condition of grant aid (Speller and Ravenscroft 2005). Friends of Parks in the UK are notably different from Friends of Parks in other countries. In the US they tend to represent a new approach to management and funding which relies on private donations. For example, in New York, the Friends of the High Line not only programme, maintain and operate this new park, they raise nearly 100% of the High Line's annual budget (thehighline.org). In the UK, Friends groups are essentially user groups, and involve volunteers who campaign to maintain and improve parks. As Whitten (2019) highlights, UK Friends groups aim to complement, rather than replace, local authority management and maintenance. However, there is considerable variation in the roles and responsibilities that these groups adopt, with some functioning as heritage appreciation societies, whilst others are more focused on campaigning, or contributing volunteer labour.

In this chapter we focus on the Friends' perspective for four reasons. First, because Friends groups have become key stakeholders in the management of parks – groups across London now help to protect, maintain and improve many of the capital's green spaces. Second, whilst they are not necessarily representative of all park users, Friends groups represent people who use parks on a regular basis. Third, because funding and organising festivals and events are activities that Friends are directly involved in. Fourth and finally, we focus on Friends groups because some of these groups have led high profile campaigns against festivals and events staged in parks (Smith 2019). As such, Friends groups offer informed and involved perspectives on festivals and events staged in London's parks – and one that has been hitherto ignored in published research.

The overriding aims of this chapter are to explore how London's parks are programmed as venues, and to establish what Friends groups think about the festivals and events that are staged in their parks. We begin with a short review of relevant literature and a synopsis of the methods used to collect data on park events in London. We then outline the range of festivals and events that were staged in London's parks in 2019 and summarise the impacts these have, according to Friends groups. The chapter also discusses how Friends groups are themselves involved in events, and how these groups are incorporated into decision making. The chapter also addresses the extent to which park events represent the communities that live nearby. We conclude that it is relevant to apply the notion of festivalisation to explain processes affecting London parks in the years preceding the Covid-19 pandemic. The outcomes of festivals and events vary and depend on the types of events and types of spaces under consideration: events are seen as good ways to attract and diversify users, but they are also associated with exclusion and environmental damage. To help address the negative impacts identified and to ensure events are more inclusive, a series of recommendations are provided to help guide future practice.

The Festivalisation of Parks

Festivalisation is a term that describes the increases in the number and size of festivals in recent years, but also the ways that culture and space is organised and presented in a festival-like way (Rönstrom 2016). The notion of festivalisation is often applied to urban public spaces, but research on urban streets and squares tends to dominate this body of work. Texts that explicitly address the festivalisation of urban green spaces are rare, even though this process seems to be equally relevant to city parks. Park settings have long been used for festivals and events but in recent years there seems to have been a marked increase in the number and range of events staged (London Assembly 2017). There are multiple, overlapping reasons for this trend: the mission to encourage more people and different types of users to parks; the aim to make parks more visible; the push to modernise outdated parks; the need to generate commercial income to offset cuts to grant funding; and increased demand for events generally. In cities like London, where there seems to be a shortage of large outdoor spaces, parks are regularly utilised as event venues, particularly in the summer months (Smith 2019).

One of the main benefits of park events at various scales is that they can attract new users and encourage social interactions between them. This allows open spaces to be reconstituted as sociable, *public* spaces that are more welcoming to a wider set of users (Barker et al. 2019). In Neal et al.'s (2015) research, organised parks events and celebratory occasions were identified as moments of diversity and amicable interaction by participants. Their findings suggest park events are effective ways of encouraging people from different ethnic groups to come to parks: indeed, interviewees talked positively about the 'ethnic diversity of park events' such as Fun Days. In Neal et al.'s research, feelings of connectivity to culturally different others were also noted as positive impacts of staging organised events. Similarly, Gobster (2002, 157) suggests that park events are effective vehicles for nurturing multiculturalism: 'the park serves as a logical centre of activity for festivals or a cultural centre that celebrates the multicultural population of park users'. There is also evidence that festivals and events can connect people with park spaces, building greater affinity, attachment and involvement. Perry, Ager and Sitas (2020, 613) note that: 'linking a cultural event with natural and/or built heritage can build people's sense of belonging and pride, especially if focused at a local or regional audience'.

The literature on parks also highlights that events and other forms of entertainment have allowed parks to transcend their origins and become more than just sites of passive leisure (Elborough 2015). This has led to more 'active' parks, with organised fun and social mixing usurping parks' traditional functions as spaces for quiet contemplation and encounters with nature (Jones and Wills 2005). An event function is now designed into many parks. Obvious examples include bandstands, event pavilions and outdoor theatres, but other design features such as sloping lawns and hard standing areas also make green spaces more suitable for large-scale events. Designing contemporary parks as eventful spaces is something indelibly associated with Tschumi's design for Parc de Villette in Paris, which was intended to be a model for the urban park of the twenty-first century (Hardingham and Rattenbury 2011). Tschumi designed an urban and dynamic park – a park of culture, not nature – which essentially provided a setting for events.

Nam and Dempsey's (2020) recent research found that residents of Sheffield, UK, were generally positive about events staged in their parks. Of the 500+ people they questioned, 79% were positive about fun days and fairs, although there was less support for music festivals (60% positive) and circuses (34% positive). Their research concluded that there is broad acceptance of events in parks amongst park professionals and community groups, a finding which is 'at odds with dominant discourses in academic literature that parks should be protected from commodification and commercialisation' (Nam and Dempsey 2020, 8). Academic texts tend to emphasise that parks are increasingly hired out for commercial events, something which provides an important income stream for sites suffering from government cutbacks and under-investment (Smith 2020). Accordingly, events have become indelibly associated with the notion of self-funded, 'entrepreneurial' parks with users increasingly regarded as consumers, rather than citizens (Loughran 2014; Madden 2010). In American examples such as Union Square and Bryant Park in New York, rental of parkland for special events is now ingrained in the governance, management and funding models, transforming them into places of leisured consumption (Zukin 2010). Lang and Rothenburg (2016, 5) discuss this trend and its consequences: 'amenity-laden parks are always facing pressure to pay for maintenance which in many cases leads to the further privatisation and commercialisation of public space'.

Although many of these ideas emanate from US research, similar approaches are increasingly prevalent in the UK, and there are now examples of parks in London that are entirely funded by the commercial income generated by events (Smith 2020). The increased use of London's parks for commercial festivals means that, whilst events are seen by some as ways of making parks more welcoming, they can also exclude people physically, symbolically and financially (Smith 2016). Large-scale festivals disrupt access to park space during events but also during the time it takes to assemble and derig temporary venues (Smith 2019). If events damage park environments, then access can be disrupted for an even longer period. Local residents in London have objected because events restrict their access, and because of the noise, anti-social behaviour and crowding linked to some events, especially music festivals (Smith 2019). Opponents tend to be dismissed as selfish, conservative NIMBYs who have an old-fashioned idea of what a park is for, but objections to events can be aligned to wider concerns about the right to the city (Harvey 2013). Intensive programming is regarded by some commentators as the antithesis of free space (Mitchell 2017) and various researchers now acknowledge that animating public parks can exclude, as well as include, even when it aims to achieve the latter effect (Glover 2019).

Research Method

The research presented here is based on the results of an online, qualitative survey which was distributed to Friends groups representing parks and green spaces across London in 2020. The survey involved a series of open-ended questions about events staged in parks which key representatives of Friends groups were encouraged to answer. To provide focus, comparability and validity, questions were asked specifically about events that were staged during one calendar year (2019). This means that the effects of the Coronavirus crisis are not addressed in the research presented here. Online surveys usually capture quantitative data but we wanted to develop a qualitative instrument that could record a) what was happening in London's parks and b) what representatives of Friends groups thought about it. We developed a qualitative survey that aimed to gather in-depth insights from informed participants on a focused topic, rather than a broader, more basic overview from the wider public. According to Braun et al. (2020), online qualitative surveys are a novel, and often invisible or sidelined method, and our survey matches many of the recommendations developed by these authors. Questions were generally open and expressed as succinctly and as unambiguously as possible. Braun et al. (2020) suggest studies include nine or ten questions, including some questions where participants are asked to explain an answer, and a final open question inviting further comments. These principles guided the design of our research instrument which included questions on the range of events staged and their impacts, plus questions about Friends' involvement both in events and in decisions about whether to stage them, and questions about how well the events staged represent local communities.

Our online qualitative survey was distributed in several different ways. The lead author attended a meeting of the London Friends of Green Spaces Network (LFGN) in March 2020 to introduce the research and to encourage participation. A link to the survey was then distributed via an email newsletter distributed regularly by the LFGN. If email addresses for Friends groups were available publicly online, emails and reminders were sent directly. This generated a good response: we received completed surveys from representatives of groups from 43 different parks and green spaces across London. This sample included a relatively even distribution of sites across different parts of London, and a mix of centrally located and more peripheral spaces (see Figure 2.1). There is an over-representation of cases in inner London Boroughs and a corresponding absence of ones located in outer London, but otherwise submissions were obtained from a good range of locations and a wide range of boroughs (17 out of 32). A range of governance modes are represented too, with local authority managed parks complemented by those run by charitable trusts, social enterprises and the Corporation of London. The sample was also varied in terms of the types of spaces represented, with responses from eight main types of urban green spaces: local parks (15); large 'destination' parks (8); small urban parks and garden squares (6); heaths and commons (6); linear parks (2); peripheral country parks (2); publicly accessible playing fields (2); plus orchards and woods (2). This produced good variety in terms of the scale of parks included, but also in terms of different types of publicly accessible urban green space.

There are inevitably some limitations with the sample. We acknowledge that Friends groups most affected by events were more likely to respond to the survey. Therefore it is not possible to claim that the sample of parks and green spaces is representative of London parks generally. This issue may have resulted in the overemphasis on inner London boroughs noted above. The high number of large municipal parks in the sample perhaps reflects the fact that events are a particular issue for more central spaces that can host large-scale festivals. Nevertheless, there were many responses from groups representing parks that staged no commercial events at all, and several responses from parks that staged very few events of any kind, which suggests that the sample of parks and green spaces obtained is varied enough to draw conclusions about the general state of park events in London.

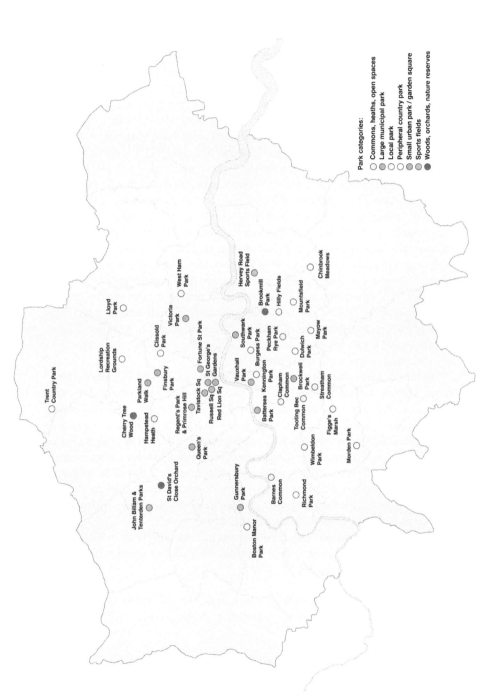

Park categories:
- Commons, heaths, open spaces
- Large municipal park
- Local park
- Peripheral country park
- Small urban park / garden square
- Sports fields
- Woods, orchards, nature reserves

Figure 2.1: The types and locations of the parks that responded to the survey. Map by Goran Vodicka.

The Range of Events Staged in London's Parks

Festivals and events come in all shapes, sizes and guises, a heterogeneity that is exacerbated by the blurring of the boundaries between everyday leisure and special events. London parks host a varied selection of events, and existing policy guidance can be used to build sustainable and varied programmes whilst minimising and mitigating negative impacts (Parks for London 2019). The events staged in London's parks can be split into three categories: free to access events; events organised by Friends groups; and paid entry events. Whilst events in the latter category tend to be the most contentious, it is useful to get a flavour of the broad spectrum of events that take place across one calendar year.

Free to access events are prevalent within London parks and green spaces, with large sites such as Hampstead Heath reporting around 100 annually, but even smaller spaces such as Cherry Tree Wood host lots of free events. These are generally received favourably. The most commonly cited free events were gardening and planting events, highlighting the important role of urban green spaces as productive, horticultural places, rather than merely sites of passive recreation. The prominence of these 'events' in responses also highlights the fine line between small scale events and scheduled activities more generally. Following Citroni and Karrholm (2017), the events staged in London's parks are not easily separated from everyday life and draw attention to ordinary activities such as sport and horticulture.

Free music events were also staged in London's parks. Five parks reported free music festivals, including Lloyd Park in Walthamstow which attracted 35,000 people over two days in 2019 (see Figure 2.2). A further five parks reported programmes of free music events staged on bandstands. Alongside the widespread provision of fairs, dog shows, running events and other sports activities, free to access parks events also included walks and talks, plus several art events. Free festivals and events dedicated to celebrating specific cultural or religious groups were common. Some parks even hosted events outside daylight hours, including light shows and stargazing gatherings highlighting the eclectic and creative ways that London's parks are programmed.

Some of the free festivals and events staged in London's parks in 2019 were events organised by Friends groups and the rationale for staging these was highlighted by this response:

> [...] the aim is to have something each month that will appeal to a wide range of the local community – volunteer gardening, history walks, bird walks, park spring clean.

Community development and social cohesion appeared to be key reasons for staging these events, with responses often mentioning the aim to 'engage', 'involve' and 'bring together' local people. Several Friends groups told us via the

Figure 2.2: The 2019 edition of the Walthamstow Garden Party in Lloyd Park, London E17. Photograph: Andrew Smith.

survey that they want to stage more events but are prevented from doing so by limited organisational capacity, low demand and unhelpful procedures. Only three Friends groups that responded to the survey did not organise any events in 2019. One group said this was because they were anticipating the start of the major redevelopment project and another stated that due to the way their park is governed, all events are organised by the city. Perhaps reflecting the different roles and functions that Friends groups may adopt, one group acted more as a campaign group that actively campaigns against inappropriate events. This opposition is useful to bear in mind as we consider commercial events.

Commercial events are undoubtedly the most contentious events staged in London's parks with music festivals and funfairs the events provoking the most negative comments from Friends groups. Some groups pinpointed specific events that caused problems, but the effects of staging multiple commercial events were also deemed to be an issue:

> *Leading up to Wireless there were a number of other events – this meant that for most of the summer our park was mostly out of bounds. The fabric of the park suffered and the noise/disruption to the local community was unacceptable. (Friends of Finsbury Park)*

Music festivals were cited by eleven groups as examples of paid for events staged in 2019, but other types of ticketed events were also staged in London's parks, with open air cinema or theatre events prevalent. Interestingly, these events were regarded more favourably by respondents. For example, The Friends of Dulwich Park reported that their Luna Cinema screenings were *'popular and had little impact on the park'*.

Whilst ticketed, paid for, events generate a lot of publicity and complaints, our survey found that around a quarter of the Friends groups that responded to our survey reported no paid entry events at all and, in most parks, only a few commercial events are staged. However, in some of London's largest parks a large number of paid entry events were held in 2019. Remarkably, The Friends of Richmond Park reported: 'Typically 170 or so events per month' – mainly running, cycling and other fitness events that required some form of entry fee. These events encourage exercise but they are disruptive to other users especially when they involve several thousand participants. Constructing large temporary arenas in parks to stage arts exhibitions, corporate events and various other commercial events was also something reported by Friends groups. These events do not relate to (or enhance) parks' status as green spaces but instead treat parks as open spaces available to hire (Smith 2019).

The Impacts of Park Events

There is considerable body of work on event impacts, which now includes considerable attention to socio-cultural impacts, alongside an established focus on economic and environmental impacts. Our survey included questions about the positive and negative impacts of events staged in London parks during 2019. The answers provide insights into how Friends groups view the events organised in their park. Seven groups were adamant that all events had positive impacts – these were mainly groups representing small urban parks or woodland spaces. A further five stated that all community/free events had positive impacts. Countering this positivity were three groups that reported that 'all' events caused negative impacts. Apart from these polarised views most answers were more nuanced, as discussed below.

Which Events are Associated with Positive Impacts and Why?

The most commonly cited events regarded as making a positive contribution were various fun days, fairs and carnivals. Friends groups also mentioned funfairs, circuses, concerts, gardening events and nature walks as events that had the most positive impact on their park. Different reasons were given to explain why certain events were regarded positively. Six groups said that events were regarded as a good way of getting more people to use the park. The Friends of Regents Park and Primrose Hill reported that:

> *The bandstand concerts were very popular – over 15,000 people came and sat on the deckchairs or the grass-brought picnics, kids etc. Klezmer on the Bandstand is a huge one-day Jewish music event that is free and very popular. It attracts around 5,000 people (many non-Jewish) during the one day.*

Attracting more users, even in large numbers, was generally seen as a positive thing. The Friends of St George's Gardens explained why: '*we want the gardens to be used*'. Other groups also saw events as good ways of promoting their parks and prompting future visits. For example, two separate parks in the Borough of Lewisham reported positive impacts from a series of talks which '*drew in a large audience and were informative and raised the profile of the park*'.

To explain positive outcomes, a number of Friends groups mentioned community cohesion and the role of events as occasions that bring people together. A related explanation for positive impacts was the contribution certain events made to inclusivity, with free events regarded as good ways of bringing '*a wider group of people into the park*'. A good example was the response from Queen's Park:

> *The most positive [event] is Queen's Park Day bringing in 17,000 [people] through [the] doors, supporting many organisations, through a range of events bringing the community together in many different ways.*

One of the most interesting positive impacts cited was the way events helped to get users more involved in their parks. The Friends of Cherry Tree Wood told us that their events programme '*engaged with the local community and involved them directly in planning a range of activities*'. At Lordship Rec, a renowned example of community-led management, the Friends group felt that their events empower communities and '*help them see that it's our park and we are the local community taking responsibility for it*'.

Nature walks were deemed to be good ways of encouraging participation, but also promoting environmental awareness and pro-environmental behaviours. One group felt these events: '*Encourage people to value biodiversity in the park, so the community is more likely to want to be involved with protecting and enhancing our biodiversity assets*'. Seven user groups cited the income generated by events as a key positive impact. Friends groups representing Gunnersbury Park, Victoria Park and Boston Manor highlighted that large music festivals generated significant sums of money for management authorities. And groups representing Victoria Park, Lloyd Park, Richmond Park and Russell Square reported that income earned had been used to upgrade park facilities, maintain environments or fund other free to access events.

Which Events are Associated with Negative Impacts and Why?

Where examples of problematic park events were reported by Friends groups, music festivals were the most commonly mentioned type. The groups most worried about these tended to be those representing some of London's largest parks such as Gunnersbury Park, Finsbury Park, Streatham Common, Peckham Rye Park, Morden Park and Brockwell Park. Other events that were also regarded as problematic by some groups included funfairs, winter festivals, religious festivals and even exercise 'bootcamps' and park runs. These caused issues in very large country parks (e.g. Richmond Park), but also in smaller parks.

The reasons events were cited as having negative impacts were varied, but three core problems were mentioned by multiple groups: excessive noise; damage to grassed areas; and restricted park access. The most frequently mentioned problem was noise, although this was usually mentioned in conjunction with other issues rather than being a standalone problem. For example, one group reported that: '*We are aware of complaints from residents relating to parking, litter and noise related to large commercial events arranged through the Council*'. Several groups highlighted that noise from events not only affected people inside the park, it impacted those living nearby, particularly when there was '*varying levels of intense bass noise*'.

The two other most commonly cited negative impacts – restricted access and environmental damage – are linked because damage (e.g. to grassed areas) means that people cannot access areas whilst repairs are made. Groups stressed that parts of their park were inaccessible or unusable for as long as six and even seven months after events because of the damage they caused. Damage to turf is caused by event attendees, installations which deprive grass of sunlight/water, and by lorries/vehicles used for events. It was noted that restrictions on park access happen both during events and during their assembly/derig. The time it takes to set up and take down events means that a weekend-long event equals '*restricted use one week before and two weeks after*'. Groups complained about the amount of space and time events take up, particularly when multiple ticketed events were staged in key spaces: '*The number of ticketed summer events restricts access to the most desirable parts of the park*'. Restricted access was noted as a particular problem in areas where few local people had private gardens: '*many people in our area live in flats and don't have private access to outdoor space, so when a fun fair or circus comes for 10 days and takes up a large portion of the park then it restricts access to outdoor space*'.

Problems with the aesthetics of 'ugly' fences were also mentioned by several groups and three groups reported problems with litter and various forms of neighbourhood disruption linked to congestion, traffic and parking. Reassuringly, crime and antisocial behaviour were only mentioned sparingly, although one group did note that a music festival staged in their park was accompanied by '*4 non-fatal stabbings*'. Another felt that music festivals were justified by the council as cultural provision, but the reality was different: '*The business of drink with loud music "festivals" has been misrepresented as a cultural expression for which space must be found*'. One other interesting issue highlighted was low level commercialisation; with one group suggesting that events mean parents are pressured to spend money when they visit the park. This suggests that the transformation of parks into sites of consumption is something not merely associated with large-scale, ticketed festivals, but smaller, free to access events too.

Concerns about the negative impacts highlighted above meant that nearly half of groups reported they had formally objected to event proposals in 2019: seventeen before, and one after specific events. One group contextualised their objections as follows:

> *Our objections are legion, extensively documented, campaigned at all levels without result. The council asserts it makes money from mega commercial events, but we have demonstrated this is false. Its insistence appears to be solely politically motivated to satisfy its supporter constituency in the east of the Borough.*

A similar number (eighteen) said they had not objected to any proposals to stage events in their park in 2019. One of these groups explained that timely consultation meant they didn't need to object: '*No. We are involved at a much earlier stage so events we are likely to object to don't happen!*' When asked about the ways they have been involved in the wider decision-making process about events staged in their park in 2019, six groups said they hadn't been involved at all and five responded 'not much'. Where groups were involved this tended to be relatively superficial involvement: eight groups told us that they were only involved in decision making related to one or a few specific events and a further ten described their involvement in the decision-making process as taking part in regular council-led park management groups or public consultation meetings. These were often criticised:

> *Invited to public consultation evenings – painful droning from dull businessmen explaining how things were going to be so much better than the previous year. Subtext – how little do we have to spend to keep you lot quiet?*

The striking number of objections raised, and the rather limited involvement of Friends in decision making, highlight an interesting contradiction: whilst these groups are increasingly relied on to provide voluntary services for parks and green spaces – including small scale event organisation – they tend to be ignored when their views on park events do not concur with the priorities of park authorities.

Festivity and Inclusivity

Parks should be designed and managed 'for the purpose of facilitating co-mingling and co-presence among loosely connected strangers from diverse parts of society' (Barker et al. 2019: 496). As discussed earlier, one key justification for programming events in parks is the potential to nurture these interactions between people from different social groups. Whilst our survey established that events can act as useful vehicles to reach out to people who might not otherwise use parks, the inclusivity of event programmes is not always so clear. We asked Friends groups how well the events staged in their parks matched the social profiles of neighbouring communities. Whilst fifteen groups felt that the events matched the social demographics reasonably well, two felt they did not and a further ten were unsure how to answer this question.

A key issue identified was the price of tickets, something several groups mentioned as presenting a barrier to inclusivity. Even free events were seen as problematic by some groups due to a perception that they tend to be focused on certain socio-economic and ethnic groups. For example, there was a critical self-awareness that events organised by Friends groups, 'tended to attract a greater proportion of white young families than is a true reflection of the socio-economic composition of the area'.

The issue as to whether events attracted people who did not usually visit the park elicited a generally positive response. However, our research participants' interpretation of this question was insightful: it was usually taken to mean people travelling from further afield, rather than people from underrepresented ethnic and socio-economic groups. This suggests that the issue of under-representation (of non-white and poorer users) might be underestimated by Friends groups. Responses to our survey suggested that park events *do* aim to achieve community cohesion and *could* have the effect of bringing people together, but there was acknowledgment that more could be done to address diversity and inclusion agendas.

> *The events have definitely introduced a greater variety of people to the park but there may be other events that would draw a more diverse group to better match the socio-demographics of the area.*

One way of doing this would be to involve a wider range of groups and communities in organising and promoting events. Indeed, whilst this research asked Friends groups about inclusivity, it is important to acknowledge that these groups have themselves been criticised for their lack of diversity as their members tend to be older and whiter than the park users they purport to represent (Whitten 2019).

Conclusions and Recommendations

This chapter has reaffirmed that London's parks are used for a wide range and large number of festivals and events. The observations made here, alongside the finding that these events are used to achieve a range of strategic objectives, support the notion that there has been a festivalisation of parks in the period leading up to 2019. According to Rönstrom (2016), festivalisation involves an unprecedented increase in the number and size of festivals staged and our survey provides evidence of such increases, with 2019 perhaps representing 'peak event' for London's parks. The other facets of festivalisation identified by Rönstrom are also evident. Following his ideas about the semantic dimension of festivalisation, what might have once been considered park activities are now regarded or rebranded as events. For example, sports activities, gardening and nature walks were regarded as events in responses to our survey. Rönstrom (2016) also considers festivalisation as something that describes the ways culture and space are now produced and organised in a festival-like way, and the research presented here suggests this also applies to London's parks and green spaces which are increasingly managed, represented and experienced as venues.

Many of the events deemed to have positive impacts (e.g. horticultural events, nature walks, fun days/runs) were those that emphasised the notion of parks as active, green, community spaces. Our research also revealed that a series of innovative events were staged: with festivals dedicated to specific communities, art exhibitions and night events all notable examples. These events disrupt traditional notions of who and what parks are for, and when they can be accessed. The significant role that Friends groups play in organising many smaller events was reaffirmed by the responses to our survey. Events, particularly those that are free to access, have a series of very positive impacts on London's parks according to Friends groups. They bring people in, diversify users, boost awareness and generate income that can be used to help maintain parks. The prevalence of nature-oriented events also highlights the role of events in promoting pro-environmental behaviours. Our findings support Nam and Dempsey's (2020) research which also revealed generally positive attitudes towards park events. The most positive outcomes seem to stem from instances where Friends and other local groups were involved in organising events.

Friends groups also feel that some events cause negative impacts with restricted accessibility, damage to park environments and disruption of surrounding neighbourhoods the key complaints. These effects are associated with large-scale festivals and, to a lesser extent, funfairs and circuses. Over a quarter of the parks that responded to the survey hosted major music festivals in 2019 and, although Friends groups were generous enough to acknowledge these mean '*three nights of 40,000 people having a good time*' (Friends of Gunnersbury Park and Museum), they do cause negative effects. For example, some groups reported access restrictions for 6–7 months post-event while park surfaces were restored. This problem and other issues meant that around half of Friends groups that responded to our survey objected to event proposals in 2019. Worryingly, many Friends groups reported that their involvement in decisions to stage park events was limited or nonexistent. There has been much written about the potential for Friends groups to play a more active role in park maintenance and fundraising, but such involvement must also be accompanied by incorporation into decision making and park governance (Speller and Ravenscroft 2005). The combination of negative effects and the perceived imposition of commercial events meant several Friends groups were very strongly opposed to the ways their parks were being exploited as commercial venues. Reflecting observations made by Smith (2019), these groups tend to be those representing large municipal parks and urban commons which have recently introduced large-scale music festivals.

Finally, our findings suggest that events have an important role to play in making parks more inclusive. Festivals and events, particularly free to access events, can attract a wider set of users in terms of their socio-economic and ethnic profiles, and they produce places where people from different backgrounds encounter one another (Barker et al. 2019; Neal et al. 2015). When they are dedicated to particular cultural or religious identities, events can help to build more cohesive and tolerant communities by ensuring marginalised people are visibly represented in prominent public spaces (Low, Taplin and Scheld 2005). However, more needs to be done to ensure event programmes represent the interests and profiles of surrounding neighbourhoods (Citroni and Karrholm 2017). It is imperative that Friends and other community groups are meaningfully involved in event planning and management decisions, that social inclusion outcomes are used in criteria to evaluate proposals for events, and that community groups organise their own events. More research is also required to understand if and how events include and exclude different groups, but also the cumulative and longer term effects that programmes of events have on the inclusivity of park spaces.

Recommendations

The following recommendations are directed towards the authorities responsible for managing parks. Some of these were suggested specifically by Friends groups in the responses they submitted. The remainder were conceived by the authors based on responses to the survey. These recommendations can be viewed in full in an online document we produced to report our findings to participants and key stakeholders (Smith and Vodicka 2020), but we have provided a short summary here.

Many of our recommendations refer to the ways events are planned and regulated. Friends groups and other user groups should be involved in event planning and management decisions. Consultations about new events or major changes to existing events need to be timely and meaningful. Decisions whether or not to stage events should be guided by an up to date events policy that is co-produced with Friends and other user groups. User friendly procedures and training in event marketing and management could encourage community groups to organise more free-to-access events.

We have also developed a series of recommendations that aim to minimise negative impacts. Parks' suitability and resilience as venues could be enhanced by providing specialised features and design adaptations. For example, simple additions such as a permanent power supply would help to reduce the need for polluting generators. In instances where park settings are irrelevant to the aims and user experience of events, alternative outdoor venues should be considered – including brownfield sites awaiting development. The relocation of the Field Day music festival from Victoria Park to an industrial site in Enfield in 2019 provides a useful example to follow. Our survey highlighted that lengthy winter events on grass surfaces (e.g. winter wonderland type events) were deemed particularly problematic so these should be avoided or relocated.

Finally, there are ways that festivals and events staged in parks could be better aligned to inclusivity objectives. Social inclusion outcomes should be included in criteria used to adjudge the merits of event proposals and, given the important roles that park settings and cultural events play in social inclusion (Neal et al. 2015), park events could be better integrated into wider social policy. The only reliable way to ensure that event programmes represent the interests and profiles of surrounding neighbourhoods is by involving local stakeholders in planning events and event programmes. We think it would be helpful to (re)consider events as powerful processes, not merely opportunistic occasions, and more could be achieved by leveraging event planning/organisation to advance social inclusion. A good way to do this would be to provide dedicated funding and support for events organised jointly between different community groups. This would encourage inter-group collaborations pre-event and address the need to engage community groups beyond Friends groups.

References

Barker, Anna, Adam Crawford, Nathan Booth and David Churchill. 2019. Everyday Encounters with Difference in Urban Parks: Forging 'Openness to Otherness' in Segmenting Cities. *International Journal of Law in Context*, 15(4), 495–514.

Braun, Virginia, Victoria Clarke, Elicia Boulton, Louise Davey and Charlotte McEvoy. 2020. The Online Survey as a Qualitative Research Tool. *International Journal of Social Research Methodology*, 24(6), 1–14.

Citroni, Sebastiano and Mattias Karrholm. 2019. Neighbourhood Events and the Visibilisation of Everyday Life: The Cases of Turro (Milan) and Norra Fäladen (Lund). *European Urban and Regional Studies*, 26(1), 50–64.

Elborough, Travis. 2016. *A Walk in the Park: The Life and Times of a People's Institution*. London: Random House.

Glover, Troy. 2019. The Transformative (and Potentially Discriminatory) Possibilities of Animating Public Space. *World Leisure Journal*, 61(2), 144–156.

Gobster, Paul. 2002. Managing Urban Parks for a Racially and Ethnically Diverse Clientele. *Leisure Sciences*, 24(2), 143–159.

Hardingham, Samantha and Kester Rattenbury. 2011. *Bernard Tschumi: Parc de la Villette, SuperCrit No. 4*. Abingdon: Routledge.

Harvey, David. 2013. *Rebel Cities: From the Right to the City to the Urban Revolution*. London: Verso.

Jones, Karen and John Wills. 2005. *The Invention of the Park: From the Garden of Eden to Disney's Magic Kingdom*. Cambridge: Polity.

Lang, Steven and Julia Rothenberg. 2017. Neoliberal Urbanism, Public Space, and the Greening of the Growth Machine: New York City's High Line Park. *Environment and Planning A: Economy and Space*, 49(8), 1743–1761.

LFGN. 2021. *Friends Groups*. Available at: http://www.lfgn.org.uk/about-us

London Assembly. 2017. *Park Life: Ensuring Green Spaces Remain a Hit with Londoners*. Environment Committee Report. London: London Assembly.

Loughran, Kevin. 2014. Parks for Profit: The High Line, Growth Machines, and the Uneven Development of Urban Public Spaces. *City & Community*, 13(1), 49–68.

Low, Setha, Dana Taplin and Suzanne Scheld. 2005. *Rethinking Urban Parks: Public Space and Cultural Diversity*. Austin, TX: University of Texas Press.

Madden, David. 2010. Revisiting the End of Public Space: Assembling the Public in an Urban Park. *City & Community*, 9(2), 187–207.

Mitchell, Don. 2017. People's Park Again: On the End and Ends of Public Space. *Environment and Planning A: Economy and Space*, 49(3), 503–518.

Nam, Jinvo and Nicola Dempsey. 2020. Acceptability of Income Generation Practices in 21st Century Urban Park Management: The Case of City District Parks. *Journal of Environmental Management*, 264, 109948.

Neal, Sarah, Katy Bennett, Hannah Jones, Allan Cochrane and Giles Mohan. 2015. Multiculture and Public Parks: Researching Super-Diversity and Attachment in Public Green Space. *Population, Space and Place*, 21(5), 463–475.

Parks for London. 2019. *Good Parks for London*. London: Parks for London. Available at: https://parksforlondon.org.uk/wp-content/uploads/2020/08/Good-Parks-for-London-2019_FINAL-updated-18th-Oct-19.pdf

Perry, Beth, Laura Ager and Rike Sitas. 2020. Cultural Heritage Entanglements: Festivals as Integrative Sites for Sustainable Urban Development. *International Journal of Heritage Studies*, 26(6), 603–618.

Richards, Greg and Robert Palmer. 2010. *Eventful Cities: Cultural Management and Urban Revitalisation*. Oxford: Butterworth-Heinemann.

Ronström, Owe. 2015. Four Facets of Festivalisation. *Puls – Journal for Ethnomusicology and Ethnochoreology*, 1(1), 67–83.

Smith, Andrew. 2016. *Events in the City: Using Public Spaces as Event Venues*. Abingdon: Routledge.

Smith, Andrew. 2018. Paying for Parks: Ticketed Events and the Commercialisation of Public Space. *Leisure Studies*, 37(5), 533–546.

Smith, Andrew. 2019. Event Takeover? The Commercialisation of London's Parks. In Andrew Smith and Anne Graham (Eds.) *Destination London: The Expansion of the Visitor Economy*, pp. 205–224. London: University of Westminster Press. https://doi.org/10.16997/book35.j

Smith, Andrew. 2020. Sustaining Municipal Parks in an Era of Neoliberal Austerity: The Contested Commercialisation of Gunnersbury Park. *Environment and Planning A: Economy and Space*, 53(4), 704–722.

Smith, Andrew and Goran Vodicka. 2020. *Events in London's Parks. The Friends Perspective*. FESTSPACE. Available at: https://zenodo.org/record/3878727# .YH71w-hKg2z

Speller, Gerda and Neil Ravenscroft. 2005. Facilitating and Evaluating Public Participation in Urban Parks Management. *Local Environment*, 10(1), 41–56.

Whitten, Meredith. 2019. Blame it on Austerity? Examining the Impetus Behind London's Changing Green Space Governance. *People, Place and Policy*, 12(3), 204–224.

Wynn, Jonathan R. 2015. *Music/City: American Festivals and Placemaking in Austin, Nashville and Newport*. Chicago, IL: University of Chicago Press.

Zukin, Sharon. 2010. *Naked City: The Death and Life of Authentic Urban Places*. New York: Oxford University Press.

CHAPTER 3

Mapping Barcelona's Cultural Event Landscape: Geographies and Typologies

Alba Colombo, Michael Luchtan
and Esther Oliver-Grasiot

Introduction

In this chapter, we analyse the relationship between public spaces and cultural events, as part of research for the FESTSPACE project funded by HERA (Humanities in the European Research Area) and as a response to the eventification of Barcelona, a process that has also been happening in many other European cities in recent years. In light of the massive changes that have affected the sector, and the renegotiations of the field of events due to Covid-19, it is necessary to critically observe the use of physical space by events and the consequences generated by that use, both positive and negative.

Barcelona, like many other cities around the globe, has experienced what Richards (2007) and Jakob (2012) have described as the festivalisation and eventification of the city. Barcelona has a long history of large-scale pulsar events (Richards 2015a), the most important arguably being the Summer Olympics of 1992, when the city emerged as an international tourist destination. Increasingly, international visitors appeared in the city streets

How to cite this book chapter:
Colombo, A., Luchtan, M. and Oliver-Grasiot, E. 2022. Mapping Barcelona's Cultural Event Landscape: Geographies and Typologies. In: Smith, A., Osborn, G. and Quinn, B. (Eds.) *Festivals and the City: The Contested Geographies of Urban Events*. London: University of Westminster Press. Pp. 39–58. London: University of Westminster Press. DOI: https://doi.org/10.16997/book64.c. License: CC-BY-NC-ND 4.0

at local celebrations in public places and at global pulsar events such as the Mobile World Congress or Primavera Sound. While large-scale pulsar events can move from location to location to different urban centres around the globe, the city of Barcelona, similar to other Mediterranean cities, has a unique feeling and way of life all its own, with a cultural agenda of iterative events that maintain social structures and promote social cohesion (Richards 2015). Barcelona has a full calendar of local celebrations, not just popular events and cultural events originating from the liturgical calendar, but traditional celebrations that have arrived with immigrant communities, arising from the fact that, during recent years, global immigration has transformed the city into a multicultural and socially diverse metropolis with multiple communities that share time and space, living together.

The growth of the city has led to an overuse of Barcelona's limited public space, not only by Barcelona citizens themselves but also by mass tourists, most explicitly illustrated in the case of Parc Guell where the once public park was enclosed to protect it from the influx of tourists (Arias-Sans and Russo 2016).

With the aim of observing the way public spaces are occupied by planned cultural events, this chapter analyses the landscape of cultural events in Barcelona. This comprehensive analysis, which we call the landscape of Barcelona's events, was generated by combining a cultural database of events in Barcelona, consisting of 349 cultural events, with their geographical references, allowing us to map the distribution of events in the city. The resulting information about cultural events and their spatial dimensions allows us to see the concentration and centralisation of cultural events in the city and to analyse the interactions between public resources and citizens within the urban environment.

In this chapter we first define diverse categories of cultural events which will allow us to see differences and similarities between them. We then illustrate the concentration, distribution and cartographies of cultural events and event spaces. Finally, this chapter develops an understanding of the distribution of cultural events in the city with insightful results which allow us to pose questions about the distribution of the public resources of time and space. By observing and analysing the concentration of cultural events and resources in the city, we provide potentially useful knowledge that could guide future decision-making processes.

Contextual Framework

When Richards and Palmer (2010) introduced the concept of 'eventful cities', not only had Covid-19 not happened yet, neither had the full effects of overtourism been felt in Barcelona. The Western world, or at least those in the most comfortable centre of it, were in the full throes of late stage capitalism. The eventful city accurately described what was going on in 2010 as the network society had enabled the rapid global movement of people, wealth, and information (Castells 2010). Historically, the notion of eventful cities describes the way that many cities, Barcelona included (Colombo 2017; Richards and Palmer 2010; Richards 2015a), were using events – both large-scale industry events and popular culture events – as an expedient resource to generate capital, development and regeneration. The overall result of this can be to produce an effect of 'festivalisation,' which can be understood as a specific mechanism to manage and organise the coalition between urban space and social activities as well as a way to entertain residents and tourists (Karpińska-Krakowiak 2009). In contrast, Richards (2007) defines 'festivalisation' mainly in terms of policies of mega-events, linking festivals to economic growth and investment attraction. Along the same lines, Häussermann and Siebel (1993) had earlier identified 'festivalisation' as a process of supporting urban policies through the staging of mega-events. Hitters (2007) also considered that 'festivalisation' implies the continuous staging of festivals and a permanent event presence in the city.

The eventful cities paradigm has often been used to describe cities that were, at least in part, trying to reproduce the so-called Barcelona Model (Monclús 2003). Authors such as Scarnato (2016) and Degen and Garcia (2012) pointed out how Barcelona's success in combining cultural strategies with urban redevelopment were tied to the city's unique political, economic and social characteristics as it emerged after Franco's dictatorship. The Barcelona Model was built mainly on large-scale, centrally planned, top-down industry events that included not just the Olympics of 1992, which cleaned up the beaches and opened up the city to a wave of international tourism, but likewise yearly and current events such as the Mobile World Congress, staged in the city since 2006. Although the effects of these strategies are contested, especially from a social point of view, this model has at least generated positive effects in the field of urban and economic development. Barcelona's events also extend well beyond this model. The city has a rich and diverse calendar of popular and traditional cultural events that take place city-wide and in local neighbourhoods, often planned and organised in a highly localised and bottom-up manner.

Both types of events involve planned occurrences at a given place and time (Getz 2007) and they compete for the limited public resources of time and space. The city's cultural event calendar therefore includes not only international pulsar or iterative events (Richards 2015a), but also the community-produced events, such as celebrations of ritualistic fire, described by Colombo, Altuna and Oliver-Grasiot (2021). These popular celebrations go beyond the promotional impact or commercial effects, and help to shape the social and cultural fabric of the city.

To compare the advantages and disadvantages of how events are distributed in and across urban public spaces, we need to consider cultural events in Barcelona beyond proposals such as the ones developed already by Getz (2007), Peranson (2009) or Wynn (2016) among others. Consequently, in our analysis we have classified each event into different categories to be able to better understand the relationship between the events and the different spaces and areas of the city, and their socio-cultural and demographic characteristics.

As cities competed on the international stage by marketing their unique histories, places and identities, a number of problems arose. Not only can a popular traditional event be taken from its original context of participation to become a spectacle (Debord 1994; Gotham 2005), but there has been an observable pattern of uneven distribution of benefits gained from mega-events. Ziakas (2014) and consequently Smith, Ritchie and Chien (2019) proposed a new framework for citizens' attitudes towards these mega-events, to understand the personal price that the average city dweller pays for large-scale events and what they get in return. It is important to ask, especially when trading the shared resources of time and space in an urban environment, who benefits and who loses, in terms of the usability, quality and accessibility of urban spaces. Smith (2017) and other scholars have attempted to uncover the long-term effects of short-term takeovers of public spaces as event venues. Lefebvre (1991) provided a phenomenological understanding of the co-production of the urban environment and various urban scholars such as Jacobs (1961) and Lynch (1960) argued that urban space can determine how we view the world. Beyond urban space, we must consider public space, and the main schools of thought concerning the public realm. Arendt's approach (1958) leaned toward the physical with a focus mostly on the political, and likewise Young (1990) advocated universally inclusive spaces that incorporate interaction of diverse citizenry to achieve a democratic ideal of the kind proposed by Arendt. Meanwhile, a dramaturgical school of thought has been more concerned with the performative aspects of the public realm and the processes that create it, and Sennett (1970) argued that spaces such as public squares and parks that allow for unplanned and unmanaged encounters are integral to a healthy urban environment. Inclusive public spaces that allow for unstructured encounters can be restricted by the festivalisation of the city, especially with mega-events, such as the Olympics, which require public resources. For example, Smith (2013) looked at the limitations on use access to Greenwich Park during the 2012 Olympics in London, when a popular park was 'borrowed' for the equestrian venue. These events restricted public access to what is perceived as a shared common good, consequently exposing a tension inherent in the eventful cities paradigm. According to Lefebvre (1968), the urban environment is co-created and belongs to the people who inhabit it, but at times it can seem as though public space is being sold without acquiescence of those who use it, or transformed into a spectacle.

In every urban settlement, different types of cultural events compete for the same time and space. As with any limited resource, the growth of one can come at the cost of the others. Arias-Sans and Russo (2016) analysed the events leading up to the enclosure of Barcelona's Parc Güell in 2013, which was receiving 25,000 visitors a day (mostly tourists). They point out how in the years leading up to the mass saturation, its role as a venue for neighbourhood popular culture events had progressively diminished. Faced with this scenario, Russo and Scarnatto (2018) attribute Barcelona en Comú's rise to power in 2015 as a reaction to the Barcelona Model and its dependence on the tourism growth machine. Wilson (2020) has done significant work to describe the effect that collaborative tourism platforms have had on the production of urban space in Barcelona. Faced with the centralisation of culture in specific districts of the city, the Barcelona City Council has, since 2016, promoted various measures and programs to decentralise and democratise culture to make cultural events and resources accessible to all residents of the city and to all neighbourhoods. An excellent example of this initiative is *La Mercè dels Barris. La Mercè* is one of the main cultural events in Barcelona and it is now being staged in different neighbourhoods of the city, and consequently has generated greater participation from different social and cultural groups. Since the 2016 edition, new peripheral locations have been used such as Parc de la Trinitat in Nou Barris and institutions like Palauet Albeniz or Fàbrica Fabra i Coats have also been involved.

The background to this study lies in the intersection of planned events and urban public space. We incorporate a phenomenological view that urban public space is more than a physical location but a result of an intersubjective reality that encompasses the social rhythms and collective patterns of movement within an inhabited space. The joint perception of that space, the social cognition and shared experience of an urban environment, is a public resource that is simultaneously tied and untied to the place and participants, creating and created by the urban environment.

Methodology and Data

The first task was to create a database about Barcelona's cultural events. The municipal government has a prominent role in supporting and disseminating cultural events, and cultural activities are coordinated by the Barcelona Institute of Culture (ICUB) which organises, supports or promotes several types of cultural events. In a complementary way, the department concerned with Social Rights, Global Justice, Feminisms and LGBTQI+ from the City Council also collaborates with the promotion, and in some cases with the organisation, of cultural events. Our database has been constructed from those cultural events which have a link with Barcelona City Council as it either organises or supports them or because they are recognised and identified by ICUB or other City Council areas such as the Department of Social Rights. Our cultural events database focuses on events held in 2019 with the aim of showing the city's distribution then, which may be affected by a possible change after a pandemic. Most of the collected data has been provided directly by the City Council, supplemented with data collected by researchers from official events dissemination portals and reports, or by contacting stakeholders.

The database consists of two groups of variables. First, descriptive variables: number of attendees; edition; frequency; season of the year; content; and the name of the organiser, among others. Second, geographic variables: the main location, neighbourhood, district, and address where the event takes place. This second group of variables has been generated with geographic information systems and facilitates the visual understanding of the distribution, and consequently the concentration, of cultural events in Barcelona. The total number of cultural events identified in our database is 340, all of which have a clear link with cultural activities, showing or promoting cultural products, representing local or newcomers' traditions, or involving community celebrations.

The quantitative event data, provided by the database, combined with data from geographical information systems, shines a light on the distribution of cultural events throughout the city by observing event distribution by typologies and districts. Geolocation has been carried out only for the events of the year 2019, identifying 2,268 different cultural events locations. Since there are events which happen in more than one space, a classification of spaces as 'main' and 'secondary' has been developed. The guidelines for identifying main spaces were made according to the following criteria: (1) the space with more activities within the event; (2) the space where the inaugural ceremony takes place (or the closing, if there is no inauguration); (3) the symbolic space as where *pregóns*, or opening speeches happen; and (4) the most important event space featured in the programme (as the first in the list of spaces) or in the festival poster. Some of the events, however, could not be identified by their main space, either because they take place in a shared way throughout the city or because they are networked, that is, in different equal locations, such as museums or civic centres. Therefore, based on the type of space used and its distribution, events have been organised into three categories that will be retrieved for mapping. These are 'general', 'massive or city' and 'networked'.

- General: designates the majority of events, those whose spaces and / or distribution do not have specific characteristics that designate them as city or network.
- Massive or city: events that have the character of a city, which are celebrations on a city scale but are concentrated in certain areas. These events are: Barcelona Carnival, Christmas cycle, La Mercè festivities, Santa Eulàlia festivities, St. John's Night, Saint George, Innocent Saints and Easter.
- Networked: events in which it is not possible to allocate a main space, but are all at the same level. These events are: Barcelona Cultural district, Barcelona Gallery Weekend, Transit Literature Festival, Album Week, Light Bcn, Barcelona screen, SYMPHONIC, Roofs in Culture, All Saints and Young Gallery Weekend.

When possible, specific locations such as squares, civic or cultural centres, museums, cinemas, etc. have been used. In cases where the location is in one street, a specific point on that street has been identified to geo-locate the space.

Barcelona Cultural Events Landscape: Events Typologies and Distribution

The landscape of cultural events in Barcelona is built through the combination of the citizens' social and cultural actions with the geographical elements involved. Characteristics of the event are as relevant as the space, as the symbiosis of both aspects draws and delimits this constantly changing landscape. It is understood that public space is all space which is open and accessible to citizens. In this sense there are different types of spaces, such as outdoor public spaces, like squares, streets, parks or beaches, while indoor public spaces are public buildings opened to the public such as libraries or museums. The latter tend to have restricted areas and greater limits upon use. With the understanding that different cultural events coexist in Barcelona, sharing space and time, and that the link between events and space depends on the typology, we present the analysis of both: characteristics of the events by typology and their distribution around the city.

Understanding Barcelona's Cultural Events by Typologies

Barcelona has a mature event calendar, filled with many types of events, from large-scale urban development events such as the Olympics (1992) to the more traditional, neighbourhood based events. Observing all cultural events developed over a year in the city, we found that events could be grouped by different variables, such as the cultural sector they relate to, the way in which they are developed, or even who is involved (actors or communities) in organising them or participating in them. Based on these parameters we identify three main cultural events typologies in Barcelona: cultural industry events; traditional and popular culture events; and cultural diversity events.

According to the data obtained based on 340 events staged in 2019, the majority of cultural events are cultural industry events (66%), followed by traditional and popular culture events (27%) and culture diversity events (6%).

'*Cultural industry events*' (also identified as festivals) are those festivities with a strong link to the commercialisation and industrialisation of culture, from festivals and fairs to diverse cultural corporate events. These events have a strong link with the so-called 'cultural industries' which share creation, production and distribution of goods and services that are cultural in nature and usually protected by intellectual property. As stressed by Throsby (2008), these industries are generally involved with certain creativity in their processes, are concerned with the creation of symbolic meanings, and have an expressive value. In this typology we included industrial or commercial festivals from performing arts, audio-visual, visual arts, literature, or music, among others. The main characteristic of this typology is the type of physical space used, as most cultural industry events in Barcelona are held in an indoor space, 74% according to our data. Indoor spaces are not homogeneous and include different formats as civic centres, theatres, cinemas, libraries, museums and some emblematic buildings, but also diverse private or public properties.

The cultural industry sector has been on the rise in Barcelona over the last decade. As in other European cities, there is an increasing interest in the production and consumption of activities related to cultural industries. According to the ICUB data on cultural festivals, in 2010, 146 festivals were identified while in 2019 there were about 214. The increase in cultural industry festivals has been accompanied by the rise of attendees, which in 2019 was almost three million while ten years before it was close to a million and a half. These events are generally organised by private institutions with strong coordination and supported by the City Council (through the ICUB). In this typology we include events with international recognition such as Mutek, Sónar or Primavera Sound, local consolidated events as the Festival International de Jazz de Barcelona (which celebrated its 51st edition in 2019), and other festivals with less recognition and shorter trajectories. According to our data, 30% of the events have occurred between one and five times.

For 'traditional and popular culture events' (identified as popular culture) we understand those social and community undertakings related to traditional or popular activities, strongly linked to locality. In Barcelona, after Franco's dictatorship, a wish to re-establish those events arose from the administration but also from citizens who wanted to reclaim the streets, expressing and reconstructing Catalan symbols and identity. The first democratic City Council (in the late 1970s) consolidated celebrations of popular culture in Barcelona as a response to different citizens' demands (Contreras 1978–1979). From that period on, traditional and popular culture activities in Barcelona constructed, reinterpreted and strengthened an annual calendar of festivities and rites strongly linked to Catalan and Barcelona culture and identity. Currently, popular celebrations attract more than 8 million people every year, and are linked to 117,000 people who belong to 500 groups and associations which work all year long to ensure that the Barcelona festive calendar is developed appropriately (Duran 2016).

Within popular culture events we include those events consolidated from the 1970s until now, created by this cooperation between social organisations, citizens and the municipal administration. With these peculiarities we identify two different groups of events: the ones arising out of the traditional Catalan and Barcelona cultural calendar, and the *festes majors*. The first group consists of the annual celebrations marked mainly by the liturgical calendar and are generally organised or coordinated by the City Council (ICUB) in collaboration with neighbourhood associations or local communities. Carnival, Sant Joan Night (June 23rd) or Christmas are some examples of this first type.

The *festa major* is a neighbourhood celebration which combines different events: traditional rites such as *Correfoc* (a traditional fireworks event, performed by citizens dressed as devils, where participants run through firelit streets during the main celebrations of the towns and cities in Catalonia), music concerts and popular events related to sports, culture or gastronomy. Each *festa major* corresponds to the celebration of the patron saint of each neighbourhood and of the city itself; a *festa major* is celebrated in each neighbourhood of Barcelona during different times of the year and with different uses of space and time. Although each *festa major* is different from the other, they are organised almost entirely bottom-up by neighbourhood organisations and some of them stand out for their colourful street decorations. The Festa Major de Gràcia and the Festa Major de Sants are the most emblematic examples of the second group. In addition, there is a *festa major* for the city itself, known as La Mercè. This is held all around the city, with an extended programme including different performances and activities, from traditional culture to cultural industries' initiatives among others.

'*Cultural diversity events*' (identified as cultural diversity) we consider as those activities linked to diverse communities in Barcelona that arrived with new citizens coming from other cultural, political and economic backgrounds. During the recent decades Barcelona has drastically changed its social structure. In 2019 Barcelona achieved its highest registered population since 1991, becoming a more diverse and international city: in 2010, 17% of the citizenry were immigrants compared to 20% in 2019. This evolution generated a transformation of the city's social and cultural life and its landscape. Celebrations with origins from these communities are represented in the city cultural calendar, although they are still isolated in many cases.

These celebrations are mostly related to political or religious issues originating from the immigrants' country of origin. Usually these events are organised bottom-up and initiated by communities or associations created by a foreign population in Barcelona, such as the Catalan Federation of Pakistani Associations or the Federation of Ecuadorian Associations in Catalonia. Those events generally take place in public open-air spaces and mostly consist of festive events with food, music, dances, etc. Observing our data we identify that the most represented community with the highest number of events in this typology are from Latin American communities (63%). Nevertheless some examples of these events also might include Pakistan Independence Day, Ecuador National Day, Chinese New Year and Eid al-Adha (Festival of the Sacrifice).

In summary, these classifications give us insight into identifying cultural events typologies, observing different aspects of cultural events in the city of Barcelona, understanding certain differentiations, from content to form and context. These events characteristics do not just differentiate events from one another, they also significantly determine the use of the space and likewise focus on the ways they are programmed, organised, and additionally by and for whom they are developed. These elements are relevant to consider when it comes to the analysis of events distribution and space used in the city: as the characteristics of an event with a strong link to the social fabric, being bottom-up created, are different to those of a commercial music festival resulting from a format imported from another European country.

Barcelona's Cultural Events: Distribution by Districts

The analysis of cultural events distribution in the city of Barcelona is a new exercise never completed before but it is necessary in order to understand the impact of cultural events, their distribution and their use of urban space. The city of Barcelona, according to 2019 data, is home to more than 1.6 million inhabitants and has 10 districts divided into 73 neighbourhoods. This is a complex context for public space management and utilisation of space. The analysis of cultural events from a spatial-geographical perspective provides an overarching view of the uses of spaces by these events.

Based on ICUB information, a database of cultural events has been constructed which presents variables such as main location or space used, giving us the possibility to map events in the city by district. The first results indicate a strong pattern of centralisation even though there are cultural events throughout the city's districts, including peripheral areas.

This map shows that of the 340 events in 2019, 322 main locations have been identified, although the majority of locations are secondary ones. It is also interesting to note that mass or networked events use many spaces in the city yet districts such as Sant Marti primarily host networked events or operate as secondary spaces whereas central districts primarily host events in their main spaces.

As Figure 3.2 shows, on a scale from one to five, the district with the highest concentration of cultural events is clearly Ciutat Vella, and those with fewer events are Les Corts and Sarrià-Sant Gervasi. This could be due to the geographically central location of Ciutat Vella, where consequently more activities take place, while those places which have fewer events are more peripheral.

Related to Ciutat Vella, it is also interesting to observe some demographic specifics. For example, although the number of residents is not high (only 6.4% of Barcelona's citizens live here), it is one of the districts with a high population density and also the district with the largest proportion of immigrants (49%). Additionally, it is the district with the second most tourist accommodation (21% of the total), and has the largest number of cultural facilities (91 out of 340) such as museums, galleries, cinemas and libraries. Most of the cultural events celebrated in the centre are cultural industry events. Les

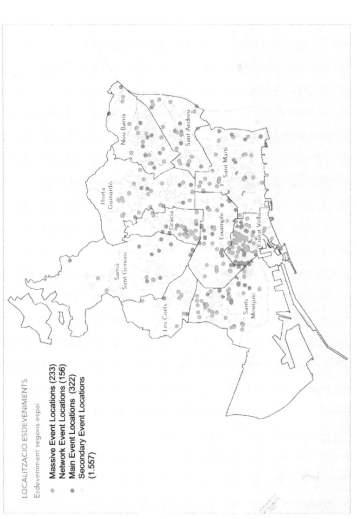

Figure 3.1: Cultural events locations in Barcelona by massive, network, principal and secondary locations. Source: the authors.

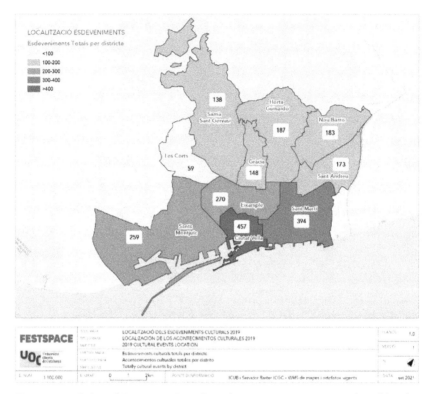

Figure 3.2: Cultural Events in Barcelona by District. Source: produced by the authors.

Corts and Sarrià-Sant Gervasi, socio-demographically, however, are the least populated districts, since only 5% of Barcelona residents live in Les Corts and not much more than 9% in Sarrià-Sant Gervasi. Even so both districts have significant tourist accommodation capacities and a small number of cultural facilities (14 in Les Corts and 22 in Sarrià-Sant Gervasi). Nevertheless, the cultural events held in those districts are mostly cultural industry and popular culture events.

What caught our attention are those districts hosting between 259 and 394 events which can be grouped into three sets: Sants-Montjuïc, Eixample and Sant Marti; Sant Andreu, Nou Barris and Horta-Guinardó; and finally Gràcia, Sarrià-Sant Gervasi and Les Corts. This map could be read as a concentric circle of concentration or of events intensification from the centre to the periphery. Nevertheless, there are exceptions with Sants-Montjuïc and Nou Barris as they are mostly peripheral and not illustrative of this intensification. Explanations can be found in dimensions such as venues, district social fabric or events typology, since Sants-Montjuïc houses a recurring event space (Poble Espanyol), and Nou Barris is one of the districts where there are more bottom-up associative institutions linked to popular culture.

Regarding Sants-Montjuïc, in relation to the socio-demographic characteristics, it is the district with the third largest population (11.2%), and the immigrant population is high compared to the city average (22.3%). Additionally, it stands out for being a district with important museum facilities, such as the Ethnological and World Cultures Museum, the National Museum of Art of Catalonia and large facilities dedicated to fairs such as Fira de Barcelona or Poble Espanyol. The majority of events held in this district are cultural industry festivals. Nou Barris, together with Sant Martí, are districts with notable differences in population and cultural equipment related to the rest of the city. In Nou Barris the presence of cultural facilities is much lower than the city average (having just 14 facilities) and the population represents just 10.4% of the total. Nevertheless, there is a clear presence of cultural events, mostly related to popular culture not determined by the availability of municipal infrastructure (Ajuntament de Barcelona 2020a; 2020b; 2020c; 2020d; 2020e).

Figures 3.3a–3.3c show how these events locations are distributed by cultural events typologies, from cultural diversity events, popular culture events to cultural industry events (identified in figure 3.3 as festivals). Illustrating the events centralisation tendency, it is clear that this centrality differs according to the typology. In the case of cultural industry events, these are clearly centralised, while those of traditional and popular culture are more widely distributed throughout the city.

It can also be seen that those traditional and popular culture events have significant representation in districts where the other typologies are not so much represented, such as in Nou Barris and Sant Andreu.

Recalling that the database of cultural events originates from those events the ICUB is aware of – or has direct participation in one way or another within its public spaces – it is worth noting that the distribution of cultural diversity events is *also* centralised. (Some non-central districts such as Horta Guinardo, Nou Barris, Sant Martí and Sants-Montjuïc are also represented). Yet in one of the districts with the largest immigrant population in Barcelona, the Eixample, there is no clear representation of cultural diversity events.

In summary, contextual data such as socio-demographic information (density and population profile), tourist accommodation data, as well as cultural facilities information, gives us a clear picture of the distribution of cultural events in the city. This articulation helps us understand the relationship that the concentration of cultural events may have to conflicts, or even disputes, between long-term residents, tourists and recent immigrants. It also highlights the Barcelona scenario, a city where the use of spaces is a shared good where everyday use by all citizens is a given within a context of different uses of public spaces, whether for cultural, commercial or tourist purposes. These factors underline the need to make further in-depth analysis drawing on the event typologies and

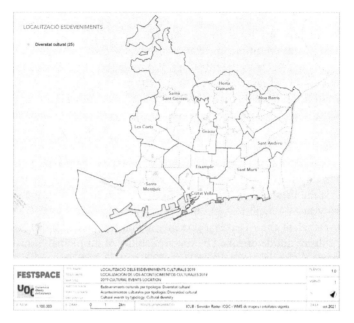

Figure 3.3a: Cultural events distribution by event typology and district (cultural diversity events). Source: the authors.

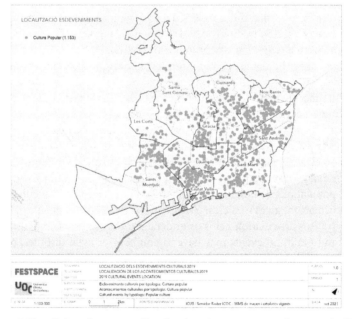

Figure 3.3b: Cultural events distribution by event typology and district (popular culture events). Source: the authors.

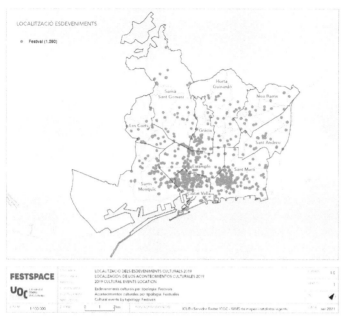

Figure 3.3c: Cultural events distribution by event typology and district (festivals). Source: the authors.

spaces used here, as a street event organised by the neighbourhood social fabric is not the same as a commercial event in a public venue organised by private companies.

Discussion and Conclusion

By trying to work out how public spaces are occupied by cultural events in Barcelona we have observed their distribution and identified cultural events typologies. We have taken into account a broader conception of cultural events that allows us to understand how Barcelona is not only an eventful city (Richards and Palmer 2010), but has also evolved into a 'festivalised' city, where space and time are resources that must be shared and negotiated, since currently festivals and cultural events constitute everyday urban life as a permanent setting (see Hitters 2007). As such, this study reveals three key reflections that may be considered by leaders and decision makers of cultural programming and urban planning.

First, the holistic understanding of the landscape of Barcelona cultural events shows how those events are distributed in terms of public space, how diverse this distribution is and how it can influence the residents' way of doing, living and coexisting in city public space. The intensity of events in the city's districts, mainly those with a high concentration, such as Ciutat Vella or Sants-Monjuïc, suggests possible imbalances between the limited public resources of space and time. An outline that could facilitate dialogue between the social activities of both city residents and tourists could be useful to maintain a better balance.

Second, the link between the nature of each type of event and the use of space facilitates or hinders the relationships between those involved, either actively or passively. Cultural industry events are primarily held in limited access spaces, making it difficult for spontaneous encounters between residents. In contrast, popular culture events by their nature – and especially because they are collective events – are mainly held in squares and streets, and allow for numerous unplanned meetings which Sennett (1970) emphasises are an integral part of a healthy urban environment. Hence, Barcelona's cultural events typologies landscape could be a useful starting point, complementing ethnographic methodologies, for uncovering what effects cultural events are having on the residents of different districts of Barcelona. This could build on the frameworks Smith, Ritchie and Chien (2019) and Ziakas (2014) have developed for mega-events.

Thirdly, with regard to the declared objective of the City Council to create a participatory democracy and just distribution of public resources, the mapping of cultural events in Barcelona displays how public resources of space and time are distributed throughout the city. However, the mapping shows there is no equitable distribution between the districts because there is a concentration of events in the city centre and in the districts with a greater population and more cultural facilities, limiting those districts with less facilities and population.

The current pandemic context and the health measures decreed by the regional government have accelerated the process of decentralisation, forcing programmers to look for new spaces for events and to distribute these for the communities that had participated in them. This circumstance has placed new locations outside the city centre as cultural spaces. A new distribution of cultural events resulting from the pandemic has forced us to ask ourselves whether these new spaces will be maintained in the future and, consequently, whether geographical access to culture by the citizens of Barcelona will be widened. The pandemic has also made the citizens of Barcelona question how they want to live in their own city as well as what functions public spaces should serve. Classic questions from urban studies regarding the effects of tourism in the city have been topics of constant debate in Barcelona, a city reacting to intense flows of tourism and its needs. As this flow alters due to the pandemic, the recovery and reclaiming of streets and the main spots of the city by the citizens must be a key element in the programming of cultural events.

The staging of events in Barcelona has changed dramatically due to the Covid-19 pandemic and the resulting 'new normality'. The trajectory of massification that had seemed unstoppable and headed for a precipice abruptly came to a halt due to unforeseen circumstances. Crowd capacities and expectations have been drastically reduced, and outdoor events have been prioritised. As the tourism industry begins to climb back from its sharp decline, it is important to observe how and where these events are held. In the post-pandemic lull of 2021, when the citizens of Barcelona were able to move about the city freely, tourists were generally absent. The citizens of Barcelona reclaimed their public spaces, using them to celebrate, albeit in a muted manner, events and festivities amongst themselves. With the data that we have collected for 2019, there is scope for research to be done on how the use of public space has changed due to the restrictions imposed on tourism, and how it will change as the tourism industry begins to reawaken.

References

Ajuntament de Barcelona. 2010. *Informes estadístics. La població estrangera a Barcelona Gener 2010*. Available at: https://www.bcn.cat/estadistica /catala/dades/inf/pobest/pobest10/pobest10.pdf

Ajuntament de Barcelona. 2019. *La població de Barcelona. Lectura del Padró Municipal d'Habitants a 01/01/2019*. Available at: https://ajuntament .barcelona.cat/premsa/wp-content/uploads/2019/07/Poblaci%C3%B3 _BCN_2019.pdf

Ajuntament de Barcelona. Departament d'Anàlisi Oficina Municipal de Dades. 2020a. *Ciutat Vella*. Available at: https://www.bcn.cat/estadistica/catala /documents/districtes/01_CiutatVella_2020.pdf

Ajuntament de Barcelona. Departament d'Anàlisi Oficina Municipal de Dades. 2020b. *Les Corts*. Available at: http://www.bcn.cat/estadistica/catala /documents/districtes/04_LesCorts_2020.pdf

Ajuntament de Barcelona. Departament d'Anàlisi Oficina Municipal de Dades. 2020c. *Nou Barris*. Available at: http://www.bcn.cat/estadistica/catala /documents/districtes/08_NouBarris_2020.pdf

Ajuntament de Barcelona. Departament d'Anàlisi Oficina Municipal de Dades. 2020d. *Sants-Monjuïc*. Available at: http://www.bcn.cat/estadistica/catala /documents/districtes/03_Sants_Montju%C3%AFc_2020.pdf

Ajuntament de Barcelona. Departament d'Anàlisi Oficina Municipal de Dades. 2020e. *Sarrià-Sant Gervasi*. Available at: http://www.bcn.cat/estadistica /catala/documents/districtes/05_Sarria_San%20Gervasi_2020.pdf

Arendt, Hannah. 1958. *The Human Condition*. Chicago, IL: University of Chicago Press.

Arias-Sans, Albert and Antonio Russo. 2016. The Right to Gaudí. What Can We Learn from the Commoning of Park Güell, Barcelona? In Claire Colomb and Johannes Novy (Eds.) *Protest and Resistance in the Tourist City* (pp. 247–263). London: Routledge.

Castells, Manuel. 2010. *The Rise of the Network Society. The Information Age: Economy, Society, and Culture, vol. 1*. Malden, MA: Wiley-Blackwell.

Colombo, Alba. 2010. El impacto social en la audiencia de un festival. In Manuel Cuadrado Garcia (Ed.) *Mercados Culturales. Doce estudios de marketing*, pp. 59–75. Barcelona, Spain: EdiUOC.

Colombo, Alba. 2017. Music Festivals and Eventfulness: Examining Eventful Cities by Event Genres and Policy Agendas. *Event Management*, 21(5), 563–573.

Colombo, Alba and Greg Richards. 2017. Eventful Cities as Global Innovation Catalysts: The Sónar Festival Network. *Event Management*, 21(5), 621–634.

Colombo, Alba, Jaime Altuna and Esther Oliver-Grasiot. 2021. Playing with Fire Collectively: Contemporary Cultural Rites as Devisers and Outcomes of Community Networks. *Event Management*, 25(1), 57–68.

Contreras, Jesús. 1979. Les festes populars a Catalunya com a manifestació de la identitat catalana. *Mayurqa: revista del Departament de Ciències Històriques i Teoria de les Arts*, 18, 217–224.

Debord, Guy. 1994. *Society of the Spectacle*. New York: Zone Books.

Degen, Monica and Marisol Garcia. 2012. The Transformation of the 'Barcelona Model': An Analysis of Culture, Urban Regeneration and Governance. *International Journal of Urban and Regional Research*, 36(5), 1022–1038.

Duran i Armengol, Teresa. 2016. *Barcelona festes, festivals, fiestas*. Ajuntament de Barcelona/Triangle Books, 223.

Getz, Donald. 2007. *Event Studies: Theory, Research and Policy for Planned Events*. Oxford: Butterworth-Heinemann.

Gotham, Kevin. 2005. Theorizing Urban Spectacles, *City*, 9(2), 225–246. https://doi.org/10.1080/13604810500197020

Häussermann, Hartmut and Walter Siebel. 1993. *Festivalisierung der Stadtpolitik: Stadtentwicklung durch grosse Projekte*. Opladen: Westdeutscher Verlag.

Hitters, Erik. 2007. Porto and Rotterdam as European Capitals of Culture: Towards the Festivalization of Urban Cultural Policy. In Greg Richards (Ed.) *Cultural Tourism: Global and Local Perspectives*, pp. 281–301. New York: Haworth Press.

Idescat, Institut d'Estadística de Catalunya. 2019. *Població estrangera a 1 de gener. Per països. 2019 Barcelona*. Available at: https://www.idescat.cat/poblacioestrangera/?geo=mun:080193&nac=a&b=12

Jacobs, Jane. 1961. *The Death and Life of Great American Cities*. New York: Vintage Books.

Jakob, Doreen. 2012. The Eventification of Place: Urban Development and Experience Consumption in Berlin and New York City. *European Urban and Regional Studies*, 20(4), 447–459.

Karpińska-Krakowiak, Małgorzata. 2009. Festivalisation of the City: Contemporary examples. *Urban People*, 11(2), 338–350.

Lefebvre, Henri. 1968. *Le droit à la ville*. Paris: Antropos.

Lefebvre, Henri. 1991. *The Production of Space*. Oxford: Blackwell.

Lynch, Kevin. 1960. *Image of the City*. Cambridge, MA: MIT Press.

Map of actual facilities. n.d. In Observatori de Dades Culturals. Ajuntament de Barcelona. Institut de Cultura de Barcelona [Database]. Available at: https://barcelonadadescultura.bcn.cat/equipaments/?lang=es

Monclús, Francisco-Javier. 2003. The Barcelona Model: and an Original Formula? From 'Reconstruction' to Strategic Urban Projects (1979–2004). *Planning Perspectives*, 18(4), 399–421.

Peranson, Mark. 2009. First You Get the Power, Then You Get The Money: Two Models of Film Festivals. In Richard Porton (Ed.) *Dekalog 3: On Film Festivals*, pp. 23–37. London: Wallflower Press.

Richards, Greg. (Ed.) 2007. *Cultural Tourism: Global and Local Perspectives.* New York: Haworth Press.

Richards, Greg and Richard Palmer. 2010. *Eventful Cities: Cultural Management and Urban Revitalisation.* Oxford: Butterworth-Heinemann.

Richards, Greg. 2015a. Events in the Network Society: The Role of Pulsar and Iterative Events. *Event Management*, 19(4), 553–566.

Richards, Greg. 2015b. Developing the Eventful City: Time, Space and Urban Identity. In S. Mushatat and M. Al Muhairi (Eds.) *Planning for Event Cities*, pp. 37–46. Ajman, United Arab Emirates: Municipality and Planning Department of Ajman.

Russo, Antonio and Alessandro Scarnato. 2018. 'Barcelona in Common': A New Urban Regime for the 21st-century Tourist City? *Journal of Urban Affairs*, 40(4), 455–474.

Scarnato, Alessandro. 2016. *Barcelona Supermodelo. La complejidad de una transformación social y urbana (1979–2011).* Barcelona: Editorial Comanegra Ajuntament de Barcelona.

Sennet, Richard. 1970. *The Uses of Disorder: Personal Identity and City Life.* New York: Alfred A. Knopf.

Smith, Andrew. 2013. 'Borrowing' Public Space to Stage Major Events: The Greenwich Park Controversy. *Urban Studies*, 51(2), 247–263.

Smith, Andrew. 2017. Animation or Denigration? Using Urban Public Spaces as Event Venues. *Event Management*, 21(5), 609–619.

Smith, Andrew, Brent W. Ritchie and Monica P. Chien. 2019. Citizens' Attitudes Towards Mega-Events: A New Framework. *Annals of Tourism Research*, 74, 208–10.

Statista. 2021. Atracciones turísticas más visitadas en Barcelona en 2019. Available at: https://es.statista.com/estadisticas/486111/atracciones-turisticas-mas-populares-en-barcelona-espana

Throsby, David. 2008. The Concentric Circles Model of the Cultural Industries. *Cultural Trends*, 17(3), 147–164.

Wilson, Julie. 2020. Collaborative Tourism Platforms and the Production of Urban Space: Tales from Barcelona In *Transforming Tourism: Regional Perspectives on a Global Phenomenon*, pp. 32–59. Brussels: Centre Maurits Coppieters.

Wynn, Jonathan R. 2016. *Music/City: American Festivals and Placemaking in Austin, Nashville, and Newport.* Chicago, IL: University of Chicago Press.

Young, Iris Marion. 1990. *Justice and the Politics of Difference.* Princeton, NJ: Princeton University.

Ziakas, Vassilios. 2014. For the Benefit of All? Developing a Critical Perspective in Mega-Event Leverage. *Leisure Studies*, 34(6), 689–702.

VVAA Cultural festivals. n.d. In Observatori de Dades Culturals. Ajuntament de Barcelona. Institut de Cultura de Barcelona [Database]. Available at: https://barcelonadadescultura.bcn.cat/festivals/dades/?lang=en

CHAPTER 4

The Contested Role of Events in Public Squares: The Case of George Square, Glasgow

David McGillivray, Séverin Guillard
and Gayle McPherson

Introduction

Urban public squares have long been important sites for festivals and events. As crucial features of urban life, many of these spaces were designed to accommodate a range of civic activities, including hosting markets, military events, protests and commemorative occasions. However, in the past two decades, they have been increasingly used as venues for an array of civic and commercial events. This new trend is part of a broader festivalisation of the city (Gravari-Barbas 2009; Richards and Palmer 2010; Gold and Gold 2020), through which festivals and events are employed as tools for the promotion and management of urban public spaces. However, the specific use of civic squares as festival and event sites has generated mixed reactions. Building on critiques of a neoliberal, entrepreneurial turn in public space management (Harvey 1989; Mitchell

How to cite this book chapter:
McGillivray, D., Guillard, S. and McPherson, G. 2022. The Contested Role of Events in Public Squares: The Case of George Square, Glasgow. In: Smith, A., Osborn, G. and Quinn, B. (Eds.) *Festivals and the City: The Contested Geographies of Urban Events*. London: University of Westminster Press. Pp. 59–76. London: University of Westminster Press. DOI: https://doi.org/10.16997/book64.d. License: CC-BY-NC-ND 4.0

1995), commentators have analysed how festivalisation contributes to the commodification (Smith 2016) and privatisation (Gomes 2019) of civic spaces. Others, especially those supporting the benefits derived by the entrepreneurial local state, laud its positive effects, including showcasing important attributes of the city to a watching global audience. In architecture and urban design texts, events hosted in civic squares have been praised as a means of facilitating the 'activation' of these spaces (Ivers 2018), creating new modes of conviviality which could contribute to their revitalisation (Gomes 2019).

Most of the recent research on the relationship between festivals, events and public space has focused either on their role in regeneration or revitalisation plans (Smith et al. 2021) or their contribution to broader urban projects (Gomes 2019). Relatively few studies have considered the role of festivals and events in the making, or remaking, of a civic public square by urban planners and designers. As civic squares are conceived as festivals and events venues, participatory planning and design processes are now utilised to include the views of the general public to inform plans (Daoust Lestage 2018; Smith et al. 2021). These processes generate strong responses, both positive and negative, providing insights into how these spaces are valued, and by whom, and for what purpose.

This chapter draws on a case study of George Square in Glasgow, Scotland, to explore citizen views of the staging of festivals and events in a historically important civic public square. Over the past few decades, Glasgow has become a prime example of a European city where festivals and events have been used to regenerate the urban environment and address the crisis associated with the loss of its traditional industries (Gomez 1998; García 2005; Mooney 2004). This strategy led to the intense utilisation of the central spaces of the city – sometimes at the expense of other areas (Paddison and Sharp 2007) – with a particular focus on a few iconic squares and parks central to the city's image and history. This is especially the case in George Square, a space which has long been crucial for the city as the home for its political headquarters, the City Chambers. Historically, George Square has been the site of many important protests and civic celebrations, and in recent years has regularly hosted a wide range of events. Some of these events have restricted access for everyday use and generated city-wide discussion about the suitability of the space as an event venue, and the appropriateness of its physical design. In this context, Glasgow City Council's announcement in late 2019 of a city-wide 'conversation' to consider the future design of the square was an important moment regarding the future role of this space, and the role that events should play within it.

The chapter starts by outlining the role festivals and events have historically played in the design and use of urban squares, and how this role has evolved and changed in recent years. It then sets out the context of the Glasgow-wide conversation that took place in 2019 to discuss the future of George Square, and the observational and interview-based fieldwork conducted on this. In the second half of the chapter, the results of the investigations are presented, with a specific focus on discussions related to 'events'. What this process revealed about Glasgow citizens' views on the role of events in the future of the square is explored, highlighting tensions between institutional actors and citizens about its purpose and use, and the sort of events which should be hosted there. The chapter concludes by arguing that the city-wide participatory process for this square revealed two dimensions of the contested geographies of festivals in the city: the contested role of events in public squares, and the contested voices of urban residents about public space.

The Historical Relationship Between Public Squares and Events

Often occupying central locations, and surrounded by major civic buildings (e.g. town halls and municipal headquarters), civic squares represent particularly 'charged public spaces' providing 'a physical, social, and metaphorical space for public debate about governance, cultural identity, and citizenship' (Low 2000, 20). Distinct from public parks, squares connect citizens 'not to manifestations of nature but to the heart of urban culture, history and memory' (Lévy 2012, 157). The history of the urban square is inseparable from its association with festivity. This situation is particularly evident in Europe, where the relationship between public squares and festive occasions represents an important moment in the making of cities. For example, the Roman Forum was historically one of the main event spaces in the city, hosting gladiatorial combats. The Forum was designed with spectacular events in mind, with monuments located at the periphery of the square rather than at its centre; columns less densely grouped so they could shelter silversmiths; and balconies on the upper floors to host viewing audiences (Sitte 1889). In the Middle Ages, civic squares represented meeting and gathering points for urban dwellers, often located in the centre of cities. This was reinforced by their status as spaces of commerce, as host sites for markets (Webb 1990).

Squares have also been the places where popular pastimes were hosted, tied to agriculture, religion and other important markers of identity. For example, the piazza in Italy is often referred to as a civic space for commerce, entertainment and strolling. Carnivals and parades have traversed through, or come to their conclusion in, squares. The Plaza del Campo in Siena represents an archetypal example of a square renowned for its association with events and popular festivity. In medieval times, the square was the centre of many sporting events which included bullfights, battles with staves and stones, and horse races in the streets around the cathedral (Webb 1990). Today, these traditions remain, attracting residents and tourists alike into this city's square during the summer. However, the historic relationship between squares and events has also been linked with the expression of power. In medieval times, many squares originated as extensions of churches, providing places for people to gather before and after worship, and a site for religious ceremonies (Smith 2016). After the end of the Renaissance period, many squares were also built or redesigned with the idea of hosting events which could showcase the power of royal authority. This is the case for Plaza Mayor in Madrid, which was reshaped on the command of Philip III so it could host major ceremonies, and this function was illustrated by the inclusion of a royal pavilion from which the King could watch spectacles. Similarly, in Paris, the Place Royale was designed by Henri IV as a setting for royal festivities (Webb 1990).

Though some of the traditional festivities that took place in public squares are centuries old, others can be traced to the mass generation of traditions which took place pre-war across Europe (Hobsbawm and Ranger 1983). These traditions represented the expression of the state's pomp and power and citizens' pleasure, and often took place in public squares as the number and scale of ceremonies and other gatherings grew. This official expression of power through events was often intertwined with more informal and spontaneous gatherings, some of which challenged established authority structures. Squares have been spaces for political demonstrations or protests, providing the focal point for collective action. Mass gatherings of people protesting political, economic or social injustices have been seen across major European and international cities, from the fall of communism across Eastern Europe, the poll tax protests across UK cities in the early 1990s, or the anti-war protests around the time of the Iraq War. In recent years, some scholars have addressed how securitisation and privatisation have threatened the politicisation of public spaces (Mitchell 1995; Low and Smith 2006), but the past two decades have also shown the importance of public squares as sites of collective gatherings. Squares continue to have a central role in these movements (e.g. the Place Tahrir as part of the Arab Spring Revolution in Cairo, the Puerta del Sol for the Indignados in Madrid, the Place de la Republique for the Nuit Debout movement in Paris) (Hristova and Czepczyński 2017). These events have put a new emphasis on the continuous role of the square as a politically contested space (Low 2010), and on the role of civic events as a crucial tool for redefining who has the right to access and use these spaces (Hancock 2017).

Squares as Contemporary Event Venues

In the second half of the twentieth century, scholars, journalists and commentators forecast a crisis for public squares which, as with many other public spaces, were thought to have lost their central role in urban life. These declarations were attributed to the increasing importance of the car, which changed squares into traffic islands or parking lots (Giddings et al. 2011). With the growth in indoor venues in major cities in the 1980s and 1990s, public squares were also said to have lost some of their importance as places of public celebration. Yet in the past two decades, researchers have identified a renewal of public squares, often related to their role as a venue for various types of events. Indeed, in the context of increased inter-urban competition, the local state has put more emphasis on making their public spaces attractive to both residents and visitors alike. That has created tensions within urban environments. For example, in Glasgow from the mid 2000's, visitor needs were perceived to be served over local citizens with the introduction of the Winter Festival in George Square (Foley and McPherson 2007). As Richards and Palmer (2010) suggest, cities have become more eventful, and civic squares and plazas have been constituted more intentionally to host a range of civic and commercial events and festivities, some rooted in the unique characteristics of the place, but many 'brought in' as part of wider event-led neoliberalised policy imperatives. Traditional festivities held in public spaces are now increasingly subject to management (in terms of risk, brand activation and media promotion) and planned in the name of instrumentalised, globalised motives when their original purpose was intentionally symbolic and locally meaningful (Foley et al. 2012).

Events are now frequently imagined as a means of 'activating' and 'animating' public spaces, including those like public squares viewed as having lost their appeal. Gomes (2019) shows how hosting atmospheric events in public squares has been part of wider promotional techniques to encourage gatherings of people as an antidote to trends of privatisation and atomisation associated with late capitalism. Yet, trends towards public squares being conceived as venues for events have also been influenced by processes of neoliberalisation and the rise of new public management models, accompanied by cuts to public funding and the need for the local state to act entrepreneurially, identifying new sources of revenue. Because the commercial entertainment and event industry is searching for more iconic, unique venues in (and on) which to host their spectacles, public squares are conceived as assets which can be sold or rented temporarily to private companies, generating much needed revenue for municipal authorities. Indeed, because of their contained nature, squares are perfect for staging commercial events. Audiences can be managed spatially and then mediated to a watching world. The civic backdrop marks the place at a time when urban uniqueness is increasingly difficult to achieve. In Glasgow, for example, tourism imagery often includes pictures from events in George Square (such as fireworks displays), which includes the backdrop of the City Chambers and a building advertising the city's official motto, 'People Make Glasgow' (Figure 4.1).

The contemporary use of events and festivals also influences the design of squares. Historically, squares have changed to reflect the evolution of their function, but new adaptations are now made with the explicit goal of hosting (commercial) festivals and events. Design adaptations take several forms. First, there are temporary interventions to mark off event sites and to limit access to those paying for tickets (Smith 2014). For example, fences and barriers are erected to limit access to events, partly on grounds of health and safety, but also to ensure exclusivity to those paying for the privilege. This demarcation of space in public squares is also intended to manage and control access

Figure 4.1: George Square Christmas Lights Switch On. Source: Glasgow City Council.

even when events are free (McGillivray 2019). Free-to-access civic events, celebrating key markers in the year, like Christmas, Halloween and New Year, are now invariably ticketed and subject to extensive regulatory interventions. Second, more and more squares are also intentionally redesigned *for* events, with public authorities adapting their physical design to accommodate a range of uses. An emblematic example is The Place des Festivals (Festival Square), within Montréal's Quartier des Spectacles, a one-square-kilometre neighbourhood which was developed around the idea of embedding culture and creativity in the experience of public space (Harrel, Lussier and Thibert 2015). The Place des Festivals is a square specifically designed to accommodate large events and gatherings (Daoust Lestage 2018). This intention is reflected in the shaping of the square as a slope which allows it to work as an amphitheatre during events, the existence of mega-lighting structures that signify the 'walls' of an outdoor theatre, and the existence of flexible landscapes which can accommodate the various uses of the space (Figure 4.2). In particular, the fountains in the middle of the square can be turned off for large events, concrete benches can be moved, and scaffolding structures, usually dedicated to host art installations, can be repurposed as kiosks (Daoust Lestage 2018).

While the design features visible in public squares are important, they mask the contested nature of discussions that take place in cities to decide who is responsible for, involved in, and left out of, decisions about how public spaces

Figure 4.2: The Place des Festivals in Montreal. The left-hand side shows the slope character of the square as well as the moveable benches, while the mega-lighting structures are displayed on the right-hand side. Source: Séverin Guillard.

are designed and managed, including their potential to host festivals and events. While it is possible to 'design-in' festivals and events to new public spaces (Smith et al. 2021) it is much more difficult to transform an historical public space into an events venue. However, it is now common to gauge public views on what uses of public spaces are appropriate, before incorporating design features like street furniture, landscaping, lighting and traffic management. Therefore, as we demonstrate through the case of George Square, Glasgow, exercises designed to consult with citizens over the most appropriate use of public space can produce responses that illustrate tensions between the trajectories of political and economic policy and the interests of the public.

Reimagining George Square: A City-Wide Conversation

George Square is a good example of the contested geographies of urban events. This is a traditional civic public space which has changed dramatically as the city has been reimagined over the last 30 years. The square has been designed and redesigned to be adapted to current uses and architectural trends: it changed from a pond with green water in the middle of a gridded New Town, to a city-centre square with a private pleasure garden, a Haussmannian-influenced piazza for the City Chambers, and finally a civic square hosting a cenotaph, green spaces, and statues of politicians, warriors, poets and scientists. These are now increasingly criticised for being exclusively male and reminiscent of Glasgow's colonial past (Murphy 2019). Throughout its history, the square has also been the site of many important political and social occasions, such as protests, demonstrations, commemorations and parades. As a civic space it has also hosted many traditional festivities to celebrate key dates in the calendar – including the switching on of the Christmas lights, Hogmanay (Scotland's New Year's Eve), and May Day. In 1990 the square was a central hub for the European City of Culture celebrations. It has also long been used as the starting point for mass running and cycling events, both elite (Tour of Britain) and participation-focused (e.g. Great Scottish Run, Santa Dash, Skyride). More recently, it has served as a Fan Zone space for major sporting and cultural events (McGillivray 2019). In 2002, the square was home to the UEFA Champions League fan zone and fulfilled the same role in 2007 when the city hosted the UEFA Cup Final. In 2014, the Commonwealth Games took over the square to host the merchandising operation and in 2018 it was again used as a fan zone and broadcast centre for the inaugural European Championships multi-sport event.

Throughout its history it has been difficult to secure consensus as to what uses should be prioritised in the square, and who has the authority to make those decisions. In 2013 there was a major consultation on the future of the square that included a design competition, only for the City Council to cancel the entire project at the last minute (Duffy 2013). Since then, the future of the square has continued to be the subject of political debate, leading to a decision in 2019 to commission an urban design agency to undertake a 'conversation' with the city's citizens about the future of the square. This decision was partly informed by concern over the way the square has been hired out for events – several of which were viewed as overly commercial – as well as its unsuitability to host major events because of its lack of proper event infrastructure. As one senior event officer in the city commented in 2019, 'George Square is ... it's a roundabout ultimately just now. So you're doing an event in a roundabout with no power, with no tech, on a slope, with lots of statues in very bizarre places' (personal interview).

The recognition that different types of events can attract different audiences and participants has impacted the way urban planners think about engaging with citizens in the design and programming of their public spaces. However, if squares are to be enlivened by hosting events, then it is imperative that a diversity of interests are included in the design process to ensure it is reflective of existing and potential users of that space. Over the last decade, the practice of urban design has been influenced by a shift towards more participative methods (Aelbrecht and Stevens 2019) which seek to incorporate a wider cross-section of non-specialist voices. These new methods include workshops, open-source participatory mapping, storytelling and related activities that put the user at the centre (Brain 2019). It is in that vein that a city-wide 'conversation' on the future of George Square was initiated over a period of 10 weeks in late 2019. This conversation took place online, and in person via a series of 'hands on workshops'. Initial responses were brought together for a final 'co-creation' workshop with a smaller 'representative' portion of the city's population. This then fed into a final report from the urban designers to the local authority.

During the city-wide conversation, the team were permitted to observe meetings and workshops, and attend public consultation sessions, comprising a total of 15 hours of observation. This enabled the team to identify tensions, conflicts and areas of consensus and assess both the effectiveness of the process and the issues participants felt were important to them, with a focus on events. A bespoke observation template was used to document the findings and research team came together to identify key issues, using a thematic analysis approach. Five semi-structured interviews were conducted. These were with those directly involved in leading the city-wide conversation (n=1), representatives from the client who commissioned the work (n=2), and the organisation responsible in Glasgow for planning and delivering events in the city (n=2). Finally, with the authorisation of the lead consultant, the team were granted access to data gathered through the online conversation, which helped inform the observations and interpretations. In each case, while interest was primarily in participants' views on every aspect of the square and its potential use(s), our focus was how the public viewed the role of events and the influence of these expressions on the institutional decision-making process about the future of George Square. In the following discussion three key themes are focused upon. First, linking the opening historical account of the role of squares to the documenting of participants' reflections on how they valued events and their relationship with George Square. Second, the study highlights participants' views on the perceived commercialisation of the square through event activity. The final theme illustrates how the process of participatory planning created tensions between what people 'want' and how this relates to the imperatives of the institutional actors involved.

Events and the Square: Perceptions of Past and Future

As previously discussed, squares are contested spaces, historically representing different functions. Similarly, the study findings illustrated a diversity of opinion on the most appropriate uses of Glasgow's George Square, informed by both historical and contemporary narratives. Participants in the 'conversation' were asked to contribute their views about George Square at present, and what they thought it should be in the future, via paper surveys passed out in the streets, online comments on social media, and individual contributions made on the consultation website. There were 2,267 submissions to the main conversation in total and the majority were online. The conversation included a mix of open-ended questions ('what brought you to the square?') which were then gathered to find a common set of purposes, and questions based on a predetermined pool of words or phrases ('words and phrases that describe George Square today'). Though there were many important reasons for respondents' visiting the square, events ranked highly in responses. When asked 'what brought them to the square?', the most popular responses were 'walking or passing through', followed by 'open space to relax, meet and socialise' and 'special events or occasions'. Also related to events, a further smaller number of respondents mentioned 'for protests, rallies and demonstrations'. The importance accorded to events was unsurprising as George Square is the location for several civic gatherings that are locked into the city's annual calendar and it has been used as a meeting point or fan zones for many mass sporting and cultural gatherings in recent years (McGillivray 2019).

The regular use of the square for festivities did not, however, prevent participants having contrasting feelings about it. In terms of people's perceptions of the square at the present time, many people expressed negative perceptions, and identified the need for change. They described the square as an overlooked place, containing 'nothing special', being 'undervalued' or 'unattractive'. More positively, the square was described as 'historic', representing a typically 'Glaswegian' place, Glasgow's 'civic heart' and an 'iconic landmark'. Reflecting people's ambitions for the future of the square, attending special events or occasions occupied an important role here, too, being the third most popular response after 'sightseeing the building or monuments' and 'open space to relax, meet and socialise'. Summarising the online conversation, attending special events or occasions were identified as being important in people's perceptions of George Square, but there were also intimations of contestation over the purpose and role of events, which were explored further in the second part of the city conversation, where more the focus was more discursive.

Civic, Not Commercial, Event Space

In the second phase of the city-wide conversation a number of hands-on workshops, and a final co-creation workshop, were held. These discussions highlighted further tensions and contestations over the purpose and role of events in George Square. In these workshops, attendees proposed different uses, often influenced by their personal or professional experiences. On one level, participants were positive about the role of events in animating the square and making it an attractive place for visitors and residents to gather, congregate and interact. This perspective was commonly voiced by participants who supported the pedestrianisation of the square and improvements to the surrounding city centre streetscape and public realm. One professional contributor (with knowledge of the design and architecture field) made the bold statement that 'George Square's function as an event space is its most important one'. Supporting that perspective, contributors suggested that 'events in George Square contain atmosphere', producing positive feelings. Management of atmosphere using events as a powerful affective component is increasingly influential in how urban places are promoted (Bille, Bjerregaarde and Sorensen 2015). When discussion focused on design ideas and potential pedestrianisation, contributors mentioned the importance of the 'flows and circulation' of people (visitors, for example) from retail and other environments close to George Square. In this context, events were viewed as a means of drawing people in, driving footfall to businesses in the surrounding area.

On the other hand, many more critical voices spoke of the dangers associated with the increasing commercialisation of the public realm, exemplified by the hiring out of the square for commercial events. There was general recognition that some civic events needed to be hosted in the square, like the annual Christmas Lights switch on, and probably had to be ticketed because this contributed to a sense of civic pride amongst citizens. However, there was concern expressed over conceptions of the square as an event space, especially when the square was effectively closed off to everyday use. Participants expressed the view that public spaces should be accessible all of the time for uses like passing through and relaxing. Strong opposition was expressed to the 'barriered marketplace' feel of the square when handed over to commercial event operators, with barriers being erected for commercial purposes, and the square becoming a building site for many months of the year in preparation for hosting events. These tensions between staging commercially valuable events in public spaces and these spaces being open, inclusive and free for all is evident in other cities too (Smith 2020). The George Square conversation reinforced the view that people wanted to access their public spaces without having to pay, to queue, or be searched.

Participants also expressed the need for events to be managed and not 'takeover the square', especially if they produced conflict between different uses and users. Some felt that the square should only be used for not-for-profit events and others wanted the square to primarily be a site for more spontaneous, convivial, pop-up events or cultural expressions that reminded them of their experiences of visiting other European plazas. Strictly regulated event activity tends to give precedence to official event organisers over informal occurrences (Foley et al. 2012). One workshop participant shared the story of a local choir who had performed in the square to entertain people but had been moved on by the police. They felt this was against the 'spirit of Glasgow' and the public use of the square. Some people felt that there were more appropriate public spaces in the city to host some types of events so as not to restrict access to George Square for extended periods of time. The theme of unrestricted access to enjoy this civic space all year round was prominent in workshop discussions (see Figure 4.3). Continuing the themes of informality and spontaneity, there

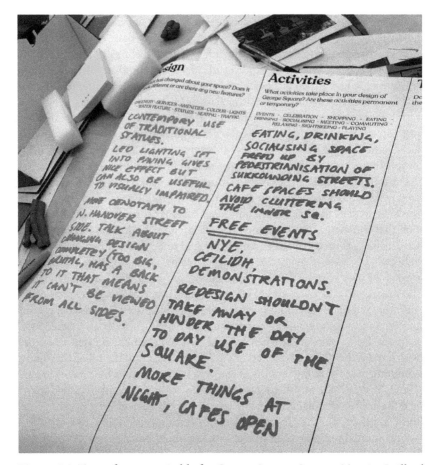

Figure 4.3: Type of events suitable for George Square. Source: Séverin Guillard.

was consensus that the square should continue to be an important space for demonstrations and protests, retaining a tradition in Glasgow for mass gatherings in George Square as a visible expression of democracy in action.

Discussions about the use of the square as an event space also veered into practical design considerations, with participants using terminology drawn from architecture and urban design about the value of events, culture and hospitality as 'interventions' that could 'activate' the square (Ivers 2018). Common to these discussions was a recognition that the physical features accommodated in public space are only part of the solution, with interactions between people and place being crucial in bringing spaces to life. In the final co-creation workshop participants were asked to produce a mock design, reflecting their priorities (Figure 4.4). This process illustrated an expressed view that George Square needed to cater for both events and more sedate uses. Indeed, most designs contained some form of event-space, though it

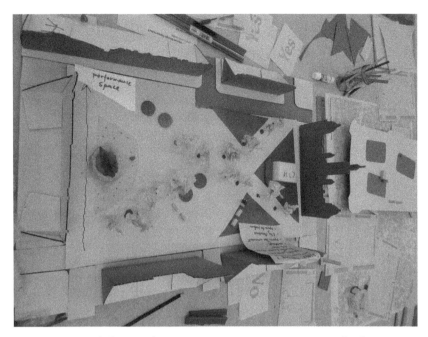

Figure 4.4: Mock design of George Square. Source: Séverin Guillard.

was often a designated area within the square, alongside other more valued elements, like greening.

Your Voice Counts: Participatory Rhetoric Meets Institutional Realities

In the context of urban planning and design, Brain (2019, 177) has identified a shift in the balance of power and locus of agency from professional design expertise to a wider public, looking to 'ground its practices in the formative aspirations of a community (rather than the technical issues of civic administration)'. The George Square city-wide conversation aligned with this trend given its emphasis on involving the general public in shaping the future of this important public space. However, this outward commitment to the formative aspirations of a community masks power relations and the continuing dominance of institutional actors in shaping the urban landscape. Despite the well-intentioned commitment to engage with the general public, the conversation was, in practice, a selective exercise with particular social groups represented more than others and the short timescales making it difficult to reach out to those less likely to participate because of lack of trust in institutions (Peinhardt and Storring 2019). While the online activities generated over 2000 contributions, the detailed workshop interventions produced relatively low levels of attendance, with only 52 attendees at hands-on workshops, 71 visitors at the pop-up exhibition and 39 attendees at the final co-creation forum. In addition, while the conversation was conceived to collect the views of 'ordinary Glaswegians' (personal interview, lead urban designer), there is an important role for professionals in the planning and design of urban space. Many participants in the co-creation workshops possessed expertise which justified their interest in attending, including professionals specialising in design or related practice (architects, designers, and transport planners). The cultural capital and social profile of workshop attendees influenced the nature of debate, reproducing power dynamics in the way they tried to exert their authority over how the square should be designed and used; for example, the male voice was dominant in at least two of the workshops. Some issues of representation were addressed in the final co-creation workshop, with a broader cross-section of Glasgow's citizenry invited to contribute, including people with disabilities, minority ethnic groups and young people. However, the short timescale, 'snapshot' approach to the George Square conversation increased the risk of tokenism, of providing merely a veneer of meaningful engagement with citizens about an important civic space (Peinhardt and Storring 2019) when decisions have already been made.

In the context of the (re)designing of a well-loved space like George Square, the city-wide conversation produced a plethora of different ideas. There was evident passion and commitment from participants, whether online or in person, to feed into a process that would help them enhance a space that has lost some of its appeal in recent years. At the conclusion of the process, recommendations to the council included: 'events that take place on the Square must benefit and be accessible to all citizens' and 'George Square should be a place for the common good of Glasgow, so that it predominantly offers free space that can be enjoyed by anyone at any time'. Crucially, it was also suggested that 'the design process for the future of George Square must be rooted in public aspirations ... designers need to work with Glasgow's citizens to ensure that their proposals have public support and reflect public aspirations'. This expressed desire for ongoing public involvement in the future (re)design of the square beyond the initial scoping exercise was reinforced by the lead urban designer who suggested that 'there does need to be a collaborative approach. And it definitely has to be collaborative approach and not a consultative approach, a collaborative approach that ... needs a design team that have that built in from the start and kind of are up for it' (personal interview). In response to these recommendations, there was recognition from the local authority in its Emerging Area Strategy (January 2020) of the need for a 'new Event Space and Management Strategy' (4), that would form part of a 'wider city centre event space plan' (4). The need for an Event Space and Management Strategy was confirmed in the Council's commitment to the recommendations emerging from the city-wide conversation (Table 4.1).

Table 4.1: Public conversation recommendations.

Management recommendation	Action
GSq is special: the main civic space and special place in citizens' hearts	Management Plan Event Space Strategy
GSq should be a place for the common good, predominantly with free space available to anyone anytime	Event Space Strategy Common Good
GSq is one of various event spaces and its role/function should be reflected in the programme of events	Event Space Strategy
GSq should offer citizens the chance to showcase Glasgow's changing creativity	Event Space Strategy

However, despite the collaborative rhetoric, the actions following the city-wide conversation ultimately showed a need to 'craft an accommodation with the dominant institutional and ideological arrangements' (Brain 2019, 177). George Square has been subjected to institutional determination for many years based on the need to use it, instrumentally, as a place for hosting events that attract incoming visitors and help project the city to an international audience. As a Senior Officer responsible for events in the city confirmed, the Square is in demand from event organisers: 'when you talk to event owners right, where do they, where do they want to bring their event? … they want tae go tae George Square … they want to be in front a' the City Chambers' (personal interview). These imperatives challenged the rhetoric of participatory planning and design processes. In the case of George Square, the City Council's elected members decided that while part-pedestrianisation of the square was possible in the short term, contractual obligations with several major sporting federations means that the square will continue to operate as a major event space until at least the end of 2023 when the UCI World Cycling Championships will take place. In awarding the design contract for the square in April 2021, the Council reinforced the importance of the square as a venue for major events, stating that 'the redesign of George Square will factor in Glasgow's hosting of major events in the coming years'. So, while the George Square conversation clearly confirmed a desire on behalf of the public for the renewal and reimagining of the square as a public space with less traffic, more green space and fewer barriered marketplace commercial events, city leaders decided that hosting events there provides a focal point for the city as a place to draw in crowds and as a space for powerful place-specific mediation.

Conclusion

Following a history in Europe where squares have long been used as a location for hosting events, George Square is valued in Glasgow as the civic heart of the city, a place where people want to relax, meet others, walk through and gather for demonstrations or special civic events. However, in the context of increasing concerns regarding the role of events in the commodification of contemporary squares, George Square is an exemplar of contested geographies in action. Since the late 1980s Glasgow has invested in culture, sport, events and tourism as a means of restructuring its economy, and George Square has been an important stage upon which this particular version of urban place-making has been performed. This has led to concerns over the commercialisation of the city's civic heart, and uncertainty over the place of the square in the city's future vision.

While George Square has been structurally and institutionally determined in recent years to suit the urban entrepreneurialism of its governing authorities, the city-wide conversation initiated by city leaders was suggestive of a move towards a wider cross-section of views and interests shaping the future design and use of the square. Indeed, the participatory engagement methods utilised in the city-wide conversation generated diverse views about the square as an event space. This approach suggested a commitment to intentional and self-conscious action, with choices articulated by a broader public and then translated into a visual and spatial order of new design. However, despite the expressed desire for the square to be a public space primarily for uses other than commercial events, economic imperatives and long-term contractual obligations with external event owners means that the public's aspirations are left largely unfulfilled.

Squares, like other public spaces, have long had contested meanings and securing consensus on their suitability for staging events is unlikely to be achieved easily. Civic events with wider historic, social or political meanings will continue to remain a prominent feature of public squares. However, this study has shown a desire from the public for more nuanced urban planning and design strategies to ensure a better distribution of events around the city, reducing the reliance on some historically valuable public spaces and the accompanying negative impacts. In realising this ambition, there is an important place for longer term engagement processes with multi-actor involvement, clear design parameters and management plans. Public squares are important sites of communal celebration, representing more than just another event venue. Reflecting public aspirations in their design and use will ensure that public squares retain their value, providing a space for public debate about governance, cultural identity and citizenship.

References

Aelbrecht, Patricia and Quentin Stevens. 2019. *Public Space Design and Social Cohesion*. New York: Routledge.

Bille, Mikkel, Peter Bjerregaarde and Tim Flohr Sorensen. 2015. Staging Atmospheres: Materiality, Culture and the Texture of the In-between. *Emotion, Space and Society*, 15, 31–38.

Brain, David. 2019. Reconstituting the Urban Commons: Public Space, Social Capital and the Project of Urbanism. *Urban Planning*, 4(2), 169–182.

Daoust Lestage. 2018. Permanent and Ephemeral Culture: La Place des Festivals – Quartiers des Spectacles, Montréal. In B. Cannon Ivers, *Staging Urban Landscapes: The Activation and Curation of Flexible Public Spaces*, pp. 282–284. Berlin: De Gruyter.

Duffy, Owen. 2013. Dumped: £15m plan to redevelop Glasgow's George Square dropped after popular backlash. *The Guardian*, 21 March. Available at: https://www.theguardian.com/uk/scotland-blog/2013/jan/21/glasgow-georgesquare-saved

Foley, Malcolm and Gayle McPherson. 2007. Glasgow's Winter Festival: Can Cultural Leadership Serve the Common Good? *Managing Leisure*, 12(2–3), 143–156.

Foley, Malcolm, David McGillivray and Gayle McPherson 2012. *Event Policy: From Theory to Strategy*. Abingdon: Routledge.

Garcia, Beatriz. 2005. De-constructing the City of Culture: The Long-term Cultural Legacies of Glasgow 1990. *Urban Studies*, 42(5/6), 1–28.

Giddings, Bob, James Charlton and Margaret Horne. 2011. Public Squares in European City Centres. *Urban Design International*, 16(3), 202–212.

Gold, John and Margaret Gold. 2020. *Festive Cities: Culture, Planning and Urban Life*. Abingdon: Routledge.

Gomes, Pedro. 2019. The Birth of Public Space Privatization: How Entrepreneurialism, Convivial Urbanism and Stakeholder Interactions Made the Martim Moniz Square in Lisbon, 'Privatization-Ready'. *European Urban and Regional Studies*, 27(1), 86–100.

Gómez, Maria. 1998. Reflective Images: The Case of Urban Regeneration in Glasgow and Bilbao. *International Journal of Urban and Regional Research*, 22(1), 106–121.

Gravari-Barbas, Maria. 2009. La « ville festive » ou construire la ville contemporaine par l'événement. (The 'Festival City': Urban Events and Contemporary City Building). In *Bulletin de l'Association de géographes français*, 2009-3, 279–290.

Hancock, Claire. 2017. Why Occupy *République*? Redefining French Citizenship From a Parisian Square, *Documents d'Anàlisi Geogràfica*, 63(2), 427–445.

Harrel, Simon, Laurent Lussier and Joël Thibert. 2015. *Le Quartier des spectacles et le chantier de l'imaginaire montréalais*. Québec: Presses de l'Université Laval.

Harvey, David. 1989. From Managerialism to Entrepreneurialism: The Transformation in Urban Governance in Late Capitalism. *Geografiska Annaler. Series B, Human Geography*, 71(1), 3–17.

Hobsbawm, Eric and Terence Ranger. 1983. *The Invention of Tradition*. Cambridge: Cambridge University Press.

Hristova, Svetlana and Mariusz Czepczyéski (Eds.) 2018. *Public Space: Between Reimagination and Occupation*. Abingdon: Routledge

Ivers, B. Cannon. 2018. *Staging Urban Landscapes: The Activation and Curation of Flexible Public Spaces.* Berlin: De Gruyter.

Lévy, Bertrand. 2012. Urban Square as the Place of History, Memory, Identity. In Dušica Dražić, Slavica Radišić and Marijana Simu (Eds.) *Memory of the City,* pp. 156–173. Belgrade: Kulturklammer, 156–173.

Low, Setha. 2000. *On the Plaza: The Politics of Public Space and Culture.* Austin, TX: University of Texas Press.

Low, Setha and Neil Smith (Eds.) 2006. *The Politics of Public Space.* New York: Routledge.

McGillivray, David. 2019. Sport Events, Space and the 'Live City'. *Cities,* 85, 196–202. https://doi.org/10.1016/j.cities.2018.09.007

Mitchell, Don. 1995. The End of Public Space? People's Park, Definitions of the Public, and Democracy. *Annals of the Association of American Geographers,* 85, 158–178.

Mooney, Gerry. 2004. Cultural Policy as Urban Transformation? Critical Reflections on Glasgow, European City of Culture 1990. *Local Economy,* 19(4), 327–340.

Murphy, Nail. 2019. The Evolution of Glasgow's George Square. George-square.com, 21 October. Available at: https://www.george-square.com/blog

Paddison, Ronan and Joanne Sharp. 2007. Questioning the End of Public Space: Reclaiming Control of Local Banal Spaces. *Scottish Geographical Journal,* 123(2), 87–106.

Peinhardt, Katherine and Nate Storring. 2019. *A Playbook for Inclusive Placemaking.* Project for Public Spaces, 31 May. Available at: https://www.pps.org/article/a-playbook-for-inclusive-placemaking-community-process

Richards, Greg and Robert Palmer. 2010. *Eventful Cities: Cultural Management and Urban Revitalisation.* Abingdon: Routledge.

Sitte, Camillo. 1889 [2013]. *The Art of Building Cities: City Building According to its Artistic Fundamentals.* Eastford, CT: Martino Fine Books.

Smith, Andrew. 2014. 'Borrowing' Public Space to Stage Major Events: The Greenwich Park Controversy. *Urban Studies,* 51(2), 247–263.

Smith, Andrew. 2016. *Events in the City: Using Public Spaces as Event Venues.* Abingdon: Routledge.

Smith, Andrew. 2020. Sustaining Municipal Parks in an Era of Neoliberal Austerity: The Contested Commercialisation of Gunnersbury Park. *Environment and Planning A: Economy and Space.* https://doi.org/10.1177/0308518X20951814

Smith, Andrew, Goran Vodicka, David McGillivray, Alba Colombo, Kristina Lindstrom and Bernadette Quinn. 2021. Staging City Events in Public Spaces: An Urban Design Perspective. *International Journal of Event and Festival Management,* 12(2), 224–239. https://doi.org/10.1108/IJEFM-10-2020-0063

Webb, Michael. 1990. *The City Square: A Historical Evolution.* New York: Whitney Library of Design.

CHAPTER 5

The Publicness of Local Libraries: Insights From Local Libraries Turned Festival Venues in Dublin

Bernadette Quinn and Theresa Ryan

Introduction

As Low and Smart (2020, 4) argue, many of the 'social spaces that are so important to societies and creativity will come back weaker, at least initially', after the Covid-19 pandemic. Public libraries constitute one of these social spaces, and as these institutions reopen, their future as public spaces is unclear. As public services reliant on public funding, recent years have already been difficult for libraries in many countries, and threats to their public funding will undoubtedly be exacerbated by the recent pandemic. In addition, it is likely that social distancing will continue to feature in public health advice for some time, and the implications of this for how libraries may function is unclear (Jaeger, Taylor, Gorham and Kettnich 2021). These new Covid-19 related challenges will compound those already faced by libraries in an increasingly digital age. They have had to adapt to immense changes in how information is produced, disseminated and consumed. This has led to questioning about whether their physical

How to cite this book chapter:
Quinn, B. and Ryan, T. 2022. The Publicness of Local Libraries: Insights From Local Libraries Turned Festival Venues in Dublin. In: Smith, A., Osborn, G. and Quinn, B. (Eds.) *Festivals and the City: The Contested Geographies of Urban Events*. London: University of Westminster Press. Pp. 77–92. London: University of Westminster Press. DOI: https://doi.org/10.16997/book64.e. License: CC-BY-NC-ND 4.0

presence matters any longer in this digital age, although some, like Houpert (2019), argue that their importance has become more vital, precisely because they are needed to help people adapt. More generally, in line with the ownership and management arrangements for many other kinds of public spaces, there are signs of libraries moving away from direct state involvement to other kinds of arrangements involving different social actors (de Magalhães 2010). In the UK, for instance, they are being increasingly transferred out of public service into arrangements that involve voluntary capacities. Developments like this which see the state reduce its oversight and involvement with public spaces have generally been interpreted negatively (Low and Smith 2006). Critics fear that it brings in its wake more social exclusion and less openly accessible communal-use space (Carmona 2010). At a time when libraries are under increasing pressure to justify their calls for public funding it is opportune to think about what would be lost if the publicness of the library was to be diminished.

This chapter investigates what it is that people value about public space and how they understand and value the kinds of publicness that library spaces foster. Conscious that libraries of the future will probably have to work harder to maintain their presence as prominent and easily accessible public spaces, this chapter is particularly interested in how libraries try to diversify the nature and reach of their activities, something they have been increasingly engaged in over recent decades (Fouracre 2015). Thus, in addition to trying to understand how people understand and value libraries as public spaces, a key aim is to investigate how functioning as a festival venue informs the publicness of libraries. Empirically, the data presented were gathered from people attending events in six local libraries as part of the Dublin Festival of History in October 2019. The chapter turns now to review literature on libraries as public spaces, before considering the implications of libraries functioning as festival venues. The data are subsequently presented and discussed.

The Importance of the Library as a Public Space

During the Covid-19 pandemic, physical access to public spaces of all kinds was severely curtailed in many jurisdictions, with indoor public spaces being particularly badly affected. People who continued to have access to open and available public spaces because of where they lived fared much better under 'lockdown' conditions than those who lived where public space was unavailable, overcrowded or otherwise problematic. This experience has underscored the importance of public space to quality of life. Public discussions about the closure and restricted nature of public space during Covid-19 have emphasised the fact that being public means open, accessible and available. It means being an identifiable place 'where the public is free to mingle in the company of strangers' (Given and Leckie 2003, 367). It has been painfully clear that these characteristics have been suspended during the pandemic and questions as to whether the restoration of these public spaces in the future will entail altered forms are now being raised (Low and Smart 2020).

Libraries constitute a type of public space that is often overlooked in discussions about the changing nature and role of public space in contemporary society (Frederikson 2015). Trying to define or classify space, including library space, in terms of its degree of publicness is a difficult, possibly futile task (Given and Leckie 2003). However, trying to understand what it is that people value about public space is important, especially for spaces like public libraries which currently face a number of threats. For Audunson et al. (2018, 774), a functioning public sphere is an essential precondition of democracy. The public sphere is always grounded in physical space (Low 2017) and, in the guise of spaces like parks, squares and city thoroughfares, public space is highly valued politically, socially and symbolically for its democratic qualities (Varna and Tiesdell 2010). For Given and Leckie (2003), the library is arguably one of the few authentic physical, public spaces left. Jaeger et al. (2021, 2) describe libraries as the 'radiant ideal of democracy' and argue that shutting their doors during the pandemic felt like democracy itself had gone into hiding. This pairing of the library with democracy points to how public libraries are fundamentally thought of as open, civic spaces that give access to information such that citizens can inform and educate themselves in true democratic fashion (Frederikson 2015). Symbolically, they are seen to epitomise politically neutral, community places that are open and accessible to all (Leckie and Hopkins 2002) and vital to the vibrancy of urban civic life. However, claims like these can unravel under deeper scrutiny. Crawford (2008, 27) drawing on Fraser (1993), wrote that 'no single physical environment can represent a completely inclusive space of democracy'. Malone (2000) has interpreted libraries as agents of social control and Frederickson (2015) has highlighted how they are strongly conditioned by institutional norms that are culturally situated. Nevertheless, the political and symbolic importance of libraries is not in doubt.

Relatedly, they are crucially important as social spaces. Libraries function as 'third spaces' where people frequently spend time. They are one of those accessible, nearby places that anchor communities and lend structure to daily life (Low and Smart 2020). Classic third spaces are welcoming and inviting places where people routinely and casually encounter others in the guise of acquaintances, friends, familiar faces and strangers. As a trusted space which facilitates the mingling and interaction of all kinds of people, libraries are associated with the development of social capital (Johnson 2012) and seen as an optimal setting for the development of objectified cultural capital (Summers and Buchanan 2018). Houpert (2019, 176) suggests that the social importance of libraries is increasing because they function as 'meeting places for a variety of people, as spaces for cooperation, connection and inspiration'. In a discussion on the changing functions of the library in the digital age, Imholz (2008) stresses the important role that the library of the future will play as a place for accessing people, as opposed to information. She argues that because technology can now deliver information directly to individuals, it is the social experience offered by the library that distinguishes it from the experience of 'sitting at home in front of a computer screen' (Imholz 2008, 338). Accordingly, Capillé (2018, 409) deduces that from the viewpoint of sociability, 'the library provision of indoor public space has become its most valuable feature'.

Libraries and Festivalisation

The political, social and symbolic value of libraries as public space is not in doubt. Yet, while libraries are widely thought to epitomise democratic public space, critical observers have long been aware that they are not, in fact, equally open and available to all (Newman 2007). This is well acknowledged within the library sector itself and efforts to widen their appeal and to draw in 'difficult to reach' cohorts of society can be tracked back to the 1970s and early 1980s in countries like the UK. Such efforts are underpinned by theoretical observations that public space is a constantly changing context (Zukin 1996), that space in general is continuously reproduced through a process of ongoing heterogeneous interrelations (Massey 1994), and that the very make-up of the interests and actors who use space strongly shape its reproduction. Varna and Tiesdell (2010) reviewed literature related to the publicness of libraries and concluded that five dimensions are thought to be central to creating publicness: ownership, control, physical configuration and animation. Of interest in this chapter is how the festivalisation of libraries might affect these dimensions.

As Ronström (2016) explains, festivals have become an increasingly important form of cultural production in recent decades, proliferating in number and type, altering cultural consumption patterns, expanding into spaces not historically associated with festivals, and serving diverse kinds of agendas at the behest of various institutions. Jordan (2016, 53) argues that 'festivalisation is both a response to and a cause of changing audience expectations and production processes within the cultural marketplace'. It brings potentially far-reaching implications for all of the actors and institutions concerned. Cultural institutions like public libraries have inevitably become festivalised, ostensibly in order to e.g. celebrate community identities, 'challenge misconceptions, break down barriers, improve community spirit and promote the local library' (Rooney-Browne 2008, 64). However, to date, relatively little is known about what this development means for how people understand, value and use libraries. In contrast, an extensive more general literature now exists on how time, space and social relations can be visibly and affectively transformed through the workings of festivals (Quinn and Wilks 2017). Temporally, festivals are often understood as a 'time out of time' (Bakhtin 1968) that are empowered with the potential to resist, challenge or reinvent normal societal routines. Festivals have the ability to temporarily alter the physical, atmospheric and affective traits of places, changing how they look, feel and sound (Johansson and

Kociatkiewicz 2011). They can create, reshape and embed new meanings of all kinds into 'place' (Weller 2013). It seems reasonable to think that the potential for transformation exists in library settings too. When libraries become an 'activity' place for staging public lectures, classes, workshops etc., and when they partner with festival organisations to serve as festival venues, they become a different kind of space. Festivals have the potential to enhance the publicness of library space, to improve its functioning as a meeting place and enhance its qualities as a public, social space. In library contexts, festival events can animate spaces that are frequently described as 'quiet' and 'calm' (Engstrom and Eckerdal 2017, 152). They can add interest and strengthen the 'third space' nature of libraries as places of encounters and interactions, as is also the case when libraries host authors' nights, programmes and courses (Aabø and Audunson 2012). Festivals can increase liveliness, especially at quieter times of the library day, for example, near closing time in the evening. They also hold the prospect of increasing diversity, drawing in clusters of people, regular and non-regular library users, in concentrated moments in time, to express a shared interest in whatever topic the festival is showcasing.

Libraries in Ireland

The public library in Ireland is a free service open to everyone and library space is public space. In 2018 there were 330 local libraries across 31 local authority areas with 1,195,909 members. The current public library strategy *Our Public Libraries: Inspiring, Connecting and Empowering Communities 2022* (Department of Rural and Community Development 2018) explains that 'the public library supports people and communities through its civic presence' (7). It describes the library as a trusted space that is 'integrated into the local community and accessible to all' (7). Indeed, the strategy's guiding vision sees public libraries as 'attractive and welcoming spaces where all members of the community can access knowledge, ideas and information, and where people can reflect, connect and learn' (15). One of its ambitions is to 'reinforce the local library as a trusted place at the centre of the community' (17). While Peachey (2017) found that almost 80% of people said that libraries were important to their communities, the public library strategy recognises that 'there is clear potential to encourage significantly greater use of the library by the public' (7).

Methods

Mixed methods were used to gather data. Eighty-six surveys were administered at six local libraries located throughout the Dublin city local authority area. The survey tool employed a series of close-ended questions to gather information on respondents' profiles, and 19 open-ended questions investigating the topic in hand. Thus, the bulk of the data was qualitative in nature and the overall approach was interpretivist. Such approaches to public space recognise that 'a place might be more (or less) public' (Varna and Tiesdell 2010, 4) depending on who you ask. As such, the study investigates what people think of public space, believing in the need to study the socially constructed meanings of libraries because these differ greatly from person to person depending on factors like age, gender, socio-economic status, ethnicity, and so on. The questions probed issues relating to the library itself, e.g. how inclusive do you think the library is? How well do libraries work as public spaces? They also pertained to the festival events, e.g. what motivated you to come to the event? What does attending an event like this mean for you? The survey was administered to people visiting the libraries to attend a free lunchtime/evening event hosted as part of the October 2019 Dublin Festival of History. This was left, along with an information note/consent form and a pen, on chairs in the rooms where the events were being held. The research project was introduced by the event organiser before the event commenced. Attendees were invited to complete the questions and were advised that a researcher would be present in the room during and after the event to take any queries. The ensuing data were collated and the open-ended responses thematically coded and analysed (Braun and Clarke 2006). The findings are presented and discussed under the themes of: the library as public space, the inclusiveness of libraries, and libraries turned festival venues.

The Festival Audience

The 86 people who participated in the study included 48 females and 38 males. It was a group of relatively older people, with just 12 people aged under 44 years, 29 aged between 45–64 years and 45 older than 65 years. This age profile is related to the fact that the festival under study is a festival of history, and the events being staged were lectures on topics that related to Ireland's Decade of Centenaries 2012–2023. In terms of party composition, 50 people were attending alone. Eighteen had come as part of a couple or with family, and three had come with friends. Not surprisingly, given the older age profile, 40 people were retired. Numerous different kinds of occupations were noted, with six people describing themselves as teachers, two as students and two as unemployed. All of the audience was white, with the vast majority of people describing themselves as Irish and not surprisingly, because the events were being held in local libraries, and related to Irish history, audiences were virtually all Dubliners.

This audience profile has some striking features, most notably the predominance of older people, the fact that so many attended the event on their own and that so many people were retired. The nature of the festival and the fact that the venues were local libraries help explain these particular characteristics. History events may appeal relatively more to older cohorts, and clearly this audience found the library venue to be accessible. The events were free of charge; they were housed in a trusted venue that is generally perceived as safe and inviting; they were local, and a large majority of attendees had found it easy to reach the venue on the evening of the event; finally, they were familiar to those audience members who were regular library users and 47 respondents used it at least once per month. The fact that so many people felt sufficiently comfortable to attend alone speaks to the safe and sociable nature of the library space and to the understanding that the easy co-presence facilitated by the library represents an attractive alternative to the isolation of loneliness (Sequeiros 2011).

Understanding the Library as Public Space

When asked about how they recognised and interpreted the library as a public space, respondents answered easily and usually with multiple responses. The characteristics that they identified can be clustered into five categories:
Varna and Tiesdell's (2010) core dimensions of public space resonate, albeit in overlapping and somewhat blurred fashion, with these criteria. Firstly, respondents instinctively recognise and clearly value the library as a publicly owned institution. This public **ownership** is critical to the publicness of the library and to people's understanding that they have every right to be there. The sense of public ownership was such that many respondents felt entitled to be critical, and to comment on the shortcomings of different aspects of the library space. Attesting to the importance of the **physical configuration** of the space in facilitating publicness, respondents most frequently critiqued the physicality of the space, explaining that 'more space' 'more different kinds of spaces', 'more sectioned off spaces' 'more places to sit' were needed. This physicality included location, as libraries need to be 'easy to get to', although overwhelmingly, respondents experienced few problems either getting to the library or negotiating the building upon arrival. Temporality was also important, with some respondents calling for 'longer opening hours' and opening hours that are consistent and predictable. In noting these shortcomings, respondents often referred to a lack of public resourcing. In terms of Varna and Tiesdell's (2010) notion of **civility**, the library's function as a welcoming, inviting centre of information and learning was extremely highly valued and beyond reproach. The six local libraries were generally viewed as being well resourced and well managed in terms of the broad access they afford to knowledge, information and learning opportunities of all kinds. It was understood that libraries section off different spaces for different activities (e.g. reading, using computers) and different users (e.g. children's section) and this was appreciated. Library staff were viewed as helpful, friendly and welcoming, and constituted an asset that was strongly linked to the perceived inclusivity of the library as a public space.
Fundamentally, there was an understanding that the library inherently promotes culture through its collections and activities. This in turn underpinned

Table 5.1: Respondents understanding of the library as a public space.

Criteria	Description
Public facility	The library is recognised as a public space because it is: unambiguously, publicly owned; free of charge, open to all, locally located, wheelchair accessible, and provides facilities like public bathrooms and drinking water.
Information and learning	Above all, the library is synonymous with 'information and resources of all kinds'. It provides study spaces, resources for children's school projects, access to technology, an array of electronic resources and helpful staff.
Social and community space	The library is understood as a social space. It functions as a community hub, offers 'company' and welcomes people of all ages. It serves to 'connect communities' and is cross-generational. Its aura of calm and quietness indicates welcome.
Community resource	The library serves the wider community as a resource centre, providing activities for all ages, venues and facilities for local groups and clubs, and spaces to host events.
Promotes culture	The library inherently promotes culture through its collections and activities.

the understanding of the library as a vital source of information and learning. There were some indications that respondents thought that the kinds of culture being promoted could be expanded or changed in some way, but no overt suggestions for change or signs of contestation were noted. The conception of the library as a public, social space was very strong. The social dimension was critical to how respondents perceived the inclusivity of the library space. In speaking about what constitutes an inclusive public space, respondents explained that inclusivity means 'a place that's available', 'where people feel welcome and comfortable', 'where all kinds of people can feel welcome, all ethnic backgrounds, all genders and ages' and 'a place where nobody feels out of place'. An inclusive library is one that cultivates sociability, that 'fosters community engagement', is 'hospitable, informative and comfortable' and acts as 'somewhere free to gather and talk'. Implicit in much of this commentary and explicit in occasional comments was the idea that inclusive library space is 'safe'. Overwhelmingly, the data showed that these respondents experienced a sense of inclusion. They felt welcomed, relaxed and comfortable.

Responses like these show that the **control** mechanisms being used in the library context were acceptable to study participants. These mechanisms constitute examples of the 'soft power': a 'particular atmosphere, a specific mood, a certain feeling' that Allen (2006, 441) notes can structure behaviour in public space. Here, sound seems particularly important, with silence and quietness normatively acting as a form of control to indicate what is (and is not) appropriate library behaviour (Sequeiros 2011). The data signalled an awareness that the sounds of the library are changing; that libraries are less silent than they have been in the past: 'I've noticed a complete change since my childhood use where the library was a very strict and silent place'. For some this is a welcome development: 'they are wonderful places, quiet and welcoming'. Others felt the opposite, 'however, a quiet area is lacking'.

Closely connected to the idea of the library as a social space is an appreciation of how it functions as a community resource. A lot of the data reported so far relates to how people actively use the library in line with Varna and Ties-dell's (2010) idea of **animation**. However, multiple respondents voiced suggestions as to how this dimension of the library's publicness could be enhanced. To attract and engage people more fully it was suggested that libraries could: provide further facilities like a café/restaurant; organise more activities like book clubs and courses; and host more events like readings, talks and exhibitions. Many respondents expressed the view that the library 'needs to be more inviting', it's 'not widely used'. There were suggestions that the library 'needs to target the youth'. Finally, there was a persistent view that libraries 'need more publicity', 'more promotion' and 'more advertising'; that the general public doesn't appreciate what the library has to offer and that this needs to be addressed. As in the data relating to sound levels in the library, here emerged signs that library space, like all public space, is open to contestation between different user groups who have different ideas about how a public library should sound, look and feel. Respondents pointed to the 'need to balance the core requirement of a library as a place for reading and research and not merely a space for public performance', and to the need to ensure that users 'are not disturbed'. One person thought that 'this library is already too packed' and so should not seek to attract further users. These views reflect a long understanding of the library as a civilising institution that provides information for the self-education of citizens in democratic societies (Frederikson 2015). However, others recognise that libraries 'may only appeal to particular audiences', and could 'be used more creatively than they sometimes have been' in how they develop, create and present culture to the public. Thus, while the data show how and why the library is much valued as a public space they also demonstrate a clear understanding that the publicness of the library is not unproblematic. Rather it is a dynamic, changing construct, characterised by tensions and possible contestation, absence as well as presence, openness as well as closure.

Libraries Turned Festival Venues

Much of the data generated in the study indicates a general understanding that library space is dynamic and constantly changes depending on what's going on and how people are using the space. Its pre-eminent function relates to information and learning, and so users engage with it cognitively, but they also experience it affectively, preferring it to sound and feel in particular ways. They greatly appreciate the sociability afforded by the library, as evidenced by the many comments about the helpful staff, the friendly interactions, the community connectedness that the local library provides and the inter-generational nature of this sociability. The data strongly suggest that these respondents use the library to meet social needs as well as to satisfy their curiosity for knowledge and search for information. However, the question remains as to how the extraordinary staging of festival events in the local libraries alters their publicness and how people perceive that publicness.

At its simplest, the Dublin Festival of History events studied attracted people to the libraries. This became clear when people were asked about their library usage. Forty-seven respondents use the library at least once a month. Among the remainder, 15 said that they use it rarely or not at all, 14 described themselves as occasional users and yet all of these attended festival events in the libraries. Furthermore, when asked for suggestions as to what might draw more people into libraries, respondents most frequently mentioned that libraries should organise 'more events like this', and more 'talks', 'events', 'readings', 'presentations'. Thus, it seems clear that hosting events opens up libraries to new and occasional users. It animates library space and makes it more inviting to more, and possibly different users.

In this case, people were attracted to the events overwhelmingly because of their interest in learning about the historical topic being celebrated, and in learning about the local area. Virtually everyone commented on how they hoped to learn more, get new insights into the topic, and enjoy some intellectual stimulation by attending the events. In the process, people were able to deepen their relationship not only with the library, but with local history, other local people and with the local area. Thus, there was a very symbiotic relationship between the festival and the libraries in that the former crystallised the local library as a forum where people can educate themselves and co-create knowledge about their local place. As such, the festivalisation of the library in this case complemented and strengthened respondents' understanding of the library as a valued community resource. It further enhanced the accessibility of the library by creating a shared space and shared opportunity to engage with locally embedded, historico-cultural imaginaries.

While these events could be seen to bring cohorts of like-minded people together over a shared interest in learning about a topic, there was also a social dimension to their motives. Respondents referred to the social dynamic of the events, saying that they were looking forward to being 'able to discuss with other enthusiasts' and to 'asking the speaker questions afterwards'. In one local library, a small cluster of audience members were members of a local historical society. In response to a question asking about the interactions with other people during the event, responses were mixed: 22 people did not answer the question while eight said they had not talked to anyone, with some noting their own inclination to 'prefer not to chat too much'. However, the remaining 53 had talked to other people who had not accompanied them to the event. This is interesting because so many audience members had come to the event on their own. By way of explanation, people commented that there was a sense that 'everyone is clearly interested in the event, (which creates an) immediate natural bond', that 'the informal atmosphere is conducive to chatting', and that 'many people are friendly at these lectures'. Overwhelmingly, people described the atmosphere using positive descriptors like 'interesting', 'friendly and welcoming', 'warm and engaging', 'courteous', 'comfortable', 'relaxed' and 'informed'. The suggestion emerging here is that transforming library space into festival venues enhances the potential for creating sociability and for generating bonding social capital (Wilks 2011). However, even as festival spaces, the controls at play in the library environment remained, constraining some people's efforts to socialise: 'formal seating – like church pews – doesn't lend itself to spontaneous outpourings of dialogue!' In addition access, in the guise of timing, was sometimes an issue. When the event ended at library closing time, audience members were given little opportunity to linger afterwards and this was noted by several respondents who commented on how there was 'little time tonight' to chat.

Concluding Discussion

The data reported here were gathered on the eve of the Covid-19 pandemic. Public libraries in Ireland closed within six months of the data being gathered and, as they cautiously reopened during 2021, the manner in which they welcomed the public was different. This underscores the pertinence of closely investigating how people use and make sense of libraries so that as they undergo reconstruction post pandemic, the important functions that they play are not lost. The clearest finding emerging from this study is that people who use libraries value them highly. The library is greatly appreciated as a public space where information and learning can be publicly and freely accessed and as a social space that is welcoming and encouraging of social interactions. The data generated here resonate with Varna and Tiesdell (2010) in finding that people clearly understand publicness in terms of public ownership, civility and accessibility. Furthermore, respondents were aware that the library space is officially controlled and animated in particular ways. Overall, they had clear ideas about how the publicness of the library could be enhanced in virtually all of these dimensions.

The fact that the data presented here were gathered in local libraries probably explains why the findings have strongly highlighted the social, as opposed to the political or symbolic, value of the library. Amin (2006) wrote that the history of urban planning is about managing public space so as to build sociability and civic engagement out of the encounter with strangers. The data reported here attest to local libraries doing exactly this. The library is further valued for its standing as a community hub where local groups (e.g. book clubs, local historical societies) hold talks and events, all of which encourages community connectedness and promotes interest in, and learning about, the local place. Klinenberg (2018) describes social infrastructures as the physical conditions that determine whether social relations and capital develop. These findings attest to the vital role that local libraries play in the social infrastructure of the city, particularly perhaps for those like the older people, so predominant in this study, and for children and young people, whose lives pivot around the local area.

Nevertheless, there was an understanding among many respondents that the popular rhetoric of the library being public and accessible to all is not always borne out in reality. Respondents were clearly of the view that the publicness of the library is not as optimal as it might be. In particular it was noted that while children are associated with libraries in the minds of respondents, young people are thought to be notable by their absence. More generally, there was a belief that the undoubted merits of the library were underappreciated and even unknown to some sections of the wider public. Accordingly, there were persistent calls for the library to raise the profile of its services and activities. These findings may point to issues with the reputational value of the library and raise questions about its profile in virtual public space. In a sense, this finding is complicated in that the library as a civic institution is widely known about, yet it is underused. This problem has already been identified in the current Irish public library strategy document (Department of Rural and Community Development 2018). The question as to why this is the case needs research. Undoubtedly, the answer is multi-faceted but this study contributes by identifying a range of suggestions that people make as to how the library could broaden its public appeal.

Prominent among these suggestions was that libraries should organise and host more events of various kinds and the findings here show that the Dublin Festival of History did entice occasional, irregular and a few new users into the library. Thus, a conclusion drawn is that events can enhance the publicness of libraries, a pertinent finding in the context where the Library Service is currently striving to increase library usage (Department of Rural and Community Development 2018). Festival attendees benefited in multiple ways through their attendance. Not only did the events 'broaden ... (their) ... knowledge', they helped them develop 'a great sense of what it is to be a Dubliner', increased their 'interest in the local area', made them 'belong more' to their area and offered them opportunities to actively participate in activities close to home: 'it's nice to do things locally instead of 'city centre''. As these quotes illustrate, the library's function as a cultural hub/resource and as a 'community connector' seems to be clearly strengthened through its association with the festival. This finding could be a starting point for further research into how festivals might help libraries surmount escalating societal challenges in keeping people socially connected, cognitively engaged and locally embedded into the future.

Overall, this particular festival did not have a radically disruptive effect on the kind of publics drawn into the libraries, or on the publicness of the library. Undoubtedly, this relates to the fact that the festival and its programme were conditioned by the same kinds of cultural norms that condition the library environment i.e. it privileged learning, about quite a serious topic, in the normal 'calm' of the library (Engstrom and Eckerdal 2017), at an event that was staged in a highly conventional way. The events appealed to an older demographic who tend to appreciate the popularly conceived understandings of libraries as civilising institutions and who may be relatively more interested in attending historical events. However, none of this is to deny the potential that festivals could play in creating a different kind of publicness, if they are specifically constructed with that end in mind.

The heightened sociability associated with attending a festival (Quinn and Wilks 2017) was evident in this study, although the material, and indeed temporal, reconfiguration of the library space into event space was found to be unhelpful in stimulating social interactions. Aspects like this require more consideration if libraries are to strategically use festivals to effectively further specific aims. Johnson (2012) has written of the social capital formation associated with libraries, and here bonding capital was apparent: like-minded people with shared interests, strengthened existing connections (e.g. local library or historical association membership) while reinforcing their cultural capital (Summers and Buchanan 2018). Again, this draws attention to the need to consider the synergy between the library's ethos and mission, and the festivals with which it collaborates, as this will have implications for the kinds of social capital generated. This study sample was particular in the extent to which it was dominated by people attending alone and by older people. Very obviously, future research could usefully focus on different types of festivals, with different audience profiles, to investigate how a greater variety of social cohorts value and engage (or not) with the library. In this instance, festival attendance was not strongly gendered, although females dominated, a finding that is in line with studies on literary festivals (Rossetti and Quinn 2019), which in the absence of much research on history festivals, might be a useful comparison.

Overall, the complex ways in which public libraries are highly valued as vital parts of a city's social infrastructure emerge strongly through this research. The study findings drew most attention to their undoubted social and cultural importance while also problematising their purported status as neutral spaces that are unequivocally open to all (Newman 2007). Like all public spaces, libraries are dynamic, and constantly being reproduced. As they negotiate an uncertain future, creative efforts to outreach, and to develop more inclusive kinds of publicness will become more prevalent. Staging festivals will likely become a strategy that will be increasingly used to this end but to date, little is known about what this might mean for the role and function of public libraries as important public spaces. This study has only begun to investigate a subject deserving of much further attention.

References

Aabø, Svanhild and Ragnar Audunson. 2012. Library Space and the Library as a Place. *Library Information Science Research*, 34(2), 138–149.

Allen, John. 2006. Ambient Power: Berlin's Potsdamer Platz and the Seductive Logic of Public Spaces. *Urban Studies*, 43(2), 441–455.

Amin, Ash. 2008. Collective Culture and Urban Public Space. *City*, 12(1), 5–24.

Audunson, Ragnar et al. 2019. Public Libraries as an Infrastructure for a Sustainable Public Sphere: A Comprehensive Review of Research. *Journal of Documentation*, 75(4), 773–790.

Bakhtin, Mikhail. 1968. *Rabelais and His World*. Cambridge, MA: MIT Press.

Braun, Virginia and Victoria Clarke. 2006. Using Thematic Analysis in Psychology. *Qualitative Research in Psychology*, 3(2): 77–101. https://doi.org/10.1191/1478088706qp063oa

Capillé, Cauê. 2018. Political Interiors: The Case of Public Libraries. *Space and Culture*, 21(4), 408–423.

Carmona, Matthew. 2010. Contemporary Public Space: Critique and Classification, Part One: Critique. *Journal of Urban Design*, 15(1), 123–148.

Crawford, Margaret. 2008. Blurring the Boundaries: Public Space and Private Life. In John Chase, Margaret Crawford and John Kaliski (Eds.) *Everyday Urbanism*. New York: Monacelli Press.

De Magalhães, Claudio. 2010. Public Space and the Contracting-out of Publicness: A Framework for Analysis. *Journal of Urban Design*, 15(4), 559– 574.

Department of Rural and Community Development. 2018. *Our Public Libraries: Inspiring, Connecting and Empowering Communities 2022*. Dublin: Government of Ireland.

Engström, Lisa and Johanna Rivano Eckerdal. 2017. In-between Strengthened Accessibility and Economic Demands. *Journal of Documentaton*, 73(1), 145–59. https://doi.org/10.1108/jd-02-2016-0013

Engström, Lisa and Johanna Rivano Eckerdal. 2019. Public Libraries as Promoters of Social Sustainability? *Proceedings of the Tenth International Conference on Conceptions of Library and Information Science*, Ljubljana, Slovenia, June 16–19, 2019.

Fouracre, Dorothy. 2015. Making an Exhibition of Ourselves? Academic Libraries and Exhibitions Today. *The Journal of Academic Librarianship*, 41(4), 377–385.

Fraser, Nancy. 1993. Rethinking the Public Sphere: A Contribution to the Critique of Actually Existing Democracy. In Bruce Robbins (Ed.) *The Phantom Public Sphere*. Minneapolis, MN: University of Minnesota Press.

Frederikson, Lia. 2015. Our Public Library: Social Reproduction and Urban Public Space in Toronto. *Women's Studies International Forum*, 48, 141–153.

Given, Lisa M. and Gloria J. Leckie. 2003. Sweeping the Library: Mapping the Social Activity Space of the Public Library. *Library & Information Science Research*, 25, 365–385.

Houpert, Cécile. 2019. The New Role of Libraries: Places for All. *European Journal of Creative Practices in Cities and Landscapes*, 2(2), 175–184.

Jaeger, Paul T., Natalie Greene Taylor, Ursula Gorham and Karen Kettnich. 2021. The Light, of Course, in the Library: Pandemic, Protests, and Being What the Community Most Needs. *The Library Quarterly*, 91(1), 1–4.

Imholz, Susan. 2008. Public Libraries by Design: Embracing Change at Low Cost. *Public Library Quarterly*, 27(4), 335–350.

Johansson, Marjana and Jerzy Kociatkiewicz. 2011. City Festivals: Creativity and Control in Staged Urban Experiences. *European Urban and Regional Studies*, 18(4), 392–405.

Johnson, Catherine A. 2012. How do Public Libraries Create Social Capital? An Analysis of Interactions Between Library Staff and Patrons. *Library and Information Science Research*, 34(1), 52–62.

Jordan, Jennie. 2016. Festivalisation of Cultural Production, *ENCATC Journal of Cultural Management and Policy*, 6(1), 44–56.

Klinenberg, Eric. 2018. *Palaces for the People: How Social Infrastructure Can Help Fight Inequality, Polarization and the Decline of Civic Life*. London: Penguin.

Leckie, Gloria J. and Jeffrey Hopkins. 2002. The Public Place of Central Libraries: Findings from Toronto and Vancouver. *The Library Quarterly*, 72(3), 326–372.

Low, Setha. 2017. Public Space and the Public Sphere: The Legacy of Neil Smith. *Antipode*, 49, 153–70. https://doi.org/10.1111/anti.12189

Low, Setha and Alan Smart. 2020. Thoughts about Public Space During Covid-19 Pandemic. *City & Society*, 32(1). https://doi.org/10.1111/ciso.12260

Low, Setha and Neil Smith (Eds.) 2006. *The Politics of Public Space*. New York: Routledge.

Malone, Cheryl. 2000. Toward a Multicultural American Public Library History. *Libraries & Culture*, 35(1), 77–87.

Massey, Doreen. 1994. *Space, Place and Gender*. Cambridge: Polity Press.

Newman, Janet. 2007. Re-mapping the Public. *Cultural Studies*, 21(6), 887–909.

Peachey, Jenny. 2017. *Shining a Light: The Future of Public Libraries Across the UK and Ireland*. Dunfermline: Carnegie Trust UK.

Quinn, Bernadette and Linda Wilks. 2017. Festival Heterotopias: Spatial and Temporal Transformations in Two Small-Scale Settlements. *Journal of Rural Studies*, 53, 35–44.

Ronström, Owe. 2016. Four Facets of Festivalisation. *Puls – Journal for Ethnomusicology and Ethnochoreology*, 1(1), 67–83.

Rooney-Browne, C. 2008. Changing the Way We Look at Libraries? An Evaluation of East Renfrewshire's Look at Libraries Festival. *Library Review*, 57(1), 50–66.

Rossetti, Giulia and Bernadette Quinn. 2019. Learning at Literary Festivals. In Ian Jenkins and Katrín Anna Lund (Eds.) *Literary Tourism: Theories, Practice and Case Studies*. Wallingford: CABI.

Sequeiros, Paula. 2011. The Social Weaving of a Reading Atmosphere. *Journal of Librarianship and Information Science*, 42(4), 261–270.

Summers, Sarah and Steven Buchanan. 2018. Public Libraries as Cultural Hubs in Disadvantaged Communities: Developing and Fostering Cultural Competencies and Connections. *Library Quarterly: Information, Community, Policy*, 88(3), 286–302.

Varna, George and Steve Tiesdell. 2010. Assessing the Publicness of Public Space: The Five Star Model of Publicness. *Journal of Urban Design*, 15(4), 575–598.

Weller, Sally, 2013. Consuming the City: Public Fashion Festivals and the Participatory Economies of Urban Spaces in Melbourne, Australia. *Urban Studies*, 50(14), 2853–2868.

Wilks, Linda. 2011. Bridging and Bonding: Social Capital at Music Festivals, *Journal of Policy Research in Tourism, Leisure and Events*, 3(3), 281–297.

Zukin, Sharon. 1996. *The Cultures of Cities*. Malden, MA: Blackwell Publishers.

PART 2

Festivals and Inclusive Space

CHAPTER 6

How Music Festival Organisers in Rotterdam Deal with Diversity

Britt Swartjes and Pauwke Berkers

Introduction

Festival spaces are often seen as arenas where diverse groups of people come together in celebration. They can be defined as regularly occurring, social occasions where 'all members of a whole community, united by ethnic, linguistic, religious, historical bonds, and sharing a worldview' meet (Cudny 2016, 16). Festivals are spaces of social bridging (inclusion) as well as bonding (exclusion) (Mair and Duffy 2017). On the one hand, music festivals have the potential to connect people and foster tolerance. Previous research, for example, shows 'acts of heightened sociability and communication' across social boundaries at music festivals (Chalcraft, Delanty and Sassatelli 2014, 120). Following Durkheim's notion of collective consciousness, festivals create a sense of community and belonging because of their rhythm and rituals (Mair and Duffy 2017). In the case of music festivals, this refers to the affective, emotional and bodily responses individuals have while listening and dancing to music. However, festivals might not quite be able to create 'real cohesion' (Crespi-Valbona and Richards 2007), due to the size of the group gathering and their ephemeral nature. As such, they may be characterised as 'sites of

How to cite this book chapter:
Swartjes, B. and Berkers, P. 2022. How Music Festival Organisers in Rotterdam Deal
    with Diversity. In: Smith, A., Osborn, G. and Quinn, B. (Eds.) *Festivals and
    the City: The Contested Geographies of Urban Events*. London: University of
    Westminster Press. Pp. 95–109. London: University of Westminster Press. DOI:
    https://doi.org/10.16997/book64.f. License: CC-BY-NC-ND 4.0

conviviality' at best (Fincher and Iveson 2008). On the other hand, previous research has shown that festival sites can be exclusionary spaces, where social inequalities are aggravated (Misener 2013). For example, quite often festival audiences have a contentious relationship with the local population (Laing and Mair 2015), gender hierarchies might be reinforced (Pielichaty 2015) or ethnically diverse populations may be excluded (Van den Berg 2012). Music, and music festival consumption, is a form of distinction, an indicator of one's social position (Bourdieu 1984). This means that music can act to exclude as well as include people who have a similar cultural taste, influencing one's feeling of belonging (or not) to a festival space.

Either way, festival spaces do not come into existence naturally. They are created, often with a particular vision in mind. As Mair and Duffy (2017) argued, for positive encounters to occur at festivals, they must be planned and managed to allow festival attendees to share the atmosphere of the festival (Arcodia and Whitford 2006). Festival organisers have the power to engage in inclusionary or exclusionary practices in event planning (Walters, Stadler and Jepson 2021). However, the efforts of organisers have been heavily understudied. For example, in their systematic literature review, Wilson, Arshed, Shaw and Pret (2017) found only two articles exploring the role of the festival founder. One exception is a study of festival organisers' perspectives on inclusion by Laing and Mair (2015). While it focuses on the organisers' intentions rather than on how they think about diversity, it does highlight several ways through which organisers felt they could produce inclusive events. These include: using local suppliers, authorities and volunteers; partnering with community-based organisations; offering internships and volunteer programmes; devising marketing strategies to reach marginalised groups; providing free or discounted tickets; and showcasing local talent and live broadcasts (Laing and Mair 2015). Diverse programming might also play a role in creating inclusive events (Harvie 2003). This chapter therefore aims to describe how music festival organisers in Rotterdam define, and deal with diversity in making their festival. In doing so, we consider many different possible categories of differentiation, for example, gender, sexuality, age, life course, class, religion, ethnicity, migrant trajectories, nationality and ability (Hoekstra and Pinkster 2019). Taking an inductive approach, we are interested in finding out how these categories are employed, by whom and in which contexts. The chapter investigates: 1) discussing diversity: what meanings do festival organisers attach to the concept of diversity, 2) organizing diversity: how they deal with diversity throughout the festival organisation process, and 3) implementing diversity: the difficulties and tensions perceived in making diverse festivals.

Data and Methods

Our study focuses on music festivals within Rotterdam for three reasons. First, the city of Rotterdam sees itself as a very diverse city, meaning that we

Table 6.1: Selection of music festivals.

	Pricing	Genres	Scale	Diversity goals	Maturity (n editions)	Number of inter-viewees
Blijdorp Festival [BF]	Paid	multiple	medium	no	7	5
Magia Festival [MAG]	paid / free	focused	small	no	3	3
Metropolis Festival [MET]	Free	multiple	medium	no	31	5
Rotterdam Unlimited [RU]	Free	multiple	large	yes	6	3
Confetti Fest [CON]	Paid	focused	small	yes	2	1
Expedition [EXP]	Paid	focused	medium	no	4	1*
Eendracht Festival [EEN]	free	multiple	medium	no	10	1
Modular [MOD]	paid	focused	medium	no	3	1
Vrije Volk [VRIJ]	paid	multiple	medium	yes	6	1*
Kralingse Bos Festival [KRA]	paid	multiple	large	no	5	1*

* One interviewee working for three festivals.

can no longer talk about distinct majorities and minorities within an urban area (Scholten, Crul and van de Laar 2019). Second, diversity and inclusion have become a policy spearhead for the Rotterdam Arts Council. Its policy programme has included research, symposia, heated debates in the (local) media, and generally more attention to the topic of inclusion in the arts and culture sector (Berkers et al. 2018). Third, Rotterdam often profiles itself as a festival city (Van der Hoeven 2016). Drawing on a dataset including all music festivals that took place in the Netherlands between 2008 and 2018, we used four criteria to select relevant music festivals in Rotterdam (see Cudny 2016, Paleo and Wijnberg 2006): pricing (paid or free entry), genres (multiple or focused), scale (large, medium or small audiences) and maturity (number of editions). Based on our interviews, we also distinguished between festivals with and without explicit diversity goals. Table 6.1 shows the selection of festivals.

Our selection of music festivals includes paid electronic music festivals, such as Blijdorp, Expedition and Modular, but also more broadly oriented free music festivals, including Eendracht and Metropolis. In addition, we have festivals clearly focusing on diversity, such as the paid electronic music festival Confetti Fest (with the slogan: 'We don't blend, we mix') and the large-scale, free festival Rotterdam Unlimited which focuses on the celebration of cultural diversity as well as Vrije Volk Festival, specifically oriented to the LGBTQI+ community. Moreover, the selection includes a smaller, free music festival focusing on non-Western music with Magia Festival, and Kralingse Bos Festival, which is paid and includes many music genres. This way, we gained a diverse selection of music festivals within Rotterdam.

In total, 20 semi-structured interviews were undertaken with music festival organisers. The number of interviewees per festival depended on the structure of the festival (division of labour) and availability of the organisers. We spoke to six festival directors, two artistic directors, three programmers, two marketeers, four producers, one artist handler, one collaborations liaison and one sustainability expert. However, roles often overlap, and these roles do not necessarily mean the same for each festival. The study sample gave us a first indication of the gendered, classed and racialised nature of the festival organisation profession. Despite the broad variety of music festivals, including music genres, included in the study, it seems that being a festival organiser mostly means being white, young and/or male, although there were some exceptions. The interviews were set up in such a way that we did not ask organisers about diversity until the very end, unless they brought it up themselves earlier in the interview. Rather, the interviews focused on the characteristics of the festival, work processes before, during and after the festival took place, and considerations regarding programming, production and marketing. This enabled the researchers to see whether diversity is part of festival organisers' rationale when developing their sites. The interviews were transcribed verbatim and afterwards coded, during which saturation was reached, in Atlas-ti in two rounds, including 1) open coding and 2) organising themes. The results will be discussed in three sections: 1) discussing, 2) organising and 3) implementing diversity.

Discussing Diversity

Different Meanings of Diversity

Our interviewees are highly aware of diversity issues within the music festival sector, often in connection with Rotterdam as a diverse city. Festival organisers are 'trying to be a festival for everyone in the city' [programmer, KRA] wanting to embrace the contemporary city which 'is formed by a wide variety of cultures and from that a new metropolitan culture emerges, a new urban culture' [festival director, RU]. Within this context, organisers are working with five types of diversity: 1) age-generation, 2) race-ethnicity, 3) gender-sexuality, 4) disability and 5) social class.

Two diversities are discussed most by organisers: age-generation and race-ethnicity. The first type is either being talked about in terms of the importance of having a young team or including young talent, as is the case with Blijdorp Festival, Eendracht Festival and Rotterdam Unlimited, but mostly it is about the composition of audiences. The artistic director of Blijdorp Festival, for example, states: 'people from 18 to 65 and that's something you see in ticket sales, the biggest part is of course the average age is 28, but really everyone comes'. The festival director of Magia also considers his audience to be diverse in terms of age, as do all organisers from Metropolis festival: 'you have the old people who have been coming to the festival for 20 years … you have a lot of families, because well we are a pretty kid friendly festival' [producer, MET]. Other festival organisers mention age/generation diversity among their audiences too, albeit less strongly.

Second, cultural diversity, or race-ethnicity, is widely discussed by festival organisers, particularly by representatives of Rotterdam Unlimited and Confetti Fest which have a specific focus on cultural diversity. As the festival director of Confetti Fest argues: 'Basically, you can see Confetti Fest as some kind of "umbrella festival", where we want to characterise ourselves as the most colourful festival of the city, in programme as well as in audiences, at least that is what we strive for'. Rotterdam Unlimited takes this several steps further and strives for diversity in terms of audiences, programming, partners and their team. Rotterdam Unlimited is one of the few festivals in our sample consciously engaging with diversity within their organising team: 'the cultural framework from not only Rotterdam, but all big cities and all cities in the Netherlands, is fairly white so we're consciously choosing a culturally mixed framework. [...] We become an open door, overcoming a threshold for those new makers, and those new, new currents and also new cultures, to give them a spot in the framework of the cultural sector which is fairly white' [festival director, RU]. He continues to talk about all the workers from varying backgrounds they work with: from an Antillean producer, to a half-Antillean/half-Surinamese social media expert, makers with a Moroccan background and entrepreneurs with a Turkish background. Magia festival mainly focuses on ethnic diversity in terms of the artists programmed, and Eendracht festival tries to be representative of all music scenes present in the city. Some other organisers are attracting a mostly white audience and are not sure if and how to change.

Third, gender-sexuality is mentioned fairly often by festival organisers, mostly in terms of their programming. For instance, the festival director of Magia states: 'the first edition I only had men on the stage. And then I thought hmmm is that necessary? […] So then I started looking a bit differently, and more, more noticing what is happening at the female side of the industry. [...] There are a lot of women in that terrain as well, so you have to search a bit better, but that, that's what I did …'. The organiser from Confetti Fest, consciously looks for female DJs to programme at his festival 'because there are fewer options to pick from'. One organiser from Blijdorp festival also talks about wanting to create a gay-queer-community stage at their festival in coming years.

Lastly, festival organisers discuss social class and disability the least. Metropolis emphasises social class in terms of their location in a working-class neighbourhood: 'Well let me put it like this, those are the people who are a bit behind compared to the rest of Rotterdam socio-economically. I'm not sure if I'm saying this very harsh now but they are not to be found at other festivals or cultural occasions. And with us they do, so we have a whole group of Feyenoord hooligans. They come to have a look. Yeah, you don't find them uhh. And we know them, the police know them. And they come in with families. And yeah, then they're not the Feyenoord hooligan for a moment but just Dad with his family' [festival director, MET]. Disability is only mentioned by four organisers, two from Blijdorp festival and two from Metropolis festival, focusing mostly on (physical) disability and spatial arrangements that have been, or could be, made for audiences with disabilities.

Reasons to Engage with Diversity

As shown above, organisers are aware of different types of diversity. But why do they engage with diversity? Firstly, addressing diversity has become a necessity within the (Rotterdam) cultural sector over past years as it increasingly became a sectoral norm. Cultural workers often describe how they have to address how they will engage with diversity in their projects, for example, when applying for funding. Even festival organisers who do not have diversity as a spearhead in their festival concept consider its importance: 'For me, it has never really been a goal, no. And at the same time I would conclude for myself that I would be doing something wrong if it wasn't the case' [festival director, EEN]. Some organisers also see themselves, or festivals in general, as front-runners in terms of diversity. For example, the festival director of Confetti Fest states: 'people are looking at festivals and organisers on things-uhh such as inclusivity and diversity and it becomes ... more of a thing'. Another organiser adds: 'it is very important for visitors to come into contact with that [diversity]. [...] I think it can be an eye-opener for many people to be confronted with new ways of thinking and new ways of listening' [collaborations liaison, MET]. Emphasising the role of festivals within society, this organiser is convinced of the value of festival spaces as learning spaces with regards to diversity.

Secondly, festival organisers are concerned with attracting more audience groups for festival growth: 'for us it is important of course for the future that every year you attract young, new visitors, to make sure that you keep those visitors later' [festival director, MET]. Here diversity is also a business decision within the commercial festival sector. As one of the organisers argues: 'it is very good that they [diverse audience groups] are there because yeah, very crudely said, you need them to grow ...' [safety producer, BF].

Third, organisers engage with diversity as it impacts the enjoyment of their audiences. For some organisers, diversity is an integral part of that story, for others it is not. For example, when the festival director of Rotterdam Unlimited talks about his festival, he says: 'they [the audiences] have fun, they mix'. By talking about this in this order, he shows how he perceives the convergence of both things: enjoyment of the festival is equal to mixing. For those who organise festivals without concrete diversity goals, it might not be inherently about diversity; yet, having fun at a festival is equated with discovering and seeing new things. As an organiser from Blijdorp describes: 'especially with a bigger festival your supply has to be more diverse, otherwise people won't think it's worth their money, and people like to be challenged and to be excited, people want to be surprised. And that's something you're only doing when you programme more broadly and you try to attract a broader audience' [Safety Production, BF]. In a way, festival organisers use diversity as a tool to create an enjoyable festival space.

Organizing Diversity

Organisers consider four different factors when trying to produce a diverse festival space.

Programming and Audiences

Programming is key to producing a diverse festival. As aptly put by the festival director of Magia: if you want any kind of diversity at your festival 'you have to change your programme accordingly'. There are multiple festival organisers who take the diversity of their line-up into consideration, mainly the backgrounds of artists in terms of race-ethnicity, gender and age. The organiser from Confetti Fest, for example, connects the diversity of artists with audience diversity: 'I think it would be nice if open-minded people were coming to our festival. People who appreciate the profile of these kind of things and one of the things that fits into that is a better balance between male and female artists and the same goes for the background of DJs'. Other organisers also see the connection between different audience groups and their musical taste. For example, as the festival director of Eendracht Festival described: 'You're gathering all these scenes, and those scenes are a mirror of the city, so then it is pretty logical that you're not just attracting white, highly educated men, you know. […] It would be that at the moment that I saw we're only attracting white people, then it would be a sign for me of how can that be, you know, how can I have a representative scene representation and only attract one group? That would not be a reason for me to think well let's advertise on FunX, but that just, that would mean that that should be a sign that something in my framework doesn't fit'. This organiser equates different music scenes with particular audiences. Thus, the audiences should match the programme they are doing and if he does not get a diverse audience, then there must be something wrong with his programme since it is supposed to reflect a city and its diverse scenes and audiences.

Partners

Collaborations, for example, with media or programme partners, are mainly based on required expertise. Even though they are not the most important diversifying strategy, some organisers see collaboration with partners as an important way to foster diversity. One festival director commented: 'We notice that through the partners we work with we attract a totally different group of people on the stages we have. [...] So we make them and they host them' [festival director, BF]. This means that by working together with a partner that has an audience you want to have at your festival, you hope to create diversity at your festival. A similar strategy is used by Confetti Fest: 'I think that's the number one way for festivals. You're buying it in. In the same way that Blijdorp Festival has a yardbird stage, they just bought in a bit of black music and that sound and in that way they're hoping to buy in that audience'. Thus, programming partners are considered to be important for producing diversity. Another example is Metropolis which collaborates with art schools in Rotterdam for poster designs, to give young talent the opportunity to work and learn at their festival.

Festival organisers talk about the media partners they work with in targeting their audiences, or how they develop their social media strategy, but this is not necessarily talked about in terms of diversity. For some, however, this is a thing they do more consciously. The festival director of Magia, for example, considers a media partner he would not work with: 'I'm not looking for collaborations with FunX for example. No. FunX, FunX, for them it is not interesting, and their audience is not interesting for me. And we both know that'. As a radio station that is mainly focusing on urban music, the director of Magia festival which focuses mainly on 'forgotten' non-Western music, is not interested in working with FunX. Rotterdam Unlimited, on the other hand, would see FunX as an interesting media partner for particular programme parts: 'Of course collaborations are an important tool in that. [...] You understand that for an act such as Erdogan I would put that somewhere else marketing-wise than a Noche de Las Chicas, because Noche de Las Chicas I put on FunX immediately and they partner up with Open. For Aktas Erdogan I would do it through website, I'd do it through ethnomedia'. Here, we can also see that the way organisers partner up with certain media partners derives from the music that is programmed, and this is considered the most important diversifying strategy.

Format

Several organisers organise music festivals that are (partially) for free. For some of them, this is related directly to their accessibility and audience diversity. The programmer of Metropolis, for example, states: 'Yeah I would say, poor, rich, but for us that's not the case because we're free for everyone so poor and rich are welcome'. One of Metropolis' organisers compares it to another paid festival she works for and argues: 'it really is a very different type of people coming there. That's often white people with money' [collaborations liaison, MET]. Organisers from Rotterdam Unlimited also consider their audiences when thinking about their festival format: 'Well actually you could say people with a migration-background, as first, but as a sub-target-group people from underprivileged neighbourhoods. And that is why we, indeed why it is a free event' [artistic director, RU]. Considering their audiences and the festival character they would like to create, they stipulate the importance of a free festival format.

Ticket prices also play a role in paid festivals. Even though one organiser of Blijdorp Festival argues that for their festival 'everyone has a nice income and that is, that is something you can see, otherwise of course it's more difficult to pay for a festival day. Because, let's just be honest, I mean fifty euros for eleven hours' [marketeer, BF]. On the other hand, the artistic director of the same festival argues that they purposefully keep their ticket prices lower: 'If you're a bit cheaper you're attracting a younger audience and uhh … you're making a different impression on people you know, you want, that fits with the brand Blijdorp too that open-minded and free and, you know down-to-earth and then you don't want-uhh … to have too expensive tickets because that doesn't fit the brand'. Here, he also directly links ticket prices to festival accessibility.

Location Within the City

For most festivals, location does not seem to be a conscious decision, but it is restricted by the municipality. Some organisers think that location matters for diversity. Metropolis has a particularly important connection to their location, as it has taken place within the same park in the South of Rotterdam for over 30 years: 'There is a strong value to Metropolis because it is Op Zuid. And that we just have a very diverse audience composition' [marketeer, MET]. The festival director adds: 'the fun thing about us is that just because we are Op Zuid and because we are free, that we serve a whole different audience. Our audience composition is way different than a festival in Kralingse Bos or … Roel Langerakpark. So yeah, that uh, and well that's also cool that you really, look people that love music will come anyway, but next to that you have a very different audience, say the families and the people from Zuid who also join our festival. And who embrace it as being their festival'. A few organisers from other festivals also see the connection between location and attendees, such as the programmer of Expedition: 'But also from the neighbourhood, so if it is in Vroezenpark, then you see that a lot of people from Blijdorp and Noord join'. Moreover, people who regularly visit the place where your festival is held, might accidentally attend, especially when the festival is freely accessible: 'A mix of the usual Witte de With visitor walking around and gives it a casual look, but also the visitors from the locations themselves where we are at. So just the regulars of Witte de With and TENT who saw it on the calendar and think oh that looks fun let's explore it a little bit' [artist handler, MAG]. In this way, location might not always be a choice that organisers get to make themselves, but it does seem to affect audience diversity.

Implementing Diversity: Ideals, Tools, Risks

Festival organisers run into three main tensions when trying to implement diversity goals, even when they are not explicitly formulated as such.

Diversity as an Ideal

Organisers tend to target a specific type of diversity with their festivals. Even the festivals with diversity goals do not provide some perfect, utopian situation where everything and anything is diverse. By focusing on one type of diversity, a particular group or community (Daspher and Finkel 2020), organisers try to create a singular identity or concept that fits their festival. As one organiser puts it: 'you can want to be for everything and everyone all the time, but that's just not always feasible and some [groups of] people don't want that [to join a festival] either' [collaborations liaison, MET]. For instance, some festivals, such as Magia, are set up because they want to celebrate a particular lifestyle or music genre. Changing the content or programme of the festival to become more diverse, is not something the organisers of Magia want to do, because that would change the identity and concept of their entire festival. This also means that there is no 'perfectly' diverse festival. As the safety producer of Blijdorp says, for example, 'In the ideal world you would want to organise a festival where literally everyone can come together. And that an EO youth day [a music event for Christian youth] and a Blijdorp festival wouldn't have to take place separately, but that they can happen on one terrain. And that's I think, that's sort of the ultimate form of diversity in my eyes that you, that you can combine that within one party. If that's ever going to happen, I think chances are small. We don't live in a utopia but that's a sort of the ideal world how I see diversity that you just, that you just, get to bring everyone in a space literally and figuratively'. Comparing an electronic music festival such as Blijdorp to a big music event for Christian youth, this organiser shows an awareness of the different types of audiences that these festivals attract and the fundamental differences between them that according to him could only be overcome in a utopian version of the world. In other words: festivals tend to focus on a specific type of diversity, serving a specific audience, often for commercial reasons as we will show below.

Diversity as a Commercial Tool

Organisers of festivals with explicit diversity goals argue that it is rather challenging to market their festival in comparison to festivals organised around a singular identity. 'Well, the wide reach of the event Rotterdam Unlimited of course makes it more complex marketing-wise. Because it has so many areas' [artistic director, RU]. Still, doing diversity is often criticised as being a good marketing trick or 'easy marketing' as 'it also sells very well at the moment' [festival director, CON]. This is partially about doing diversity for the wrong (read: commercial) reasons: 'I think that the value is about that you keep moving as a festival and go along with the current affairs of certain things and that, also understanding the urgency. So not only going along with it because it is a trend in the cultural sector or because subsidies want that from you and because you wrote a plan so now you have to do it. But just, feeling that it must. Feeling. […] So that it is not a gimmick or a hype or trending but just really, get the urgency of it' [collaborations liaison, MET]. This organiser, and some others, share their frustration with the trendiness that surrounds the topic of diversity. From their point of view, festivals should not engage with the topic because they have to, but because they want to.

Additionally, doing diversity is also criticised by festival organisers when it is done in the wrong way. For instance, when talking about gender and sexual orientation, the festival director of Magia shares his annoyance: 'In the festival I'm doing, it's [diversity] not playing a role in my take on it. [It is] not that I'm working with that in my communication, it is not that I'm thinking about that in my programme that I purposefully book a transgender artist because I'm, no … I think it's a bit cheap, because a lot of festivals know that it's trendy and they use that'. Other organisers also criticise the 'quota-politics' they say some cultural organisations tend to wield: 'Cultural organisations have to be diverse. So everyone threw themselves at the token black person. I'm saying that kind of disrespectfully but, it seems like it really works that way. Like oh god we need one, could you, you have that black guy couldn't we just? That's the way it works most of the time' [artistic director, RU].

Diversity as a Risk

A few festival organisers note that bringing together diverse audience groups also creates safety risks. According to the festival director of Rotterdam Unlimited 'a culturally diverse event like this, is also a risk event. Of course, diverse cultural groups have a high risk. And they are all walking there at the same time. So, if it is about the sensitivity of public order, then we're more sensitive than De Havendagan or De Marathon. We have to invest a lot in safety. And there are a lot of demands put on us in terms of safety and that influences your budget'. The artistic director of the same festival also considers the prejudices she sometimes comes across in the organisation of their festival: 'We notice that a lot of people don't know or are pre-programmed with prejudice to the group we work with. And if you, for example, want to work with a certain theatre and they say, yeah but do you know how expensive our furniture is? As if my audience would ruin furniture any more than a Western audience would.' One other organiser argues: 'there are certain groups we do not want at our festival. [...] Those are groups that hang outside of my house, for example, guys that don't have anything to do in their lives. Certain people between 12 and 27, who do petty crime, who come to our event with another reason than we want them to come. [...] But in that we're not diverse, no, that's something we're very strict on, we keep an eye on that. [...] But that is a certain type of people and that is very annoying because that does not mean that other people would not do that, that's an important thing, and that's why in my eyes it is not discrimination. But it is unfortunately a stigma that is based on a certain type of person, and that's not what someone looks like, but that's about behaviour right, how does someone move around an event? Yeah, and that is a certain group of guys' [festival director, BF]. It seems that, even though organisers themselves might not always feel this way or conceptualise it differently, diversity is equated to conflict and danger and safety measures are therefore perceived as a necessity.

Conclusion and Discussion

In this chapter, we examined how music festival organisers in Rotterdam discuss, organise and implement diversity in the making of their festivals. First, our respondents primarily discuss diversity in terms of age-generation and race-ethnicity, mostly in relation to their audiences. One could say these are dominant diversities in the Rotterdam festival context. On the one hand, this makes sense in a young and diverse city like Rotterdam, where the arts council has pushed arts organisations to diversify. Indeed, festival organisers recognise diversity as a sectoral norm as well as crucial to staying commercially relevant, in a rather competitive festival world. On the other hand, Rotterdam still has a reputation as an, albeit transforming, working-class city (Van den Berg 2012), making the absence of diversity in terms of social class somewhat surprising (cf. Bourdieu, 1984).

Second, festival organisers discuss four diversity strategies: 1) programming and audiences, 2) partners, 3) format and 4) location within the city. The link that can be made to cultural sociology is significant in the organisation of diversity through programming and audiences. Generally speaking, there are music genres that can be distinguished along racial, classed and gendered lines (Schaap and Berkers 2019; Vandenberg, Berghman and van Eijck 2020), which is a rationale that organisers use or think of in creating diversity at festivals. Bourdieu refers to this overlap as homology. And, as Laing and Mair (2015) noted before, partnerships are considered of importance in diversifying festivals too. Here we can also see the organisers' concern with creating accessible spaces (Zhang and He 2019), which is often defined as a political and ideological decision. As we have seen, organisers argue that the format of their festival and the location within the city affects the accessibility of the festival to certain groups of people.

However, even if organisers have found diversity strategies, they also indicated difficulties in implementing diversity. Several organisers struggle with the inability to achieve 'perfect' diversity as music taste inherently discriminates, i.e. one cannot programme a music festival that caters for all tastes. Moreover, as diversity has become a buzzword, some organisers see it as a marketing trick. Finally, bringing people together also creates a risk in terms of public order. Indeed, diversity can foster creativity but also result in conflict (Government Equalities Office 2013).

Future research might consider how effective such diversity strategies are in making an inclusive festival community. Do particular strategies 'merely' foster conviviality, while others lead to a collective conscience? Interviews with some festival organisers indicated a concern with the diverse range of festivals in the sector resulting from the Corona crisis. The survival of many festivals is an issue, possibly reducing overall diversity within the festival sector in the coming years. Future research should consider how the crisis may possibly affect organisers' diversity strategies.

References

Arcodia, Charles and Michelle Whitford. 2006. Festival Attendance and the Development of Social Capital. *Journal of Convention and Event Tourism*, 8(2), 1–18.

Berkers, Pauwke, Koen van Eijck, Rento Zoutman, Wilma Gillis-Burleson and Diana Chin-A-Fat. 2018. De cultuursector is als een alp, hoe hoger je komt hoe witter het wordt. *Boekman*, 115, 20–24.

Bourdieu, Pierre. 1984. *Distinction: A Social Critique of the Judgement of Taste*. Cambridge, MA: Harvard University Press.

Chalcraft, Jasper, Gerard Delanty and Monica Sassatelli. 2014. Varieties of Cosmopolitanism in Art Festivals. In Andy Bennet, Jodie Taylor and Ian Woodward (Eds.) *The Festivalization of Culture*, pp. 109–131. Surrey: Ashgate.

Crespi-Vallbona, Montserrat and Greg Richards. 2007. The Meaning of Cultural Festivals. *International Journal of Cultural Policy*, 13(1), 103–122.

Cudny, Waldermar. 2016. The Concept, Origins and Types of Festivals. In Waldermar Cudny (Ed.) *Festivalisation of Urban Spaces: Factors Processes and Effects*, pp. 11–42. Cham: Springer. https://doi.org/10.1007/978-3-319 -31997-1_2

Daspher, Katherine and Rebecca Finkel. 2020. Accessibility, Diversity, and Inclusion in the UK Meetings Industry. *Journal of Convention and Event Tourism*, 21(4), 283–307.

Fincher, Ruth and Kurt Iveson. 2008. *Planning and Diversity in the City: Redistribution, Recognition and Encounter*. Basingstoke: Palgrave Macmillan.

Government Equalities Office. 2013. *The Business Case for Equality and Diversity: A Review of the Academic Literature*, 11 January. London: Department for Business, Innovation and Skills. Available at: https://assets.publishing .service.gov.uk/government/uploads/system/uploads/attachment_data /file/49638/the_business_case_for_equality_and_diversity.pdf

Harvie, Jen. 2003. Cultural Effects of the Edinburgh International Festival: Elitism, Identities, Industries. *Contemporary Theatre Review*, 13(4), 12–26.

Hoekstra, Myrte and Fenne M. Pinkster. 2019. 'We Want to Be There for Everyone': Imagined Spaces of Encounter and the Politics of Place in a Super-Diverse Neighbourhood. *Social and Cultural Geography*, 20(2), 222–241.

Laing, Jennifer and Judith Mair. 2015. Music Festivals and Social Inclusion – The Festival Organizers' Perspective. *Leisure Sciences*, 37(3), 252–268.

Mair, Judith and Michelle Duffy. 2017. *Festival Encounters: Theoretical Perspectives on Festival Events*. Abingdon: Routledge.

Misener, Laura. 2013. Events and Social Capital. In Rebecca Finkel, David McGillivray, Gayle McPherson and Peter Robinson (Eds.) *Research Themes for Events*, pp. 18–30. Ashgate: CABI.

Paleo, Iván Orosa and Nachoem M. Wijnberg. 2006. Classification of Popular Music Festivals: A Typology of Festivals and an Inquiry into their Role in the Construction of Music Genres. *International Journal of Arts Management*, 8(2), 50–61.

Pielichaty, Hanya. 2015. Festival Space: Gender, Liminality and the Carnivalesque. *International Journal of Event and Festival Management*, 6(3), 235–250.

Schaap, Julian and Pauwke Berkers. 2019. 'Maybe It's… Skin Colour?' How Race-Ethnicity and Gender Function in Consumers' Formation of Classification Styles of Cultural Content. *Consumption Markets and Culture*, 23(6), 599–615. https://doi.org/10.1080/10253866.2019.1650741

Scholten, Peter, Maurice Crul and Paul van de Laar (Eds.) 2019. *Coming to Terms With Superdiversity: The Case of Rotterdam*. Cham: Springer.

Vandenberg, Femke, Michaël Berghman and Koen van Eijck. 2020. 'Wear Clogs and Just Act Normal': Defining Collectivity in Dutch Domestic Music Concerts. *Cultural Sociology*, 15(2), 233–255. https://doi.org/10.1177 /1749975520961618

Van den Berg, Margeurite. 2012. Femininity as a City Marketing Strategy: Gender Bending Rotterdam. *Urban Studies*, 49(1), 153–168.

Van der Hoeven, Arno. 2016. Het levend erfgoed van Rotterdam. *Puntkomma, 10*, 20–22. https://www.puntkomma.org/artikelen/het-levend-erfgoed-van -rotterdam

Walters, Trudie, Raphaela Stadler and Allan Jepson. 2021. Positive Power: Events as Temporary Sites of Power Which 'Empower' Marginalized Groups. *International Journal of Contemporary Hospitality Management*, 33(7), 2391–2409. https://doi.org/10.1108/IJCHM-08-2020-0935

Wilson, Juliette, Norin Arshed, Eleanor Shaw and Tobias Pret. 2017. Expanding the Domain of Festival Research: A Review and Research Agenda. *International Journal of Management Reviews*, 19(2), 195–213.

Zhang, Xuefan and Yanling He. 2020. What Makes Public Space Public? The Chaos of Public Space Definitions and a New Epistemological Approach. *Administration and Society*, 52(5), 749–770.

CHAPTER 7

Atmospheres of Belonging? Exploring Ambient Power Through Manchester's Craft Beer Festivals

Chloe Steadman and Anna de Jong

Introduction

This chapter explores how craft beer festivals in Manchester, UK, are made and unmade through atmospheres, in ways that inform, and are informed by, a broader urban politics of belonging. We are witnessing the atmospherisation of places (Thibaud 2014), with ambiences increasingly engineered within urban regeneration schemes to render cities attractive on the 'global catwalk' (Degen 2003). Indeed, for Thrift (2004, 57), cities are 'roiling maelstroms of affect', which can be 'forged into economic weapons' (ibid, 58). Cultural festivals are increasingly used in cities' regeneration efforts (Finkel and Platt 2020) and are thus crucial generators of the atmospheres flowing across our cities. This includes craft beer festivals, the focus of this chapter, which have become part of Manchester's cultural-led regeneration (de Jong and Steadman 2021); constructing the urban landscape as creative, innovative and experiential to attract visitors, residents and investors.

How to cite this book chapter:
Steadman, C. and de Jong, A. 2022. Atmospheres of Belonging? Exploring Ambient Power Through Manchester's Craft Beer Festivals. In: Smith, A., Osborn, G. and Quinn, B. (Eds.) *Festivals and the City: The Contested Geographies of Urban Events*. London: University of Westminster Press. Pp. 111–128. London: University of Westminster Press. DOI: https://doi.org/10.16997/book64.g. License: CC-BY-NC-ND 4.0

When utilising cultural events within urban regeneration, however, there is a tendency that certain identities (e.g. middle class, male, heterosexual, white, and employed) are favoured (Young 2008), producing a politics of belonging within the spaces and places of cities. And yet, inclusionary and exclusionary festival atmospheres are far from predetermined; they are processual and porous, flowing across the cities in which they take place and influenced by pre-existing power relations. The unique spatial and temporal affordances of specific festivals likewise influence the ways through which belonging unfolds in unequal ways.

Accordingly, this chapter shifts the focus away from binary, static accounts that position events, such as beer festivals, as either inclusive or not; towards understanding the ways that atmospheres assemble and flow through porous networks of spaces, informing a politics of belonging. To do this, we turn to literature on urban atmospheres and Allen's (2006) concept of 'ambient power', to inform a study of two craft beer festivals in Manchester (Independent Manchester Beer Convention, and Summer Beer Thing). We reveal how the ambient power working through the festivals informs, and is informed by, the broader geographies of craft beer, as well as attendees' memories and anticipations. Importantly, however, we also demonstrate how, despite the two craft beer events sharing a number of similarities, different atmospheres are produced through contrasting embodied performances, materiality and multi-sensory affordances. We conclude by reflecting on how more inclusive atmospheres might be crafted through festivals, in cities like Manchester.

Atmospheres, Ambient Power and Festivals

We have witnessed a so-called 'atmospheric turn' (Gandy 2017), with bourgeoning literature exploring 'affective atmospheres' (Anderson 2009) across the social sciences. Indeed, atmosphere is regularly used, and variously interchanged with affect, ambience, tone and mood (ibid), to describe everyday embodied encounters within spaces and places. We hear, for example, of the 'stressful' atmosphere of busy cities (Brighenti and Pavoni 2017), or 'cosy' candlelit atmospheres of homes (Bille 2015). Whilst atmospheres can be vague, ambiguous and indeterminate (Anderson and Ash 2015), the term is typically deployed to express how a place feels, with atmosphere conveying the affects, emotions and sensations flowing between bodies and places (Edensor 2012).

Accordingly, atmospheres have an inherently spatial quality (Wilkinson 2017), being variously described as a 'spatially extended quality of feeling' (Böhme 1993, 118), 'spatially discharged affective qualities' (Anderson 2009, 80), and 'spatial bearers of moods' (Biehl-Missal and Saren 2012, 170). For instance, playful and sensuous art installations help to create atmospheres of conviviality and sociability along Blackpool Promenade (Edensor and Millington 2018), while colourful Middle Eastern furnishings, low seating and communal dining tables together inform a welcoming, warm and inclusive atmosphere in a Danish neighbourhood café (Kuruoğlu and Woodward 2021). Indeed, there is vast literature around 'atmospherics' (Kotler 1974), and hence how consumption environments can be designed through spatial layout, material artefacts and ambient qualities to shape people's cognitions, emotions and behaviours (Turley and Milliman 2000).

Atmospheres also have an important temporal quality, since they are '… always in the process of emerging and transforming … taken up and reworked in lived experience' (Anderson 2009, 79). Bissell (2010) finds atmospheres can shift over the course of a train journey, owing to delays and the embodied behaviours of passengers. Steadman et al. (2021) highlight how football stadium atmospheric intensities can swing between elation and boredom during matches due to unfolding events on the pitch and spectator (inter) actions. May and Lewis (2021) further reveal how movements between light and dark in a housing scheme can inform contrasting atmospheres for some residents, feeling welcoming in the daylight, yet foreboding as darkness sets in. Edensor (2015a) similarly observes how, during light festivals, participants can experience fluid affective intensities, shifting between calm absorption and excitement, as the lighting fluctuates.

Whilst much work on atmosphere and sensory places focuses on more discrete space-times (Degen and Rose 2012; Paiva and Sánchez-Fuarros 2020), emergent literature considers not only how atmosphere changes over time, but also its temporal and spatial 'porosity' (Steadman et al. 2021). Regarding the former, Edensor (2012), for instance, employs the term 'atmospheric attunement' to explore how past encounters with Blackpool Illuminations can condition the affective experiences and anticipations of repeat attenders. Accordingly, past memories of places have been found to spill into, and hence shape, the present-day atmospheres of town centres (Degen and Rose 2012), markets (Degen and Lewis 2020), housing schemes (May and Lewis 2021) and football stadia (Steadman et al. 2021). Equally, nascent literature observes how atmospheres have a spatial porosity, flowing out of cafés (Kuruoğlu and Woodward 2021) and tourist areas (Paiva and Sánchez-Fuarros 2020), into surrounding streets and neighbourhoods, with Paiva and Sánchez-Fuarros (2020, 10) introducing the concept of 'collateral atmospheres' to capture how produced (tourist) atmospheres are '… boundless phenomena that leak into the boundaries of everyday life'.

Atmospheres are not just a passive backdrop of experience, and their 'forceful' quality is also recognised (Bissell 2010). Atmospheres encompass an 'action potential' (Duff 2010, 885), whereby certain atmospheres render '… particular kinds of embodied experience more or less likely' (Duff and Moore 2015, 303). Darkness, for instance, can create uneasy atmospheres provoking young people to walk home more quickly after a night out drinking (Wilkinson 2017); while atmospheres of frustration can emerge when waiting for public transport after drinking, sometimes rendering conflict (Duff and Moore 2015).

It is also important to consider how atmosphere has the power to both include and exclude, as reflected in Allen's (2006) concept of 'ambient power' as defined below:

> [...] There is something about the character of an urban setting – a particular atmosphere, a specific mood, a certain feeling – that affects how we experience it and which, in turn, seeks to induce certain stances which we might otherwise have chosen not to adopt. (ibid, 445)

Rather than power working via more explicit forms of exclusion, therefore, such as walls, fences and security (Thörn 2011), Allen (2006) argues urban spaces today encourage and/or inhibit certain behaviours through the affects they produce to ensure spaces, on the surface, feel 'open, accessible, and inclusive' (ibid, 445). For Allen (2006), power works in spaces through their ambient and sensory qualities; yet such inclusive affects are a seductive illusion, a new form of atmospheric power is instead being wielded.

Accordingly, ambiences are increasingly staged through sensory manipulations to create attractive and competitive cities (Thrift 2004) or, what Thörn (2011, 1004), informed by Allen, refers to as 'soft policies of exclusion'. Focusing on the city of Gothenburg, Thörn explains how urban regeneration often involves 'imagineering strategies' (ibid, 997), such as creating attractive window displays and appearance improvements, to form an environment '... seductively inclusive for some and at the same time mak[ing] others feel uncomfortable' (ibid, 1001). Degen (2003) similarly reveals how sensory manipulations in public spaces to regenerate Manchester and Barcelona, inform power relations by working to insidiously deter 'undesirable' social groups from these spaces. Elsewhere, Kärrholm (2008) illustrates how the materiality of a pedestrian precinct in Mälmo is crafted to generate ambient power that encourages certain behaviours and users (e.g. walking, shopping), whilst discouraging others.

Reflecting the festivalisation of the city, whereby festivals are increasingly leveraged to position cities as attractive, creative hubs (Finkel and Platt 2020), festivals play an important role in this strategic creation of atmospheres. Indeed, atmosphere is crucial in influencing perceptions of food and drink festivals (Axelsen and Swan 2009), with sensorial immersion of festival attendees deemed important to festival enjoyment (Davis 2016). Festival atmospheres can also create feelings of belonging. For example, the light festival Spectra produces a 'shared atmospheric event' (Edensor 2015a, 339); similarly, community light festival Lighting the Legend can help forge 'neighbourliness between disparate adjoining communities' and a 'shared place identity' (Skelly and Edensor 2020, 259). However, despite cultural events often being promoted as diverse and inclusive (Duffy, Mair and Waitt 2019), their ambiences can equally exclude. Davis (2016) observes, for example, how communal atmospheres can be disrupted at music festivals, when tensions around belonging arise between locals and visitors, and younger and older groups. Similarly, Paiva and Sánchez-

Fuarros (2020) found that the 'premium' atmosphere of touristic events and spaces in Lisbon could spill out into surrounding neighbourhoods, rupturing feelings of community, well-being and cosiness for local residents.

Despite Jamieson's (2004) related reference to how Edinburgh Fringe Festival atmospheres can spread across the city, and Stevens and Shin's (2012, 16) insights into how the 'social atmosphere' of Glasgow's West End Festival parade 'spill[s] over into adjoining spaces', studies into atmospheres are typically bounded within the time and space of the event. However, as the nascent literature on atmospheric 'porosity' (Steadman et al. 2021) highlights, festival atmospheres are not impermeable to other temporalities, nor their broader urban context. How atmospheres might spill out of festival time and space, informing a broader politics of belonging, is underexplored. Equally, notwithstanding references to 'micro-atmospheres' in football stadia (Edensor 2015b) and on housing schemes (May and Lewis 2021), 'multiple atmospheres' of hospitals (Anderson and Ash 2015), and 'pools of affect' at the Blackpool Illuminations (Edensor 2012), there is little research revealing the multiplicity of atmospheres. Little is said about how spaces and places do not typically contain a singular atmosphere; nor is a festival atmosphere necessarily fixed as inclusive or exclusive for all, which we now further reveal through our study of craft beer festivals.

Researching Festival Atmospheres

This chapter explores atmosphere, ambient power and (not) belonging through two craft beer festivals in Manchester: the Independent Manchester Beer Convention and the Summer Beer Thing, both directed by Jonny and Charlotte Heyes – key players in Manchester's food and drink scene (Confidentials 2020a). Taking an initial broader focus on investigating processes of inclusion and exclusion at craft beer festivals, during the project it became clear that atmospheres were important in informing how belonging unfolded at the events. Given they have the potential to dissipate at any moment, atmospheres are challenging to research (Anderson and Ash 2015; Hill, Canniford and Mol 2014). The multiple qualitative methods we utilised attended to their complex and in-between quality which blurs the affective and emotional, pre-cognitive and reflective, individual and collective (Edensor 2012).

Following the idea of *knowing in* atmosphere (Sumartojo and Pink 2019), and hence to attain first-hand embodied, emotional and affective experiences of craft beer festivals, we attended both festivals in 2018 and 2019, including daytime and night-time sessions, with Anna serving as a volunteer during one 2018 Indy Man session. This involved exploring the festival venues, consuming and/or serving craft beers, and chatting to other attendees and volunteers. Our resultant fieldnotes observe the: music; chatter; food and drink smells and tastes; lighting; architecture and spatial layout; objects, signage and furnishings;

embodied performances, density and social interactions; reflections and emotions, which can together contribute to consumption atmospheres (Turley and Milliman 2000). Photographs and videos were also taken to capture the festivals' ambient qualities, since videos are useful for accessing pre-cognitive, affective and embodied experiences of atmosphere (Hill, Canniford and Mol 2014) and, like photographs, can evoke multi-sensory memories of research encounters (Pink 2015).

To access reflections of festival experiences and the craft beer 'scene', which relates to the idea of *knowing about* atmosphere (Sumartojo and Pink 2019), we collected over 5,000 social media posts about the festivals using Keyhole software, spanning two weeks before, during and two weeks after the 2019 events. This technique thus also attended to the temporal unfolding of atmosphere (Anderson 2009), anticipations and memories. As Pink (2015) elucidates, our experiences of physical places are often accompanied by 'digital traces', such as social media posts, with material and digital spaces melding together, further justifying the inclusion of online methods.

Due to the large volume of online posts, these were divided in half between the researchers and analysed thematically, alongside fieldnotes and visual materials, initially independently and then shared in discussions. Belonging and atmosphere emerged as important themes. Whilst possessing the ability to submerge groups into a shared ambience, atmospheres can also be experienced personally, based on individual perceptions and embodied sensations (Thibaud 2014). It is important, therefore, to be reflexive about our positionality as two white, female academics in their early 30s, the intersection of which conceivably led to a particular sensitisation to the gendered aspects of belonging in these spaces. Further, whilst social practices around drinking beer fit with our British (Chloe) (Thurnell-Read 2016a) and Australian (Anna) identities, and we have attended beer-related events, we both identify as sitting at the margins of the craft beer 'scene'. This was reflected upon in our fieldnotes, when analysing data and in writing the chapter.

We now explore each festival in turn, before pulling together thematic threads to identify how, whilst both events are informed by broader power relations, their contrasting atmospheric affordances meant that belonging (or not) unfolded in different ways.

Segregated Atmospheres at Indy Man Beer Con

The Independent Manchester Beer Convention ('Indy Man') takes place annually every autumn in Manchester's Victoria Baths: an Edwardian Grade II listed building constructed in 1906, and once considered 'Manchester's Water Palace' (for more detailed information, see de Jong and Steadman 2021). Beginning in 2012 with 500 attendees, the 2019 Indy Man hosted six sessions at the baths, from Thursday to Sunday, with around 1,000 people at each (Manchester Evening News 2017). Indy Man prides itself on being 'open-minded, inclusive and modern' (Indy Man 2020), and indeed, for some, the festival produces atmospheres of belonging, with references in online spaces to how there is 'always a great atmosphere and always amazing beers', and 'great beer, atmosphere, and people'. Yet, we find there is not a fixed nor singular atmosphere of belonging at Indy Man. Reflecting Kuruoğlu and Woodward's (2021) contention that some bodies can more comfortably extend into certain spaces, it is observably male, white and middle-class bodies who are most frequently encountered at Indy Man. Those falling outside of this 'somatic norm' may instead feel like 'bodies out of place' (Puwar 2004, 8).

Accordingly, considering the porosity of atmospheres (Steadman et al. 2021), feelings of exclusion arising for some at Indy Man can be informed by past memories and future anticipations. For instance, associations are often formed between men and (craft) beer, based on historical drinking experiences and discourses; as one attendee remarked online, 'I am at @IndyManBeerCon and I have a beard and I am blending in'. Feelings of not belonging can thus emerge for some women pre-event, which in some cases could mean they do not attend at all, or, when they do attend, potentially feel like 'space invaders' (Puwar 2004, 8). For example, Chloe was 'feeling quite anxious' on the morning of a 2019 session, inspired by '… anticipations of the high proportion of men I am imagining will be dominating the place, based on my past experiences at beer festivals' (*Chloe's fieldnotes*). We can see here how spaces can take '… the shape of the bodies that inhabit them' (Kuruoğlu and Woodward 2021, 4) whilst 'folding' back upon others, who can instead be 'flushed out by affects of discomfort' (ibid, 13). Such anxious emotions can surge into festival time and space, and spread to others considering the 'porous boundaries' (Hill, Canniford and Mol 2014, 387) between bodies, through which atmospheres can flow:

> I go off downstairs to select our first beer. I'm feeling a bit anxious as I enter the busy room below. What if the person serving me realises I know nothing about beer? What if I make a fool of myself … ? Which counter should I even go to? … Anna notes how she is glad I am there with her, or otherwise she would probably … leave the convention quite quickly. (*Chloe's fieldnotes*)

Yet, as Wilkinson (2017, 753) contends, '… spaces and places are not passive backdrops … they are active constituents with the ability to shape drinking occasions'; and Jayne, Valentine and Holloway (2008) similarly foreground the importance of attending to the 'place of drink'. Pre-event anticipations, memories and related emotions further intertwine with the unique architectural and multi-sensory affordances of the Victoria Baths to generate the atmospheres simmering, swirling and seething at Indy Man – influencing how belonging unfolds in different ways over time. As an attendee commented, reflecting a sentiment shared by others online, Victoria Baths is 'surely one of the most beautiful beer festival locations', given it boasts many historical features such as stained glass windows, high ceilings, green tiled walls, crumbling changing cubicles and a Turkish rest room. It provides a patchwork of rooms and passageways: large and small; open and intimate; light and dark, with most brewers located in the three large swimming bath rooms at the centre of the building.

Illustrating how ambient power (Allen 2006) works through the festival's material and multi-sensory affordances, Indy Man's design, on the surface, conveys inclusivity. Indeed, it aims to provide a 'multisensory, headlong, hop-forward beer extravaganza', for all (Indy Man 2020). Wooden benches and relaxed beanbags are dotted around the venue fostering sociality, with colourful bunting strewn overhead in the main rooms, and cosy fairy lights twinkling during evening sessions. Yet the production of 'sensescapes' (Degen 2003) can insidiously ensure the 'flows of "the right people"' into places (Thörn 2011, 994), whether intentionally or not. In Indy Man's case, rustic chalkboards advertising beers on offer, quirky event branding, street food trucks and wooden furniture create a palpable 'hipster' vibe, reminiscent of fixed food and drink-scapes spreading across Manchester's trendy Northern Quarter, attracting the city's young(er) creatives.

Yet owing to its labyrinthine layout, each festival micro-space produces different embodied sensations, through contrasting music styles, volume and tempo, colours and lighting and material artefacts (Figure 7.1), further emphasising how Indy Man is not fixed as either inclusive or exclusive. 'Micro-atmospheres' (May and Lewis 2021) can be sensed at Indy Man, with the potential to experience a greater sense of belonging in some of the festival spaces, dependent on the performances and density of other bodies, the size of the space, and contrasting 'affective tonalities' (Thibaud 2015), as revealed below:

> Each room and passageway has its own unique combination of multi-sensory elements intermingling to create different vibes. The *'token room'* overwhelming, with bright lighting, tightly packed crowds, and thundering music. The *'Deya room'* playing funk and soul music, with inflatable crocodiles flying overhead creates a quirky ambience. Whilst the quiet and dingy *'white room'* [as I referred to it] where people seem to be hiding from the crowds, appears sterile and lifeless. In some of these rooms I feel more comfortable than others. (*Chloe's fieldnotes*: see also de Jong and Steadman 2021, 13)

Observations indicated that some attendees preferred to 'hide' in peripheral rooms, away from the loud and busy crowds that primarily constituted men, further foregrounding atmospheric multiplicity. Thus, 'interstitial' – or in-between – spaces (Kärrholm 2013) were sometimes intentionally crafted, producing and diffusing temporary micro-pockets of affective belonging. For example, female-only craft beer groups utilised online spaces and social media

Figure 7.1: The multi-sensory affordances of Indy Man and the Victoria Baths. Photographs: Chloe Steadman.

hashtags, such as #womeninbeer and #beeryladies, to organise a meet-up at the 2019 event (see de Jong and Steadman 2021). Such planning enabled the women associated with these groups to apparently generate feelings of belonging and negotiate preconceived ideas regarding the exclusive, masculinised atmosphere at the event. The unique festival space lends itself particularly well to crafting such comforting interstices of belonging, especially the traditional changing cubicles and upper mezzanine decks, as captured below:

> Instead of choosing to stand with our beer in this crowded room, we decide to find somewhere quieter to sit on the upper level … There are a couple of young families with babies on this upper deck, who presumably also had the same idea of escaping the crowds of men drinking beer in the room below. (*Chloe's fieldnotes*)

Moreover, echoing how Wilkinson (2017, 752) identified some young people who '… found "refuge" in quiet and affective spaces of gloom' in bars, Chloe also felt 'calmer' in Indy Man's more intimate, darker spaces, in which she was 'thankful for the dim lighting', since it enabled her to 'hide away' from the conspicuous and brighter, larger rooms and minimise any feelings of not belonging (*Chloe's fieldnotes*). Whilst darkness can create uneasy atmospheres (Bille 2015; May and Lewis 2021), at Indy Man, shadow can 'craft a secretive drinkscape' (Wilkinson 2017, 751) for those who might not necessarily feel a sense of belonging within the primary event spaces.

As well as morphing through the festival's micro-spaces, Indy Man atmospheres shift through the festival's annual temporality, due to fluctuating constellations of bodies and multi-sensory elements, and can transform during a five-hour drinking session, reaffirming the temporality of atmosphere (Anderson 2009). Cultural capital regarding different brewers and beers is central to belonging within the craft beer scene. Such pre-existing power relations led many attendees to strategically plan beers in advance through the Indy Man smartphone beer list. Like the civilised drinking practices witnessed at real ale festivals (Thurnell-Read 2016b), atmospheres of serious contemplation were observable in the initial hours of drinking sessions. Anna, for example, noted 'no loud punters, drinking too much … it was a very relaxed atmosphere, but a business-like approach to it …' (*Anna's fieldnotes*); whilst Chloe likewise observed:

> Everything is quite civilised at the beginning of the evening, with people politely sipping their beer, seeming more contemplative. However, as the night progresses and more beer is consumed, the lighting in the room seems to become dimmer; the music and chatter louder. People appear more animated … sometimes swaying along to the music … It's starting to get a bit unrulier … the rooms getting increasingly packed, and some spilling drinks from being bashed by others. (*Chloe's fieldnotes:* see also de Jong and Steadman 2021, 13)

Whilst more serious and civilised atmospheres can potentially generate exclusive affects for those without the requisite cultural capital to fold in, we can see from the above how more convivial atmospheres of belonging can spread over time. Yet, just as pre-event anticipations, memories and emotions can flow into the time and space of Indy Man, its atmospheres can equally swirl out of the festival, across its wider urban context. Indy Man forms part of a broader network of fixed and temporary craft beer spaces and events taking place across Manchester, including Summer Beer Thing – now explored.

Relaxed Atmospheres at Summer Beer Thing

The Summer Beer Thing (SBT) is also the brainchild of Indy Man founders Jonny and Charlotte Heyes, which they refer to as a 'little sister event' and 'offshoot' of Indy Man (Confidentials 2020a). Indeed, the couple is also behind a number of other fixed food and drink venues, including Common, Port Street Beer House (both Manchester's Northern Quarter), and the Beagle (Chorltoncum-Hardy). Alongside Indy Man and SBT, they feed into '… a burgeoning scene of breweries, bars and events across the city and the region' (Heyes, in Confidentials 2020a) – aligning with the broader gentrification claimed to be currently taking place in Manchester (Myles and Breen 2018).

Beginning in 2016, SBT aims to provide a 'three-day Summer celebration of the best beer that the North and beyond has to offer' (Summer Beer

Thing 2020). Contrasting with the crumbling splendour of Indy Man's Victoria Baths, SBT is housed each year at the contemporary Pilcrow pub and its surroundings of Sadler's Yard square (Figure 7.2), located near Victoria Station in the city centre. Dubbed as 'the pub that Manchester built' (Connolly 2019), Pilcrow opened in 2015, (co)created by a team of Manchester residents who took part in workshops to voluntarily craft chairs, tables, tiles, wooden beer pump handles and woven flower baskets. As Connolly (2019) explains:

> The idea was that there are now people in the city who have bragging rights over the bar-stool they put together, or that beer pump handle they helped make. Everything about The Pilcrow screams Manchester … The building is long and thin with floor to ceiling glass panels spaced out along the side encouraging you to look out into Sadler's Yard, but also to draw the neighbourhood in.

Compared to the more serious atmospheres sometimes simmering at Indy Man, which can result in exclusionary affects for some, relaxed summer-day ambiences flow around SBT, enabling even those with a more peripheral location within the craft beer scene to be submerged into atmospheres of belonging. As one attendee remarked online, '#summerbeerthing is understated, relaxed and just brilliant for craft fans without even a hint of self-importance'; whilst a brewer promised online to deliver a 'super chill, laid back, and free pop-up tasting' at SBT. Although 76% of online posts about Indy Man analysed were from male identified accounts, for SBT this notably dropped to 59%, thus indicating potentially greater inclusivity felt by the women attending – at least *relative* to Indy Man. Moreover, tickets into Indy Man cost £10–15 for a five-hour drinking session, with beer tokens being required in addition for 1/3 pint servings; in contrast, tickets into SBT are £7 for all-day entry, with tokens and drinks then purchased. As well as being held in different seasons, such contrasting ambiences are, arguably, also partially related to the festivals' opposing layouts, materialities and multi-sensory affordances.

Diverging from Indy Man's labyrinthine layout and segregating atmospheres, SBT is primarily held outside of the Pilcrow Pub in its Sadler's Yard surroundings, filled with numerous wooden benches, several street food stands and a stage at the far end (Figure 7.2). This bright, open layout can, in turn, generate shared atmospheres of belonging. Anna, for instance, noted:

> Groups weren't spatially separate … the venue itself … didn't really allow for this – with it being open and outside, and not particularly large. IMBC [Indy Man], by contrast, having a number of rooms, and mezzanine spaces, with different lighting, music and beers, allowed distinct configurations of attendees. (*Anna's fieldnotes*)

Figure 7.2: Sadler's Yard during Summer Beer Thing. Photograph: Chloe Steadman.

Unlike Indy Man, SBT appeared less about the craft beer itself than the sociality that drinking practices can afford. No material beer list was provided to encourage the ticking off of beers during the event and advertising of breweries was limited. Accordingly, Anna noticed how '… there didn't seem to be conversations between those working on the stalls and the attendees in regards to the beers that were on offer' (*Anna's fieldnotes*). Chloe echoed, 'I can hear no chatter around me about beer types or breweries; people just seem to be here for a summer day out …' which led to her 'feeling in general much more relaxed' due to experiencing '… less pressure to be a beer aficionado' (*Chloe's fieldnotes*). This resonates with Kuruoğlu and Woodward (2021) who found that cafés foregrounding appreciation and knowledge of coffee (as Indy Man does with craft beer), are not necessarily conducive to producing convivial and inclusive atmospheres. Inside the Pilcrow Pub, an assortment of alcohol types was offered, with a cocktail bar in the outdoor space. Craft beers were housed under outdoor marquees, loosely organised by strength and flavour ('session', 'hoppy & hoppier', 'sour & fruit', and 'other'), rather than having distinct spaces for different brewers. This made it difficult to discern which beers were on offer until first in line, and thus it was challenging to strategically plan beers in advance:

In contrast to IMBC [Indy Man], where each of the stalls was shared by just two breweries, with branding everywhere and attendees seeking out specific breweries … this seemed to be noticeably lacking at SBT. It was difficult to really know what breweries were on offer, with limited promotional information … The beers themselves were categorised by type, rather than brewer … (*Anna's fieldnotes*)

Subsequently, one could conclude that SBT characterises what Tani (2015) refers to as a 'loose' space, enabling a range of embodied (drinking) performances and singular atmospheres of belonging. Yet following the logic of ambient power (Allen 2006), SBT's relaxed summer atmospheres and open spaces might potentially mask exclusionary processes. There is evidence of some people using online spaces during the festival, such as online beer platform Untappd, to track and share beers tasted, and knowledge of craft beer with others in the wider 'scene'. For example, echoing other online posts, one attendee shared: 'Boozy, coffee, malty. Can't taste much rum but it's a stand out imperial stout. Drinking a *Things We Summon* by @lhgbrewingco at @summerbeerthing'. To further illustrate how festivals cannot arguably be fixed as either inclusive or exclusive, Anna observed:

[…] In a lot of ways, this was very much business as usual … There were a few groups of just women – but this was rare. This became even more noticeable the couple of times I headed to the bathroom. As is a social rule, at most drinking style venues or events … as a woman, one must line up to use the bathroom. The high number of liquids being consumed conflicts with the small number of cubicles generally available to create a line that takes at least a few minutes to move through. Heading to the bathroom at SBT, there was no line … Further to the dominance of men, was that of whiteness, youth (30s/40s), and a 'hipsterism' that indicated a certain class … (*Anna's fieldnotes*)

We must not lose sight of how SBT does not exist as a standalone craft beer festival; rather, alongside Indy Man, it forms part of a broader, porous, interweaving network of temporary and permanent, online and offline, craft beer spaces, across which atmospheres can flow, beyond festival time and space, and through their urban contexts. Such festivals are, importantly, always in the making, and their outcomes are never assured. This has become explicit through the cancellation of both 2020 events, in response to Covid-19 restrictions. Further, despite the cultural value associated with the community-made Pilcrow Pub, it may not remain – with planned development set to extend into the space (Confidentials 2020b), meaning SBT will perhaps need to find a new venue. This highlights the ways culture is managed and required to align with the prioritisation of economic development within Manchester's urban landscape.

Conclusions

Atmospheres, ambiences and affects are increasingly engineered within urban regeneration schemes, enabling cities to create certain identities. This is evident in Manchester's cultural-led regeneration, whereby craft beer events have become entangled within the landscape as creative and innovative, in ways that produce ambient powers (Allen 2006) that flow across the spaces of the city; informing, and informed by, a politics of belonging. What we illustrated in this chapter, however, is that the experiences unfolding at festivals are not predetermined. The politics of belonging within the context of cultural events is, rather, processual, fluid and becoming, which tells us things about how we might assist in enabling inclusivity at cultural festivals.

Indy Man and SBT are both annual festivals produced by the same artistic directors, taking place in Manchester, and aiming to be inclusive events which anyone can enjoy. At both events, the requirements for belonging were evident. Entrance fees, alongside the capacity to consume alcohol and the necessity to possess leisure time to attend, ensure that from the outset, these are events for certain types of individuals. Alongside pre-existing associations between (craft) beer and men, the above can contribute to greater feelings of belonging for male, middle-class and white bodies at the craft beer festivals. However, it can also potentially lead to discomfort for those falling outside of this 'somatic norm' (Puwar 2004), with affects of belonging (or not) potentially seeping into festival spaces to shape their atmospheres. Indeed, contrasting with the wider spaces of Manchester, a city known for its ethnic diversity, where the proportion of residents identifying as 'white' was 19.4% below England's national average in 2011 (Manchester City Council 2011), both festivals were also observably 'white spaces' (Francis and Robertson 2021). This signals an opportunity for future research to foreground how race and ethnicity intersect with belonging at craft beer events, and to examine how drinking practices and atmospheres unfold over a more diverse array of urban spaces.

There were also important distinctions in the ways that atmospheres of inclusion and exclusion emerged at each event, dependent upon their contrasting spatial and temporal affordances. For instance, hosting SBT within the Pilcrow Pub facilitated an element of relative inclusivity. This was a space built by community volunteers, facilitating a pre-existing sense of belonging, felt materially when dwelling within the event space. The festival also took place during the height of summer, in the centre of the city, and was well served by public transport. Craft beer branding was notably lacking, reducing opportunity for attendees to display discursive knowledge regarding breweries and beer types. Instead, such performances took place in online spaces, e.g. beer review sites, not explicitly visible during the festival itself. All of this ensured that greater feelings of belonging were experienced and observable at SBT. At Indy Man, the cost of entry was higher, and craft beer discourse and performance were centred. However, unlike at SBT, which took place in an open space, at Indy

Man interstitial spaces (Kärrholm 2013) became important ways through which attendees created micro-atmospheres of inclusivity, demonstrating how feelings of belonging could also be experienced. This points to how research around 'atmospherics' (Turley and Milliman 2000) could further investigate how such design choices in consumption environments intersect with processes of inclusion and exclusion for consumers.

In conclusion, our aim in presenting these two case studies was not to claim that either are necessarily fixed as inclusive or exclusive; nor that one is necessarily more inclusive than the other. Rather, we have hoped to highlight how ambient power intersects with the spatialities and temporalities of festivals, producing varying outcomes regarding the politics of belonging. Therefore, whilst ambient powers influence who feels belonging within the city, belonging is not always, necessarily predetermined. Attending to the varying spatial and temporal affordances of specific events, alongside the ways they entangle with broader urban atmospheres, arguably presents opportunity to curate and manage festivals and event portfolios in more inclusive ways, with learnings to be taken from both cases about how to craft atmospheres of belonging.

References

Allen, John. 2006. Ambient Power: Berlin's Potsdamer Platz and the Seductive Logic of Public Spaces. *Urban Studies*, 43(2), 441–455.

Anderson, Ben. 2009. Affective Atmospheres. *Emotion, Space, and Society*, 2(2), 77–81.

Anderson, Ben and James Ash. 2015. Atmospheric Methods. In Phillip Vannini (Ed.) *Non-Representational Methodologies: Re-envisioning Research.* Abingdon: Routledge.

Axelsen, Megan and Taryn Swan. 2009. Designing Festival Experiences to Influence Visitor Perceptions: The Case of a Wine and Food Festival. *Journal of Travel Research*, 49(4), 1–15.

Biehl-Missal, Brigitte and Michael Saren. 2012. Atmospheres of Seduction: A Critique of Aesthetic Marketing Practices. *Journal of Macromarketing*, 32(2), 168–180.

Bille, Mikkel. 2015. Lighting Up Cosy Atmospheres in Denmark. *Emotion, Space, and Society*, 15, 56–63.

Bissell, David. 2010. Passenger Mobilities: Affective Atmospheres and the Sociability of Public Transport. *Environment and Planning D*, 28(2), 270–289.

Böhme, Gernot. 1993. Atmosphere as the Fundamental Concept of a New Aesthetics. *Thesis Eleven*, 36(1), 113–26.

Brighenti, Andrea and Andrea Pavoni. 2017. City of Unpleasant Feelings. Stress, Comfort, and Animosity in Urban Life. *Social & Cultural Geography*, 20(2), 137–156.

Confidentials. 2020a. Meet the man behind Common, Port Street Beer House, Indy Man Beer Con and more. Available at: https://confidentials.com /manchester/meet-the-man-behind-common-port-street-beer-house -indy-man-beer-con-and-more (accessed 17 September 2020).

Confidentials. 2020b. Property: Rochdale refurb, Pilcrow Pub and Manchester stands head and shoulders above the rest. Available at: https://confidentials .com/manchester/property-rochdale-town-hall-refurb-pilcrow-pub -glassed-manchester-so-much-taller-than-other-cities (accessed 3 November 2020).

Connolly, Christopher. 2019. The Pilcrow. Available at: https://www.creative tourist.com/venue/the-pilcrow/ (accessed 17 September 2020).

Davis, Andrew. 2016. Experiential Places or Places of Experience? Place Identity and Place Attachment as Mechanisms for Creating Festival Environment. *Tourism Management*, 55, 49–61.

Degen, Monica. 2003. Fighting for the Global Catwalk: Formalizing Public Life in Castlefield (Manchester) and Diluting Public Life in el Raval (Barcelona). *International Journal of Urban and Regional Research*, 27(4), 867–880.

Degen, Monica and Camilla Lewis. 2020. The Changing Feel of Place: The Temporal Modalities of Atmospheres in Smithfield Market, London. *Cultural Geographies*, 27(4), 509–526.

Degen, Monica and Gillian Rose. 2012. The Sensory Experiencing of Urban Design: The Role of Walking and Perceptual Memory. *Urban Studies*, 49(15), 3271–3287.

de Jong, Anna and Chloe Steadman. 2021. Recrafting Belonging: Cultural-Led Regeneration, Territorialisation and Craft Beer Events. *Social & Cultural Geography*. https://doi.org/10.1080/14649365.2021.1939126

Duff, Cameron. 2010. On the Role of Affect and Practice in the Production of Place. *Environment and Planning D*, 28(5), 881–895.

Duff, Cameron and David Moore. 2015. Going Out, Getting About: Atmospheres of Mobility in Melbourne's Night-Time Economy. *Social & Cultural Geography*, 16(3), 299–314.

Duffy, Michelle, Judith Mair and Gordon Waitt. 2019. Addressing Community Diversity: The Role of the Festival Encounter. In Rebecca Finkel, Briony Sharp and Majella Sweeney (Eds.) *Accessibility, Inclusion and Diversity in Critical Event Studies*. Abingdon: Routledge.

Edensor, Tim. 2012. Illuminated Atmospheres: Anticipating and Reproducing the Flow of Affective Experience in Blackpool. *Environment and Planning D*, 30(6), 1103–1122.

Edensor, Tim. 2015a. Light Design and Atmosphere. *Visual Communication*, 14(3), 331–350.

Edensor, Tim. 2015b. Producing Atmospheres at the Match: Fan Cultures, Commercialization, and Mood Management in English Football. *Emotion, Space, and Society*, 15, 82–89.

Edensor, Tim and Steve Millington. 2018. Learning from Blackpool Promenade: Re-Enchanting Sterile Streets. *The Sociological Review*, 66(5), 1017–1035.

Finkel, Rebecca and Louise Platt. 2020. Cultural Festivals and the City. *Geography Compass*, 14(9), 1–12.

Francis, June N. P. and Joshua T. F. Robertson. 2021. White Spaces: How Marketing Actors (Re)Produce Marketplace Inequities for Black Consumers. *Journal of Marketing Management*, 37(1–2), 84–116. https://doi.org/10.1080/0267257x.2020.1863447

Gandy, Matthew. 2017. Urban Atmospheres. *Cultural Geographies*, 24(3), 353–374.

Hill, Tim, Robert Canniford and Joeri Mol. 2014. Non-Representational Marketing Theory. *Marketing Theory*, 14(4), 377–94.

Indy Man. 2020. About and Contact. Available at: https://www.indymanbeercon.co.uk/contact/ (accessed 20 March 2020).

Jamieson, Kirstie. 2004. Edinburgh: The Festival Gaze and its Boundaries. *Space and Culture*, 7(1), 64–75.

Jayne, Mark, Gill Valentine and Sarah L. Holloway. 2008. The Place of Drink: Geographical Contributions to Alcohol Studies. *Drugs: Education, Prevention and Policy*, 15(3), 219–232.

Kärrholm, Matthias. 2008. The Territorialisation of a Pedestrian Precinct in Malmö: Materialities in the Commercialization of Public Space. *Urban Studies*, 45(9), 1903–1924.

Kärrholm, Matthias. 2013. Interstitial Space and the Transformation of Retail Building Types. In Andrea Brighenti (Ed.) *Urban Interstices: The Aesthetics and Politics of the In-between*: Farnham: Ashgate.

Kotler, Phillip. 1974. Atmospherics as a Marketing Tool. *Journal of Retailing*, 49(4), 48–64.

Kuruoğlu, Alev P. and Ian Woodward. 2021. Textures of Diversity: Socio-Material Arrangements, Atmosphere, and Social Inclusion in a Multi-Ethnic Neighbourhood. *Journal of Sociology*, 57(1), 111–27. https://doi.org/10.1177/1440783320984240

Manchester City Council. 2011. Ethnic Group Summary: 2011 Census. Available at: https://www.manchester.gov.uk/downloads/download/6833/2011_census_-_summary_by_topic (accessed 30 April 2021).

Manchester Evening News. 2017. Five of the best beers coming to Indy Man Beer Con. Available at: https://www.manchestereveningnews.co.uk/whats-on/food-drink-news/indy-man-beer-con-manchester-13653565 (accessed 10 October 2020).

May, Vanessa and Camilla Lewis. 2021. Micro-Atmospheres of Place: Light and Dark on a Modernist Housing Scheme. *Cultural Geographies*, 29(1), 83–98. https://doi.org/10.1177/14744740211005521

Myles, Colleen and Jessica Breen. 2018. (Micro)movements and Microbrew: On Craft Beer, Tourism Trails, and Material Transformation in Three Urban Industrial Sites. In Carol Kline, Susan Slocum, and Christina Cavaliere (Eds.) *Craft Beverages and Tourism*. Cham: Palgrave Macmillan.

Paiva, Daniel and Iñigo Sánchez-Fuarros. 2020. The Territoriality of Atmosphere: Rethinking Affective Urbanism Through the Collateral Atmospheres of Lisbon's Tourism. *Transactions of the Institute of British Geographers*, 46(2), 392–405. https://doi.org/10.1111/tran.12425

Pink, Sarah. 2015. *Doing Sensory Ethnography*. London: Sage Publications.

Puwar, N. 2004. *Space Invaders: Race, Gender, and Bodies Out of Place*. Oxford: Berg.

Skelly, Gail and Tim Edensor. 2020. Routing Out Place Identity Through the Vernacular Production Practices of a Community Light Festival. In Cara Courage et al. (Eds.) *The Routledge Handbook of Placemaking*. Abingdon: Routledge.

Steadman, Chloe, Gareth Roberts, Dominic Medway, Steve Millington and Louise Platt. 2021. (Re)thinking Place Atmospheres in Marketing Theory. *Marketing Theory*, 21(1), 135–154.

Stevens, Quentin and HaeRan Shin. 2012. Urban Festivals and Local Social Space. *Planning Practice and Research*, 29(1), 1–20.

Sumartojo, Shanti and Sarah Pink. 2019. *Atmospheres and the Experiential World: Theory and Methods*. Abingdon: Routledge.

Summer Beer Thing. 2020. Summer Beer Thing: About. Available at: https://www.summerbeerthing.co.uk/about-summer-beer-thing (accessed 17 September 2020).

Tani, Sirpa. 2015. Loosening/Tightening Spaces in the Geographies of Hanging Out. *Social & Cultural Geography*, 16(2), 125–145.

Thibaud, Jean-Paul. 2014. Urban Ambiences as Common Ground? *Lebenswelt: Aesthetics and Philosophy of Experience*, 4, 282–296.

Thibaud, Jean-Paul. 2015. The Backstage of Urban Ambiences. *Emotions, Space and Society*, 15, 39–46.

Thörn, Catharina. 2011. Soft Policies of Exclusion: Entrepreneurial Strategies of Ambience and Control of Public Space in Gothenburg, Sweden. *Urban Geography*, 32(7), 989–1008.

Thrift, Nigel. 2004. Intensities of Feeling: Towards a Spatial Politics of Affect. *Geografiska Annaler*, 86(1), 57–78.

Thurnell-Read, Thomas. 2016a. Beer and Belonging: Real Ale Consumption, Place and Identity. In Thomas Thurnell-Read (Ed.) *Drinking Dilemmas: Space, Culture and Society*. Abingdon: Routledge.

Thurnell-Read, Thomas. 2016b. 'Did You Ever Hear of Police Being Called to a Beer Festival?' Discourses of Merriment, Moderation and 'Civilized' Drinking Amongst Real Ale Enthusiasts. *The Sociological Review*, 65(1), 83–99.

Turley, L.W. and Ronald E. Milliman. 2000. Atmospheric Effects on Shopping Behavior: A Review of the Experimental Evidence. *Journal of Business Research*, 49(2), 193–211.

Wilkinson, Samantha. 2017. Drinking in the Dark: Shedding Light on Young People's Alcohol Consumption Experiences. *Social & Cultural Geography*, 18(6), 739–757.

Young, Greg. 2008. *Reshaping Planning with Culture*. Aldershot: Ashgate.

CHAPTER 8

'Messing About in Boats': The Heritage Livescape of Glasgow's Canal and Clydebuilt Festivals

Eleni Koumpouzi, Katarzyna Kosmala and Gareth Rice

Introduction

Heritage urban waterscapes are perceived as contested territories, where spatial politics of different scales are set in motion (Clark, Kearns and Cleland 2016; Pollock and Paddison 2014). In deprived areas, neglected post-industrial urban heritage environments experience regeneration. In Glasgow, the 'reinvention' of these environments as festival locations occurs in places where, in recent memory, people created and sustained their livelihoods (Bruttomesso 2004). Once providing the area with its livelihood and identity, the festivals' heritage waterscapes are now employed in renewing meanings of community ownership. As in other cities, Glasgow's renewal process engages culture in an attempt to solve socio-economic issues (Tretter 2009). The Glasgow Canal Festival (GCF) emerged as part of the Speirs Locks and the Applecross Street basin developments on the Forth and Clyde Canal (FCC) in north Glasgow (Gray 2018). On the north bank of the River Clyde, the Clydebuilt Festival's (CF) location on the

How to cite this book chapter:
Koumpouzi, E., Kosmala, K. and Rice, G. 2022. 'Messing About in Boats': The Heritage Livescape of Glasgow's Canal and Clydebuilt Festivals. In: Smith, A., Osborn, G. and Quinn, B. (Eds.) *Festivals and the City: The Contested Geographies of Urban Events*. London: University of Westminster Press. Pp. 129–145. London: University of Westminster Press. DOI: https://doi.org/10.16997/book64.h. License: CC-BY-NC-ND 4.0

Riverside is integral to the Clyde Waterfront Project (2003–2011). Billed as the biggest regeneration project in Scotland (Pollock 2019), it also includes the new iconic Riverside Museum alongside the Tall Ship and Kelvin Harbour.

This study involved two transient and marginalised community groups and investigated the nature of their engagement with the two festivals, based at two locations along the FCC. Over twelve months from October 2019, the groups were involved in a National Lottery Heritage funded project, CanalCraft, run by the Forth and Clyde Canal Society (FCCS) and during that project, the groups engaged in boat building and boating activities. The groups took their boats to the two festivals which served as a platform for them to showcase their achievements through participation in the community and to re-activate these urban waterways.

We argue that the re-activation of the waterways, and direct community engagement with the post-industrial landscape of the River Clyde and the Forth and Clyde Canal and the barriers and tensions that derive from it, form the *livescape*. This re-activation demands an understanding of the complex perceptions of the locality. Stevenson (2013) has argued that this understanding should include the present, as well as the historical, use value of the waterways for the local community. The question of how transient and marginalised communities have fostered a sense of belonging by removing barriers of access and facilitating use of the waterways was therefore central to the study. In this context, we also examined how place-making processes and hierarchical knowledge based agency are challenged in the contested heritage livescape. Overall, the chapter focuses on the use value of participation in the festivals, the integration opportunities which they offered to the transient communities, and the livescape as an emerged framework.

The chapter is structured in the following way. First, an account of the context and methods of data collection and analysis is provided. Second, an analysis of the conceptualisation of the heritage waterscape as livescape is presented; this is linked to the identification of tensions and place activation in the festivals. We focus on the activation of these two heritage livescapes in the process of place-making, highlighting issues of agency and the impact on the transient communities in facilitating place-making in the localities they occupy. Third, we discuss the participants' interactions at the GCF at Speirs Lock and CF at the Riverside. Finally, we argue that viewing the festivals as livescapes contests knowledge ownership and agency by providing a platform for a bottom up place making process.

Context and Methods

FCCS's history of boating informed the study and its volunteers facilitated the two community groups in taking their boats to events. The two community groups in the study were recruited from Maryhill and Kirkintilloch, both historically significant boat building areas through which the canal runs. The localities from which the groups came were significant in terms of transiency in the communities' mobility and also in respect of changes due to urban renewal (Ferguson 2011). Participants volunteered for the study by accepting the invitation to engage with the festivals with the use of 'their' boats.

Maryhill is an area in North Glasgow with high concentrations of refugees and asylum seekers, due to housing provision arrangements (Hill, Meer and Peace 2021). One of the participating groups was recruited with the help of a Maryhill migrant community organisation which included long-term residents as well as those with insecure immigration status. Achieving integration through culture is a place-making tactic where marginalised and transient communities such as refugees and asylum seekers are given opportunities to engage creatively with their locality (Ferguson 2011). Some participants took the boats to the GCF and others took them to the CF.

Kirkintilloch is an area on the outskirts of Glasgow, with strong post-industrial connections with the Forth and Clyde Canal (the town is marketed as the 'Canal Capital of Scotland'). Despite its more stable and established community setting, Kirkintilloch has acquired new spaces through canal regeneration, including a towpath development, a new marina, and even canal-front facing schools. The Kirkintilloch participants came from community youth groups in the area, with most members coming from the local LGBT+ community. They expressed an interest in the study as they did not have any opportunities to engage with the canal in general and boating activities in particular. The group built one boat and four members of the group took it to the CF. The outcomes of the boat building workshops were celebrated at the GCF and CF, in July and September 2019 respectively.

One of the authors was part of the organising committee in the CF's inaugural year. This facilitated access to the festival for the participants, and also presented an opportunity to examine whether the festival's initial values had been maintained in its third year. Most data were gathered while the two festivals were ongoing. Additionally, data collected from the CanalCraft project, starting from October 2018, were also used. Participatory action research and ethnography were the main methodological approaches adopted, with emphasis on boat handling as the core activity. This provided the platform for our observations of the community groups (hereafter 'participants') who used the boats they built to engage and interact with festival visitors. We followed Herbert's (2000, 557) approach to ethnographic research because it was suitable for 'disentangling and explaining [these] interconnections'. Observations of how the interactions took place were based on a variety of methods such as field notes (including direct comments) from activities (planned and impromptu), participation in meetings, informal conversations with professionals from voluntary organisations operating in the area, and engagement with volunteers from charities involved. Additionally, multiple text data (photographs, emails, social media and videos) were collected and analysed.

The 'multiple texts' (Keats 2009) collected were interpreted using content analysis: codes of concepts (Yin 2018), such as 'Activation', 'Familiarity' and 'Inclusion' were applied. Furthermore, as Banks and Zeitlyn (2015) point out, when analysing visual content such as researcher-generated photographs, the subject's motivations for being photographed is important, thus the analysis used triangulation of data from different sources.

Furthermore, as one of the authors had previous experience of the study area for more than four years having had a leading role in CanalCraft, the research methods were informed by a model of reflexivity and positionality discussed by England (1994). The position in CanalCraft gave the opportunity to form close working and friendship relations with a range of participants, professionals and volunteers. Reflexivity is important in this study, as, according to England, the researcher acquires a position of knowledge exchange and shared emotions with the researched.

The Heritage Waterscape as Livescape

We argue that festivals in heritage locations are not only environments celebrated because of their history, but realms where everyday, lived experiences and contemporary conflicts occur. Together, these form the *livescape*. Conflicts in the localities are manifested as transiency leading to complexities in the identification of 'local community'. Furthermore, place-making developments in the post-industrial heritage waterscape are being constantly negotiated in their everyday usage, while at the same time, processes of publicness (Varna and Tiesdall 2014) appear to operate within structures of power, finance and class.

Transience in the Activated Livescape

Evidence from observations at the festivals suggests that barriers to direct participation for transient and marginalised community groups include financial exclusion, physical barriers, lack of familiarity with the place and, connected to this, transience of community experience. The two places where the participants built the boats, Maryhill and Kirkintilloch, were chosen for their significant history of boat building and boating along the waterways. Both groups in the study exemplify local communities who, on the whole, are not currently engaged in regeneration discourses. As Gray (2018) argues, even after communities have been consulted about urban regeneration, tensions can still arise over the struggle for agency. Maryhill has a high incidence of locales that fall into the lowest quintile on the Scottish Index of Multiple Deprivation (SIMD 2020). Although Kirkintilloch is less 'deprived' overall according to SIMD measures, it includes neighbourhoods that are amongst the lowest quintile, and some of the participants came from these areas.

We argue that both groups involved in the study, migrant and youth, can be regarded as transient. The migrant community in Maryhill exhibits many transient qualities, not least their migration experiences and, for some, the possibility of further onward migration or return. The group, primarily of young LGBT+ identifying people, is transient both in the sense that, as young adults they are likely to move on, and also in the sense that the environment with which they engage is ever changing and under pressure from urban regeneration. Bauman's argument (2001) about 'aesthetic or peg' communities was relevant for the community groups here. For Bauman, aesthetic communities are short-lived groups that gather for a specific purpose, for example, to deliver a festival or event. Peg communities, whilst they may be involved in similar activities, have more established connections to an action (Bauman 2001) such as festival-making. Our observations highlighted the interplay between the two kinds of communities during the festivals, including the aesthetic community formed by participants through 'one-off' involvement with the events, and peg communities such as local residents who volunteer year on year for festival activities. The events created 'aesthetic' communities who interacted within an impermanent framework, although they were less successful in creating new 'peg' communities within marginalised groups. These communities required ease of access, familiarity and a sense of belonging in interactions with the livescapes of the festivals. Transience emerges in communities through ease of access, and as Hall (2012) explains, the interplay among 'the familiar and the unfamiliar'. As well as the participant groups studied, other local residents who were relatively new to the area also participated in the festivals. However, some of the latter residents were more successful in forming a 'peg' community as the locality in transit had been reinvented to fit this new community's needs. This was particularly evident in the GCF where the new residents of Speirs Locks formed a 'peg' community in contrast with both of the community groups' participants' transient 'aesthetic' community experience. The area has changed and according to Gray (2018), the injection of new residents in the space of the festival has created a confused notion of the locality and active engagement within it.

Manifestly, at one of the festival committee meetings, one Speirs Locks' resident and festival volunteer exclaimed:

> *What do you mean by 'local community'? We are the local community.*
> (GCF Volunteer 1)

It seems apparent that the new residents benefited from the activation of the festival livescape as it contributed to their bonding with 'their' place (through volunteering at the event or by having a cultural event on their doorstep). Observations showed that the new locals had the resources to volunteer and participate directly without having to be represented through an organisation.

The activated, contested livescape and place-making processes

According to Vallerani (2018), waterways invoke meanings of belonging. Vallerani's (2018, 2) 'fluvial sense of space' has significance in place-making, as cultural events encouraged by cultural strategies in cities aim to provide new meanings for post-industrial spaces (Hutton 2016). According to del Barrio, Devesa and Herrero (2012) cultural festivals bring together, display and reinterpret a cultural legacy, and in Glasgow, this legacy is the historic industrial activity that has defined urban waterscapes. Within this framework, the participating groups were provided with opportunities to engage directly with the waterways and in doing so engaged directly with the place-making process 'on the ground'.

In their study on issues of social 'connectivity' and access to urban rivers, Kondolf and Pinto (2017) point out that connections with urban waterways and consequently waterscapes can be blocked by road systems and constructions that raise barriers to accessing the water. The Clydeside Expressway (built in the 1970s) and a series of newly built high-rise buildings created a physical and visual barrier to the river that was further reinforced by restricted, gated access to the water from the raised waterfront development around the Riverside Museum. Parking fees and a considerable walking distance from the train station contributed to the blockade, which affected engagement with the waterfront and consequently the festival. On the River Clyde, familiarity with the place was also problematised by limited use of the waterway. The Riverside Museum and the waterfront were used for activities such as events and street sports, whereas access to the water is usually limited to boaters who are affiliated with boating clubs, and being a member involves a fee.

Familiarity with the environment and the publicness of the river and canal were central to the activation of the livescape. Both of these factors contributed to the level of festival participation, and here, participating community groups' unfamiliarity with the festivals' locations appeared to affect overall engagement. Similar findings have been noted in a study of the use of urban blue spaces. Haeffner et al. (2017) argue that access to urban waterways depends on opportunities to interact with the water and on socio-economic status, thus living and working adjacent to waterways does not necessarily indicate interaction. They go on to explain that the increased value of a blue space area affects its accessibility for communities who lack resources to interact with the urban waterways. These findings point to the contested nature of the livescape.

As part of the formation of the festivals' heritage livescape, affectual relationships (Müller 2015) between places, human and non-human, small and large-scale elements (including traditional tools and the historic river) challenge hegemonic knowledge approaches to participation, in this case through the activation of the waterscape (use of boats). Lorimer (2005) and Ingold (2000; 2012) have, in different contexts, observed how an environment is sensed and worked by interactions of matter of the 'lifeworld' (Ingold 2012). We argue that the heritage livescapes of the two festivals have emerged and continue emerging from relationships such as boat building and boating. Consequently, departing from Ingold's notion of 'taskscapes', implying landscapes' processual nature as environments worked through time, it is suggested that the traditional craft of using boats activates the waterscape and therefore, the livescape – the (crafted) place which, continually, implicates the dweller in consistent 'life activity' (Ingold 2000). Applying this notion to the realm of the two festivals, the events activate the livescapes in two ways: through the water of the historic environment, and through the lifeworld of the festivals. Where boating occurs, this recreates knowledge and social space, as one of the Clydebuilt festival producer's explained:

> With boat building going on and also activity in the river outside with the rowing, with Clydebuilt Festival we wanted to celebrate these two things together. (CF Producer 1)

Thus, reproduction, exchange and celebration of knowledge through boating stimulates the production of a shared space (Lefebvre 1991). In this context, and developing from Lefebvre's notion of 'lived space', 'space is not a thing among other things, nor a product among other products, rather, it subsumes things produced, and encompasses their interrelationships in their coexistence and simultaneity … Social space implies a great diversity of knowledge' (Lefebvre 1991, 73). As contested livescapes, the festivals challenge hierarchical knowledge over the historic environment as they develop from the idea of knowledge transmission through community participation. These are the spaces where objects such as boats, and interactions with them, form a platform where participants contribute their own knowledge and understanding of the place, by claiming use of its urban waterways. Through their acquired new craft skills participants were able to claim ownership of an unfamiliar and potentially dangerous space:

> Come and try our boat. It is safe. (GCF Participant /Boat builder 1, inviting visitors)

Agency and the activated livescape

Varna (2016) and Hall (2012) both recognise public space and its diversity in terms of community and place. This diversity and fluidity have been analysed by Neimanis (2016, 55) vis-a-vis the entitlement to knowledge: 'Somewhat ironically, unknowability refers to water's capacity to elude our efforts to contain it with any apparatus of knowledge'. We juxtapose this notion with how the public realm of the waterways underpins the livescape, being a place where the examination of macro- and micro- entanglement of matter and interactions with transient outcomes provide a challenge at a detailed and accurate level to the less nuanced strategies of renewal processes in public space (Gray 2018). If knowledge of the watery environment is 'fluid', why is agency of heritage waterscapes hard to access, and do festivals celebrating waterways challenge this?

In Glasgow, the heritage environments of the River Clyde and its canal provide exemplars of this reality (Gillick and Ivett 2018), as the livescape is subjected to place-making processes, '[t]he impact of culture-led regeneration is clearly closely tied up to a localised sense of place' (Miles and Paddison 2005, 836). Culture has played an important role in the regeneration process of Glasgow, and particularly the Clyde's waterfront (Pollock and Paddison 2014; Gray 2018).

This interaction and knowledge exchange between visitors, participants, canal, river and boats demonstrates the transformation of the sense of place through the sharing of information and experiences, stimulating the livescape through celebratory practices (visitors at a festival, in a celebratory mood and ready to try new things). The interaction relates to Lorimer's argument that in order to understand the 'ecologies of place' one needs to recognise the processual element of the formation of the place through activities (Lorimer 2005). In this study, it implies that knowledge transmission and ownership, from the human geographical perspective, is understood by activating the livescape through the use of boats. As expressed by one CF visitor;

> *I have never been on a boat before. I don't know how to swim and this river feels big.* (CF Visitor 1)

Matter such as the river, the boat and the rope that ties the boat to the shore for extra safety, or the oars which are essential in moving it, all have a political, active role (Bennett 2010), contributing to a sense of place. According to one of the young CF's participant's comments, the use of the boat they created is their way to claim a right to be on the river, with the festival providing the motivation for the activity.

> *I built the boat so I could go on the water. Without the boat I would have never been here.* (CF Participant/Boatbuilder 2)

As the use of the boat stimulates a sense of belonging and the act of claiming space, the political implications of being on a boat challenge dominant forms of agency in the historic environment by exposing tensions in engagement with the livescape in terms of decision making. The design and delivery of the two festivals point to hierarchical attitudes, even if unintentional, because in both festivals, participants were not included in the production of the event from the outset. Decision-making powers were exclusively retained by the most 'knowledgeable' – the festival producers. In this sense, it has been observed that knowledge ownership in the livescape is contested and some participants possibly gained more knowledge about the canal and the river than the festival producers through their boating experience, challenging authority in the livescape. Thinking about decision-making processes through the notion of the livescape being contested exposes barriers in engagement with the festivals and the sense of belonging. Subsequently, considering the festivals' livescape and its complexity in terms of authoritative knowledge, governance and on how access to participation is managed, taking the boats on the water could be viewed as an act of 'disruption' of authority (Keating, Portman and Robertson 2012). Festival participants used their new skills to reinvent the place and their own position within it, and their agency in introducing it to others.

> Rowing the boat is more than a skill. I want to teach people to accept others by using the boat. (CF Volunteer 1)

Additionally, the festival participants' sensory experience of the environment as a 'learned ability' (De Matteis 2018) turns the focus to the mundane and the ordinariness of everyday life in the landscape in transit, compared to the contested livescape of the festivals, as occasional occurrences. As well as feelings of ownership of the festival environment, familiarity with the livescape in everyday life provide a basis for developing a sense of belonging. An example of this notion is Hall's study of Walworth Road in London (2012), where the urban condition of another locality (or livescape), similar to the festivals', is framed. Hall argues that since nuanced margins exist in the city, there is an ever-changing environment of the locality which calls for 'the ability to live with combinations'. Hall's approach to Walworth Road is close to the conceptualisation of the livescape as she recognises that the road is a meeting place where interactions occur, and where matter and activities have opportunities to transform each other through time. Hall employs the *table* in a café as an example, where members of a family gather and interact and where conversations unravel. The *table*, in this instance, functions like the *boat*, as a place-making and belonging tactic in a livescape. Hall considers the local to be the life realm. Interaction here is significant because it occurs from repeated use of the public space. In the case of waterscapes, regular engagement with the water, whether through organised or informal activity, builds familiarity with and ownership of the space. Being in the waterways regularly, one gains familiarity and a sense of belonging in the festival and subsequently in the urban environment.

In sum, conceiving of festival places as livescapes offers a holistic approach to understanding the historic environment which develops through contestation and negotiations of tensions over time.

The Festivals

Glasgow Canal Festival (GCF)

GCF was established in 2017 to celebrate the renewed environment of the canal and its local communities in North Glasgow. The event in 2019, as mentioned before, was driven by Glasgow Canal Co-op with the support of Scottish Canals, the agency which manages the Scottish canal network. The festival was organised by a collective of local ventures as well as housing associations representing the locality.

In 2018, GCF ran alongside another event which had an urban games theme. During an informal conversation, a professional who participated in the event from a local voluntary organisation observed that, although the two events succeeded in advertising the area as a sought-after place to 'hang around', members from disadvantaged communities who lived, worked in and used the place around the canal were underrepresented;

> *I reckon only around 20% of the people who spoke to me came from the local community. I let the organisers [of the canal festival] know about it. One would need targeted surveys to prove that that only a small percentage of the local community comes to these events.* (Community Professional 1)

Speirs Locks is near public transport routes, however it is not a familiar place to people from the participant communities. Speirs Locks is a private development and normally limits general public access. This discourages people from casually using the place.

> *There is no point in coming here for any reason other than this time at the festival. We never come here and the cafes must be dear.* (GCF Participant 4)

In April 2019, three months before the event, the festival organisers, through social media, invited wider community involvement in the organisation of the event. It was suggested that participants in the study should respond to this call. However, many of the boat building participants were vulnerable and faced language barriers in engaging with the festival steering group. Provision of interpreters, childcare and travel expenses help in overcoming barriers in participation of marginalised groups (Ferguson 2011). As there was no such provision in place for attending the steering group's meetings, one of the authors and a professional from the participatory community group agreed to join the festival steering group meetings, while the participants themselves engaged directly with the festival activities. Because the festival was at the weekend, participants with no childcare were restricted in how much they could engage with the festival. One female participant, for example, could not interact with visitors as she had her young family with her.

The programme for the festival included free activities provided by professionals, food stalls (with festival prices), other cultural productions (ticketed but at affordable prices) and exhibitions that were already part of the core activities happening in the area. Essential costs for study participants were covered by public funding from CanalCraft and by the Maryhill community group, and this subvention was critical in enabling them to take part.

If it wasn't for the funding from the boat-building project (CanalCraft) or the refugee organisation covering travelling expenses, these people [participants] wouldn't be able to be at the festival. (Community Professional 2)

Because of a time shortage, the study group's participation was not mentioned in the festival programme and there was no signage to guide visitors to the group or to their boats. Fortunately, the tent and the boats were given a space at the edge of the festival, at a spot where there were enough passers-by to notice the group, which gave visibility to the boats. Nevertheless, the lack of signage meant that at the beginning of the festival, it was unclear to visitors that the activity was an official part of the festival, thus they reluctantly approached the boats and participants:

They (visitors) couldn't understand what it was about at first, but when they eventually figured it out, they wanted to go in [the boat]. (GCF Participant/Boatbuilder 3)

Despite obstacles to participation, participants felt confident to have visitors on their boat and those who were more confident with conversational English connected with the visitors through discussions about boat building and rowing experiences. Some visitors even allowed their children to sit in the boat with the boat-builders:

I didn't know that this group existed. It must have been very hard building a boat without understanding the language. (GCF Visitor 1)

The boat is the connection when language is a barrier; I've never been in a small boat before. (GCF Visitor 2)

The group appeared to take ownership of the space through being on boat:

I can't believe I'm in the canal in our boat! (GCF Participant/ Boatbuilder 2)

Now that we have the boat, we can get to know the canal better. (GCF Participant/ Boatbuilder 3)

Many visitors queued to get on the boat and from the participants' body language it was apparent that they felt part of the event. Although they didn't have the opportunity to be part of the organisation for the festival, they felt appreciated and accepted:

People asked if we will build more boats. (GCF Participant/Boatbuilder 3)

Although observations and other data suggested that participation in the festival induced a sense of place and integration for the transient communities who would not have had the chance to interact with visitors in this event otherwise, it was evident that this participation was only possible with organisation from the community group's professionals and with resources unrelated to the festival's budget. Participants had limited resources to support themselves being there. Most of them were in receipt of limited government asylum support, or engaged in very low-paid employment, which excluded them from being in events away from their neighbourhoods. In summary, participants felt included in the festival event despite barriers of language based communication, resource provision and unfamiliarity with the place of the festival. Through their engagement with the festival, they felt connected with Speirs Locks and a sense of ownership in the spots where their boats were placed for that day. They expressed their desire to participate again, and there was a suggestion from the organisers that they would be open to it.

> *I think that it would be great if the Glasgow Canal Project [Glasgow Canal Coop] can build on the relationship for next year and perhaps a little further in advance of the festival.* (GCF Festival Producer 1)

Clydebuilt Festival (CF)

CF also started in 2017 and takes place in the area around the Riverside Museum, including the Tall Ship at Riverside. As already mentioned, the festival was established to mark the end of a three year project to encourage wider participation in boat building and boating activities with the aim of making them accessible to marginalised and disadvantaged communities.

> *The legacy of the project [Anchor and Sail] gave us Clydebuilt Festival, where we want to encourage people use boats, make boats accessible to all.* (CF Producer 1)

All groups' boats were transported to the area around the Riverside Museum. The group from Maryhill (with different participants from GCF as the previous participants' circumstances had changed) and the group from Kirkintilloch participated. As with GCF, the budget didn't cover travel expenses for participants, however, this time they could get food at subsidised prices. There was a mixture of private and commercial stall holders, relevant community projects, free activities for all and food venders (at festival prices).

> *On the shore, we wanted to have something for everyone, kids, women, we wanted to get away from the white beard ... people connect boats with old men with white beards.* (CF Producer 1)

Access to the river from the group's tent was not as easy as it was on the canal, due to stricter rules about safe access. Consequently, festival visitors who wanted to get into the boats had to arrange to do so at a specific time.

We can't see the water from here; if we want to go to the boats we need to leave the tent for a while. (CF Participant/Boat builder 1)

The fact that there was no visual connection with the water affected interaction between visitors and the community groups. Taking visitors to the pontoon to board the boats was time consuming, plus the boats had to be handled by a more experienced rower, as the river presented a higher safety risk than the canal. Due to insurance restrictions, children were not allowed on the boats. Therefore, interaction on the water was restricted as participants didn't have the same opportunities to experience the extensive interaction they had had with the visitors inside their boats at the other festival. Most interactions took place instead around the tent area, where there were discussions with visitors about boat building and the boats themselves:

The weather is sunny and it seems all Glasgow is here today. I'm exhausted talking to so many people but it has been rewarding. People love the boats. (CF Participant/ Boatbuilder 2)

The event organisers visited the tent several times and met with the participants. Other community projects at the festival were also represented by their own participants, too, which created a sense of inclusion and belonging.

The GalGael folk came over and gave us a hand with the boats. It's good to see other people with similar projects. (CF Participant/ Boatbuilder 3)

Accessibility to the Riverside also presented a barrier for people from outside Glasgow, as noted by participants from the Kirkintilloch group;

I've never been here before and I have no reason to come again. (CF Participant/ Boat builder 4)

If it wasn't for the project, I wouldn't have visited the festival. (CF Participant/ Boat builder 2)

The cost of travelling to the Riverside and further spending at the event created barriers for communities who faced financial limitations.

I would come again if it's free to go on the river. I love the river. (CF Participant/ Boat builder 5)

Celebration for wider inclusion in boating activities underpinned the festival's priorities. The festival producers (officers from the Tall Ship at Riverside, officers from GalGael, and independent event producers) appeared to prioritise and encourage direct participation from community projects in the festival's programme. Nevertheless, the core activity of the festival was a river race for rowing activity that presented obstacles for independent rowers who wanted to participate and were not a member of an established club. CF is part of the place-making process for the river waterfront encouraged by the City of Glasgow and the Lord Provost visits the event every year. Despite the intention of the producers to create an inclusive event, the festival's location still feels unfamiliar to some marginalised community groups who live in other locations, due to lack of available incentives for them to visit the area, such as directed promotions and easy access for groups who require extra resources to visit and feel welcomed (Hassanli, Walters and Friedmann 2020). Kelvin Harbour is used by rowing clubs, although for anyone to be regularly involved in a club requires resources and free time. CF organisers are boaters themselves. The Castle to Crane race at the festival meant that being on a boat and interacting with the waterway was one of the main values of the festival. However, safety on boats on the river required special training and usually membership of a club, which was prohibitive for the community groups in this study. Additionally, restrictions in 'messing about in boats' on the river – despite festival participation – creates barriers in knowledge ownership and consequently agency in the decision making of the event. Furthermore, familiarity with the livescape of the river and the wider festival itself were difficult to achieve due to the lack of access to resources and opportunities for engagement with the fluvial environment.

It could be argued that activation of the livescape during CF encouraged prolonged interaction with boats and their use, inspiring ownership and a sense of belonging. However, this study showed that to regularly engage with the river required time and resources, as access was only feasible through organised boating activities, such as being a member of a rowing club. This discourages regular engagement with the river for marginalised groups and therefore direct participation and activation of the livescape.

Conclusion

This chapter discussed the festival space as a livescape, and how festivals celebrating urban waterways are employed as place-making processes, achieving a sense of belonging and ownership of spaces, particularly for community groups affected by marginalisation and transiency.

This study observed two transient and marginalised community groups' efforts to plan and directly participate in two urban community festivals by using boats they had built on the water of the canal and the river. Understanding these festivals as livescapes problematises place-making processes by exposing the complexity of the publicness of space, as this is underpinned by notions of access, familiarity and connectivity via ownership of the events. Observations of participants, visitors, organisers and others involved with community work revealed the challenges faced by the community groups in their attempts to integrate localities through participation in the festivals' environments. This was contrasted with the festival producers' aims and objectives which were manifested in terms of knowledge ownership, a different connectivity with the places, and notions of agency and apprehension. In this context, and following a holistic approach of understanding the heritage livescape, it appears that marginalised communities (that have experienced transiency in their environment through urban renewal, forced migration and their struggle for inclusion and agency), achieved a sense of belonging by directly engaging with the festivals for the duration of the study. Their engagement showed that the livescape was the worked, activated and constantly changing environment – consisting and emerging from relationships, interactions, tensions and a distinctive sense of place. It was contested *qua* the challenges of hegemonic knowledge and ontological certainties.

Both historic places where the festivals took place in Glasgow have been significant for their regeneration initiatives (Mooney 2004; Gillick and Ivett 2018). However, there is evidence that the place-making process has been misaligned with transient communities' opportunities for engagement. This exposes tensions in the Glasgow Canal Festival and the Clydebuilt Festival livescapes, as the study suggested that each festival is itself an activated livescape presenting its own tensions, including barriers to participation, gaps in interactions with authorised decision making, and transient communities' attempts to have direct control over the engagement. Observations from these two livescapes support the notion that their activation provides a platform where expertise is asymmetrically shared between decision makers and the communities. Knowledge (and consequently agency) within the livescape depends on the vigour of bottom up interactions and activities, such as 'messing about in boats'. Considering the festive space as a contested livescape in the planning of urban community festivals has the potential to enhance the place-making process. This approach situates a sense of familiarity and ownership of social spaces with community groups who experience alienation in regenerated urban spaces.

References

Banks, Marcus and David Zeitlyn. 2015. *Visual Methods in Social Research* (2nd edn). London: Sage.

Bauman, Zygmunt. 2001. *Community: Seeking Safety in an Insecure World*. Cambridge: Polity.

Bennett, Jane. 2010. *Vibrant Matter: A Political Ecology of Things*. Durham, NC: Duke University Press.

Bruttomesso, Rinio. 2004. Complexity on the Urban Waterfront. In Richard Marshall (Ed.) *Waterfronts in Post-Industrial Cities*, pp. 47–58. New York: Taylor and Francis.

Clark, Julie, Ade Kearns and Claire Cleland. 2016. Spatial Scale, Time and Process in Mega-Events: The Complexity of Host Community Perspectives on Neighbourhood Change. *Cities*, 53, 87–97.

Clyde Waterfront. 2003–2011. Available at: http://www.clydewaterfront.com (accessed June 2018).

del Barrio, María José, María Devesa and Luis César Herrero. 2012. Evaluating Intangible Cultural Heritage: The Case of Cultural Festivals. *City, Culture and Society*, 3(4), 235–244.

De Matteis, Federico. 2018. The City as a Mode of Perception: Corporeal Dynamics in Urban Space. In Francesco Aletta and Jieling Xiao (Eds.) *Handbook of Research on Perception-Driven Approaches to Urban Assessment and Design*, pp. 436–457. Hersehey, PA: IGI Global.

England, Kim V.L. 1994. Getting Personal: Reflexivity, Positionality, and Feminist Research. *The Professional Geographer*, 46(1), 80–89.

Ferguson, Jennifer. 2011. Weaving a New Tartan in Scotland: The Role of Arts and Culture in Refugee Integration. *Line* (formerly *West Coast Line*), 68, 24–33. Available at: https://journals.lib.sfu.ca/index.php/wcl/article/view/3688/2951

Gillick, Ambrose and Lee Ivett (Eds.) 2018. *Test Unit*. Glasgow: Glasgow Urban Lab, dpr-barcelona.

Gray, Neil. 2018. Neither Shoreditch nor Manhattan: Post-Politics, 'Soft Austerity Urbanism' and Real Abstraction in Glasgow North. *Area*, 50(1), 15–23.

Haeffner, Melissa, Douglas Jackson-Smith, Martin Buchert and Jordan Risley. 2017. Accessing Blue Spaces: Social and Geographic Factors Structuring Familiarity With, Use of, and Appreciation of Urban Waterways. *Landscape and Urban Planning*, 167, 136–146.

Hall, Suzanne. 2012. *City, Street and Citizen: The Measure of the Ordinary*. Abingdon: Routledge.

Hassanli, Najmeh, Trudie Walters and Ruth Friedmann. 2020. Can Cultural Festivals Function as Counterspaces for Migrants and Refugees? The Case of the New Beginnings Festival in Sydney. *Leisure Studies*, 39(2), 165–180.

Herbert, Steve. 2000. For Ethnography. *Progress in Human Geography*, 24(4), 550–568.

Hill, Emma, Nasar Meer and Timothy Peace. 2021. The Role of Asylum in Processes of Urban Gentrification. *The Sociological Review*, 69(2), 259–276.

Hutton, Thomas A. 2016. *Cities and the Cultural Economy*. Abingdon: Routledge.

Ingold, Tim. 2000. *The Perception of the Environment: Essays on Livelihood, Dwelling and Skill*. Routledge: New York.

Ingold, Tim. 2012. Toward an Ecology of Materials. *Annual Review of Anthropology*, 41, 427–442.

Januchta-Szostak, Anna B. and Anna M. Biedermann. 2014. The Impact of Great Cultural Projects on the Transformation of Urban Water-Side Spaces. *Czasopismo Techniczne*, Architektura Zeszyt 1 A (1), s. 69–87.

Keating, Richard, Kel Portman and Iain Robertson. 2012. Walking the Wateryscape: Exploring the Liminal. *Journal of Arts & Communities*, 4(1–2), 10–31.

Keats, Patrice A. 2009. Multiple Text Analysis in Narrative Research: Visual, Written, and Spoken Stories of Experience. *Qualitative Research*, 9(2), 181–195.

Kondolf, G. Mathias and Pedro J. Pinto. 2017. The Social Connectivity of Urban Rivers. *Geomorphology*, 277, 182–196.

Lefebvre, Henri. 1991. *The Production of Space*. Oxford: Blackwell Publishing.

Lorimer, Hayden. 2005. Cultural Geography: The Busyness of Being 'More-Than-Representational'. *Progress in Human Geography*, 29(1), 83–94.

Miles, Steven and Ronan Paddison. 2005. Introduction: The Rise and Rise of Culture-Led Urban Regeneration. *Urban Studies*, 42(5–6), 833–839.

Mooney, Gerry. 2004. Cultural Policy as Urban Transformation? Critical Reflections on Glasgow, European City of Culture 1990. *Local Economy*, 19(4), 327–340.

Müller, Martin. 2015. More-Than-Representational Political Geographies. In John A. Agnew et al. (Eds.) *The Wiley Blackwell Companion to Political Geography*, pp. 407–423. Chichester: Wiley Blackwell.

Neimanis, Astrida. 2016. Water and Knowledge. In Dorothy Christian and Rita Wong (Eds.) *Downstream: Reimagining Water*, pp. 51–68. Waterloo: Wilfrid Laurier University Press.

Pollock, Venda Louise. 2019. Revisiting the Creative City: Culture and Regeneration in Post-Industrial Glasgow. In Keith Kintrea and Rebecca Madgin (Eds.) *Transforming Glasgow: Beyond the Post-Industrial City*. Bristol: Policy Press.

Pollock, Venda Louise and Ronan Paddison. 2014. On Place-Making, Participation and Public Art: The Gorbals, Glasgow. *Journal of Urbanism: International Research on Placemaking and Urban Sustainability*, 7(1), 85–105.

Scottish Index of Multiple Deprivation. (revised 2020). Scottish Government. Available at: https://www.gov.scot/collections/scottish-index-of-multiple-deprivation-2020 (accessed June 2021).

Stevenson, Deborah. 2013. *The City*. Cambridge: Polity Press.

Tretter, Eliot M. 2009. The Cultures of Capitalism: Glasgow and the Monopoly of Culture. *Antipode*, 41(1), 111–132.

Vallerani, Francesco. 2018. Introduction: Flowing Consciousness and the Becoming of Waterscapes. In Francesco Vallerani and Francesco Visentin (Eds.) *Waterways and the Cultural Landscape*. Abingdon: Routledge.

Varna, Georgiana. 2016. *Measuring Public Space: The Star Model*. Abingdon: Routledge.

Varna, George and Steve Tiesdell. 2010. Assessing the Publicness of Public Space: The Star Model of Publicness. *Journal of Urban Design*, 15(4), 575–598.

Walters, Trudie and Allan Stewart Jepson (Eds.) 2019. *Marginalisation and Events*. Abingdon: Routledge.

Yin, Robert K. 2018. *Case Study Research and Applications*. Washington DC: Sage Publications.

PART 3

Images and Narratives of Festival Cities

CHAPTER 9

Longevity and Reinvention: Venetianization and the Biennale

John R. Gold and Margaret M. Gold

'There were so many Venetian festivals that, in the end, one day was chosen to commemorate several different celebrations. It had become in essence a ritual city. That is why certain pathways were chosen. Churches were sited at focal points, where theatre and piety converged. Public spaces became ceremonial axes, part of the vast geometry of the sacred city. It was a society of the spectacle. Land and water were conjoined …'

Ackroyd (2010, 81)

Introduction

Had it not been for the Covid-19 pandemic, Thursday 25 March 2021 would have been a day of memorable festivity in Venice. According to the *Chronicon Altinate*, a thirteenth-century compilation of urban myths and realities, the city was founded at noon on 25 March 421 with the dedication of its first church, San Giacomo di Rialto (Ammerman et al. 2017, 1625). The advent of the city's 1600th anniversary had therefore encouraged local, national and international bodies to

How to cite this book chapter:
Gold, J. R. and Gold, M. M. 2022. Longevity and Reinvention: Venetianization and the Biennale. In: Smith, A., Osborn, G. and Quinn, B. (Eds.) *Festivals and the City: The Contested Geographies of Urban Events*. London: University of Westminster Press. Pp. 149–167. London: University of Westminster Press. DOI: https://doi.org/10.16997/book64.i. License: CC-BY-NC-ND 4.0

collaborate in arranging a celebratory programme to recognise this remarkable longevity. At the outset, the programme contained 235 events ranging from talks and exhibitions to waterborne processions and treasure hunts in the Basilica but, in the circumstances, changes had to be made. In particular, the opening celebrations were scaled down to anticlimactic levels, with lockdown provisions and travel restrictions in the face of a third wave of Covid-19 infections meaning empty streets and concerts attended by small, socially distanced audiences.

There was nothing new, of course, in Venetians choosing to stage festivals to celebrate landmarks in the city's history or in using it as a backdrop for those festivities. Venice was ever the Ur-city of festivals. Each phase of its development from a small settlement built on 118 islands off Italy's northern Adriatic coast to a Mediterranean maritime power had been observed by initiating festivals. Many would stand the test of time. The Candlemastide Festa delle Marie, for example, originated in the late tenth century; the Festa della Sensa, commemorating the city's symbolic 'marriage' to the sea, emerged around the year 1000 (Korsch 2013); and Carnival, in its earliest forms, was already celebrated by the mid-eleventh century (Gold and Gold 2020, 41). In due course, these and other popular festivals were conjoined into a formidable annual schedule that was organised, *inter alia*, around saints' name days, plentiful local feasts, increasingly extended Carnival celebrations, special events recording civic allegiances and military victories, and thanksgivings to mark deliverance from plague and pestilence. To these would be added La Biennale di Venezia – the Venice Biennale – in the late nineteenth century; the gathering commonly regarded as the world's greatest art show.

This chapter, which is set against this longstanding tradition, explores the development and urban implications of the Biennale. It contains five main parts. After considering the events and circumstances that led to the Biennale's foundation in 1895, the ensuing section examines the politically inspired festivalisation that characterised the 1930s, its growth after 1945 and its increasing 'Venetianization' – the term used by Clarissa Ricci (2010, 105) to describe the festival's tendency to spread spatially from its original hub in the Giardini into locations scattered throughout the rest of the city. The final parts look at current issues, including the problems facing the city's historic core and the rising disquiet of citizens feeling themselves overwhelmed by the impact of mass cultural tourism on the city's everyday life. It is noted that the hiatus in activity caused by the response to Covid-19 has fed calls for rethinking Venice's relationship with art, tourism and urban development. The desire for a 'new normal' that is expressed in some quarters, juxtaposed with the views of those who wish to restore the *status quo ante*, provides an important dynamic for future discourse and practice.

Origins

The notion that Venice should stage a regular arts exhibition had various nineteenth-century antecedents (Holt 1983; Fyfe 1984; Ward 1996). These included the salons convened by national academies of fine art, the exhibitions routinely added as visitor attractions to the Expositions Universelles and, more specifically, a series of exhibitions hosted by Italian cities from 1858 onwards as part of a carefully orchestrated strategy of political unification and state formation. Cities with a modern industrial base held national exhibitions (Esposizioni Nazionali) that covered agriculture, industry and the fine arts. By contrast cities like Venice, which lacked such sectors, proffered smaller and more specialised exhibitions. For its part, Venice had staged an Esposizione Artistica Nazionale in 1887. Opened by King Umberto I on 2 May 1887, this immediate predecessor of the Biennale displayed around 1800 pictures and 170 sculptures. Significantly for future developments, it was held in an elongated temporary structure in the Giardini, the parkland peripherally located on the eastern tip of the main island (Bowness 1995; May 2009).

The Esposizione proved a popular success, drawing 100,000 visitors and attracting strong representation from Venetian artists. Admittedly it incurred heavy financial losses and showed the need for improved display and marketing strategies, but it demonstrated the virtues of mounting a regular and prestigious art exhibition. *Inter alia*, such an event could radically enhance the city's position in the art market, create opportunities for local artists to sell their work to an international clientele, and attract wealthy and high-spending visitors to supplement Venice's already substantial presence in the world of tourism (Davis and Marvin 2004).

The ensuing Biennale embraced the key points from this experience. It was first proposed at a meeting of civic dignitaries at the Caffè Florian on St Mark's Square in April 1893 (May 2009). Although they first contemplated staging a more limited Biennial Exhibition of Italian Art (Esposizione Biennale Artistica Nazionale), the final decision was in favour of a more ambitious International Art Exhibition of the City of Venice (Esposizione Internazionale d'Arte della Città di Venezia). It was in this form that the event opened in the Giardini on 30 April 1895. By the time that it closed on 22 October 1895, it had attracted 224,327 visitors. In contrast to its 1887 precursor, it recorded an overall profit, with sales of more than a third of the artworks on display. The pattern was now set. By the time that war broke out in September 1914 there had been eleven Biennales, firmly launching Venice as a centre for the international art market venue and attracting more than 400,000 visitors in both 1909 and 1912.

Display space was at a premium. Quickly outgrowing the facilities provided for the 1887 exposition, additional space was found, first, by substantially extending the central pavilion (Martini 2010, 69–70) and later, by copying the policy pioneered by the Expositions Universelles, whereby nation states provided their own pavilions. This innovation simultaneously achieved two goals: it pragmatically delegated the handling and expense of exhibiting foreign art to national commissioners who worked independently of the Biennale's committees (Alloway 1969, 112); and it freed up space in the central pavilion for Italian artists. Seven national pavilions had appeared by 1914 and, by the mid-1920s, this had become the standard method for displaying exhibits (Figure 9.1). From

Figure 9.1. French Pavilion. Designed by Fausto Finzi, chief engineer for the Venice municipality, the neoclassical French Pavilion houses France's national representation during the Venice Biennale festivals. Opened in 1912, it was one of the first seven pavilions constructed in the Giardini before the First World War. Photograph: John and Margaret Gold.

the outset, too, the new festival's impact on the wider city went beyond the indirect changes brought about by increases in tourist numbers. For example, further attractions such as exhibitions of Murano glass were presented during festival time and a new Galleria Internazionale d'Arte Moderna was introduced to house a permanent collection – a feature deemed essential if the city was to be taken seriously as a centre for contemporary art.

Politicisation and Festivalisation

The Biennale changed radically after Mussolini's ascent to power in October 1922. The Partito Nazionale Fascista (National Fascist Party) quickly recognised the potential that art, culture and tourism afforded as media for reinforcing the Party's cultural hegemony, for fostering a new relationship with the Italian people, and for representing Italy to the world. Festivals were now formally reorganised on a quadripartite hierarchical basis. The Venice Biennale of International Art was at the apex of the new structure, with Rome's National Art Quadrennial as the next level down, then four-yearly interprovincial exhibitions, and finally annual provincial festivals as its bottom tier. For its part, Venice benefitted greatly from having Italy's only designated international arts festival, since it was protected from the ambitions of rival cities that might want to develop something similar (May 2009, 21). In due course, too, management of the Biennale was prised away from the control of the Venetian authorities, with a directly funded body headed by a government appointee, Count Giuseppe Volpi, set up to manage it in early 1930.

These political changes affected the Biennale's contents, albeit mostly indirectly. In the first place, while not facing the proscriptions of modern art that operated in Germany's Third Reich, artists laboured under new regulations concerning their eligibility to submit work. Secondly, the introduction of prizes for contributions that celebrated Fascist ideology clearly impacted on the subjects chosen by artists, just as the dominant role exercised by state agencies when purchasing artwork impacted on the type of art supported and made available for display. Thirdly, the ruling regime's wish to display decorative as well as fine arts in the Biennale would not only change the balance of exhibited materials, it also added to the demands for space, which was already under pressure given the increasing numbers of nations wanting their own pavilions. The immediate solution was to expand the showground on to the island of Sant'Elena, with improved access achieved by providing a new road to link the lagoon side of the Giardini to the historic city. Finally, the regime wished to diversify the Biennale's scope by adding new art forms that covered a wider span of media. After 1930, the creation of ancillary festivals covering film, theatre and music broadened the scope of the Biennale as well as supplying after-hours evening entertainment for its visitors.

These new events took the Biennale to new districts of the city with, for example, the Film Festival establishing its base on the Lido – the leisure resort island in the lagoon. They also boosted visitor numbers in years when the Art Biennale was not taking place, although attendances at all events dropped markedly given the deteriorating political situation of the late 1930s. The Art Biennales' visitor numbers, which had risen steadily from 172,841 in 1928 to 361,917 in 1934, declined sharply in 1936 due to boycotts imposed as a response to the 1935 Italian invasion of Abyssinia (Ethiopia). The Film Festivals also experienced decreasing participation as various national delegations, production companies and foreign journalists stayed away in the late 1930s due to accusations of political bias in the awarding of prizes.

After 1945, efforts were quickly made to re-establish the Biennale and shake off any associations with its Fascist past, but reinstatement could not be immediate. Apart from the harbour area, Venice had escaped major wartime damage, but the physical decay and non-availability of some of the venues posed problems. During the war, for example, the Giardini had been the centre of the Italian film industry when the Società Italiana Cines and Istituto Nazionale Luce were moved there from Rome. When film production began in February 1944, the pavilions were used as film sets, film processing laboratories and dubbing studios (Di Martino 2005, 36). Although the film industry had vacated the site by 1946, many of the pavilions needed repair, which their owners were often unwilling to do given the prevailing austerity.

The Film Festival was the first to recommence in August 1946, making use of the Cinema Teatro San Marco and the courtyard of the Doge's Palace in the historic city because the Lido's Palazzo del Cinema and Casino remained occupied by the American forces. The festival only returned to the Lido in 1949. The Art Biennale returned in 1948. While it attracted 216,471 visitors – a number unsurpassed in the post-war period until 1972 – just fifteen nations attended. In these circumstances, empty pavilions were commandeered when necessary. Hungary, for instance, used the Romanian pavilion rather than repair its own (Bódi 2019, 277). Other pavilions staged specialist exhibitions. The Yugoslav pavilion offered a retrospective for the Expressionist painter Oskar Kokoschka, the German pavilion showed work by Impressionists, and the Greek pavilion displayed 136 items from Peggy Guggenheim's collection of contemporary art. Significantly, the Italian pavilion showed works by German artists banned as 'degenerate' in the 1930s along with a retrospective of nineteen canvases by Picasso; his first return to a Biennale since his work had been removed before the opening day in 1910.

Venetianization

The numbers of participating nations, artists and visitors steadily grew during the early post-war years. The Summer of 1968, however, acted as a watershed with student groups leading protests about the anachronistic structure of the Biennale organisation (unchanged since the 1930s) and the commercialism of an art exhibition that profited from selling the art that it displayed. Resulting reforms started to address the content and organisation of the exhibition, especially with an eye to the competition arising from newly created rival international art exhibitions (Gold and Gold 2020, 92–3, 103). However, the two developments that impacted most on Venice itself were, first, the establishment of the Architecture Biennale with its pioneering role in regenerating the Arsenale dockyards and, secondly, finding premises for temporary national pavilions and so-called 'collateral events' (see below) in other parts of the city in order to alleviate the pressure on space in the established showgrounds.

Arsenale

Traditionally, the Venice Biennale lacked a distinct architectural dimension, although the work of architects had occasionally featured. In 1972, for example, the 'Four Projects for Venice' exhibits featured unrealised buildings for the city designed by Frank Lloyd Wright, Le Corbusier, Louis Kahn and Isamu Noguchi. In 1974, the newly appointed Biennale President Carlo Ripa di Meana built on this underlying interest by inviting the architect Vittorio Gregotti to become the first director of Art and Architecture. While Ripa di Meana envisaged this as simply extending the existing Biennale, Gregotti recognised the difficulty of incorporating architecture into the Biennale's existing structure, especially due to its extensive requirements for space. He organised small exhibitions in

1975, 1976 and 1978, but these were spatially detached from the rest of the Biennale, using the former salt warehouse (Magazzini del Sale) in the Zattere district. Yet quite apart from the need to find space, this symbolic detachment addressed two distinct goals: first, to meet a commitment to take the Biennale to the people in the wake of the 1968 protests and, secondly, to show that the architectural component would eventually support a distinctive and separate event (Gregotti 2010, 22–3).

The latter took two further decades to be fully realised, but 1980 saw the creation of a separate architecture department, headed by Paolo Portoghesi, who curated what was later regarded as the first Architecture Biennale. Its theme was 'The Presence of the Past' (Portoghesi et al. 1980). This explored the recent trajectory of architectural practice, with its most notable feature being a faux street, the Strada Novissima, in which twenty invited architects each produced a building façade or a 'self-portrait' of their distinctive architectural styles. These measured up to three storeys high, behind which was an exhibition of that architect's work (Portoghesi 2010, 39). Needing a building with generous dimensions to house this installation and given that Giardini was already fully occupied by the Art Biennale, Portoghesi turned to the Arsenale.

Conveniently located within walking distance of the Giardini, the Arsenale was once Venice's largest industrial space. Occupying 48 hectares and comprising almost seventeen per cent of the city's land area, the Arsenale was historically the heart of Venice's naval and mercantile power. In the fourteenth century, its shipyards were the wonder of Europe with capacity to construct 60 galleys simultaneously (Menichelli 2014, 29). Over the centuries, it had been expanded and modernised, culminating in the production of submarines during the Second World War with total employment of around 5000 workers (ibid, 33). Thereafter decline was rapid. Public sector work ceased in 1957 when the strategic naval command role was transferred to Ancona (Pazeri 2009, 56) and although some naval activity and private sector businesses continued, many of the older buildings fell into disrepair. Yet the general state of dilapidation also presented an unprecedented opportunity. The growing appreciation of the potential of redundant industrial facilities for urban regeneration would clearly earmark the Arsenale as a possible candidate for redevelopment despite the problems of the expenditure needed for a site of this scale, the difficulties of split ownership and multiple agencies, and heritage considerations (given that demolition was not an option).

The ideal space within the Arsenale for the Strada Novissima was the Corderie (the ropeworks). The authorities were initially hesitant about granting permission to use these spaces, since they were still 'full of tanks and armaments' (Portoghesi 2010, 36). Persistence, however, paid off and led to a groundbreaking exhibition that attracted 40,000 visitors and captivated the design world by promoting a nascent postmodernism. In strategic terms, however, moving to the Arsenale transcended just being a pragmatic solution. Rather the Architecture Biennale was likened to a 'Trojan horse', giving Venetians access to a part

Figure 9.2: The Gaggiandre. In Venice's Arsenale, the Gaggiandre, built between 1568–73 to designs attributed to the sculptor and architect Jacopo Sansovino, overlook a large internal dock. Photograph: John and Margaret Gold (July 2015).

of the city from which they had previously been excluded (Portoghesi et al. 1980, 13) and shifting the centre of gravity of the Biennale closer to the heart of the city. Ricci (2010, 105) heralded this locational shift as initiating the 'Venetianization' of the Biennale, ending the Biennale's detachment from the rest of Venice in the Giardini (Ricci 2010, 105).

Despite the 1980 exhibition's success, the Arsenale spaces remained unsuitable for regular public use for some time. Renovation only started in earnest in 1983, with work to stabilise and restore the Corderie. The Art Biennale used the buildings in 1986, 1988 and 1990 for the Aperto, an exhibition of work by young artists, with the Architectural Biennale using the Arsenale regularly from 1991 onwards. In 1998, by which time the Arsenale's regeneration had gathered pace, a new law codified the formal relationship between the Arsenale and the Biennale. The Biennale was transformed into a Culture Company from an autonomous body and the southern half of the Arsenale was transferred to the Biennale, with access to funding that allowed it to become directly involved in restoration work. In 1999 it instigated major renovations of buildings shown in Figures 9.2 and 9.3, respectively, the Artiglierie (gunneries) and the Gaggiandre (wet docks). This was followed by creation of two performance spaces in the old navy cinema (the Piccolo Arsenale) and the Teatro alle Tese in 2000

Figure 9.3: Strada Campagna. View along an internal street in Venice's Arsenale looking towards the former Gunneries (Artiglierie). The north and south armaments (Sale D'armi) are, respectively, on the left and right. Photograph: John and Margaret Gold (July 2015).

(di Martino 2005, 100). Between 2012–2019, more substantive restoration works took place on the Sale d'Armi (armaments) complex to create flexible exhibition and performance spaces. This now allows five of the Biennale festivals – Art, Architecture, Theatre, Dance and Music – to use the Arsenale.

National Pavilions

Although offering a recipe for encouraging international participation while keeping the cost of staging the festival at a minimum, recourse to national pavilions has critics who maintain that the buildings symbolise imperialism, support an anachronistic approach to art in a more integrated world, and proffer a model that favours certain nations over others. Despite this, national pavilions remain a popular medium for display, with persistent demand for pavilions from new states that seek to showcase their art in this way. The fact that only Venice among art festivals now retains this exhibitionary form has become part of its unique attraction in providing a distinctive national showcase for countries wanting to promote their artists and art credentials. Nine national pavilions were added to the Giardini between 1952 to 1964, with

Australia building a temporary pavilion in 1988 (replaced by a grander structure in 2015) and Korea in 1995 (Catenacci 2010, 88).

By the 1990s the Giardini was deemed full, with the issuing of protection
orders on twelve of its older structures in 1998 ensuring that there was even less
room for manoeuvre. In short, there is now virtually no possibility of demol-
ishing, radically changing or altering the layout and structure of the Giardini
in any major way (Martini 2010, 73). While extra space for national contributions was eventually made available in the Arsenale, continuing requests
from nations to participate in the Biennales has led to the relaxation of the
geographical strictures on the festival by allowing nations to establish pavilions
beyond the confines of the existing showgrounds. In the process, the festival
would become a truly city-wide event rather than being confined to a marginal
location. Under the 1998 institutional reforms, therefore, nations were formally
permitted to set up pavilions in the wider city. The Art Biennale in 2019, for
instance, saw 36 countries have national pavilions in the city along with a further 21 collateral events. This is in addition to the 30 national pavilions represented in the Giardini and 25 in the Arsenale.

The Contemporary Festival

As currently constituted, the Art and Architecture Biennales each have three
main elements. The first are the curated international exhibitions, for which
guest curators are appointed and given responsibility for devising a theme
that might lend coherence to the exhibition and engage with cutting edge contemporary artistic themes. Artists are then invited to contribute to the exhibitions, which are staged in the Giardini's Central Pavilion and the Corderie
and Artiglierie in the Arsenale. The second element comprises the pavilions
run by nation states, which as noted above, commission work and then fund
and administer their own spaces. The third element consists of collateral events
put forward by not-for-profit international bodies and institutions, individual
artists or groups of artists, as well as territories that are not recognised as independent states. In recent years, for example, these have included projects from
Catalonia, Hong Kong, Macau, Scotland, Wales, Newfoundland and Labrador.
In 2003 pressure from the People's Republic of China forced Taiwan's exhibition to be permanently reclassified as a collateral event (Wei 2013, 480). Once
accepted and an admission registration fee is paid, the collateral event appears
in the Biennale brochure, catalogue and promotional literature and may use
the Biennale logo (FBV 2019, 8). It is then the responsibility of the project to
find appropriate accommodation. The distinctive geography of each Biennale
is thus shaped by the national pavilions and collateral events that spread themselves throughout the city, using the historic centre, islands and occasionally
beyond. Finally, as with other major festivals, a sizeable 'fringe' of unofficial

exhibitions and events appear annually in the city, trading ambiguously on the image of the Biennale although not actually part of the festival.

In this process of Venetianization, the Biennale has occasionally spilled over from the islands on to the mainland. In 2008, for instance, the Biennale moved its historical archive to Port Marghera. This was done as part of a broader trade-off of interests. For the city, the archive's removal to the VEGA (the Venice Gateway for Science and Technology) Science Park provided support for an ongoing regeneration project designed to arrest the industrial decline of the waterfront area (Il Quotidiano Immoboliare 2014). For the Biennale, the move allowed its archival holdings to be brought together for the first time in custom-built premises. Previously housed in scattered locations in the city and not always in ideal conditions, the move to the VEGA was able to accommodate historic documents, Biennale records, the film library, music collection, media library, and poster collection along with research facilities and a conservation workshop.

At the start of 2020, the future for the Biennale seemed assured. The finances of the Biennale were stable, its international scope had expanded, the Architecture Biennale had developed into the premier global architecture exhibition, the Arsenale's buildings were transformed, the exhibition had spread into the city, visitor numbers had risen, and the Biennale's outreach to schools, colleges and community groups had greatly improved. The Covid-19 pandemic, however, quickly challenged the unalloyed positivity of this assessment. Although the shorter Biennales held primarily in the Autumn went ahead with appropriate safeguards, the other festivals were curtailed. Venice was one of the first European cities to enforce restrictions when case numbers in the north of Italy rose dramatically in February 2020. This immediately impacted on the timetable of the Carnival and the Architecture Biennale. The former was ended two days early on 23 February. The latter, due to open on 23 May was initially retimetabled to 29 August and then, when that was not feasible, postponed again to May 2021.

As elsewhere in the world the changes wrought by Covid-19 on everyday life led to discussions on how the pandemic might affect society in the medium and longer terms, especially regarding broader issues of urban form, work-life balance and environmental sustainability. For the *centro storico* (historic centre of Venice), the challenge brought by the pandemic reinforced existing debates about housing, population change, the dominance of tourism in the economy, the environment, and conservation of the built heritage. These had been building in intensity since the Millennium, but there was now an added urgency to debate about how the future should look; a future in which the Biennale was also part of the discussion.

To elaborate, this particularly involved the relationship between tourism and the *centro storico*. Venice was already beset by a complex skein of economic, social and environmental problems, which revolved around the interlinked issues of population numbers, housing, the economy, regular flooding and the growth of tourism (Nolan and Séraphin 2019; Séraphin, Sheeran and Pilato 2018; Bertocchi and Visentin 2019). Certainly, the decline and aging of the population in the historic core of the city had been a concern since the 1950s. Caused by overcrowding, the poor condition of the buildings, and the attraction of new housing developments on the mainland, the phenomenon was accelerated by the severe floods of 1966 (Città di Venezia 2017, 22). Over the past thirty years this has been exacerbated by the growth of tourism. Fuelled by cheap air fares and the growth of new tourist flows (particularly from Southeast Asia), this 'overtourism' or mass cultural tourism was greater than the facilities and amenities of the city could support. The carrying capacity of the historic city is calculated at 52,000 tourist presences a day while an estimated 77,000 were recorded in 2018 (Smith and Da Mosto 2020, 11). Apart from the pressure this puts on the pedestrian pathways and open spaces particularly in the 'Bermuda Shorts triangle' – the area between the Rialto Bridge, St Marks's Square and the Galleria dell'Academia (Davis and Marvin 2004, 79) – it also overloads the water transport system creating difficulties for residents and workers to get around the city. Moreover, cheap cafes, restaurants and souvenir shops have replaced the convenience stores and services that typically served the resident population. Changes to the housing regulations in 1998 and 2002 encouraged landlords to move away from residential leases in favour of short-term tourist lets, exhibition spaces and, since 2008, Airbnb. It is calculated that by 2019 there were more tourist beds available for rent in the historic city than residents' beds (Smith and Da Mosto 2020, 13).

Against this background, the triangular relationship between the city, the Biennale and tourism is clearly of considerable importance. As a festival that now lasts roughly six months (May–November), the Biennale spans the city's peak tourist season and, although a source of visitor numbers in its own right, is also well positioned to help to ameliorate some of the pressures of overconcentration. In its early days, the Biennale had an important role in promoting tourism but, given that tourism has now reached problematic proportions, current debate now revolves around how the Biennale could play a more constructive role in helping to alleviate rather than exacerbate the difficulties which the historic city is experiencing. To do so requires encouragement of the positive aspects of the Biennale while mitigating the negative.

The positive aspects of the Biennale are usually framed in terms of the economic and regenerative role that the festival plays. When discussing the current tourism crisis, the characteristic types of tourists visiting the Biennale are often contrasted favourably with those stereotypically supposed to flood the *centro storico*. Often depicted as the 'wrong type' of tourist or 'hit and run day trippers' (Smith and Da Mosto 2019, 7), their sundry misdemeanours are said to include not being interested in culture and lacking appreciation or respect for the city and its heritage (Giuffrida 2021). By contrast, those attending the Biennale are seen as wealthier, as spending money on accommodation and hospitality in the historic city and as engaging with Venice's artistic heritage. The Biennale readily chimes with the goals of Venice's campaign for responsible tourism. This sets out a code of behaviour for visitors and seeks to encourage them both to visit less well-known districts of the city and to consider arriving at quieter times of the year (Città di Venezia 2021). Biennale visitors heading for the Giardini and Arsenale or hunting for the pavilions and collateral events spread around the city fulfil this agenda and, given the length of the Biennale, they also visit in the spring and autumn. The 'Detourism' campaign run by the City of Venice, which lists its goals as promoting:

> slow and sustainable tourism, encouraging travellers to go beyond the usual tourist sights, stumble upon unique experiences and see Venice with new eyes. (Città di Venezia 2014)

specifically identifies the Biennale as a focus for responsible tourism. It is an example of what Venice's tourism minister Simone Venturini terms 'quality tourism', with the recommendation that Venice needs to 'promote international events and exhibitions and to attract visitors who want to stay for more than a quick visit' (Ghiglone 2021).

A further positive feature of the Biennale stems from the fact that it is large enough to make a significant contribution to the local exchequer, with a discernible impact on employment patterns in the city. While the numbers employed in full time positions by the Fondazione La Biennale di Venezia varies throughout the year from around 50 to 200, there is also a small army of temporary and part time staff whose livelihoods depend on the various Biennale Festivals. *Inter alia*, this ranges from curators, designers and researchers to the service roles of room attendants, caretakers, catering staff, retail, teachers and exhibition guides. The Venetianization of the Biennale has made opportunities available for consultancies, events companies, and freelancers who, collectively, work to support nations and artists looking to locate outside the Giardini and Arsenale, helping them to navigate the rules and regulations involved in planning, setting up and staging exhibitions. It was estimated in 2013 that the value of contracts to Venetian businesses was around €25 million (AN 2013).

The final positive aspects linked to the Biennale stems from its links with urban renewal. As noted, it has played a major role in regenerating the Arsenale and creating access to a part of the city that previously lay behind closed doors. More incrementally perhaps, landlords have been able to rent property for exhibition spaces supported by the noticeboard system of listings run by the Biennale. The income generated by these lets has been a major source of funds for maintaining and renovating buildings in the historic city that are costly to maintain due to their age, proximity to saltwater and propensity to flood periodically. In these sundry ways, the Biennale can be conceived as an event that has fitted into the historic fabric of the city and uses existing infrastructure sustainably.

Nevertheless, while the Biennale seems to constitute a perfect fit for the city, more radical voices challenge the real extent of the festival's impact on the city, indeed identifying an 'increasing awareness of the disconnect between the Biennale and Venice' (Smith and Da Mosto 2019, 3) that runs counter to the Venetianization narrative. These arguments are bound up with the relentless growth in the size and geographical spread of the Art and Architecture Biennales under the long-term reign of the Biennale's President, Paolo Baratta (2008–20). This, for example, has a notable effect on the property market, in which the Biennales are seen, first, as encouraging landlords to take premises out of the permanent residential sector in favour of short lets or, secondly, renting out space for exhibition purposes.

The former relates to the demand for short-let accommodation from the cadre of 'creatives' associated with the preparation, running and dismantling of the pavilions and exhibitions of the Biennale and fringe events, not to mention the dealers, agents and collectors who attend the Biennale preview. Landlords can gain greater returns from these weekly and monthly lets than from leasing residential properties to permanent residents. Pre-Covid-19, at least, the demand generated by the Biennale had helped fuel rent rises in the historic core and had boosted property prices by attracting the interest of foreign buyers (Roberts 2019).

The latter relates to the opportunities afforded to landlords to rent sites for national pavilions and collateral events. Doing so takes properties out of alternative long-term uses, not only as residential accommodation but also for equally needed spaces for local businesses such as retail services for local residents or workshops for services and craftspeople (Smith and Da Mosto 2019, 8). In 2017, Scheppe (2018, 25) calculated that 472,867 square metres of exhibition space were listed on the Biennale website as available for rental in the city outside the Giardini and Arsenale, at prices that far outweigh rents possible from local businesses.

While widely earning credit for reinvigorating part of the city and for providing public access, the Biennale's pivotal role in the regeneration of the Arsenale is also not without criticism. For all that is said about increasing access, the Biennale effectively takes over these spaces for around two-thirds of the year effectively removing them from the public realm. There is also frustration with the slow pace of regeneration and lack of strategic vision for the whole complex, with an influential local pressure group (FFA 2016, 2) maintaining that:

> this area [is] possibly the last chance to forge a healthy future for Venice as a city. So far, isolated from the negative effects of mass tourism that are manifest throughout the rest of Venice, the Arsenale is a large

enough area to significantly influence the socio-economic development of the city and yet sufficiently self-contained to be administered with a unified and integrated vision.

It is argued, for instance, that the Arsenale's renewal fails to engage with residents in the sense of providing leisure spaces that could improve quality of life. In addition, despite the Biennale clearly being a major player in the city's creative economy, critics maintain that more could be done to foster employment. This might be supplying much needed studio space for artists, musicians, dancers, and theatre groups or initiating projects that would boost jobs in the non-tourist economy which would resonate with Venice's traditional industries and craft skills (FFA 2016 5–18).

Conclusion

The disruption wreaked by Covid-19 on the festival and cultural calendar has led to much soul-searching globally over ways of delivering the arts to local and international audiences. For the historic centre of Venice where the art and cultural sector is faced with the demands of tourism, questions of sustainability, and conservation of the built heritage, the events of 2020 seemed an historic opportunity for reflection and action to bring about a change of direction. Commentators sensed the possibility of a 'new normal', with words such as resetting, rebooting, rethinking, or reimagining being mobilised in support of a more sustainable future for the city of Venice (Allnut 2021, 6; see also Armstrong 2021 and Momigliano 2020).

The postponement of the Architecture Biennale to 2021 primarily meant presenting exhibits that had already been prepared, although adjustments were necessary to navigate Covid-19 restrictions on travel to Italy, shipping problems and funding issues (Karanja and Mutegi 2021). While some pavilions provided digital content in parallel with the physical exhibition, most did not. Some critics bemoaned the failure to respond to a changing world in which architectural practices had been forced to find new and innovative ways of working, where attitudes to urban life were in flux, and where environmental attitudes were changing (Walsh 2021, Zancan 2021). The lack of engagement with residents and local businesses at a time when the collapse of travel had removed international tourists was seen as a wasted opportunity (Smith 2021). However, there was a strong presumption that 2021 marked the end of an era and that change was inevitable.

This was certainly the case in terms of the management of the Biennale. Its newly appointed president, Roberto Cicutto had stated the Biennale should seek a more central role in the city's economy and promote greater collaboration with Venice's arts institutions and universities. Nevertheless, such goals are not always easy to achieve. One of the first projects under Cicutto's regime, for example, will be to move the Historical Archives of Contemporary Arts (ASAC) from Porto Marghera on the mainland to the Arsenale, to create a research hub, with a conservation centre, professional residencies, conference and exhibition spaces. This is designed to attract 'students, talent and investment to the city, repopulating the historic centre and diversifying its economy' (Imam 2021, 12). Together these facilities would 'push' the Biennale's activity 'beyond the shows of the festival' bringing people to Venice 365 days of the year to teach, learn and research' (Spence 2021, 4). Yet, as noted previously, part of the archive had been deliberately moved to custom-designed premises in Port Marghera in 2008 as a headline component of that area's regeneration strategy. Its further relocation little more than a decade later can only serve to undermine that strategy, but it does chime with calls for the Biennale to connect with the non-tourist economy.

The Biennale is undoubtedly vital for the Venetian economy. It received a major grant in early May 2021, which amounted to 12 per cent of the Italian Government's culture budget. This was designed to maintain its international standing (Zancan 2021). For the Deputy Mayor of Venice whose portfolio includes tourism, the post-Coronavirus imperative is to:

> reinforce Venice as a major European centre of culture – including avant-garde. This would turn us into a world capital of the arts. We also want to be one of Europe's fashion centres'. (ITB 2021)

This is a return to reliance on international tourism, albeit aimed at visitors who will engage with its festivals, events and cultural offerings. Yet, as has been seen in this chapter, how these festivals and exhibitions are staged and how well they connect to both the Venetian non-tourist economy and Venetians themselves will determine whether events can provide a stable and sustainable future that addresses the complex needs of the city.

References

Ackroyd, Peter. 2010. *Venice: Pure City*. London: Vintage Books.

Allnut, Chris. 2021. Can Venice reinvent itself? *Financial Times, Weekend House and Home*, 26 February.

Alloway, Laurence. 1969. *The Venice Biennale 1985–1968: From Salon to Goldfish Bowl*. London: Faber and Faber.

Ammerman, Albert J., Charlotte L. Pearson, Peter I. Kuniholm, Bruce Selleck and Ettore Vio. 2017. Beneath the Basilica of San Marco: New Light on the Origins of Venice. *Antiquity*, 91(360), 1620–1629.

Armstrong, Mark. 2021. Venice considers a new tourism model after Covid-19 lockdown. *Euronews*, 21 April. Available at: https://www.euronews.com/2020/04/19/venice-considers-a-new-tourism-model-after-covid-19-lockdown

AN (*Art Newspaper*). 2013. Venice banks on Biennale profits. *The Art Newspaper* 22(248), 8.

Bertocchi, Dario and Francesco Visentin. 2019. 'The Overwhelmed City': Physical and Social Over-Capacities of Global Tourism in Venice. *Sustainability*, 11(24), 6937. https://doi.org/10.3390/su11246937

Bódi, Kinga. 2019. Looking Forwards or Back? Shifting Perspectives in the Venice Biennale's Hungarian Exhibition: 1928 and 1948. In Beáta Hock, Klara Kemp-Welch and Jonathan Owen (Eds.) *A Reader in East-Central-European Modernism 1918-1956*, pp. 268–282. London: Courtauld Books.

Bowness, Sophie. 1995. The British Pavilion Before the British Council. In Sophie Bowness and Clive Phillpot (Eds.) *Britain at the Venice Biennale 1895-1995*. London: British Council, 17–36.

Catenacci, Sara. 2010. Beyond the Giardini of the Biennale: Some Considerations on a Supposed Model. In Clarissa Ricci (Ed.) *Starting from Venice: Studies on the Biennale*, pp. 78–88. Milan: Et Al Edizioni.

Città di Venezia. 2014. Detourism: Travel Venice like a local. Available at: https://www.veneziaunica.it/en/content/detourism-venezia

Città di Venezia. 2017. Project of territorial governance of tourism in Venice. Available at: https://www.comune.venezia.it/sites/comune.venezia.it/files/documenti/documenti/territorial%20governance%202017.pdf

Città di Venezia. 2021. Good Rules for the Responsible Visitor. Available at: https://www.comune.venezia.it/en/content/buone-pratiche-il-visitatore-responsabile

Davis, Robert C. and Garry R. Marvin. 2004. *Venice, the Tourist Maze: A Cultural Critique of the World's Most Touristed City*. Berkeley, CA: University of California Press.

Di Martino, Enzo. 2005. *The History of the Venice Biennale, 1895-2005: Visual Arts, Architecture, Cinema, Dance, Music, Theatre*. Venice: Papiro Arte.

FBV (Fondazione La Biennale di Venezia). 2019. *58th International Art Exhibition, 11th May to 24th November 2019, Procedure for Collateral Events*. Venice: Visual Arts and Architecture Department, La Biennale di Venezia.

FFA (Forum Futoro Arsenale). 2016. *The Venetian Arsenale and the City*. Venice: Forum Futoro Arsenale.

Fyfe, Gordon J. 1984. Art Exhibitions and Power During the Nineteenth Century. *Sociological Review*, 32(S1), 20–45.

Ghiglone, Davide. 2021. Venice braced for tourists' return as liner sail into hot water. *Financial Times Weekend* 26/27, 4 June.

Giuffrida, Angela. 2021. Venice renews crackdown on bad behaviour as tourists return. *The Guardian*, 22 June. Available at : https://www.theguardian.com/world/2021/jun/22/venice-renews-crackdown-on-bad-behaviour-as-tourists-return

Gold, John R. and Margaret M. Gold. 2020. *Festival Cities: Culture, Planning and Urban Life*. Abingdon: Routledge.

Gregotti, Vittorio. 2010. Vittorio Gregotti in conversation with Aaron Levy and William Menking. In Aaron Levy and William Menking (Eds.) *Architecture on Display: on the History of the Venice Biennale of Architecture*, pp. 21–33. London: Architectural Association.

Holt, Elizabeth Gilmore. 1983. *The Triumph of Art for the Public, 1785–1848: The Emerging Role of Exhibitions and Critics*. Princeton, NJ: Princeton University Press.

Il Quotidiano Immoboliare. 2014. The VEGA Waterfront Project. Available at: https://www.vegapark.ve.it/wp-content/uploads/2017/03/VEGA-WATER FRONT-EBOOK-eng-light.pdf

Imam, James. 2021. The man looking to the Venice Biennale's past to ensure its post-pandemic future. *Art Newspaper*, 333, (April), 12.

ITB (Internationale Tourismus-Börse Berlin). 2021. Venice aims to create a brighter, more sustainable tourism future. Available at: https://news.itb.com /regional-spotlight/europe/venice-tourism-autonomy

Karanga, Kabage and Stella Mutegi. 2021. 'We should allow an African curator to turn the whole thing on its head'. Available at: https://www.dezeen .com/2021/06/07/venice-architecture-biennale-african-contribution/?li _source=LI&li_medium=bottom_block_1

Korsch, Evelyn. 2013. Renaissance Venice and the Sacred-Political Connotations of Waterborne Pageants. In Margaret Shewring (Ed.) *Waterborne Pageants and Festivities in the Renaissance: Essays in Honour of J.R. Mulryne*, pp. 79–97. Farnham: Ashgate.

Martini, Vittoria. 2010. A Brief History of How the Exhibition Took Shape. In Clarissa Ricci (Ed.) *Starting from Venice: Studies on the Biennale*, pp. 67–77. Milan: Et Al Edizione.

May, Jan Andreas. 2009. La Biennale de Venezia: The Evolution of an Institution. In Elke aus dem Moore and Ursula Zeller (Eds.) *Germany's Contributions to the Venice Biennale, 1895–2007*, pp. 17–30. Cologne: DuMont Bucheverlag.

Menichelli, Claudio. 2014. The Arsenale Yesterday and Today: History of a Complex in Transition. In Margherita Venore (Ed.) *Heritage and Architecture of Urban Landscape Under Production*, pp. 29–42. Tricase: Libellula Edizioni.

Momigliano, Anna. 2020. Venice tourism may never be the same: it could be better, *The New York Times*, 2 July. Available at: https://www.nytimes.com /2020/07/02/travel/venice-coronavirus-tourism.html

Nolan, Emma and Séraphin, Hugues. 2019. Venice: Capacity and Tourism. In Rachel Dodds and Richard Butler (Eds.) *Overtourism: Issues, Realities and Solutions*, pp. 139–151. Berlin: De Gruyter.

Panzeri, Lidia. 2009. The Arsenale: A 50-year Stalemate Over its Change of Use. In Jane Da Mosto (Ed.) *The Venice Report: Demography, Tourism, Financing and Change of Buildings*, pp. 56–58. Cambridge: Cambridge University Press.

Portoghesi, Paolo. 2010. Paolo Portoghesi in Conversation with Aaron Levy and William Menking. In Aaron Levy and William Menking (Eds.)

Architecture on Display: on the History of the Venice Biennale of Architecture, pp. 35–47. London: Architectural Association.

Portoghesi, Paolo, Vincent Scully, Charles Jencks and Christian Norberg-Schulz. 1980. *The Presence of the Past: The First International Exhibition of Architecture, the Corderia of the Arsenale*. London: Academy Editions.

Ricci, Clarissa. 2010. Installation and Display Strategies at the Venice Biennale: Prolegomenon. In Clarissa Ricci (Ed.) *Starting from Venice: Studies on the Biennale*, pp. 99–108. Milan: Et Al Edizioni.

Roberts, Hannah. 2019. The role of arts in Venice's property market. *Financial Times*, 21 June. Available at: https://www.ft.com/content/124ba730-8dc0 -11e9-b8cb-26a9caa9d67b

Scheppe, Wolfgang. 2018. *The Ground-Rent of Art and Exclusion from the City*. Available at: https://www.arsenale.com/downloads/Ground-Rent_and _Exclusion_from_the_City_2018.pdf

Seraphin, Hugues, Paul Sheeran and Manuela Pilato. 2018. Over-Tourism and the Fall of Venice as a Destination, *Journal of Destination Marketing and Management*, 9, 374–376.

Smith, Carolyn. 2021. The Venice Biennale Needs Radical Changes to Maintain its Relevance and Respond to Local Needs, *Architectural Review*, 1482 (June), 66–67.

Smith, Carolyn and Jane Da Mosto. 2019. How was it for you? Available at: https://drive.google.com/file/d/1vaIiVqxMaXWo7NMNagH6T2lz8yjh9ws8 /view

Spence, Rachel. 2021. A place for us? *Financial Times, Weekend House and Home*, 22/23 4 May.

Walsh, Niall Patrick. 2021. The Venice Biennale Pressed Pause, While Everyone Else Changed the Game. Available at: https://archinect.com/features /article/150271426/the-venice-biennale-pressed-pause-while-everyone-else -changed-the-game

Ward, Martha. 1996. What's Important About the History of Modern Art Exhibitions? In Bruce W. Ferguson, Reesa Greenberg and Sandy Nairne (Eds.) *Thinking about Exhibitions*, pp. 331–340. London: Routledge.

Wei, Chu-Chiun. 2013. From National Art to Critical Globalisation: The Politics and Curatorial Strategies of the Taiwan Pavilion at the Venice Biennale. *Third Text*, 27(4), 470–84.

Zancan, Roberto. 2021. Venice Biennale. Biennale, Stop Making Sense! Available at: https://www.domusweb.it/en/speciali/venice-architecture -biennale-2021/2021/biennale-stop-making-sense.html

CHAPTER 10

Limerick City Stories: The European Capital of Culture Bid Process and Narratives of Place

Niamh NicGhabhann, Annmarie Ryan
and Stephen Kinsella

Introduction

'Limerick has always been sharp, lively, passionate, proud, historic, funny opinionated, welcoming, even occasionally pure awkward and a wonderful place of culture'.

Limerick.ie (2020a, 3)

This description opened the Social Impact Report published in the wake of Limerick's year as the inaugural Irish National City of Culture[1]. The report, which examined the year of events and actions held throughout 2014, clearly communicates a sense of self-confidence and a distinctive identity. The opening lines of Limerick's 2020 European Capital of Culture (ECoC) bid book, by

How to cite this book chapter:
NicGhabhann, N., Ryan, A. and Kinsella, S. 2022. Limerick City Stories: The European Capital of Culture Bid Process and Narratives of Place. In: Smith, A., Osborn, G. and Quinn, B. (Eds.) *Festivals and the City: The Contested Geographies of Urban Events*. London: University of Westminster Press. Pp. 169–185. London: University of Westminster Press. DOI: https://doi.org/10.16997/book64.j. License: CC-BY-NC-ND 4.0

contrast, reflect a sharp change of direction. The opening paragraph notes that 'Limerick had been a non-place in Europe, in Ireland for a long time' (ECOC Bid Book 2016 (Limerick.ie 2020b) – hereafter 2020 Bid Book, 3). The ECoC process is explicitly framed as a positive opportunity for change: 'Limerick is creating a place of belonging in Europe', with the competition offering an 'invitation to all of Europe to celebrate our transformation' (2020 Bid Book, 3).

While the reflection on 2014 offers a celebration of what *is*, therefore, the 2020 bid book suggests a process that addresses a deficit, a lack of definition resulting in it being a 'non-place'. The term 'non-place' stems from the work of Marc Augé and is 'taken to mean places divested of meaning, homogenous, and largely interchangeable' (Trigg 2017, 127). Indeed, by the end of the opening paragraph, the idea of the 'non-place' is superseded by the phrase Ireland's 'problem city', strongly suggesting that the transformation required is not one of creation *ex nihilo*, but one of rehabilitation and reconstruction. This chapter focuses attention on the development of place narratives as part of the ECoC bidding process. It provides a close analysis of one case study, which allows us to examine the development of place narratives in a specific historic and cultural context, and to consider the ECoC process within this localised frame. We examine the interwoven relationships between city branding and city narratives in the context of the liminality afforded by the bidding process.

Throughout our analysis, the ECoC process is not considered as an isolated event, but is located within the longer context of past and current city branding and city narrative development in Limerick. We examine the tensions that can arise between the construction of city narratives in the context of a bidding process, and the different stakeholder perspectives on these narratives. In particular, we take account of the past perceptions and narratives associated with Limerick, in terms of increased unemployment, socio-economic disadvantage, and violence during periods of economic recession, when the city was badly impacted by the closure of large industries (Hourigan 2011).

In our analysis, we look at planned and realised festival events associated with the ECoC bid as arenas for mobilising new or alternative city narratives for Limerick, and at festivity as a process through which these dynamics are enacted in the theatre of the city itself. Our consideration of the reception and response to these new city narratives for Limerick explores the extent to which they can undermine – rather than support – the themes of social inclusion and engagement commonly associated with ECoC bidding processes. This approach builds on the work of Ooi, Håkanson and LaCava (2014) in examining the tensions between what they term the 'poetics' and the 'politics' of the ECoC programme as it plays out in local contexts. It also draws on the work of Liu (2019) on the processes of 'culture-led regeneration' in Liverpool during 2008.

Our approach is situated within the broad frame of festival studies. This is an arena which is informed by disciplines such as urban studies and cultural policy studies, but which pays attention to the cultural meanings, dynamics and impacts of festivity. Here, the ECoC bidding process is considered within the methodologies of urban and festival studies, allowing us to examine issues such as the liminality facilitated by a period of festivity, the relationships between festivals and the creation and expression of place identity, as well as the well-established and often contentious relationships between festivals, cultural investment, and ideas of transformation and social regeneration (Picard and Robinson 2006). It also allows us to consider the dynamics of festival experience as performed and enacted on the city streets.

The sources used to inform this exploration include the official bid book materials produced by the Limerick 2020 team, media reports of the bidding process which took place between 2015 and 2017, and photographs from the city environment reflecting the bidding process. The methods we have employed reflect those used in urban studies and festival studies more broadly, and involve the identification, description and critical analysis of relevant discourses, media and images. In doing so, this chapter contributes to existing research on the ECoC event, as well as to the research on bidding, on festivals, and on place narratives.

Limerick, Place Narratives and the European Capital of Culture

Liminality, Festivity and Place Identity

Festivals as social and cultural practices are often linked to the articulation and definition of a sense of place. As De Bres and Davis have noted, 'community festivals frequently celebrate both group and place identity', citing Alessandro Falassi's observation that festivals 'renew periodically the life stream of a community' (De Bres and Davis 2001, 327). Falassi describes the different 'rites' which can be observed as part of festivity, including 'ritual dramas'. These, he notes, can take the form of a 'creation myth, a foundation or migratory legend, or a military success particularly relevant in the mythic or historical memory of the community staging the festival' (Falassi 1987, 4). This component of Falassi's festival typology relates closely to the expression or performance of identity through a festival, including group and place identities from local to national and supranational levels, and has informed many aspects of festival studies.

In this context, festivals often connect with particular historical narratives at local or national scales to articulate specific facets of communal identity, often linked to place. As Brüggemann and Kasekamp argue in their exploration of Estonian singing festivals and national identity, the corporeal, communal and emotional dimensions of festival are what make them so impactful in 'creating cultural memory as a foundation for a national identity in a continuous work-in-progress process' (Brüggemann and Kasekamp 2014, 261).

As examined by Scully (2012), this festival dynamic can also be observed in the expression and construction of diaspora connections to specific places, with festival narratives reiterating a narrative of connection. Festival programming has also been explored as a creative process in expressing hitherto overlooked aspects of place history, as in Hunter's (2004) examination of the 1996 Adelaide Festival. The examples chosen here reflect the growing literature on the topic of festivals and the expression of place identity within festival studies, which often includes themes of regeneration, migration and diaspora, nationalism, and contested or conflicting interpretations of place expressed through festivals by different groups.

The ECoC project is, by its very nature, closely linked to the expression and articulation of place identity. It differs from festivals that are drawn from existing place-based traditions, as the designation is temporary, moving a spotlight onto specific cities across Europe. However, as well as expressing or articulating a sense of place identity, the ECoC process has become associated with an opportunity to significantly reposition place identity on an international stage. The use of the Capital of Culture designation as a catalyst for image change has been examined by several scholars, with a focus on Glasgow (1990) and Liverpool (2008) in particular. Beatriz Garcia notes that 'since Glasgow, image transformation has been a primary objective for many ECoC hosts', but that these claims to change the image of cities are rarely evidenced in a concrete or robust way (Garcia 2017, 3179). Garcia describes these image transformation claims as 'self-fulfilling prophecies', with local agencies and event organisers projecting a 'city renaissance' narrative, resulting in a media discussion that 'echoes, amplifies and legitimates' this idea (Garcia 2017, 3179).

The narrative of renaissance and regeneration has been attached to cities who have gone on to win these titles. However, in this chapter we argue that the process of bidding can be regarded as a transformative period in its own right; that is, regardless of whether the city goes on to win the title. Our close study of an individual case study builds on existing work on ECoC bidding, such as that by Richards and Marques (2016), and Åkerlund and Müller (2012). This chapter adds to this literature through its engagement with the concept of liminality (after Turner 1974, 1987) in the context of the Limerick case study. This is used to consider the ways in which the bidding process became a time where the city, its identity and the role of culture in its (regenerative) future came under discussion amongst a wide group of stakeholders. The concept of liminality has long been associated with festivity, something best expressed in Falassi's (1987) representation of festivals as a 'time out of time'. Liminal periods are regarded as transformative where the 'old' rules of cultural organising are put into flux, and where novel or creative futures can be imagined (Turner 1982). Given the need for wide stakeholder engagement and space for innovation and change, the bidding period has the potential to progress agendas of developing socially inclusive events and spatial environments.

Drawing on van Heerdon (2009) we can point to liminality experienced during a competitive bid process such as that involved in the ECoC, one marked by a 'heightened sense of now' and intensified by the ever-present deadlines throughout the bidding process. The liminal quality of the bid phase plays a role in the mobilisation and enrolment of key multi-agency actors required to be involved in the bid process (e.g., community and civic groups, the business community, elected local politicians, members of the cultural community/ artists). Further, any transformation in a liminal time is not a *fait accompli* and requires much effort to realise (Ryan 2019). This was echoed throughout the bid book, with phrases such as 'we are ready to meet the challenge' and 'we have a lot to do' peppered throughout the text (2020 Bid Book, 6). As Kinsella, NicGhabhann and Ryan (2017) identified in relation to the cultural policy formation process, the time-bound nature of the bid period enabled a space for 'lean' policy engagement, with clear expectations from stakeholders that the process would produce positive outputs for the city. The same heightened, accelerated process can be observed in relation to the process of articulating place narratives, with a usually slow, fragmented or incremental process being made explicit and formalised in the liminal context of the ECoC bid. As will be outlined below, this more explicit process of place narrative development makes space for both consultation as well as tension.

In Limerick's attempt to become the Irish city designated as ECoC in 2020, both the bid period and the imagined year as designated city were explicitly envisaged as liminal periods of potential and transformation, made possible through the festive opportunity. The chance offered to the city by this liminal festive opportunity was of reshaping the city narrative on both a national and an international stage. This narrative shift, as will be explored below, was aligned with imagined and projected futures of prosperity and activity for the city, futures that according to the internal logic of the bidding process, required significant change to be achieved. As McGillivray and Turner have highlighted, 'frequently, a successful bid will make use of an emotional "narrative" to supplement its professional-technical competencies and to convince awarding bodies to choose it over similarly technically capable candidates' (McGillivray and Turner 2018, 55). This perspective provides valuable context for the bidding team's decision to foreground this narrative of transformation for Limerick at the centre of their ECoC application. One strand of the emotional narrative centred economic and social regeneration and renewal as a key concept in the bid book.

Limerick 2020 and City Narratives

Although Limerick's bid for the ECoC designation was ultimately unsuccessful – Galway was chosen as the winning city – the bidding process can be seen as a period during which multiple diverse stakeholders came together, focused on the potential of culture to transform or change the city and region in specific ways. In this context, festivals and festivity are seen explicitly as opportunities to change the meaning and perception of the host city. This emphasis on redefinition and narrative was evident in the opening paragraphs of the Limerick 2020 bid book, which expressed a sense of the city as an 'up-and-coming cool urban space'. It also included the statements that 'Limerick had been a non-place in Europe for a long time', that the 'power of culture made us discover our city as a place on the European map', and that 'we are ready for a new Limerick' (2020 Bid Book, 3). The different strands of Limerick's bid reflect the pressure to engage with the different agendas and priorities of the programme itself, which as Immler and Sakkers (2014) have demonstrated, shift between celebrating local culture and celebrating a 'universal' sense of shared European cultural identity.

The Limerick 2020 Bid Book, titled 'Belonging', was made available to the public in July 2016. It included key demographic information on Limerick city and county, insights into the existing cultural infrastructure and information on the proposed governance and delivery structures should it be awarded the ECoC designation. Proposed events are described in some detail, including the opening ceremony and a street spectacle titled 'Lifting the Siege'. This is described as a city-wide performance involving multiple groups and street spectacle theatre companies, reflecting the historic sieges of seventeenth-century Limerick, but also the idea that 'in modern times, large areas have been under siege from crime, social disadvantage and economic deprivation'. The aim of this spectacular event would be to raise 'a new flag to celebrate the flight, song, dance, and colour that will lift the siege – allowing our citizens to emerge brighter, happier, more confident, proud of our people and place' (2020 Bid Book, 33). These images and ideas of transformation, overcoming, and renaissance inform the creative content of the proposed programme as much as the positioning statements that open the document.

The desired outcome of Limerick's proposed ECoC programme as articulated in the bid book was a transformed city with a transformed 'brand' or presence on a European stage. The bid book referenced the impact of globalisation, migration and new community formation on the city's social and economic fabric and sought to incorporate these new elements into Limerick's transformed and explicitly 'European' brand (2020 Bid Book, 17). This new city brand, encapsulated in and expressed through the Limerick 2020 logo, was to communicate this narrative of triumph over past adversity, as well as the associated values of a creative city, an 'edgy' city, and a more prosperous city. The projected programme outlined in the bid book for Limerick's year, with its anticipated economic and social benefits, was explicitly intended to enact this process of transformation. The Limerick 2020 brand was underpinned by this narrative of transition from problem to success city. As Lichrou, O'Malley and Patterson (2008) have pointed out, place marketing can be supported by utilising narrative as a frame for the dynamic and multifaceted nature of

Figure 10.1: 'Ní neart go cur le chéile'. Irish *seanfhocal* or proverb broadly translated as 'there is no strength without unity', with Limerick 2020 logo on the side of a Georgian red-brick building taken from Limerick's O'Connell Street. Photograph: Niamh NicGhabhann (July 2016).

places. Bendix (2002) points to the consumption of place as mediated by narratives 'through the narrative morsels it plants itself or that are put in circulation by others' (Bendix 2002, 476, as cited by Lichrou, O'Malley and Patterson 2010).

Throughout the bid year, the Limerick 2020 logo was made visible across the city in multiple ways, reinforcing this narrative for citizens and visitors alike (Figure 10.1). For example, businesses displayed Limerick 2020 stickers on their shop windows. The bid team also used a range of city surfaces – the sides of Georgian buildings and the river walls, for example – to write messages ('narrative morsels') associated with the Limerick 2020 brand, using the distinctive Limerick 2020 font. In this way, the Limerick 2020 brand was embedded in the experience of the city itself, encouraging people to engage with the liminality of the bid period, and with the ideas of potential and change offered by the ECoC designation. By embedding this brand into Limerick's urban fabric, the city itself could be read as being in a liminal state, awaiting transformation into something else.

However, while this narrative of transformation from a 'non-place' or 'problem city' certainly provides an example of the 'emotional' content aimed at convincing bid adjudicators (McGillivray and Turner 2018), this narrative was more complex for local stakeholders. Given the need to maintain competitive advantage over the other Irish bidding cities, the bid book itself was not made public until after the adjudication process. At the point that the bid book was released, the narrative of change that had been presented to the judges was made available more broadly. On 22 September 2016, the *Limerick Leader* newspaper reported that 'a number of locals were astonished, shocked, and saddened' by the characterisation of Limerick as a 'problem city'. The article quoted a local councillor as stating that 'we all supported #Limerick2020 with such a great enthusiasm, and people are now asking how many of us, the Limerick audience, would support or share the view that Limerick is or has ever been a "non-place"?' (*Limerick Leader*, 22 September 2016).

At a local level it can be argued that the Limerick 2020 brand had been understood as celebratory, as an opportunity to build on unique strengths and existing cultural richness, and to enact transformation through greater strategic focus by the local authority on the creative and cultural sectors. This was evidenced by the formation of new local groups during the bidding process, such as PLAN (Professional Limerick Artists' Network) and LACE (Limerick Arts and Culture Exchange). These groups focused on showcasing and supporting local arts and capacity-building across the creative sector in the city and region (Limerick Arts and Cultural Exchange 2021). However, the local media coverage of the bid book release made it clear that significantly different interpretations of the Limerick 2020 brand that had been in operation throughout the bidding period. In their analysis of the dynamics of Limerick's year as 2014 National Capital of Culture, Dillane, Power and Devereux (2017) identify and describe similar tensions between celebrating and enhancing the city and its communities as they are, and an emphasis on regeneration led by a 'top-down' management process. This analysis highlights the questions raised in 2014 by the artistic community as to whether 'the project was primarily about rebranding the stigmatised city or about being truly participatory', reflecting many of the critical disconnections also evident in 2020.

For the PLAN and LACE groups, the brand reflected an opportunity to showcase and develop existing strengths, but the bid book narrative foregrounded ideas of absence or deprivation. The *Limerick Leader* article noted the response of the bid team, who argued that cities who had identified challenges had been most successful, citing the examples of Glasgow and Linz, and added that it was 'important to be honest when referring to our city' (*Limerick Leader*, 2016). These comments reflect an understanding of the bid book as being aimed primarily at the adjudicating team, rather than acting as a meaningful cultural strategy and action plan for local stakeholders. Ultimately, however, those local stakeholders held expectations that the bid book would be representative of the process of engagement and inclusion that had been undertaken, and that it would reflect their perspectives. As Dillane et al. (2017) note, these expectations were reinforced by the 2020 slogans of 'Belonging' and 'We

Are Culture' used throughout the campaign. It is worth noting that Limerick's cultural strategy process was not launched until 2016, after the ECOC bidding process had finished. Therefore, while the ostensible function of the bid book is to act as a persuasive document aimed at winning over the judges, it can also be seen as 'acting' as a strategy for the region. These different interpretations of the bid book, or implicit expectations of its function, are further consequence of the accelerated planning process and network-building necessitated by the ECoC programme.

The Limerick 2020 brand had been able to act in different capacities throughout the bid period, articulating a narrative of transformation (from negative to positive) for the adjudicators, and quite a different narrative of transformation (celebrating, enriching and enhancing) for the local stakeholders. An analysis of community stakeholder-focused, as opposed to adjudicator-focused communications around the brand also reflect this change in emphasis. For example, a communication to local communities from the bid campaign published on 3 June 2015 invited the 'broader Limerick community to engage, discuss, and get involved in Limerick's bid', noting that the bid 'needs to reflect the ideas, ambitions, and values of its communities, and what Limerick can offer to the common European culture' (Limerick.ie 2015). This text reflects a shift in emphasis from that displayed in the bid book, from transformation towards celebration.

This tension that emerged between these perspectives reflects the pressure on the ECoC bid team to highlight the narratives that they felt would be most persuasive and impactful, drawing on the 'city renaissance' strategies that had been successfully used elsewhere. These tensions are one result of the specific conditions of the bid period, with its accelerated pace and fast-paced formation of new stakeholder groups, all with high expectations of return. Bid teams need to work within this accelerated context while ensuring that different agendas are met – for instance, return on investment for certain stakeholders, and enhanced social inclusion for others. Participants are therefore invited into a process of time-pressured 'liminal' thinking and transformative imagining shaped by the rhetoric of genuine inclusion and collaboration. However, it is worth considering that the tensions that often result from this accelerated process could undermine relationships and trust built throughout the bidding period, particularly in relation to developing new, sustainable stakeholder relationships and engagements across communities.

In this context, the pressure to use specific 'emotional' or persuasive narratives to drive the bid book could have a negative impact on long-term stakeholder relationships in the area. Indeed, following the splintering of the accepted meaning of the Limerick 2020 brand (from city celebration to city renaissance) the installations throughout the city would be read quite differently, as citizens continued to encounter the branding, now fading, across the urban fabric and in shop windows (Figure 10.2). However, as is discussed in more detail below,

Figure 10.2: Faded Limerick 2020 logo. Photograph: Niamh NicGhabhann
(November 2016).

the sometimes-competing priorities of different stakeholders, and the different
agendas that the bid team must attempt to satisfy, can be veiled in the image of
the 'festive city', with the symbols and images of festivity and conviviality being
used to represent coherence, inclusion and collaboration.

To understand the local reception of a narrative of transformation from
problem to success city, it is important to put the dynamics of the ECoC bid
and Limerick 2020 brand into broader local context. As Devereux, Haynes and
Power (2011) note, specific areas and Limerick city more broadly had been
associated via media coverage with violence, social exclusion, social disorder
and criminal gang activity. Indeed, some news coverage explicitly linked Limerick's year as 2014 National City of Culture as an attempt to 'reinvigorate an
identity that was not defined by crime' (*Euronews* 2020, 2 January). The Limerick Regeneration Agency, launched by the then President of Ireland Mary
McAleese in 2008, was tasked with a process of transforming 'some of the most

deprived areas of Limerick city' (*Irish Examiner* 2008, 11 February). However, media coverage of the process reflects some of the tensions experienced by residents of the 'regeneration' areas, who expressed a sense of frustration and disillusion with the process, and in particular with the gap between the narrative of renewal and improvement, and the slow pace of progress on the ground (*Irish Examiner* 2012, 28 March 2012).

Further to this process of regeneration, Limerick has also been the subject of a number of different branding campaigns led by the local authority and aimed at increasing both local and international tourist footfall, as well as promoting the city more broadly as a place for investment (Power, Haynes and Devereux 2021). Examples include the designation of Limerick in 2011 as European City of Sport, the '061' campaign (reflecting the area telephone code), and the roll-out of Limerick's 'Edge Embrace' brand in 2020 (*Irish Examiner* 2020, 30 January). Indeed, the strong reaction and pushback from residents and public representatives in response to a *Forbes* article published in April 2021 which reiterated and exaggerated associations between the city and gangland violence reflects ongoing local concern with place identity and the external perception of the city (*Irish Examiner* 2021, 11 April). The local reaction involved the sharing of images of the city and region using the #limerickandproud hashtag, which received over 8.6 million impressions on Twitter (*Irish Examiner* 2021, 21 April). Local response to the narrative of transformation embedded in the ECoC Limerick 2020 brand, therefore, must be considered in the context of these broader histories of rebranding, reshaping and repositioning. While attention has been paid in previous scholarship to the viability or otherwise of the 'renaissance narrative' associated with the ECoC designation, we argue here that close attention to local context and to prior stakeholder experiences with urban revitalisation or city rebranding processes is valuable in understanding the local resonance of such bid campaigns.

Articulating and Performing Transformation in Limerick

Performing the Festive City

Our exploration of the different perceptions of the Limerick 2020 brand and its associated values and narratives reflects specific facets of festival studies: the exploration of stakeholder relationships, festival impacts, and the perceived agency of festivals and festivity within a regional context. In our final section, we wish to draw on critical insights from festival studies in relation to festivity as a performed activity, and to consider how this approach enables further examination of the Limerick 2020 ECoC bid. This approach attends to festivals and festivity as performed, experienced and enacted in public space by visitors and citizens alike. It connects us to the 'corporeal, communal, and emotional dimensions of festival' mentioned by Brüggemann and Kasekamp (2014), and the role that these play in enabling the intended outcomes of festivals such as the ECoC itself.

The bid process itself took the form of meetings, consultations and world café events, with public festivity being engaged following the submission of the bid and on the eve of the judging and announcement of the successful candidate. To mark this milestone, the city hosted a street party which included public music celebrations, aerial dancers, the closure of the main city streets to traffic allowing pedestrian access and street performers. The city was festooned with green Limerick 2020 bunting and flags, and people wore green Limerick 2020 t-shirts, mobilising the brand further across the city streets. According to the Limerick council website, 'thousands of people enjoyed the carnival atmosphere at a street celebration and thank-you to the public for its support of the European Capital of Culture bid' (Limerick.ie 2016, 13 July).

The decision to use festivity in this way is, on one hand, an obvious choice, but it also reflects the desire to present the city to its citizens and to visitors as a 'festival city'. This draws on Kirstie Jamieson's analysis of the Edinburgh festivals, and the way in which this city 'self-consciously adopts the identity of 'Festival City'', with its centre becoming a stage for colour and revelry. As Jamieson points out, while the aesthetics and dynamics of festivity suggest freedom, the 'upside down' world of carnival, potential transgression and play, and seem 'spontaneously formed by the company of strangers and the collective experience of performances', the 'city *en fête* is also the result of painstaking planning that seeks to control the ways in which public spaces change' (Jamieson 2004, 65).

As well as marking the shared effort, the use of festivity as part of the ECoC bid encouraged people to engage emotionally with the bid message and to associate communal celebration in public space with the Limerick 2020 message, as well as further amplifying this message and the associated images across social media. The use of festivity also allowed the bid team to capture a series of images that framed the city in relation to festivity, with festival encounters across the city streets being photographed and shared widely. These images became an important tool in further positioning Limerick as a 'festival city', with the associated values of conviviality, inclusivity and excitement (Figure 10.3). As noted above, these images also elide many of the tensions inherent in the bid process into a public image of festive conviviality, community and inclusion.

The use of festive events to create iconic images which can further be used as part of city narratives was also evident during Limerick 2014, in particular in relation to the images generated during the Royal DeLuxe 'Giant Granny' event. This event, which featured oversized puppets making their way through the streets, drew thousands of people, and these images of the city '*en fête*' have been widely used by city authorities since (*Limerick Post* 2019, 30 March). While this was a powerful communal event for citizens and visitors alike, and was an example of creative street spectacle and narrative on a grand urban scale

Figure 10.3: Street performer July 2016 street party. Faces blurred to protect privacy concerns. Photograph: Niamh NicGhabhann (July 2016).

working extremely successfully, it also provided an opportunity for the city to position itself as a city with festive space. Jamieson argues that such images produce 'a distinct way of looking at the city' that 'insinuates the freedom of festivalized streets', suggesting that such festivalised spaces are the safer, risk-free environments sought by cultural tourists (Jamieson 2004, 69). Furthermore, Jamieson notes that these highly visible, festivalised spaces also act to eclipse the 'social worlds that are not neatly assimilated to a festival gaze', and that exist beyond these 'spontaneous' festival environments (Jamieson 2004, 70).

The festive event itself, therefore, can be seen as an opportunity for communal celebration but also as a way to deepen engagement with the Limerick 2020 brand, and as an opportunity to create and gather valuable images of the spectacular event which can be circulated via print and social media, and used in city branding and other promotional materials. This reflects what Jamieson has termed the 'fetishized' image of creative expression and liminal excess that have come to be associated with the 'Creative City' as an urban type within global networks, with festival performers and audiences required to be complicit in 'spatializing and temporalizing city brands' (Jamieson 2014, 299). In the economy of global city reputations, therefore, the street festival provided city administrators with an opportunity to enhance Limerick's reputation as a cosmopolitan, safe, creative environment.

Conclusion

This chapter has focused on the 'city stories' that are produced in the context of an ECoC bid process. It has explored some of the pressures and conflicts that can emerge in the time-bound, liminal, context of the bidding window. While Limerick was ultimately unsuccessful in winning the designation, a close focus on the bidding process itself allows us to examine the 'imagined city' that is created during this process, through brands, stories, enactment, and images. Through a close focus on one city, we point to the importance of examining ECoC bidding dynamics within longer histories of city narratives. We also point to the importance of considering the impact of 'emotional', persuasive bid narratives in the context of unsuccessful bids, and what this may mean for trust relationships between stakeholders as they move onwards.

For regional cities like Limerick, the ECoC bid process was a period of intense focus on its cultural offering, requiring the bid team to negotiate the expectation of inclusion together with agendas of ensuring return on investment with a successful bid. This period also required stakeholders to form into new groups with sometimes competing agendas, and to create a coherent sense of place in a relatively short period of time. Reflecting on our exploration of Limerick's experience in the ECoC bid process, it is worth considering the aftermath of such a process on cultural infrastructure, the dynamics of inclusion, and communities at a regional scale, and whether changes could be introduced to support the transition from an imagined 'creative city' renaissance to a more sustainable set of ongoing conversations and relationships.

Notes

[1] In April 2014, Ireland was announced as one of two countries that would host the 2020 European Capital of Culture. This was during the year that Limerick was awarded (without a competition) the inaugural Irish National City of Culture. The competition to decide which Irish city to host ECoC was open to all cities.

References

Åkerlund, Ulrika and Dieter K. Müller. 2012. Implementing Tourism Events: The Discourses of Umeå's Bid for European Capital of Culture. *Scandinavian Journal of Hospitality and Tourism*, 12(2), 164–180. https://doi.org/10.1080/15022250.2011.647418

Bendix, Regina. 2002. Capitalizing on Memories Past, Present, and Future. *Anthropological Theory*, 2(4), 469–487.

Brüggemann, Karsten and Andres Kasekamp. 2014. 'Singing Oneself into a Nation'?: Estonian Song Festivals as Rituals of Political Mobilisation. *Nations and Nationalism*, 20(2), 259–276.

De Bres, Karen and James Davis. 2001. Celebrating Group and Place Identity: A Case Study of a New Regional Festival. *Tourism Geographies: An International Journal of Tourism, Space, Place and Environment*, 3(3), 326–337.

Devereux, Eoin, Amanda Haynes and Martin J. Power. 2011. At the Edge: Media Constructions of a Stigmatized Irish Housing Estate. *Journal of Housing and the Built Environment*, 26(2), 123–142.

Dillane, Aileen, Martin J. Power and Eoin Devereux. 2017. Locating Culture, Making Soundscapes and Activating Critical Social Relations: A Case Study from Limerick Soundscapes. *Portuguese Journal of Social Science*, 16(3), 343–358.

Euronews. 2020. Galway is a European Capital of Culture 2020. But how do other Irish cities feel about it? 2 January. Available at: https://www.euronews.com/2020/01/01/galway-is-a-european-capital-of-culture-2020-but-how-do-other-irish-cities-feel-about-it (accessed 19 May 2021).

Falassi, Alessandro. 1987. *Time Out of Time: Essays on the Festival*. Albuquerque, NM: University of New Mexico Press.

García, Beatriz. 2004. Cultural Policy and Urban Regeneration in Western European Cities: Lessons from Experience, Prospects for the Future. *Local Economy*, 19(4), 312–326.

Garcia, Beatriz. 2017. 'If Everyone Says So …' Press Narratives and Image Change in Major Event Host Cities. *Urban Studies*, 54(14), 3178–3198.

Hourigan, Niamh. 2011. *Understanding Limerick: Social Exclusion and Change*. Cork: Cork University Press.

Hunter, Mary Ann. 2004. Utopia, Maps and Ecstasy: Configuring Space in Barrie Kosky's 1996 Adelaide Festival. *Australasian Drama Studies* 44(4), 36–51.

Immler, Nicole L. and Hans Sakkers. 2014. (Re)Programming Europe: European Capitals of Culture: Rethinking the Role of Culture. *Journal of European Studies*, 44(1), 3–29.

Irish Examiner. 2008. Limerick lesson for blighted area, 11 February 2008. Available at: https://www.irishexaminer.com/opinion/columnists/arid-20054892.html (accessed 19 May 2021).

Irish Examiner. 2012. Shattered Dreams, 28 March. Available at: https://www.irishexaminer.com/opinion/commentanalysis/arid-20188552.html (accessed 19 May 2021).

Irish Examiner. 2020. Atlantic Edge, European Embrace: Limerick unveils €1m branding, 20 January. Available at: https://www.irishexaminer.com/business/arid-30978675.html (accessed 19 May 2021).

Irish Examiner. 2021. '#LimerickAndProud hashtag blows up worldwide following Forbes article on Collison brothers', 21 April. Available at: https://www.irishexaminer.com/news/munster/arid-40271918.html

Jamieson, Kirstie. 2004. Edinburgh: The Festival Gaze and its Boundaries. *Space and Culture*, 7(1), 64–75.

Jamieson, Kirstie. 2014. Tracing Festival Imaginaries: Between Affective Urban Idioms and Administrative Assemblages. *International Journal of Cultural Studies*, 17(3), 293–303.

Kinsella, Stephen, Niamh NicGhabhann and Annemarie Ryan. 2017. Designing Policy: Collaborative Policy Development Within the Context of the European Capital of Culture Bid Process. *Cultural Trends*, 26(3), 233–248.

Lichrou, Maria, Lisa O'Malley and Maurice Patterson. 2008. Place-Product or Place Narratives(s)? Perspectives in the Marketing of Tourism Destinations. *Journal of Strategic Marketing*, 16(1), 27–39.

Lichrou, Maria, Lisa O'Malley and Maurice Patterson. 2010. Narratives of a Tourism Destination: Local Particularities and Their Implications for Place Marketing and Branding. *Place Branding and Public Diplomacy*, 6(2), 134–144.

Limerick Arts and Culture Exchange. 2021. Limerick.ie (www.limerick.ie). Available at: https://www.limerick.ie/lace (accessed 28 October 2021).

Limerick.ie. (www.limerick.ie). 2015. Engage, discuss and get involved in Limerick's bid for European Capital of Culture 2020', 3 June. Available at: https://www.limerick.ie/engage-discuss-and-get-involved-limericks-bid-european-capital-culture-2020 (accessed 19 May 2021).

Limerick.ie. (www.limerick.ie). 2016. Photo gallery: Limerick 2020 Street Party, 13 July. Available at: https://www.limerick.ie/discover/living/news/photo-gallery-limerick-2020-street-party (accessed 19 May 2021).

Limerick.ie. 2020a. Limerick National City of Culture 2014 Social Impact Study (published 15 June 2015). Available at: https://issuu.com/limerick2020/docs/lncc_report_digitalprint

Limerick.ie. 2020b. ECoC Bid Book. Limerick 2020 – Belonging, 15 July. Available at: https://issuu.com/limerick2020/docs/lmk_2020 (accessed 19 May 2021).

Limerick Leader. 2016. Councillor claims Limerick 2020 bid book left public 'shocked and saddened', 22 September. Available at: https://www.limerickleader.ie/news/home/216853/councillor-claims-limerick-2020-bid-book-left-public-shocked-and-saddened.html (accessed 19 May 2021).

Limerick Post. 2019. Giant Granny left a rich cultural legacy in Limerick, 30 March. Available at: https://www.limerickpost.ie/2019/03/30/giant-granny-left-a-rich-cultural-legacy-in-limerick (accessed 19 May 2021).

Liu, Yi-De. 2019. Event and Sustainable Culture-Led Regeneration: Lessons From the 2009 European Capital of Culture, Liverpool. *Sustainability*, 11(7), 1–18.

McGillivray, David and Daniel Turner. 2018. *Event Bidding: Politics, Persuasion and Resistance*. Abingdon: Routledge.

Ooi, Can-Seng, Lars Håkanson and Laura LaCava. 2014. Poetics and Politics of the European Capital of Culture Project. *Procedia: Social and Behavioral Sciences*, 148, 420–427.

Picard, David and Mike Robinson. 2006. *Festivals, Tourism and Social Change: Remaking Worlds*. Clevedon: Channel View Publications.

Power, Martin J., Amanda Haynes and Eoin Devereux. 2021. Indelible Stain: Territorial Stigmatization and the Limits of Resistance. *Community Development Journal*, 56(2), 244–265.

Richards, Greg and Lena Marques. 2016. Bidding for Success? Impacts of the European Capital of Culture Bid. *Scandinavian Journal of Hospitality and Tourism*, 16(2), 180–195. https://doi.org/10.1080/15022250.2015.1118407

Ryan, Annmarie. 2019. Guiding and Enabling Liminal Experiences Between Business and Arts Organisations Operating in a Sponsorship Relationship. *Human Relations*, 72(2) 344–369.

Scully, Marc. 2012. Whose Day is it Anyway? St. Patrick's Day as a Contested Performance of National and Diasporic Irishnes. *Studies in Ethnicity and Nationalism*, 12(1), 118–135.

Trigg, Dylan. 2017. Place and Non–place: A Phenomenological Perspective. In Bruce B. Janz (Eds.) *Place, Space and Hermeneutics. Contributions to Hermeneutics*. Cham: Springer. https://doi.org/10.1007/978-3-319-52214-2_10

Turner, Victor. 1974. Liminal to Liminoid, in Play, Flow, and Ritual: An Essay in Comparative Symbology. *Rice Institute Pamphlet-Rice University Studies*, 60(3), 53–92.

Van Heerden, Esther. 2009. *Liminality, Transformation and Communitas: Africaans Identities as Viewed Through the Lens of South African Arts Festivals: 1995–2006*, unpublished PhD. Stellenbosch: Stellenbosch University. Available at: https://scholar.sun.ac.za/handle/10019.1/1487

Semiotics of Edinburgh's Festival City Place-Myth: Management and Community Stakeholders' Visual Representations of Festival Spaces

Louise Todd

Introduction

As Scotland's capital, Edinburgh's identity is forged from multiple sources, drawing upon its rich built, political, cultural and artistic heritage. These qualities are embraced, and utilised, by management stakeholders to maintain the city's contemporary destination brand image, forming present-day place-myths. These images are perceived cultural realities created through dominant discourses and folklore (Barthes 1993) and are subject to orders of meaning where semiotic cultural codes are perceived as factual (Gaines 2007). One of Edinburgh's most persistent identities is its self-proclaimed role as the world's leading festival city (Jamieson and Todd 2020). Edinburgh's long and illustrious history of urban festivals has constructed its festival city identity, something that can be understood as a place-myth.

How to cite this book chapter:

Todd, L. 2022. Semiotics of Edinburgh's Festival City Place-Myth: Management and Community Stakeholders' Visual Representations of Festival Spaces. In: Smith, A., Osborn, G. and Quinn, B. (Eds.) *Festivals and the City: The Contested Geographies of Urban Events*. London: University of Westminster Press. Pp. 187–208. London: University of Westminster Press. DOI: https://doi.org/10.16997/book64.k. License: CC-BY-NC-ND 4.0

Eleven annual city-based arts and cultural festivals currently sit within the 'Festivals Edinburgh' strategic brand umbrella (see later discussion). In recent years, the festivals have attracted approximately 4.5 million attendees from 70 countries worldwide; and have generated £313 million for Scotland's economy annually (BOP Consulting and Festivals Edinburgh 2016a). Edinburgh's evolution as the festival city has involved destination managers leveraging the festivals to drive event tourism (Todd, Leask and Ensor 2017). Indeed, recent strategic plans recommend strengthening its festival city status, alongside active promotion of this brand worldwide (BOP Consulting and Festivals Edinburgh 2016b).

Edinburgh's festival city identity and place-myth underpin this chapter, which considers the conflicting stakeholder narratives regarding Edinburgh's contested places and spaces. The chapter opens with an overview of the festival city construct, followed by a discussion of Edinburgh's eponymous title. Informed by festival city discourses, a consideration of place-myth, and an event tourism stakeholder typology (Todd et al. 2017), the chapter then considers the semiotics of Edinburgh's place-myth as the world's leading festival city (Festivals Edinburgh 2020a).

The chapter considers Edinburgh's visual culture as the festival city through a semiotic lens. As a hermeneutical approach to understanding phenomena, semiotics uncovers layers of meaning and myth by studying systems of communicated 'signs' (MacCannell 1999). The foundation of semiotics is thus humans' interpretation of encountered signs (Peirce 1992). In semiotic terms, signs may be written, spoken, or performed; and be visual, audio-visual, or aural. Signs can be natural or created, living or inanimate and, significantly for the present chapter, signs include places and spaces (Gaines 2006). The chapter also explores how two distinct stakeholder groups engage with Edinburgh as the festival city through the semiotics of their imagery. It draws from two discrete, but related, projects. The first is an ongoing study which explores a selection of online digital images shared by destination management stakeholders, via the Instagram social media platform. The second project involves studying visual elements of a participative visual map of the festival city. The map was co-created by members of the Wester Hailes community, an area situated in southwest Edinburgh, which is well beyond designated festival spaces. Wester Hailes is one of the most deprived areas in Scotland (Scottish Government 2020) and contrary to the festival city place-myth, its folklore is marked by this deprivation (Anderson et al. 1994; Grandison 2018).

The analysis also considers the projected and portrayed imagery of both stakeholder groups, and two key narratives of Edinburgh's festival city place-myth are consequently identified. The first narrative is *staging the festival*, communicated via semiotic signs of Edinburgh Castle during the festivals. The second narrative is *performing the festival*, through the semiotics of festivalgoers in the city's streets and spaces. There are other festival city visual narratives but these two were selected to illustrate the present discussion. Additionally, these narratives are synonymous with two of Edinburgh's most enduring festivals – Edinburgh's International Festival (EIF) and the Edinburgh Festival Fringe (the Fringe). Similar staging and performing the festival narratives of festival city place-myth were shared between the two stakeholder groups, but the distribution of such semiotic imagery across urban space in the city varied significantly. In exploring management and community stakeholders' images of signs, spaces and places, the chapter concludes by reflecting upon the idealised view of Edinburgh as the festival city, alongside its contemporary socio-political and cultural context of inclusion and accessibility. The chapter closes with a consideration of the semiotics that sustain the visual culture, consumption and place-myth of the festival city.

The Festival City

The template for today's European city-based festivals evolved from the mid nineteenth to early twentieth centuries. At this time, festivals were created to surpass physical and metaphorical city and national boundaries, and to engender freedom from previously dominant societal institutions (Quinn 2005). These festivals emerged from the modern era, when sport and culture assumed a greater societal presence (Smith 2016), and with an emphasis on cultural internationalism (Jamieson and Todd 2019). The Salzburg Festival, for example (established in 1920), is recognised as the first of these festivals. It was followed by post-war urban festivals in other European cities, including Edinburgh, with the aim of 'staging the international and hosting cosmopolitan audiences' (Jamieson and Todd 2019, 4).

In contemporary strategic management practice, the festival city has become a relatively common element of cities' destination branding. The term points towards a vibrant and cosmopolitan urban setting where the collective and experiential consumption of events is encouraged and supported. Apart from Edinburgh, numerous other cities around the globe adopt this title (or similar ones) in their destination branding and marketing efforts. Indeed, the use of festival city titles includes endorsements from external bodies including, for example, the International Festival and Event Association's 'World Festival and Event City Award'. Since 2010 this scheme has recognised approximately 100 cities that fit with IFEA's competitive criteria (IFEA 2020).

The practical implementation of festival city branding is traceable to key strands of academic discourse. In tourism and event studies literature, festival and eventful city concepts have been debated for some time. Much of this discussion is concerned with the measurable parameters of the festival city as a managed destination, consumed by tourists and visitors. Consequently, there is emphasis upon characteristics such as the variety, impact, contribution, scale and annual provision of festivals. Additionally, there is concern over associated tourism volume (Getz and Page 2016; Colombo and Richards 2017; Richards 2017), alongside clear top-down stakeholder support through strategic event portfolio development (Antchak and Pernecky 2017; Ziakas 2020). Within these discourses, prominence is given to the branding potential of the festival city, alongside place-making within the context of festivalised urban space (Prentice and Andersen 2003; Richards and Palmer 2012).

Another perspective highlights the symbolic and creative promise of the festival city for staging the temporal, experimental and conceptual (Dooghe 2015). With less emphasis on tourism potential, the use of public urban space for festivals and events is debated here from a broader perspective (Gold and Gold 2020; Jamieson 2004; Jamieson and Todd 2019; Smith 2019). Similar themes are echoed in popular management literature, considering cities and the creative characteristics of their inhabitants (Florida 2002; Landry 2012).

Essentially, the festival city construct grew from the late twentieth-century concept of 'festivalisation', which describes the use of events within urban policy (Häussermann and Siebel 1993). In this sense, festivalisation refers to a particular means of staging and consuming urban space (see Chapters 1 and 2 for further discussion of the term). However, it has become a contested concept due to the, often, exclusive nature of festivals and their contribution to the commercialisation of urban public spaces (Smith 2014, 2016). Furthermore, the process and associated outcomes of festivalisation may lead to permanent physical change to the cityscape, which can be resisted by local communities and other stakeholders (McGillivray, Guillard and Reid 2020). This chapter now examines the case of Edinburgh, one of the world's most famous festival cities, beginning with an analysis of the city's identities.

Edinburgh's Identities

Today, Edinburgh is regarded as a diverse and vibrant city with a high proportion of residents with international origins, younger people, and residents educated to higher degree level (City of Edinburgh Council 2019). As one of the UK's leading tourism destinations, visitors are drawn to the city's heritage and cultural provision; its location as a gateway to Scotland and beyond, and to its renowned portfolio of festivals (City of Edinburgh Council 2019).

Edinburgh's contemporary identities are grounded in its history, cultural heritage, physical architecture and eternal festivalisation (Smith 2016). Its urban centre is comprised of two UNESCO designated World Heritage Sites: the medieval Old Town, dominated by Edinburgh Castle, which serves as a backdrop to the historic centre, and the neoclassical New Town, which was designed and built in the eighteenth century (UNESCO 2021). Around this time, Edinburgh fostered a reputation as the 'Athens of the North', in response to its architectural and cultural identities. This was complemented by the emergence of the allegorical imagery of a romantic 'Baronial' Scotland, as curated by Sir Walter Scott (Lowrey 2001). In the context of post-World War II Europe, and on the eve of the first of its festivals, Edinburgh was repositioned by its civic stakeholders as 'the cultural resort of Europe' (Bartie 2013: 37). Edinburgh's identity as 'the world's leading festival city' (Festivals Edinburgh 2020a) is underpinned by this cultural heritage.

Edinburgh's contemporary festival city identity emerged from the post-war shadows of the 1940s, amidst the prevailing climate of cultural international-ism (Jamieson and Todd 2020). Unlike other European cities, Edinburgh sur-vived the war relatively intact. Yet, far from being associated with festivals, it was viewed as a particularly sombre setting in comparison to some other Euro-pean capitals. The city's identity was underpinned by the continuing influence of the eighteenth- and nineteenth-century Scottish Enlightenment; alongside the dominant institutional presence of the Church, and professions such as law and medicine (Bartie 2013).

Edinburgh's first festivals originated in 1947 – EIF, the Fringe and the Inter-national Film Festival. All three remain key to the city's festival portfolio to this day. The EIF and the Fringe are crucial to facilitating the Edinburgh festival city place-myth. Edinburgh's festivals occur throughout the year, with the most intense festival period in the late summer, between July and September.

Despite their long history, Edinburgh's festivals were, until recently, managed in a discrete, although collaborative, way. It was not until 2006, on recognising the strategic development of event tourism in competitor destinations, that key government, civic, tourism and arts stakeholders, as well as the festivals' lead-ers, commissioned industry research to investigate the future of Edinburgh's Festivals. One of the outcomes was the establishment of Festivals Edinburgh, which was founded in 2007 and is overseen by the festivals. Today it represents them collectively, and strategically, to develop and promote the festival city brand internationally (Festivals Edinburgh 2020b).

The tangible impacts of Edinburgh's festivals are reported widely. Until the festivals were interrupted by 2020's global Covid pandemic, there were annual increases in attendee numbers, tickets distributed and economic contribution. The intangible, socio-cultural outcomes of the festivals are less documented, but a Festivals Edinburgh-led industry survey of 29,000 respondents revealed that 89% of local festivalgoers agreed that the Festivals increased people's pride in Edinburgh as a city. Furthermore, 94% of respondents agreed the festivals position Edinburgh as an attractive, creative, international destination (BOP Consulting and Festivals Edinburgh 2016a)

While Edinburgh's festivals bring significant socio-cultural and economic benefits to the city, the festivals, or rather their popularity, have also led to some discord amongst local community stakeholders. Cultural, social and economic engagement is listed as a strategic priority for Festivals Edinburgh (2020a) and the recently published 'Festival City Vision to 2030' Festivals Edinburgh (2020b) emphasises a commitment to public spaces and infrastructure, along-side inclusive cultural provision, with increased opportunities for community-led culture and creativity. Further, Festivals Edinburgh (2016, 3) maintain the festivals combine 'outward-looking internationalism with a deep commitment

to Edinburgh and Scotland' and report widening access and community participation initiatives undertaken by the festivals. Nevertheless, since late 2019
some local communities and the media (McGillivray, Guillard and Reid 2020),
have been critical of the commercial agendas of staging year round festivals in
the city's historic public spaces (Quinn 2005; Smith 2016). There is a growing
feeling that Edinburgh is for tourists rather than its communities (Leask 2019).
Following a series of particularly busy summer festival seasons that raised initial concerns, opposition was fuelled by the management of Edinburgh's Christmas and Hogmanay (New Year) festivals in 2019–2020. Being concentrated in
the historic Princes Street Gardens, these events reportedly caused significant
negative environmental impacts. Issues regarding crowding, noise and distur-
bance in the compact city centre were also reported. As a result, media and
public voices accused destination managers of commodifying these spaces for
festivals and event tourism, dubbing Edinburgh as 'the city for sale' (Cockburn
Association 2020). Debate has since continued with reports that Edinburgh's
destination managers recognise a need for more balanced festival provision in
the future (Ferguson 2021).

In terms of Edinburgh's much documented history (Gold et al. 2020), and
titular role of world leading festival city, this chapter aligns with the position
that the festivals are 'central to contemporary politics of representation where
identities, encounters and mobilities are staged' (Jamieson and Todd 2020, 1).
In this context, it is important to note that despite Edinburgh's present-day
cosmopolitan image as a cultural capital, it is well-documented as being 'the
most sharply divided of any British settlement' (McCrone and Elliot 1989, 66).
Indeed, its status as a world leading festival city (Jamieson and Todd 2020),
alongside other branding-friendly urban identities, may be viewed as evidence
of destination management stakeholders' enthusiastic adoption of neoliberal
'competitive cities' titles (Kallin and Slater 2014). Having considered issues of
identity, the chapter now turns to explore the notion of place and myth.

The Festival City Place-Myth

When viewing Edinburgh's festival city place-myth through a semiotic lens,
it is important to consider the term 'myth', which originates from the Greek
'mythos' – meaning what could not really exist (Williams 1985). Myth is often
related to folklore and legend, which have similar meanings and are narratives
that are co-created in social contexts. In essence, myths are perceived cultural
realities with layers of meaning. They become authoritative through their social
persistence (Gaines 2007). Myths exist therefore in the imagination as much
as in reality, and this duality is similarly true of place-myths (Shields 1992)
which are defined as meanings ascribed to places through discursive narratives.
These narratives evolve a dominant set of collected core images, including ste-
reotypes and clichés, that refer to the place. As these images are disseminated,

circulated and repeated within social contexts, they become durable, widespread and commonly ascribed, thus creating place-myths. This happens whether the narratives are faithful to the realities of the place to which they refer, or not (Crouch and Lübbren 2003; Scarles 2014; Urry and Larsen 2011).

As a place-myth, the festival city is relatively unusual as it is not exclusively aligned to one urban location. This was considered by Thomasson (2015) in the context of the place-myths of Edinburgh and Adelaide as festival cities. She noted that place-myths evolve over time, with certain images more enduring than others. In Edinburgh's case, heritage, culture and literature contributed to the formation of its festival city place-myth, and this was revitalised through its contemporary identity. This chapter builds upon this to consider the semiotics of Edinburgh's festival city place-myth, and specifically, the layers of meaning within discursive visual images portrayed by festival management and local community stakeholders. This is undertaken through visual research methods within a semiotic methodology. The resulting key narratives that are uncovered each contribute to Edinburgh's festival city identity and place-myth.

The Semiotic Lens and Myth

Semiotics is concerned with the study of 'signs' and their layers of meaning (Banks and Zeitlyn 2015). Human communication relies upon signs in visual, verbal or other forms. Modern semiotics is commonly viewed to have been developed in the 1930s by the Swiss linguist Ferdinand de Saussure and American philosopher Charles Saunders Peirce (Echtner 1999; MacCannell 1999). Being concerned with language, Saussure proposed an analytical framework which presented any sign as being the relationship between the signifier (the sound and/or image) and the signified (concept/object being referred to). In proposing his framework, Peirce included a third element. This was an interpretant, which was added to his presentamen (signifier) and designatum (signified), to contemplate the interpretative meanings of a sign. The addition of an interpretant allowed the consideration of connotative (deeper) layers of meaning. These had capacity to become myths, later described by French philosopher Roland Barthes (1993), as bearing an order of cultural signification, where semiotic code is perceived as fact. Barthes added to Saussure's framework, while building upon Peirce's interpretant, by enabling different layers of denotative and connotative meaning or myths. Significantly, in the semiotic paradigm, signs therefore point towards the mythologies of the phenomenon which is under consideration (Barthes 1993).

Semiotics has been applied in, and is relevant to, tourism studies (see Albers and James 1988; Berger 2011; Culler 1981; Echtner 1999; Pennington and Thomsen 2010, amongst others) and space as a semiotic sign has been subject to academic analysis (e.g. Gaines 2006; Lagopoulos 1993, 2014; Murray, Fujishima and Uzuka 2014). Nevertheless, physical space and geographical place are generally understood in relation to other semiotic signs that exist within physical and symbolic boundaries. To date, there has been little consideration of the semiotics of place-myth, or to studying festival contexts through signs within space. This method is particularly novel, therefore, in considering the place-myth of the festival city.

Adding to this study's semiotic paradigm are visual methods in each of the stakeholder settings. Visual methods involve the incorporation of visual materials in research. These can be the part of the process, the analysis, or both (Banks and Zeitlyn 2015) and are concerned with narratives inherent to visuals. In the remainder of this chapter, visual methods in general – and semiotics techniques in particular – are used to explore Edinburgh's status as a festival city.

Edinburgh Festival City Stakeholders

Stakeholders are defined here in terms of their continuous and dynamic roles within the Edinburgh festival city setting. This chapter adapts a stakeholder typology developed in Edinburgh's event tourism context (Todd, Leask and Ensor 2017). By examining the Fringe as a hallmark event, this research identified primary and secondary stakeholders, and is applicable to the wider festival city context. Primary stakeholders are those essential to festivals occurring, whereas secondary stakeholders are not fundamental to festivals taking place. They are, nevertheless, contextually unique, and thus crucial to their setting. This chapter is concerned with findings from two projects, each concerned with distinct stakeholder groups and specifically, their visual representations of festivalised spaces. These are primary festival management stakeholders and secondary community stakeholders. Firstly, by drawing from an ongoing study, this chapter refers to online digital images shared by festival management stakeholders via the Instagram social media platform. It then considers visual elements of a map of the festival city. This was co-created by members of the Wester Hailes community in Edinburgh. Although these projects are discrete and distinct, both stakeholder groups' portrayals are viewed through a semiotic paradigm where signs were sought to uncover key narratives that contribute to Edinburgh's festival city place-myth.

Festival Management Stakeholders

In its aim to consider the conflicting narratives of management and community stakeholders over the contested places and spaces of Edinburgh, this chapter draws firstly from a current study which considers Edinburgh's visual culture as the festival city (Todd and Logan-McFarlane 2019). Images depicting the festivals in the city's spaces were collected from Instagram accounts managed by Edinburgh's festivals. These were categorised on the bases of displaying semiotic signs fitting with Peirce's (1992) triadic typology of iconic (similar), indexical (causal), and symbolic (arbitrary) semiotic signs. All referred to the festival city in some way, whether by visual similarity, social agreement or cultural learning (Echtner 1999).

As 'digital media are part of how events are conceptualised, made, and experienced by participants, viewers and users' (Pink et al. 2015, 165), Instagram was selected as an appropriate platform. It has an inherently visual culture (MacDowell and deSouza 2018), where meanings are portrayed through sharing images, alongside limited text, and hashtags, to provide contextual details. Further, using Instagram images was useful in the visual analysis to fit with Pearce's (1934) typology of signs, (Laestadius 2017). While it is not possible to include a large sample of the specific Instagram images in this chapter, as discussed later, two examples of management stakeholders' images are included. These depict the festival city place-myth narratives of staging and performing the festival.

Initial findings revealed that images across all festivals' accounts are particularly rich in terms of presenting key semiotic narratives of the festivals and spaces of central Edinburgh during the festivals. Images commonly include Edinburgh Castle; fireworks; crowded streets in the Old Town, festivalgoers, and street performers; alongside iconic festival venues. Imagery is concentrated within Edinburgh's central Old Town area, and the main festival settings. It is important to note that, as management-portrayed images, these are curated, top-down, visual representations of the festival city. Although Instagram is designed as a democratic platform for sharing user-generated imagery, it has been widely adopted by managers in portraying idealised destination images as marketing communications tools. This draws upon the perspective that the distribution of destination images becomes a hermeneutic circle of representation (Albers and James 1988; Urry 1990).

Community Stakeholders

The second study this chapter draws from was a participative public engagement (and research) initiative undertaken with community stakeholders. Participants were residents of Wester Hailes, which lies around five miles to the southwest of Edinburgh's centre, outside of the festival areas. Wester Hailes was conceived in the mid twentieth century as one of a series of council residential developments on the urban periphery of the city. These were designed as 'slum clearance' projects, where many of the city's most deprived residents were rehoused from poor-quality, outdated, tenement housing (Glendinning 2005). Nevertheless, alongside other similar developments (Sighthill, also west; Craigmillar, south; Granton and Muirhouse, to the north) it became part of 'Edinburgh's other fringe – a belt of poor and intensely stigmatised peripheral housing estates' (Kallin and Slater 2014, 1356).

Despite its tourism-focused brand identity, Edinburgh remains a city segregated by class, and deprivation has remained a defining characteristic of some communities (Lee and Murie 2002). Today, Wester Hailes occupies the first decile of the Scottish Index of Multiple Deprivation (SIMD), deeming it one of the most deprived areas in Scotland in terms of the extent to which it is disadvantaged across seven domains: income, employment, education, health, access to services, crime and housing (Scottish Government 2020). Contrary to Edinburgh's festival city place-myth and identity, the 'folklore' of Wester Hailes is thus constructed from crime, poverty, drug abuse and undesirable behaviour (Anderson et al. 1994; Grandison 2018), presenting a countervailing place-myth of deprivation.

Throughout the city, including the less deprived areas of southwest Edinburgh, between 65% and 70% of residents have attended a festival in the past two years, (City of Edinburgh Council 2018). This total is only 50% for Wester Hailes residents. A similar disparity is seen in respect of residents who believe the festivals make Edinburgh a better place to live. Seventy-two per cent agree with this across the city but only 58% in Wester Hailes (ibid). Anecdotally, engagement with the festivals is not high in Wester Hailes, although it should be noted that many of Edinburgh's festivals undertake community engagement initiatives and most maintain school outreach programmes to engage children and younger people.

Wester Hailes Festival City Map

Selected images from the festival management stakeholders' Instagram accounts informed the first stage of the festival city map, which was drawn by the author as a simplified, large-scale map of Edinburgh (See Figure 11.1). This focused on Edinburgh's central Old and New Towns, as discussed above; and included collaged images and sketches of key attractions, alongside mappings of local communities of the greater Edinburgh area. This initial map then formed the basis of the participative public engagement research initiative, undertaken by the author and members of the Wester Hailes community. As a participative form of gathering data, beyond dissemination, public engagement is 'a two-way process, involving interaction and listening, with the goal of generating mutual benefit' (NCCPE 2017). The aim was to co-design an Edinburgh festival city map for Wester Hailes. Public engagement as an approach includes a dyadic approach and involves equitable and democratic partnerships amongst researchers and participants to empower the wider research community (Evans and Jones 2004). The initiative was undertaken during a day-long community festival in September 2019, at WHALE Arts, a community-led charity and social enterprise in Wester Hailes. During the festival various arts, entertainment, collaborative projects and a community meal took place. Attendees were adults and families with children who were members of the Wester Hailes community. They were provided with arts materials including stickers, colouring pens, photographic images from brochures and magazines; and invited to co-create the festival city map. Above the map was the heading: 'Make an Edinburgh festival map for Wester Hailes', alongside questions, placed around the map, including:

- What is a festival?
- What should a festival be like?
- What do you want to see/do at the Edinburgh festivals?
- Where do you want to see the festivals?

The author discussed Edinburgh's festivals with attendees and encouraged them to contribute their images and written ideas around these themes. The Wester Hailes festival city map emerged over the duration of the event. Figure 11.1 shows the festival city map and the section of the map depicting Wester Hailes. At the top of Figure 11.1 is the map as it developed. Edinburgh Castle is situated near the centre of the map, while Wester Hailes is in the lower left corner of the map. It was between these two areas that many of the festival city activities were depicted by the participants. The castle was portrayed as surrounded by fireworks and other activities; illustrated by images and words, including a request for a 'fun fair', a performance by 'animatronic dinosaurs', 'arts and crafts stalls' and a 'talent show'. Nearby, an 'animal parade' from Edinburgh Zoo was requested alongside 'flashmobs', 'more bagpipes' and 'busking' throughout the city centre streets. These were similar semiotic signs to the images depicted in the festival managers' Instagram accounts, being iconic, symbolic, and indexical images of the festival city (Pearce 1992). As signs, these communicated meanings around the staging of the festival and the performance of the festival in the city centre.

The lower part of Figure 11.1 is the section of the map depicting Wester Hailes. This part of the map received the most attention from participants who created images and requests for more festival activity around the Wester Hailes area. Many of the adult participants when asked said they rarely attended Edinburgh's festivals, with one saying they had never been to the festivals. There were requests for more 'Fringe' and 'Science festival events outside the city centre'; a 'circus around Wester Hailes'; 'music on a barge' (on the nearby canal); 'plays at the WHEC' (Wester Hailes Education Centre); 'free clubs for kids'; alongside other music, entertainment, and science activities. In these images and words, there were also similar signs to those depicted in the Instagram images. Nevertheless, while there was recognition of the value of these festival city signs of staging and performing the festival, it was clear such signs were currently largely absent from this corner of the city during Edinburgh's festivals.

Figure 11.1: The Festival City Map (top) and the section depicting Wester Hailes (below). Photograph: Louise Todd.

Edinburgh Festival City: Place-Myth Narratives

It is possible to uncover two narratives that underpin the Edinburgh festival city place-myth and these have been developed from the semiotics of the stakeholders' visual images. Both narratives reveal the visual culture of Edinburgh's festivals are part of the process of forming place-myths (Crouch and Lübbren 2003). These may be framed by performance theory (Goffman 2002; Schechner 1977), viewing Edinburgh's festivals as socially constructed phenomena. They are inclusively staged and performed by their producers and consumers as they co-construct the semiotic narratives of the festival city place-myth through their gaze (MacCannell 1999; Urry and Larsen 2011). The first narrative is 'staging the festival', which is communicated through the semiotic sign of Edinburgh Castle. In the festival management Instagram accounts, the castle is depicted frequently. It is generally immersed in light, or surrounded by fireworks, while overseeing the city. It is often depicted as the centre of festival activity. This was a similarly common portrayal for the community stakeholders.

The second narrative is 'performing the festival': seen through the semiotics of festivalgoers, consuming the festival in the city's places and spaces – alongside depictions of arts and entertainment performances on the streets and elsewhere. This aspect of *performing the festival* is largely absent from Wester Hailes during the festivals. However, community stakeholders added iconic, symbolic and indexical semiotic signs of performing the festival to their festival city map, and these were more concentrated around Wester Hailes than in the city centre. These narratives will now be discussed. Both are related, respectively, to two of Edinburgh's most enduring festivals, and their associated myths, as outlined below. Figure 11.2 depicts exemplars of the management-created narratives and semiotic signs of staging and performing the festival. These images are typical both of the Instagram images as discussed earlier; and of the co-constructed signs on the community map.

Staging the Festival

The narrative and semiotic sign of staging the festival – which contributes to Edinburgh's festival city place-myth – has origins in Edinburgh's International Festival, Edinburgh's first festival. EIF's establishment (in 1947) is associated with Rudolf Bing (1902–1997), the general manager of Glyndebourne Festival Opera, which had become renowned for its own summer festival, before closing during the war. EIF folklore recounts a romantic narrative which contributes to Edinburgh's modern festival city place-myth. Here, Bing was visiting Edinburgh in 1942 with his friend, the soprano, Audrey Millman. Having attended an opera, the pair were walking in Princes Street. On seeing Edinburgh Castle, bathed in moonlight, Ms. Millman remarked the city would be an ideal setting for an arts festival (Edinburgh International Festival 2018). This legend

Figure 11.2: Staging and performing the Festival. Examples of semiotic narratives contributing to Edinburgh's festival city place-myth. Photographs: 'Czech Dancers' © the Royal Military Tattoo and 'Street Performance at the Fringe 2', David Monteith Hodge, courtesy of Festivals Edinburgh.

(Bartie 2013) was later referred to by Bing (1972, 70) who noted that Edinburgh's castle, positioned above the city on a hill, gave it a 'Salzburg flavour'. However, despite being an enduring myth of today's Edinburgh festivals, the view of the romantic light-bathed Edinburgh Castle and its visual similarity to Salzburg was not truly behind the choice of Edinburgh to host the first edition of the EIF.

According to historical records, EIF was established for more prosaic reasons. As noted earlier, Edinburgh was viewed as a rather sedate and formal capital. At this time 'culture' was considered as attractive to affluent city residents and international visitors. The Scottish Tourism Board was established in 1946; and following this, to reposition Edinburgh's image, EIF was created by civic leaders and a group of world-leading artists as a post-war approach to enrich the cultural context of Edinburgh, while attracting tourism-related revenue to the city and to Scotland as a whole. As leader of the new EIF, Bing sought to rekindle Glyndebourne through the establishment of a European arts festival. Edinburgh was however below Oxford, Bath, Chester, Cambridge and Canterbury on the list of cities he would have chosen to host this festival (Bartie 2013). Nevertheless, due to the forces at play, EIF was created, and has remained one of Edinburgh's leading festivals. Its founding vision persists in its aim: to reunite people through great art and 'provide a platform for the flowering of the human spirit' (Edinburgh International Festival 2018).

Performing the Festival

The second place-myth narrative of Edinburgh as the festival city is that of performing the festival as people perform places in semiotic self-constructed encounters with the festivals (Crouch and Lübbren 2003). This narrative is illustrated by the semiotics of festivalgoers in the city's spaces and places. While busy streets are a visual marker of festivalisation in any city, this enduring narrative of Edinburgh's festivals can be traced to the evolution of the Fringe. Also conceived in 1947, unlike EIF the Fringe was not planned by civic stakeholders or artists, and its origins relate to a different chronicle of Edinburgh folklore. That year, eight groups of performers that had not been invited to appear at the EIF decided to take advantage of the Festival atmosphere in Edinburgh and travelled to the city to perform independently (Edinburgh Festival Fringe 2020). The results were said to engender a sense of spontaneity and transience, different to other festivals. Indeed, in 1948, the title of 'Fringe' festival was conceived by the playwright and journalist, Robert Kemp, of the Edinburgh Evening News, writing: 'round the fringe of the official Festival drama there seems to be a more private enterprise than before' (Moffat 1978, 17).

The Fringe is now the world's largest multi-arts festival and accounts for more than half of Edinburgh's annual visitors (BOP Consulting and Festivals Edinburgh International 2016a). It is supported by the administrative Festival

Fringe Society which was established in 1958 and has responsibility for centrally supporting the functions of the festival. Rather than curating the Fringe, the Society ensures the festival retains its open-access constitution, maintaining that 'anyone can take part in the Fringe' (Edinburgh Festival Fringe 2020). This narrative of the Fringe being for everyone readily contributes to Edinburgh's festival-city place-myth, where anyone can perform and consume the festivalised city. While the Fringe itself is not curated, this is not the case for many of its 300 or so venues. Often, performances and entire programmes are curated as part of venues' Fringe festival offers. Nonetheless, the Fringe itself has in recent years built upon its open-access origins by facilitating and managing street performance spaces in the centre of the city. These can be booked by anyone wishing to perform (Edinburgh Festival Fringe 2020), and in this context they lend an embodied sense of performance as they are produced and consumed in city centre spaces. In recent years, there has been some Fringe activity delivered outside of Edinburgh's centre, but this has not yet extended to Wester Hailes.

Conclusions

This chapter has considered the semiotic narratives of management and community stakeholders regarding the contested places and spaces of Edinburgh as the festival city. These narratives of *staging* and *performing the festival* and their contribution to Edinburgh's Festival city place-myth have been discussed. These are based on myths associated with EIF and the Fringe; and are founded upon post-war cultural internationalist notions of bringing people together and being for everyone. It is possible to reflect upon this idealised view of Edinburgh as the festival city, alongside the contemporary socio-political and cultural context of inclusion and accessibility. Arguably, these narratives and their associated semiotic signs have been instrumental in contributing to Edinburgh's place-myth of being the world's leading festival city. It is clear, however, that for members of one community based to the southwest of the city, the festivals are not viewed as being for everyone. In other words, the places and spaces of Edinburgh the festival city are contested.

In terms of methodological significance, as mentioned, there has been some use of semiotics to understand urban and tourism settings. This approach has not been used previously in understanding place-myths or the layers of meaning associated with the festival city as a construct, beyond the brand. The present semiotic approach would lend itself to further studies in this area. Images may be objective and material or subjective and intangible: all crucial components of place-myths (Crouch and Lübbren 2003). Furthermore, those who create and consume such images are themselves semioticians who engage with a hermeneutical and circular process of collecting and communicating these place-myths (MacCannell 1999; Urry and Larsen 2011; Scarles 2014).

There are practical implications of this study that are significant to the use and management of urban space. As highlighted earlier, Edinburgh's festival and destination management stakeholders face criticism for the concentration of festival activities in the historic centre of the city, and the associated negative impacts. Conversely, communities outside the city centre, such as Wester Hailes, would value more inclusive and localised festival activity. At the time of writing, Edinburgh's festivals remain threatened by the ongoing global pandemic. Rather than event tourism activities being of strategic concern, Edinburgh's festival managers, and other city-based festivals stakeholders, could shift focus towards stronger engagement with local communities. As highlighted by the semiotics of the Wester Hailes festival city map, residents are keen to highlight their preferred festival activities and locations. Managers could collaborate with community stakeholders therefore to co-design the staging and performing of the festival within local communities, to build upon the current centre-focused Edinburgh festival city identity and place-myth.

The similarity of semiotic signs between stakeholder groups was striking, but their locations varied. The narrative of staging the festival was communicated through the semiotics of Edinburgh Castle surrounded by light, fireworks and images of festivalisation. Such signs were dominant in the festival managers' Instagram images. It is notable however, that similar signs were depicted by the Wester Hailes community stakeholders on their map. This was interesting as it supported the notion of the city effectively staging the festivals from the platform of Edinburgh Castle, in the centre, itself on a raised volcanic rock of a stage. Both groups presented iconic, symbolic and indexical signs that communicated layered narratives of staging through fireworks, light, festival activities and performances around the castle. It was clear, however, that these were very much confined to the Old Town in the city centre, where most of the activity is concentrated. The festival city map replicated these signs but concentrated in the Wester Hailes area. This supports the value of some festival activity being redistributed away from the centre to better engage with communities.

The narrative of performing the festival was significant in its tangible absence from Wester Hailes, and its presence in the various requests and suggestions for more festivals, arts, performances and other types of activities locally. Practical suggestions of festival activities, along with suitable places and spaces to perform the festivals in Wester Hailes were offered. This too may be of relevance to festival managers in future planning for more inclusive festivals for local community stakeholders; and in continuing to develop Edinburgh as the world's leading festival city.

References

Albers, Patricia and William James. 1988. Travel Photography: A Methodological Approach. *Annals of Tourism Research*, 15(1), 134–158.

Anderson, Simon, Richard Kinsey, Ian Loader and Connie Smith. 1994. *Cautionary Tales: Young People and Policing in Edinburgh*. Aldershot: Avebury Publishing.

Antchak, Vladimir and Tomas Pernecky. 2017. Major Events Programming in a City: Comparing Three Approaches to Portfolio Design. *Event Management*, 21(5), 545–561.

Banks, Marcus and David Zeitlyn. 2015. *Visual Methods in Social Research*. London: Sage.

Barthes, Roland. 1993. *Mythologies*. London: Vintage.

Bartie, Angela. 2013. *Edinburgh Festivals: Culture and Society in Post-War Britain: Culture and Society in Post-War Britain*. Edinburgh: Edinburgh University Press.

Berger, Arthur Asa. 2011. Tourism as a Postmodern Semiotic Activity. *Semiotica*, 183, 105–119. https://doi.org/10.1515/semi.2011.006

Bing, Rudolf. 1972. *5000 Nights at the Opera*. Garden City, NY: Doubleday.

BOP Consulting and Festivals and Events International. 2016a. *Edinburgh Festivals 2015 Impact Study*. Available at: https://www.edinburghfestivalcity .com/assets/000/001/964/Edinburgh_Festivals_-_2015_Impact_Study _Final_Report_original.pdf?1469537463 (accessed 6 September 2020).

BOP Consulting and Festivals and Events International. 2016b. *Thundering Hooves 2.0: A Ten-Year Strategy to Sustain the Success of Edinburgh's Festivals*. Available at: http://www.edinburghfestivalcity.com/about/documents/196 -thundering-hooves (accessed 6 September 2020).

City of Edinburgh Council. 2018. *Edinburgh People Survey 2018 Results*. Available at: https://www.edinburgh.gov.uk/downloads/download/13249 /edinburgh-people-survey-2018-results (accessed 11 December 2020).

City of Edinburgh Council. 2019. *Edinburgh by Numbers: Overview of Statistics*. Available at: https://www.edinburgh.gov.uk/downloads/file/25200 /edinburgh-by-numbers-2019 (accessed 8 December 2020).

Cockburn Association. 2020. 'City for Sale': The Commodification of Edinburgh's Public Spaces. Available at: http://www.cockburnassociation .org.uk/blog/91/41/City-for-Sale-the-commodification-of-Edinburgh-s -public-spaces-publication-of-presentations (accessed 23 March 2020).

Colombo, Alba and Greg Richards. 2017. Eventful Cities as Global Innovation Catalysts: The Sónar Festival Network. *Event Management*, 21(5), 621–634.

Crouch, David and Nina Lübbren (Eds.) 2003. *Visual Culture and Tourism*. Oxford: Berg.

Culler, Jonathan. 1981. Semiotics of Tourism. *The American Journal of Semiotics*, 1(1/2), 127–140.

Dooghe, David. 2015. Festival City, Rotterdam. In Chris Newbold, Christopher Maughan, Jennie Jordan and Franco Bianchini (Eds.) *Focus on Festivals*, pp. 26–27. Oxford: Goodfellow Publishers.

Echtner, Charlotte. 1999. The Semiotic Paradigm: Implications for Tourism Research. *Tourism Management*, 20(1), 47–57.

Evans, Claire and Ray Jones. 2004. Engagement and Empowerment, Research and Relevance: Comments on User-Controlled Research. *Research Policy and Planning*, 22(2), 5–13.

Edinburgh International Festival. 2018. *A Festival of Stars.* Available at: https:// 70years.eif.co.uk/history/#a-festival-of-stars (accessed 8 December 2020).

Ferguson, Brian. 2021. Edinburgh tourism chief admits rethink is needed on how its festivals impact on the city, *The Scotsman.* 1 February 2021. Available at: https://www.scotsman.com/whats-on/arts-and-entertainment/edin burgh-tourism-chief-admits-rethink-needed-how-its-festivals-impact-city -3120372 (accessed 1 February 2021).

Festivals Edinburgh. 2016. *Edinburgh's Festivals Engaging Communities Changing Lives.* Available at: https://www.edinburghfestivalcity.com /assets/000/002/846/Engaging_Communities_-_July_2017_original .pdf?1499869060 (accessed 16 May 2021).

Festivals Edinburgh. 2020a. Welcome to Edinburgh, the world's leading festival city. Available at: https://www.edinburghfestivalcity.com (accessed 13 October 2020).

Festivals Edinburgh. 2020b. Festival City Vision to 2030. Available at: https:// www.edinburghfestivalcity.com/about/vision (accessed 16 May 2021).

Florida, Richard. 2002. *The Rise of the Creative Class.* New York: Basic Books.

Gaines, Elliot. 2006. Communication and the Semiotics of Space. *Journal of Creative Communications*, 1(2), 173–181.

Gaines, Elliot. 2007. The Semiotic Analysis of Myth: A Proposal for an Applied Methodology. *The American Journal of Semiotics*, 17(2), 311–327.

Getz, Donald and Stephen J. Page. 2016. Progress and Prospects for Event Tourism Research. *Tourism Management*, 52, 593–631. https://doi.org/10.1016 /j.tourman.2015.03.007

Glendinning, Miles. 2005. Housing and Suburbanisation in the Early and Mid-20th Century. In Brian Edwards and Paul Jenkins (Eds.) *Edinburgh: The Making of a Capital City*, pp. 150–167. Edinburgh: Edinburgh University Press.

Goffman, Erving. 2002 [1959]. *The Presentation of Self in Everyday Life.* London: Penguin.

Gold, John Robert and Margaret Gold. 2020. *Festival Cities: Culture Planning and Urban Life.* Abingdon: Routledge.

Grandison, Tanis. 2018. Folklore and Digital Media: Unpacking the Meaning of Place Through Digital Storytelling. In Rebecca Rouse, Hartmut Koenitz and Mads Haahr (Eds.) *International Conference on Interactive Digital Storytelling, ICIDS 2018, Dublin, Ireland, 5—8 December 5–8, Proceedings*, pp. 652–656. Cham: Springer.

Häussermann, Hartmut and Walter Siebel. 1993. Festivalization of Urban Policy: Urban Development Through Major Projects. *Leviathan*, 13, 7–31.

IFEA. 2020. *International Festivals and Events Association: Past IFEA World Festival & Event Cities.* Available at: https://www.ifea.com/p/industryawards /worldfestivalandeventcityaward/pastrecipients (accessed 23 November 2020).

Jamieson, Kirstie. 2004. Edinburgh: The Festival Gaze and its Boundaries. *Space and Culture*, 7(1), 64–75.

Jamieson, Kirstie and Louise Todd. 2019. The Transgressive Festival Imagination and the Idealisation of Reversal. *Leisure Studies*, 40(1), 57–68. https://doi.org/10.1080/02614367.2019.1693090

Jamieson, Kirstie and Louise Todd. 2020. Negotiating Privileged Networks and Exclusive Mobilities: The Case for a Deaf Festival in Scotland's Festival City. *Annals of Leisure Research*, 1–18. 25:1, 5–22 [2022]. https://doi.org/10.1080/11745398.2020.1809478

Kallin, Hamish and Tom Slater. 2014. Activating Territorial Stigma: Gentrifying Marginality on Edinburgh's Periphery. *Environment and Planning A*, 46(6), 1351–1368.

Laestadius, Linnea. 2017. Instagram. In Luke Sloan and Anabel Quan-Haase (Eds.) *The SAGE Handbook of Social Media Research Methods*. Los Angeles, CA: Sage.

Lagopoulos, Alexandros. 1993. Postmodernism, Geography, and the Social Semiotics of Space. *Environment and Planning D: Society and Space*, 11(3), 255–278.

Lagopoulos, Alexandros. 2014. Semiotics, Culture and Space. *Σημειωτκή-Sign Systems Studies*, 42(4), 435–486.

Landry, Charles. 2012. *The Creative City: A Toolkit for Urban Innovators*. London: Earthscan.

Lee, Peter and Alan Murie. 2002. The Poor City: National and Local Perspectives on Changes in Residential Patterns in the British City. In Peter Marcuse and Ronald Van Kempen (Eds.) *Of States and Cities: The Partitioning of Urban Space*, pp. 59–87. Oxford: Oxford University Press.

Leask, Anna. 2019. Case Study Edinburgh City Tourism in 'Overtourism'? In *Understanding and Managing Urban Tourism Growth Beyond Perceptions – Volume 2: Case Studies*, pp. 44–46. Madrid: UNWTO.

Lowrey, John. 2001. From Caesarea to Athens: Greek Revival Edinburgh and the Question of Scottish Identity within the Unionist State. *The Journal of the Society of Architectural Historians*, 60(20), 136–157.

MacCannell, Dean. 1999. *The Tourist: A New Theory of the Leisure Class*. Berkeley, CA: University of California Press.

McCrone, David and Brian Elliott. 1989. *Property and Power in a City*. Basingstoke: Macmillan.

MacDowall, Lachlan John and Poppy de Souza. 2018. 'I'd Double Tap That!!': Street Art, Graffiti, and Instagram Research. *Media, Culture & Society*, 40(1), 3–22.

McGillivray, David, Severin Guillard and Emma Reid. 2020. Urban Connective Action: The Case of Events Hosted in Public Space. *Urban Planning*, 5(4), 252–266.

Moffat, Alistair. 1978. *The Edinburgh Fringe*. London: Johnston and Bacon.

Murray, Garold, Naomi Fujishima and Mariko Uzuka. 2014. The Semiotics of Place: Autonomy and Space. In Garold Murray (Ed.) *Social Dimensions Of Autonomy In Language Learning*, pp. 81–99. London: Palgrave Macmillan.

NCCPE. 2017. *What is public engagement?*. Available at: https://www.publicen gagement.ac.uk/about-engagement/what-public-engagement (accessed 7 February 2021).

Peirce, Charles Sanders. 1992. *The Essential Peirce: Selected Philosophical Writings*. Vol. 2. Bloomington, IN: Indiana University Press.

Pennington, Jody and Robert Thomsen. 2010. A Semiotic Model of Destination Representations Applied to Cultural and Heritage Tourism Marketing. *Scandinavian Journal of Hospitality and Tourism*, 10(1), 33–53.

Pink, Sarah, Heather Horst, John Postill, Larissa Hjorth, Tania Lewis and Jo Tacchi. 2015. *Digital Ethnography: Principles and Practice*. Los Angeles: Sage.

Prentice, Richard and Vivien Andersen. 2003. Festival as Creative Destination. *Annals of Tourism Research*, 30(1), 7–30.

Quinn, Bernadette. 2005. Arts Festivals and the City. *Urban Studies*, 42(5–6), 927–943.

Richards, Greg. 2017. Emerging Models of the Eventful City. *Event Management*, 21(5), 533–543.

Richards, Greg and Robert Palmer. 2012. *Eventful Cities: Cultural Management and Urban Revitalisation*. Oxford: Butterworth-Heinemann.

Scarles, Caroline. 2014. Tourism and the Visual. In Alan C. Lew, Michael Hall and Allan M. Williams (Eds.) *The Wiley Blackwell Companion to Tourism*, pp. 325–335. Chichester: John Wiley & Sons.

Schechner, Robert. 2003. *Performance Theory*. London: Routledge.

Shields, Rob. 1992. *Places on the Margin: Alternative Geographies of Modernity*. London: Psychology Press.

Scottish Government. 2020. SIMD: *Scottish Index of Multiple Deprivation*. Available at: https://www.gov.scot/collections/scottish-index-of-multiple -deprivation-2020/ (accessed 5 January 2021).

Smith, Andrew. 2014. 'Borrowing' Public Space to Stage Major Events: The Greenwich Park Controversy. *Urban Studies*, 51(2), 247–263.

Smith, Andrew. 2016. *Events in the City: Using Public Spaces as Event Venues*. Abingdon: Routledge.

Smith, Andrew. 2019. Event Takeover? The Commercialisation of London's Parks. In Andrew Smith and Anne Graham (Eds.) *Destination London: The Expansion of the Visitor Economy*, pp. 205–224. London: University of Westminster Press. https://doi.org/10.16997/book35.j

Thomasson, Sarah. 2015. *Producing the Festival City: Place Myths and the Festivals of Adelaide and Edinburgh*. PhD thesis, Queen Mary University of London.

Todd, Louise, Anna Leask and John Ensor. 2017. Understanding Primary Stakeholders Multiple Roles in Hallmark Event Tourism Management. *Tourism Management*, 59, 494–509.

Todd, Louise and Ashleigh Logan-McFarlane. 2019. Iconicity and Myth-making: Exploring Visual Representations of Edinburgh as the Original 'Festival

City'. Academy of Marketing, 18th Annual Colloquium on Arts, Heritage, Nonprofit and Social Marketing, University of Stirling, September 2019.

Turner, Victor. W. 1982. *From Ritual To Theatre: The Human Seriousness of Play*. New York: PAJ Press.

Turner, Victor. W. 1987. The Anthropology of Performance. In Victor Turner (comp.) *The Anthropology of Performance*. New York: PAJ Publications.

UNESCO. 2021. Old and New Towns of Edinburgh. Available at: https://whc .unesco.org/en/list/728 (accessed 15 January 2021).

Urry, John. 1990. *The Tourist Gaze: Leisure and Travel in Contemporary Societies*. London: Sage Publications.

Urry, John and Jonas Larsen. 2011. *The Tourist Gaze 3.0*. Los Angeles: Sage.

Williams, Raymond. 1985. *Keywords: A Vocabulary of Culture and Society,* Oxford: Oxford University Press.

Ziakas, Vassilios. 2020. Event Portfolio Management: An Emerging Transdisciplinary Field of Theory and Praxis. *Tourism Management*, 83, 104233.

PART 4

Festivals, Events and Economic Development in Towns and Small Cities

Unravelling the Complex Nature of Events-Focused Policy: A Framework to Aid Understanding

Elaine Rust

Introduction

This chapter explores the events-focused policy often adopted by local authorities, the aim of which is usually to attract visitors into town centres in the hope that additional economic activity will result. This is one of a range of tools employed by town centre managers (TCMs), buisness improvement district (BID) managers or local authority officials as they attempt to animate urban spaces and add vibrancy to what can sometimes be perceived as mundane or functional town centres, while at the same time demonstrating to local businesses that they are implementing policies that help to drive up footfall and support local economic activity. High profile, large-scale annual festivals, such as the Edinburgh International Festival or Notting Hill Carnival have done much to promote the success of such a policy, with commercial economic impact studies indicating significant revenue benefits (e.g. London Development Agency 2003; SQW Consulting 2005). As attractive as they may seem, large-scale events such as these are rarely attainable for smaller cities and towns.

How to cite this book chapter:
Rust, E. 2022. Unravelling the Complex Nature of Events-Focused Policy: A Framework to Aid Understanding. In: Smith, A., Osborn, G. and Quinn, B. (Eds.) *Festivals and the City: The Contested Geographies of Urban Events*. London: University of Westminster Press. Pp. 211–230. London: University of Westminster Press. DOI: https://doi.org/10.16997/book64.l. License: CC-BY-NC-ND 4.0

Further, not all towns have the existing infrastructure to enable an events-focused policy to be successful. The research presented here explores how one local authority in the south of England implements its local economic development policy through an events programme, in order to demonstrate the complexities involved: complexities of place as well as event, and the interconnected nature of both. Serving as a cautionary example for TCMs, BID managers and local economic development officers alike, a framework to aid understanding of the delicate balance is proposed.

The framework comprises a set of factors based on empirical research undertaken at three different events in separate market towns within the Test Valley Borough Council (TVBC)[1] area of Hampshire. The aim of this framework is to provide policymakers and other local decision makers with a structure that facilitates understanding of the implications of hosting events in their respective town centres and high streets. In addition, it is intended to help such decision makers reflect on what they aim to achieve by hosting an event or series of events and encourages them to consider that increased footfall may not necessarily result in increased economic activity for the town's retail and service provision. This framework is at an early stage of development and although it would benefit from further testing, global events have, unfortunately, overtaken the ability to do this. Consequently, a Covid-19 recovery consideration may need to be accounted for, incorporating factors such as perceived risk, health and safety issues and crowd management.

The British Town Centre Predicament

The crisis facing British town centres and high streets has been well-documented for more than a decade, with considerable debate at all levels of government, as well as much academic study. Various issues have contributed to this crisis, not least of which is the Covid-19 pandemic. The resulting landscape is very complex, and more than one strategy will be needed to provide a means of recovery for the ailing town centres, the number of which continues to rise. First came the effects of the 2008 financial crisis, combined with historical issues centred on disputed planning laws (PP21), which resulted in large out-of-town developments and the resulting move away from traditional centres. Then came the internet revolution, partnered with changing consumer behaviour, which saw the advent of 'click and collect' and home delivery services, both of which have grown significantly during the Covid-19 pandemic (ONS 2021). Until this pandemic all but closed down Britain's high streets and town centres, the most pressing problem concerned uncertainty and weakening consumer confidence brought about as a result of the Brexit vote and the ongoing lack of decisive action. In addition to this, retailers and service providers in town centres were often saddled with lengthy leasehold contracts and excessive local taxation. These combined issues were sufficient to cause many town centres and high streets to suffer from increasing and long-term vacancy rates. TCMs and other local decision makers thus began to seek additional means of attempting to attract more footfall into these places in the hope that additional spend by visitors would boost the local economy.

Town Centre Revitalisation Attempts

There have been numerous efforts over the last decade to increase understanding of how to support town centre revitalisation, for example the Portas Review published in 2011 (Portas 2011), which resulted in 28 recommendations, some of which were successful, others less so. The recommendations acknowledged the importance of markets, one of which was to create a national market day (recommendation no 4). Acknowledging that not all towns were suffering either in the same way or to the same extent, Wrigley and Dolega (2011, 2538) determined that a town's 'adaptive capacity and resilience' were contributory factors to its ability to survive at times of crisis.

In response to the Portas Review, Grimsey (2013) outlined an alternative vision for the future of town centres and saw them becoming community hubs with less reliance on the traditional retail provision. This review also called for a step change in the way business rates were charged. More recently, in 2019, the High Streets Task Force (HSTF) was created with membership from industry, government and academia to tackle the systemic problems experienced by some town centres and high streets.

An update to the 2013 Grimsey Review was published in 2018, followed by a Covid-19 Supplement in June 2020 (Grimsey 2020). This latest publication emphasises the need to put the community at the centre of the reimagined town centres and high streets – much the same role performed by town and village centres in centuries gone by. Grimsey further recommends the creation of more green space and cites an example from Belgium, where a town centre car park that has been transformed into green space now provides an area for events to be located (Grimsey 2020, 27). Accordingly, small-scale events, such as food festivals, markets and music or arts festivals have a role to perform in this reimagined town centre of the future, supporting a Covid-19 recovery.

The Appeal of an Events-Focused Policy

A wide assortment of events punctuates the everyday familiarity of numerous town centres and high streets in the UK, adding vibrancy and providing the opportunity to create memorable experiences for all involved – from the weekly market, some of which can trace their origins back at least to the Middle Ages, when authority to hold a market or fair was granted to landowners or the monarch's representative by Royal Charter (Letters 2005; Stanley, 1889), through to monthly speciality markets, such as farmers' markets, to the less frequent annual arts or music festivals, or Christmas markets. These are all occurrences that resonate with many and are used by TCMs and the like to perpetuate interest and encourage repeat visits. Some extend to just a few hours, while others may continue for a number of weeks. This variance of timescales offers a flexible approach to local policymakers, as costs and resources vary accordingly.

Festivals and events are known to provide a focal point for local communities, often bringing diverse groups together to create a 'heterotopia'; even if only for a limited time (Quinn and Ryan 2019). Further, they are capable of engendering a sense of place (Derrett 2003) or civic pride (Gration et al. 2016), and offer a forum for creating or strengthening social capital (Wilks 2011). Festivals and events have the potential to transform the image of a place, which in turn leads to renewal, even in small, rural towns (Connell and Gibson 2011). For town centre visitors, the overall experience is enhanced when events take place (Stocchi, Har and Haji 2016), as they offer a stimulus for excitement and encourage interaction with supplementary activities. Recognising the significance of town centre events, the British Government has published advice for town centre management relating to the benefits of developing an events programme (Housing Communities and Local Government Committee 2019). Taking all of this into consideration, it is hardly surprising that a crammed events programme is a popular feature of most places – or at least until the Covid-19 pandemic halted such endeavours, once public gatherings were prohibited.

Covid-19 and its effects aside, an events-focused strategy seems particularly appealing when they are seen to achieve a high profile and demonstrate success in one form or another elsewhere. Well-known examples include Hay-on-Wye Literary Festival, Notting Hill Carnival and Edinburgh International Festival. These festivals take over the host location and its environs for a period of time and act to promote the place to a wider, often global, audience. In turn, this activity serves as a tourist promotion to attract visitors long after the festival is over. Such a prominent legacy effect is a driver for other towns to engage in similar ventures (Finkel and Platt 2020; Richards 2017).

At a smaller, and arguably more widely accessible scale, research has found that regular markets (e.g. weekly charter markets, which sell a wide and varied assortment of goods) increase footfall (Hallsworth et al. 2015). Grimsey has acknowledged the 'crucial role' played by events in driving increased footfall in his supplement and, indeed, his case study of Roeslare, Belgium, explicitly alludes to a coordinated series of events (2020, 43).

The theory is clear; that an events-focused policy need not be an onerous venture in order to reap the benefits. In reality, many other factors are at play. A vital caveat is this: simply because an event is successful in one place, assumptions should not be made that success will be repeated if the event is replicated elsewhere. Success can be measured in multiple ways, for example: increased footfall; consumer/visitor/retailer satisfaction or cooperation; intention for repeat visits; increased turnover in host retail and service provision. TCMs and local decision makers need to consider these different measurements prior to embarking on an events-focused policy and, in addition, manage expectations of all stakeholders in order that priorities can be set accordingly.

The additional complication now is that although events are significant contributors to driving footfall into town centres, with distancing measures and additional health and safety requirements, events that are likely to attract large crowds are going to remain challenging for the foreseeable future. The topic of Covid-19 in Britain has been notably confused by the perception that Government policy may have ignored prevention (Scally, Jacobson and Abbasi 2020) and because communications appear to change with some regularity. Ntounis et al. (2020) have attempted to provide clarity with regard to social distancing measures for individuals and groups in 'dynamic spaces' (i.e. where people are constantly moving), such as town centres. With the arrival of the so-called 'Freedom Day' on Monday 19 July 2021 in England, when most legal restrictions were removed (Cabinet Office 2021), including the compulsory maintenance of a two-metre distance between individuals, this advice may not be necessary in the longer term. Despite criticism of the Government's decision to proceed with this decision (Ball 2021), the relaxation of legislation should come as welcome news for smaller towns, such as traditional market towns with narrow street patterns, some of which introduced one-way pedestrian traffic at the start of the pandemic.

Test Valley Borough Council's Approach to Events-focused Policy

TVBC is a semi-rural borough within the county of Hampshire, in the south of England, with three main urban centres of differing sizes. Andover to the north is the largest, both geographically and in terms of population; Romsey to the south is somewhat smaller; and Stockbridge, located in the centre is the smallest. Each of these places was considered historically to be a market town, having been granted a Royal Charter to hold markets and fairs during the twelfth and thirteenth centuries (Letters 2005; Stanley 1889). Both Romsey and Stockbridge retain many historic characteristics, including for Romsey, narrow winding streets. Although Andover also has some historic remnants, it has largely been engulfed by modern development, including a covered shopping centre, which has moved the focal point of the town away from the traditional square.

The borough's Local Economic Development team considers their events programme to perform a vital role in the broader economic development policy, to the extent that its expansion has been included in the third action point of the Economic Development Strategy Action Plan 2016–19, along with environmental enhancement, 'to improve the offer of our town centres' (Test Valley Borough Council 2016, 1). The borough-wide calendar of events includes weekly charter markets, monthly farmers' markets and annual festivals, including an agricultural show. These are included in tourist promotion literature, in conjunction with details of visitor attractions and historical information, as a means of illustrating the vibrancy and character of the area, in order to attract visitors.

The size, layout and infrastructure of the towns is such that any event held within them is going to be limited in scope. It is worth mentioning, therefore, that the earlier examples provided of large-scale city-centred festivals are unrealistic for places such as these. Market towns are much smaller, in terms of population and geographic size, so present different characteristics, opportunities and challenges.

Three Different Events for Three Different Market Towns

This research examines a separate one-day event that takes place in each of the three market towns described above. As one of the project sponsors, TVBC originally requested an economic impact assessment of the borough's annual events to be undertaken. It transpired, however, that there was no annual event of note held in Andover, so a monthly event was included instead. A brief overview of each event and respective town now follows, while a more comprehensive account can be found in Rust (2017).

The Beggars Fair: Romsey

This annual folk and roots music festival takes place on the second Saturday of July. However, it was cancelled in 2020 and has been cancelled for 2021, owing to ongoing uncertainty about public gatherings. The event has a chequered history, having originated as a weekend festival in 1993. It is organised by a committee of local community groups, businesses, residents and town councillors, and is free to attend. A road closure enables the various musicians and performers to be located at numerous sites around the town centre, while the mediaeval street pattern facilitates the containment of sounds, yet simultaneously provides enticement to visitors as they wish to discover the origin of music heard in the distance, or around narrow turns. A pedestrianised area in front of the Abbey provides space for a stage and a curtain-sided trailer is used for this purpose (see Figure 12.1). The town's public houses also play host to bands during the day and into the evening. In addition, a recreation ground adjacent to the town centre is used for children's activities and a forum to showcase young musicians, as well as to provide an area for visitors to sit and absorb the atmosphere.

Although the Beggars Fair is promoted as a family event, it has experienced troubles in the past and began to develop a reputation as an event for drunkards. This culminated in a serious public order incident in 2011, reported

Figure 12.1: Beggars Fair, Romsey. Photograph: Elaine Rust.

as a 'mass brawl' in the local press (Russell 2011). As a result, the event was reviewed and reduced to a single day. Further mitigations were implemented to prevent similar behaviour in future, for example, an alcohol ban in public open spaces and all pubs required to install fencing and employ security guards for the duration of the event. The memory of this incident endures and has created division within the local community.

Trout 'n About: Stockbridge

Trout 'n About is an annual food and craft festival, which has taken place on the first Sunday in August since 2008. Perhaps unsurprisingly, it was cancelled as a live event in 2020, however it relocated online as a virtual event spanning 16 days and it is planning to resume the live version in 2021. The festival is organised by a committee of local volunteers and a salaried event manager, and draws on additional support from local community groups. Trading stalls, vintage farm equipment displays and musicians are located along both sides of the long, straight Georgian High Street but owing to the nature of the road and the absence of alternative routes, it is not possible to close the road (see Figure 12.2). Traffic congestion can be a problem, as the event draws in large numbers from a wide area.

The name of the festival originates from the historic connection between the River Test, which runs through the town, and trout fishing. Stockbridge is

Figure 12.2: Trout 'n About, Stockbridge. Photograph: Elaine Rust.

renowned in the fly-fishing fraternity, with the Grosvenor Hotel in the High Street providing a home for the historic and exclusive Houghton Fishing Club. This connection is not clearly understood by many visitors and is not especially aided by the lack of trout-related produce available to purchase at the event. A concern that has not gone unnoticed by the organisers, however, they struggle to include the local fish-related producers.

Andover Farmers' and Crafts Market

The market was introduced by the local authority in an attempt to draw visitors to the town on Sundays, which have seen lower footfall than other days of the week. It is located along the part-pedestrianised High Street, adjacent to a covered shopping centre and takes place once a month between February and December. Prior to the introduction of the market, a countywide rotating farmers' market, run by an independent organisation, visited once a month. With disappointing sales and despite the offer of a financial incentive to retain Andover on its circuit, it withdrew as members felt they would benefit from increased business elsewhere in the county. The current market is managed by a member of TVBC staff. Although the market aims to attract visitors to the town in order to support the existing retail offer, during its earlier days many of the retailers remained closed on Sundays, thus losing out on potential business. Attempts have since been made to encourage Sunday opening, with varying levels of success. Andover has suffered from higher than average, as well as

Figure 12.3: Andover Farmers' and Crafts Market. Photograph: Elaine Rust.

long-term vacancy rates (Carter Jonas 2018) and Marks and Spencer, one of the town's major retailers, closed their store in April 2018.

The stalls offer a mix of fresh locally sourced produce, confectionery, art and crafts, and offers space to local charities wishing to promote themselves (see Figure 12.3). The market also provides low-cost opportunities for emerging local businesses that may not be in a position to commit to a permanent retail space.

Research Methods and Data Collection

As previously mentioned, TVBC requested an economic impact assessment be undertaken of the three events, to produce evidence of how interventions such as those included in the study contribute to the borough's economic vitality. In order to develop a more 'holistic and contextualised picture' (Peperkamp, Rooijackers and Remmers 2015, 147) of how the studied events contributed in a broader social and cultural sense, a qualitative component was added. Thus, a mixed methods approach was taken and implemented across all three locations. Data were collected via two primary methods: semi-structured interviews with event organisers, local councillors, local government officers and event sponsors; and questionnaire surveys of event attendees, event traders/ performers, local businesses and residents. The purpose of the interviews was to develop an understanding of how and why the events were created; how they have evolved over time; perceived benefits and any associated issues. The questionnaires captured attitudinal data, the purpose of which was to aid understanding of likes, dislikes and behaviours connected to the events. In addition to this, expenditure data were also collected from event visitors, performers and traders, which contributed to the economic impact assessment.

Findings and Discussion

Economic Impact

The results indicate that it is the *type* of event that influences the level of economic benefit the host location receives. Events with a predominantly selling focus have the potential to draw expenditure away from the town's retail offer. Such was the case for both the farmers' market and the food festival (Trout 'n About). In contrast, an event that is predominantly entertainment-focused (i.e. the folk music festival – the Beggars Fair) can result in the opposite, although expenditure is likely to occur mainly in the food and drink service providers. Specifically, these results indicate that the expenditure ratio of event:town provision is approximately 2:1 for selling-type events and reversed for entertainment events (Rust 2017).

The attendant advice is that if a policymaker introduces a speciality market, or food-related event or festival in order to increase footfall and by association, to increase turnover for the host town's retail offer, this could be an erroneous strategy, unless other factors are accounted for and priorities adjusted accordingly. If, however, the local authority, BID Manager or TCM works with the relevant stakeholders to develop a mutually beneficial event, then it could prove to be successful. The Beggars Fair organising committee membership includes representatives from the local authority, local businesses and community groups (e.g. the local scout group), who each work together to ensure cooperation, which supports the mutual benefit. For example, the local food service providers can be overwhelmed on the day of the event, so the scout group runs a barbeque to alleviate pressure. The scout group benefits financially from the income to their organisation, as well socially, by connecting with the community. A further example presented itself at Trout 'n About, whereby the local football club provided car parking stewards and as a result, it benefited from a small funding grant donated by Trout 'n About's organising committee from surplus event income.

Social and Cultural Impacts

In terms of the social and cultural impacts, four key factors emerged from the interpretation of qualitative data. These suggest that a combination of each contribute to the ability of a town centre or high street to be able to provide an event that is both suitable for the host and that will be able to benefit the local economy and community satisfactorily. The key to success is finding the appropriate balance between each of these factors, in conjunction with the requirement to support the local economy. The four factors are now discussed.

Atmosphere or 'Buzz'

Atmosphere in this context is connected to enjoyment, which contributes to the overall visitor experience (Getz 1989). This pleasant 'feel good factor' (Crompton 2004) has also been referred to as 'psychic income' in the literature (Crompton 2004; Gibson et al. 2014; Kim and Walker 2012). Not always easy to define, it is nevertheless closely connected to the way in which events can generate a positive feeling for all stakeholders involved, whether this is event attendees, event traders/performers, sponsors, organisers, or local businesses.

Evidence emerged from the three events that the positive atmosphere created by the events animated the towns, at least for a temporary period, and contributed to positive memories of the events and the places in which they were located. This was strongest at the Beggars Fair and Trout 'n About, as illustrated by an attendee's remark of the Beggars Fair: *'Romsey comes alive with a lovely friendly musical atmosphere.'* This emotion was much weaker at the farmers' market, where no such comments were made.

Belonging

This factor can be divided into two separate forms: the first is the level to which the event generated a sense of belonging for those involved: becoming a temporary 'insider', whether the attendee was from the local community or a visitor to the area. Cultural events provide the opportunity for out-of-the-ordinary, shared experiences and can generate a sense of belonging (del Barrio, Devesa and Herrero 2012; Getz 1989). This seemed to be strongest in relation to the annual events (i.e. the Beggars Fair and Trout 'n About), demonstrated by a resident's comment that the Beggars fair *'brings [the] community together.'* For a limited time, visitors to the towns of Romsey and Stockbridge felt as though they were locals, owing to the friendly and open environment in which the events were located. Some attendees additionally remarked that they deliberately scheduled their visit to the area to coincide with the events taking place; a suggestion that they wished to rekindle the sense of belonging they felt while at the event. Further, there was a suggestion that arrangements need not be made in advance to meet acquaintances, as a respondent noted: *'it's a very social event; I might see somebody I know.'*

The concept of exclusivity, by its very nature, implies there are outsiders – those who are not members of the group. The feeling of exclusivity can enhance the sense of belonging (Richards and Palmer 2010), but for the outsiders – those who do not attend or wish to be involved – the events can become problematic. This was displayed in various ways. First, local residents who disliked the town being taken over, particularly in Romsey where there was a history of antisocial behaviour at the Beggars Fair:

> I just don't think it's 'Romsey'. It attracts undesirables – why do we want that and the trouble it brings?

Second, at Trout 'n About, elderly or vulnerable residents in particular felt as though they were unable to leave their homes for the day owing to the crowded pavements, as demonstrated by an elderly resident: *'I only get out when someone takes me in my wheelchair and I never go to Trout n About, as it is impossible to get through the crowds with a wheelchair.'* Finally, the farmers' market was not popular with some Andover residents, who expressed their feelings of exclusion by commenting that it was either selling goods already available in the town's shops or the produce was overpriced. The latter sentiment was clearly evident in the following: *'due to the price they tend to attract a certain type of customer, which makes the atmosphere quite snobby.'*

The second form in which belonging emerged as a key factor, is the connection or fit of the event to the place – the level to which the event 'belongs' to the host location. This overlaps with place, which is discussed next.

Place

Place can also be divided into two components: First, in relation to the host town and second in relation to the physical location of the event within the host town.

Place (a): Geographic location of the host town

Powe and Hart (2008) and Powe, Pringle and Hart (2015) have discussed the characteristics of market towns and their varying ability to attract visitors, proposing that those with historic buildings, natural features or neighbouring connections to visitor attractions are most likely to benefit. Gibson et al. (2009) argue that place features strongly in the connection between culture and economic development and Richards, de Brito and Wilks (2013) observe that cultural events enable people to create their own connections to place. This latter observation has been discussed in the previous factor, however, altogether, the literature clearly connects place and events.

In this study, all three towns are considered to be market towns by the local authority and are promoted as such. Each was granted a charter centuries ago to hold markets and fairs at various times throughout the year, so became focal points for their respective communities. Over time, this dependence has diminished, however, at different rates in each place.

Both Romsey and Stockbridge align with the findings of Powe and Hart (2008) and Powe, Pringle and Hart (2015) in that they retain historic characteristics and benefit from natural features and neighbouring attractions, so are already popular with visitors. The events are a natural fit with these locations and so, place and event are connected. Contrastingly, the farmers' market in Andover struggles, despite TVBC's consideration that it remains a market town in the traditional sense. The town has retained some historic features, for example, a museum and a former mill, which has been converted to multiple retail units. With much modern development, including the covered shopping centre, it struggles to retain the market town image, leading to a lack of connection for visitors between the farmers' market and the town. In essence, the event has an unnatural fit with the town and the sense of belonging is absent.

Place (b): Spatial location of the event

The physical spaces occupied by the events within each of the towns influence the ways in which they are experienced. The Beggars Fair is spread around the mediaeval town, with its narrow winding streets, as well as other locations, such as the recreation ground and pedestrian area in front of the Abbey. The buildings act as natural sound barriers, so noise is contained yet wafts around the street corners, enticing visitors to follow the source and discover the particular act. Trout 'n About is structured in a linear fashion, along both sides of the Georgian High Street, offering the visitor a clear line of sight along all of the stalls, enabling them to absorb everything easily. Both locations suit their respective events. Andover's farmers' market, on the other hand, is located in what would once have been the focal point of the town: a paved open area in front of the former town hall, now a café, slightly offset from the modern centre. Although a large expanse of open space, it can act as a wind tunnel, causing traders problems as they struggle to keep their gazebos secured, along with their produce. In addition, the micro locations matter: concerns were raised that consideration should be given to the location of stalls selling produce which is also on sale in the host town, for example, at Trout 'n About, a cheese stall was located directly in front of the delicatessen. Whilst the delicatessen recognised the value of the event and was in favour of it, the owner would have preferred the cheese stall to be located elsewhere. Another local independent business owner expressed frustration by stating that '*organisers should NOT duplicate goods or produce already sold in Stockbridge shops. It's just not fair!*' A small, yet clearly significant consideration.

Reputation

Bradley and Hall (2006) argue that a town's public image can be enhanced by a public event, however, an event's previous reputation can also be sufficient for it to be considered unwelcome by the community (Hubbard 2013). Antisocial behaviour, or the anticipation of it, can damage an event's reputation more than any other negative attribute, for example congestion or noise (Deery and Jago 2010). This final factor – reputation – can also be separated into two: the reputation of the event and of the place.

In terms of the event, TVBC uses all of the events in its tourist promotion material. In this way, it expects the event reputation to act as an incentive for visitors to come and contribute to place promotion. Unfortunately, in the case of the Beggars Fair, a reputation of excess alcohol consumption leading to antisocial behaviour has spread around the local community and to the neighbouring towns and villages. No serious incident has been recorded since the one mentioned earlier, however, the reputation seems to endure, as demonstrated by an attendee's comment; *'when it gets to the evening you're not so keen to stay because of the – you know – possibility of perhaps not feeling quite as safe.'* The mere thought of antisocial behaviour seems to be sufficient reason not to linger.

With regard to Trout 'n About, the name is a reference to the River Test, on which Stockbridge is located. The Test enjoys international renown for trout fishing, a day licence for which costs many hundreds of pounds. This reference is sadly lost to many visitors who are unfamiliar with this local speciality, with some visitor respondents querying the absence of trout. This is in contrast with a similar event held in Alresford, around 15 miles away, which holds an annual watercress festival, acknowledging the local connection to watercress production. The majority of the stallholders offer watercress-related products, including watercress flavoured ice cream, and cookery demonstrations using watercress are a feature of the day.

In terms of the place, how the locations are perceived is important. Romsey and Stockbridge already benefit from the characteristics discussed earlier that serve to make these towns attractive to visitors. In contrast, Andover suffers from a poor reputation, and the impression of an uninspiring town emerged from the study, as one resident remarked; *'Unfortunately, the town centre has been allowed to degenerate because of the quality of shops … this makes us avoid the town centre.'* The perception that a town will have little to offer prospective visitors may outweigh any attraction the market provides.

Understanding Event Contributions in a Town Centre Context: A Framework

The factors discussed above can combine to form a framework for policymakers, TCMs, BID managers and other decision makers to use when developing

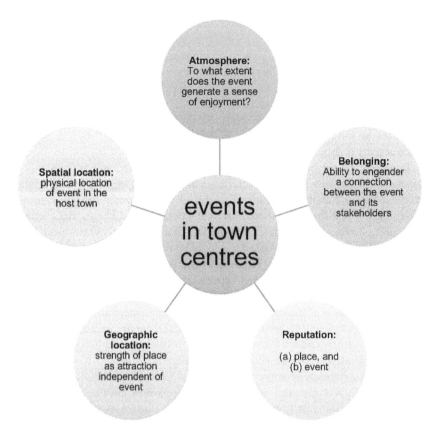

Figure 12.4: Framework for understanding town centre event contributions.

an economic strategy centred on a programme of events. When used alongside the common aim of generating economic activity, local decision makers should gain a clearer understanding of events-focused policy outcomes. The framework, shown in Figure 12.4, demonstrates the interconnected relationship between each of the factors discussed above, with place separated into the two components identified. By applying the framework, potential problems and mistakes may be avoided, particularly if an attempt is made to replicate an event that has been seen to be successful elsewhere. Most importantly, before doing this, the decision maker should consider what it is they are aiming to achieve: increased footfall, economic activity, or community well-being.

Conclusion

The study presented here has demonstrated how one local authority in the south of England supports an events-focused policy in its three main urban centres by exploring a different event in each of the towns. A complex illustration has emerged, suggesting that many factors contribute to the success or otherwise of such events, which is not always thoroughly appreciated by the local decision makers who develop these strategies. At the simplest level, events attract people, which increases footfall. There is an expectation that this additional footfall should result in increased economic activity for the host location's businesses. This is the prominent perspective adopted, at least by TVBC and potentially representative of many local authorities in the UK. Such an expectation may, however, be misguided. Evidence included here suggests that any increase in such activity is dependent upon the type of event.

Events can perform other roles within a market town setting, especially those events that complement the characteristics of the host town. There is no doubt that events such as those examined in this chapter animate their host locations, even if just for a few hours, but policymakers should be cautious when attempting to create an artificial fit, especially if a successful event – whatever 'successful' may mean – is repeated in a location that appears to possess similar characteristics – at least superficially – as the venture may not be replicable. Although the framework proposed here requires further exploration it, nonetheless, provides initial focus for local policymakers and other decision makers to aid prioritisation of the reasons for wanting to implement an events-focused policy and second, to gain an understanding of likely consequences.

There are clearly challenges ahead for the towns included here; challenges that are replicated across the entire United Kingdom. Further insights may be gathered by extension of survey work beyond the south of England but the level to which attitudes and perceptions of events may have been altered by the Covid-19 pandemic is not known. This aspect increases the value of the current findings that were obtained via face-to-face interviews and interviewer-administered surveys.

An uncertain future adds another dimension to the existing complications. Although the current Government legislation on distancing and group gatherings is to be relaxed, there is no guarantee that tighter restrictions will not be reinstated should another Coronavirus outbreak emerge. However, those centres that possess the 'adaptive capacity and resilience' (Wrigley and Dolega 2011, 2358), as discussed earlier, may be in a better position to survive such turbulence. The ability to adapt events in accordance with the respective guidelines may be an additional factor to include in a refined framework. Thus, this research offers the potential for additional work in the context of Covid-19 recovery strategies.

Notes

[1] The project was mainly funded by the Economic and Social Research Council (ESRC) with TVBC (Test Valley Borough Council) acting as an industry sponsor, which was a condition of the ESRC funding.

References

Ball, Philip. 2021. Why England's COVID 'Freedom Day' Alarms Researchers. *Nature*, 2021 (14 July). Available at: http://www.nature.com/articles/d41586-021-01938-4 (accessed 16 July 2021).

Bradley, Andrew and Tim Hall. 2006. The Festival Phenomenon: Festivals, Events and the Promotion of Small Urban Areas. In David Bell and Mark Jayne (Eds.) *Small Cities: Urban Experience Beyond the Metropolis*, pp. 75–90. Abingdon: Routledge.

Cabinet Office. 2021. *Guidance: Coronavirus: how to stay safe and help prevent the spread from 19 July* Cabinet Office. Available at: https://www.gov.uk/government/publications/covid-19-response-summer-2021-roadmap/coronavirus-how-to-stay-safe-and-help-prevent-the-spread#contents (accessed 16 July 2021).

Carter, Jonas. 2018. *Andover and Romsey Retail Capacity and Leisure Study.* Available at: https://www.testvalley.gov.uk/planning-and-building/planning policy/evidence-base/evidence-base-local-economy

Connell, John and Chris Gibson. 2011. Elvis in the Country: Transforming Place in Rural Australia. In Chris Gibson and John Connell (Eds.) *Tourism and Cultural Change: Revitalising Rural Australia*, pp. 175–193. Bristol: Channel View Publications. http://site.ebrary.com/lib/soton/docDetail.action?docID=10478184

Crompton, John. 2004. Beyond Economic Impact: An Alternative Rationale for the Public Subsidy of Major League Sports Facilities. *Journal of Sport Management*, 18(1), 40–58.

Deery, Margaret and Leo Jago. 2010. Social Impacts of Events and the Role of Anti-Social Behaviour. *International Journal of Event and Festival Management*, 1(1), 8–28.

del Barrio, María José, María Devesa and Luis César Herrero. 2012. Evaluating Intangible Cultural Heritage: The Case of Cultural Festivals. *City, Culture and Society*, 3(4), 235–244.

Derrett, Ros. 2003. Festivals & Regional Destinations: How Festivals Demonstrate a Sense of Community & Place. *Rural Society*, 13(1), 35–53. https://doi.org/10.5172/rsj.351.13.1.35

Finkel, Rebecca and Louise Platt. 2020. Cultural Festivals and the City. *Geography Compass*, 14(9), e12498. https://doi.org/10.1111/gec3.12498

Getz, Donald. 1989. Special Events: Defining the Product. *Tourism Management*, 10(2), 125–137. https://doi.org/10.1016/0261-5177(89)90053-8

Gibson, Chris, Gordon Waitt, Jim Walmsley and John Connell. 2009. Cultural Festivals and Economic Development in Nonmetropolitan Australia. *Journal of Planning Education and Research*, 29(3), 280–293. https://doi.org/10.1177/0739456x09354382

Gibson, Heather, Matthew Walker, Brijesh Thapa, Kiki Kaplanidou, Sue Geldenhuys and Willie Coetzee. 2014. Psychic Income and Social Capital

Among Host Nation Residents: A Pre-Post Analysis of the 2010 FIFA World Cup in South Africa. *Tourism Management*, 44(Oct), 113–122.

Gration, David, Maria Raciti, Donald Getz and Tommy Andersson. 2016. Resident Valuation of Planned Events: An Event Portfolio Pilot Study. *Event Management*, 20(4), 607–622. https://doi.org/10.3727/152599516X14745497664596

Grimsey, Bill. 2013. *The Grimsey Review: An Alternative Future for the High Street*. vanishinghightstreet.com. Available at: http://www.vanishinghigh street.com/wp-content/uploads/2016/03/GrimseyReview04.092.pdf

Grimsey, Bill. 2020. *Build Back Better, Covid-19 Supplement for Town Centres*. vanishinghightstreet.com. Available at: http://www.vanishinghighstreet.com /wp-content/uploads/2020/06/Grimsey-Covid-19-Supplement-June-2020.pdf

Hallsworth, Alan, Nikos Ntounis, Cathy Parker and Simon Quin. 2015. Markets Matter: Reviewing the Evidence & Detecting the Market Effect. Institute of Place Management blog. Available at: http://blog.placemanagement .org/2016/04/28/markets-matter-reviewing-the-evidence-detecting-the -market-effect

Housing Communities and Local Government Committee. 2019. *High Streets and Town Centres in 2030* (Eleventh Report of Session 2017–19 HC1010), 21 February. Available at: https://publications.parliament.uk/pa/cm201719 /cmselect/cmcomloc/1010/full-report.html

Hubbard, Philip. 2011. Carnage! Coming to a Town Near You? Nightlife, Uncivilised Behaviour and the Carnivalesque Body. *Leisure Studies*, 32(3), 265–282. https://doi.org/10.1080/02614367.2011.633616

Kim, Woosoon and Matthew Walker. 2012. Measuring the Social Impacts Associated with Super Bowl XLIII: Preliminary Development of a Psychic Income Scale. *Sport Management Review*, 15(1), 91–108. https://doi.org /10.1016/j.smr.2011.05.007

Letters, Samantha. 2005. Gazetteer of Markets and Fairs in England and Wales to 1516. Available at: http://www.history.ac.uk/cmh/gaz/gazweb2.html (accessed 23 December 2014).

London Development Agency. 2003. *The Economic Impact of the Notting Hill Carnival*. London: LDA.

Ntounis, Niko, Christine Mumford, Maria Loroño-Leturiondo, Cathy Parker and Keith Still. 2020. How Safe is it to Shop? Estimating the Amount of Space Needed to Safely Social Distance in Various Retail Environments. *Safety Science*, 132, 104985. https://doi.org/10.1016/j.ssci.2020.104985

Office of National Statistics (ONS). 2021. *Retail Sales in Great Britain, January 2021*, 19 February. Available at: https://www.ons.gov.uk/businessindustry andtrade/retailindustry/bulletins/retailsales/january2021

Peperkamp, Esther, Margo Rooijackers and Gert-Jan Remmers. 2015. Evaluating and Designing for Experiential Value: The Use of Visitor Journeys. *Journal of Policy Research in Tourism, Leisure and Events*, 7(2), 134–149. https://doi.org/10.1080/19407963.2014.951938

Portas, Mary. 2011. The Portas Review: An Independent Review into the Future of Our High Street. Available at: http://www.bis.gov.uk/news/topstories/2011/Dec/portas-review

Powe, Neil, and Trevor Hart. 2008. Market Towns: Understanding and Maintaining Functionality. *Town Planning Review*, 79(4), 347–370. https://doi.org/10.3828/tpr.79.4.2

Powe, Neil, Rhona Pringle and Trevor Hart. 2015. Matching the Process to the Challenge Within Small Town Regeneration. *Town Planning Review*, 86(2), 177–202. https://doi.org/10.3828/tpr.2015.11

Quinn, Bernadette and Teresa Ryan. 2019. Events, Social Connections, Place Identities and Extended Families. *Journal of Policy Research in Tourism, Leisure and Events*, 11(1), 54–69. https://doi.org/10.1080/19407963.2018.1465067

Richards, Greg. 2017. From Place Branding to Placemaking: The Role of Events. *International Journal of Event and Festival Management*, 8(1), 8–23. https://doi.org/10.1108/ijefm-09-2016-0063

Richards, Greg, Marisa P. de Brito and Linda Wilks. 2013. *Exploring the Social Impacts of Events*. Abingdon: Routledge.

Richards, Greg and Robert Palmer. 2010. *Eventful Cities: Cultural Management and Urban Revitalisation*. Oxford: Butterworth-Heinemann.

Russell, Tara. 2011. Drunken thugs go on rampage at festival. *Southern Daily Echo*. 11 July. Available at: https://www.dailyecho.co.uk/news/9134484.drunken-thugs-go-on-rampage-at-romseys-beggars-fair (accessed 14 January 2021).

Rust, Elaine. 2017. *The Impacts of Small-Scale Cultural Events on Market Town Vitality*. PhD, Publication Number BLL01018722196. Southampton: University of Southampton.

Scally, Gabriel, Bobbie Jacobson and Kamran Abbasi. 2020. The UK's Public Health Response to Covid-19. *BMJ,* 369, m1932. https://doi.org/10.1136/bmj.m1932

SQW Consulting. 2005. *Edinburgh's Year Round Festivals 2004–2005 Economic Impact Study*. Edinburgh: SQW Ltd /TNS Travel and Tourism. Available at: https://www.efa-aef.eu/media/12314-sqw_economic_impact_report__01.09.05_original.pdf

Stanley, E. H. 1889. *Royal Commission on Market Rights and Tolls. First Report of the Royal Commission on Market Rights and Tolls … Relating to the History of Fairs and Markets in the United Kingdom. Vol. I.* London: Her Majesty's Stationery Office.

Stocchi, Lara, Cathay Har and Iftakar Haji. 2016. Understanding the Town Centre Customer Experience (TCCE). *Journal of Marketing Management*, 32(17–18), 1562–1587. https://doi.org/10.1080/0267257X.2016.1242510

Test Valley Borough Council (TVBC). 2016. *Test Valley Economic Development Strategy 2016–19 Action Plan*. Available at: https://www.testvalley.gov.uk/business/businessgrantsandsupport/test-valley-economic-development-strategy-2016-19

Wilks, Linda. 2011. Bridging and Bonding: Social Capital at Music Festivals. *Journal of Policy Research in Tourism, Leisure & Events*, 3(3), 281–297. https://doi.org/10.1080/19407963.2011.576870

Wrigley, Neil and Les Dolega. 2011. Resilience, Fragility, and Adaptation: New Evidence on the Performance of UK High Streets During Global Economic Crisis and its Policy Implications. *Environment and Planning A*, 43(10), 2337–2363. https://doi.org/10.1068/a44270

CHAPTER 13

Come Enjoy the Craic: Locating an Irish Traditional Music Festival in Drogheda

Daithí Kearney and Kevin Burns

Introduction

Fleadh Cheoil na hÉireann (hereinafter 'the Fleadh') is a festival of Irish traditional music, begun in 1951 by the organisation Comhaltas Ceoltóirí Éireann (CCÉ), to promote Irish traditional music, song and dance that they believed were in danger of dying out. The Fleadh is an integral element of a revival in these traditions and has been held since in many parts of the country often located in a town for two or three consecutive years at a time (Kearney 2013). It was held in the town of Drogheda on the east coast of Ireland for the first time in 2018. The Fleadh has a very significant economic impact on the host town or city, and audiences have grown substantially from earlier events to reach reported crowds of 500,000 (CCÉ 2019a) and 750,000 for the two years the event was held in Drogheda. An estimated €50 million was generated in the host region (CCÉ 2019b). Although the competitions held on the concluding weekend of the event provide the major foci for the organisers, the Fleadh typically runs for eight days with visitors lingering for a day or two afterwards and continuing to engage in musical activity. The early part of the week involves

How to cite this book chapter:
Kearney, D. and Burns, K. 2022. Come Enjoy the Craic: Locating an Irish Traditional Music Festival in Drogheda. In: Smith, A., Osborn, G. and Quinn, B. (Eds.) *Festivals and the City: The Contested Geographies of Urban Events*. London: University of Westminster Press. Pp. 231–247. London: University of Westminster Press. DOI: https://doi.org/10.16997/book64.m. License: CC-BY-NC-ND 4.0

workshops in various instruments and formal events including dinners and gatherings that honour people involved in the promotion of Irish culture and traditions. The post-Fleadh activity primarily involves musicians and is evident in the ongoing sessions of Irish traditional music in public houses and some public spaces.

The Fleadh is a multi-faceted festival and this chapter focuses on the use and reconfiguration of public spaces rather than the music, workshops, competitions, or ticketed concerts. The importance of music in public spaces at the Fleadh is significant as, despite the very large numbers attending the Fleadh, ticket sales for formal events are typically low. This leads to greater engagement with public spaces and 'free' entertainment, with large numbers of people busking or engaging in 'live music' sessions in public houses or other available spaces. One of the key challenges for any town hosting the Fleadh or a similar music festival is to adapt the use of public spaces to facilitate a large number of people and music-making on the streets. Fundamental to overcoming this challenge is the engagement of all stakeholders; and management is often complex due to relationships with, and amongst, stakeholders.

The research for this project involved interviews with representatives of the local authority and festivals organisers and is also informed by ethnographic reflections. The individuals quoted in this chapter represent one group of decision makers, and were chosen to reflect official attitudes to and plans for the reconfiguration of public spaces in the town. The researchers provide emic (within social group) and etic (observer) perspectives. One of the authors (Daithí) is an Irish traditional musician and was involved in the organisation of some of the events at the Fleadh and attended events at each of the three spaces examined during both years of the festival. He had particular responsibility for the programming of the Gig Rig, on which he also performed and acted in the role of MC (in rotation with others). As a member of the organising team for the event, he has a particular insider perspective. The second researcher (Kevin) is not involved in Irish traditional music and did not have an active role in the event but engaged with the festival as a participant from the area who is active in research and teaching. The research collaboration sought to balance emic and etic perspectives of the event. Both authors visited the town together during the summer of 2020, observing changes or remaining evidence of the presence of the Fleadh in the streetscape (see Figure 13.1).

In this chapter, the study focuses on three reconfigured spaces: the Fleadh Gig Rig in Bolton Square, St Laurence's Gate, and the Main Street including St Peter's Plaza. These spaces were chosen as they are the main spaces for free public engagement, contrasting with paid venues or competition spaces. They were reconstructed to allow for elements of the Fleadh to be superimposed on a host town to allow for very large crowds to experience the festival. These temporarily created performance spaces demonstrate potential alternative uses of these public spaces. The survival and success of events similar to the Fleadh

Figure 13.1: Evidence of the efforts to enliven derelict buildings for the Fleadh that have been neglected since. Photograph: Daithí Kearney.

are dependent on those 'primary' stakeholders who are most involved and engaged (Reid 2007). This chapter primarily documents the views of the local authority with subsequent studies required to engage with other stakeholders.

The Fleadh and Drogheda

Being granted the opportunity to host the Fleadh is a very competitive process, reflecting increasing inter-urban competition for large-scale events that are not always located in the same place (see also MacLeod 2006). The Fleadh is a partnership between CCÉ and the local authority and a Drogheda Fleadh Bid Committee that first met in the D Hotel, Drogheda, on 24 January 2012 (Robinson 2020). Drogheda applied for five successive years before being selected by CCÉ, losing out to Sligo and Ennis before being selected ahead of a bid from Cork City. The bid was led by the volunteer chairperson of the local branch of CCÉ, Lolo Robinson, and the Chief Executive of Louth County Council, Joan Martin. Martin was Town Clerk for Drogheda Borough Council at the time of the first bid but, with changes to the structures of local government in Ireland, became Chief Executive of Louth County Council during the period. Martin took a keen personal interest in the bid and ensured support from the council, including the assignment of one of her management team, Paddy Donnelly,[1] to the Fleadh Executive Committee (FEC).

The Local Authority emphasised creating an economic impact, in contrast with the cultural aspirations of CCÉ who aspired to promote the traditional arts. The location of Drogheda between the major cities of Dublin and Belfast and the existence of a large town centre that could be adapted (and pedestrianised) for an event such as the Fleadh were significant in planning for the event. It is noteworthy that Drogheda is Ireland's largest town by population but located in the smallest county by area (Louth, 827km^2), although the town is partially located in the neighbouring county of Meath. There are conflicting messages within the Fleadh promotional material that describes Drogheda as 'a small town with lots to offer' (CCÉ 2018a: 7) but also 'the biggest town in Ireland, a vibrant cosmopolitan town with two of the largest shopping centres in the country nestled among countless artisan retailers' (CCÉ 2018b: 5). Between 2017 and 2019 there were several unsuccessful representations from local groups to the national government to declare Drogheda a city.

The Fleadh committee in Drogheda recognised that many attendees of the Fleadh go for the live music, the street entertainment and to consume alcohol and do not attend competitions or ticketed performances. Thus, there was a need to give considerable attention to the use and accessibility of public spaces and the provision of free entertainment, some of which is provided by the attendees themselves who require suitable spaces for performance. Preparations included the renovation, repurposing and painting of derelict buildings, while a massive street cleaning effort was undertaken each night by the local authority.

Reconfiguring Public Spaces

Unlike cities such as Oslo (Smith and von Krogh Strand 2011) or Bilbao (Ockman 2004), where music and art centres have become emblematic of the cities and play a key role in their regeneration, or in cities that have hosted major events such as World Expo or the Olympic Games and for which large buildings were constructed that remain part of the city's landscape (Smith and von Krogh Strand 2011), no new building was constructed in Drogheda for the Fleadh. However, existing structures and public spaces were utilised both as performance spaces and in imagery. Thus, the Fleadh festival space was socially constructed. Space was created, co-constructed and subverted by participants and attendees as a result of their engagement and participation in the music event. Drawing on the classification of space put forward by Lefebvre (1991), this chapter evaluates how the Fleadh embodied the triad of space – conceived, perceived and representational space – and explores how the social landscape of the Fleadh was formed.

The Fleadh is a multi-faceted event that requires a significant number of spaces to cater for different types of activities including performances, competitions, workshops, radio broadcasts and television recordings. Many activities take place in public spaces and Donnelly noted: 'there was an exercise done initially about identifying a number of the public spaces and open spaces that could be utilised to address the elements of the Fleadh' (7 July 2020). The main spaces initially considered included the location of a large Dome for ticketed performances and competitions, a Gig Rig for free open-air performances, and smaller stages for Fleadh TV, live broadcasts from the event. There was also a need to have other spaces where 'events could take place in a public street and that would be safe for pedestrians and participants' (Donnelly 2020). There was competition between various stakeholders for the use of spaces. There was a need to facilitate the crowds, large stages for performances and broadcasts, and for visitors who wished to perform on the street. Fleadh TV was a major stakeholder and they sought, early in the planning process, to use an open space near the river that might otherwise have been utilised for the Gig Rig. Instead, the Gig Rig was located in Bolton Square, with porous barriers erected to aid the delineation of space and management of people.

For the Fleadh, one key perceived space is that of the fences, the physical setting and security at the various events. These elements or 'architectures' give the sense of an inaccessible space that is rooted in the festival. Narrative mapping uncovers a more porous, produced space, what Lefebvre calls 'representational' space, that extends beyond the space and time of the Fleadh; thus the Fleadh has a legacy for the destination. The representational space created by the Fleadh conceptualises how participants alter, change and construct space through actions. Lefebvre's triad of space implies that each element informs the other; thus the lived experience at one stage in the Fleadh inspires the representational spaces which is co-constructed with and by those that are active in the space – be it impromptu performances or traditional music buskers creating their subverted space.

The ever-increasing control and regulation of festival spaces leads to what Lefebvre (1991) terms commodified or conceived space, which is structurally and socially controlled. Such a process began with the movement from free elements of the festival to the commercialisation of music festivals, and with which came an increase in health and safety regulations, codes and guidelines. This was evident during the Fleadh and due to an increase in health and safety regulation, codes and guidelines, the space in front of St Laurence's Gate was not used during the second year of the Fleadh. Lefebvre (1991) notes that architecture shapes the conceived space. In this way increased barriers and gatekeepers all act as architecture that informs the conceived space of the festival shaping how it is experienced. The parameters of the festival are heavily policed and this takes place in two ways. First by those seeking to keep people out, stopping the movement of people without tickets into the space. Secondly by security staff and barriers, and sometimes the police, that attempt to control the movement of contraband, or in this case performers, into the space.

This chapter identifies these elements of Lefebvre's triad of spaces, be it the sense of control portrayed by the Fleadh organisers and authorities or the space which is subverted by attendees and performers; or the conceived space which is structurally and socially controlled. The different spaces reflect differing social, cultural and political agendas and the interests of different groups of stakeholders. The streetscape outside St Peter's Church, which had been divided by a railing signifying the separation of Church and Public Property until the early 2000s, was utilised for broadcasts and by visiting performers. The Crescent Concert Hall was renovated and opened in time for the 2018 event. Furthermore, St Laurence's Gate, which had been recently pedestrianised and opened to the public for tours, was a significant presence in marketing. Bolton Square, location of the Gig Rig, was a car park and the location of a market since the fourteenth century.

Gig Rig, Bolton Square

The potential of Bolton Square as a location for events was identified in the 2013 Urban Design Framework (Louth County Council 2013). It is a large public space in the centre of the town that is easily accessible from several points. Its role in the Fleadh was significant as it was a space that provided live music free of charge for very large numbers of people. The acts included a mix of local artists and community arts groups and leading professional musicians. As Gibson and Connell (2005, 255–256) note, the importance of entertainment and the opportunity to hear good live music is often overlooked. The Gig Rig at Bolton Square provided access to free entertainment professionally presented, even when performed by community groups, which caught the attention of a lot of local people who may not otherwise have engaged in the Fleadh. It provides a snapshot of the diversity of the Fleadh, encapsulating both the community focus and the wider reach of the event (i.e. national radio broadcast and international performers).

For the stage in Bolton Square, Martin (2020) highlights the significant investment in a professional and high spec Gig Rig, which created a very positive impression and attracted people. It was the first aspect of the Fleadh that many people encountered for the opening of the Fleadh on Sunday 12 August 2018. For the Fleadh the location of Bolton Square was significant. Donnelly (2020) noted that:

Bolton Square then quickly became the preference for the Gig Rig as it was referred to because it was town centre, within the centre of that Fleadh

Figure 13.2a: Bolton Square Car Park. Photograph: Daithí Kearney (2020).

Figure 13.2b: The view from backstage on the Gig Rig during the Fleadh. Photograph: Robin Barnes (2019).

village type approach that we were taking and it was an area that could be easily managed. The challenges around it were the residents that surrounded it and the traders that face onto to site. So we engaged very early on with the residents on that.

Donnelly engaged in individual correspondence with the residents as the Runaí of the Fleadh committee, informed by his role with the Local Authority. He remembers that there was some concern from residents about the impact of activities in Bolton Square but they were reassured by the plan for managing activities and the benefits it would bring to the area. Their cooperation 'evolved in the months and particularly the last few weeks coming up to it when all of the houses surrounding it decked their houses out in flags and bunting for the Fleadh' (Donnelly 2020). Donnelly noted that there was a greater challenge with the businesses as, in some cases, there was reduced access to their normal customers, particularly at weekends, but the Council facilitated deliveries and worked 'to convince them that the benefits … they would get from people attending the Gig Rig would outweigh any shortcoming there was from the closure of traffic through traffic for the duration of the Fleadh'.

The Official Fleadh Opening each year was held on the Gig Rig Stage in Bolton Square and presided over by the President of Ireland, Michael D. Higgins. The attendance of the President, favourable weather and curiosity surrounding the opening event contributed to a large crowd estimated at 15,000 in the square. In advance of the President's arrival in 2018, music, song and dance was performed by staff, students and graduates from Dundalk Institute of Technology and members of Nós Nua – the Louth Youth Folk Orchestra. In 2019, the entertainment was provided by resident musicians in the Oriel Centre, Dundalk Gaol, a regional centre for CCÉ. The Taoiseach (Irish Prime Minister) Leo Varadkar also visited Drogheda both years and began a public walkabout from the Gig Rig. The Gig Rig provided a focal point for thousands of Fleadh visitors and was a popular attraction for locals with 80 performances and 59 hours of programming throughout eight days of the Fleadh.

There was an effort to encourage participatory activities at the Gig Rig. Dancing featured prominently in Bolton Square and local dance schools featured each day. The large square also made it possible to incorporate participatory dancing and a céilí[2] was held on a Wednesday night each year. Singing was also encouraged and, in 2018, the Monday night featured Cas Amhrán,[3] the culmination of a project whereby schoolchildren in Louth were taught several Irish-language songs in preparation for the Fleadh. The audience at the Gig Rig were encouraged to sing along. Although the schools' project did not take place in 2019, the event at the Gig Rig took place again. As well as Irish traditional music groups, two of the local brass bands and the Royal Meath Accordion Orchestra performed and included some Irish traditional music in their repertoire for the occasion. Groups from Korea and Turkey also added an international flavour with music from their respective traditions. Other international groups included Irish traditional music ensembles 'Ceoltóirí Óg na Breataine' and 'Feith an Cheoil' from Britain and the 'Centre for Irish Music Minnesota' from America.

While the Gig Rig did not feature on television broadcasts from the Fleadh, it did facilitate a live radio broadcast of RTÉ's *Céilí House* on the Saturday night each year, continuing a longstanding tradition. The official end of the Fleadh, a performance by the newly crowned All-Ireland Céilí Band Champions, also took place as the last event on a Sunday night at the Gig Rig. In 2019, this included a formal act of 'handing over' the Fleadh to the town of Mullingar for 2020. The focus on the Gig Rig for the opening and closing events of the Fleadh underlined its significance and, reinforced by the large numbers in attendance, ensured that it dominated many peoples' memories of the event.

'Music at the Gate', St Laurence's Gate

St Laurence's Gate is one of the most striking architectural structures in Drogheda and an important part of the tourism infrastructure. Smith notes 'the relationship between monuments, capital city status and tourism marketing' stating 'Monuments have always been useful promotional tools for cities; employed both in traditional advertising literature and as a more subtle form of place marketing' (Smith 2007, 79). St Laurence's Gate was utilised when CCÉ sent their selection panel to the town. Laurence Street became 'Fleadh Street', where a mini-Fleadh was presented for a day to the adjudicators. Martin (2020) stated: 'We used the spectacle of the street leading to the gate as part of our bid that year.' The Gate itself had been open to traffic until recently and this presented challenges for the utilisation of the space and the preservation of the building. Commenting on the potential to have music activities located at this space during the Fleadh, Donnelly noted that the pedestrianisation of St Laurence's Gate was 'ongoing before the Fleadh but the Fleadh was seen as something that was hopefully going to come to Drogheda'. Before and during the 2018 Fleadh, an event entitled 'Music at the Gate' took place.

Established independently of the FEC by local uilleann piper Darragh Ó Héiligh in September 2017 in anticipation of the Fleadh in Drogheda, 'Music at the Gate' took place on the pedestrianised area in front of St Laurence's Gate. Ó Héiligh noted that the first event was in response to the closure of the gate to traffic in the preceding weeks and was an effort to involve the local community in Irish traditional music and promote cooperation amongst stakeholders (interview, 27 August 2020). Despite the success of the event in attracting an audience, as well as performers who gave their time voluntarily, Ó Héiligh did not consider the space particularly suitable and organisers and performers had to negotiate several challenges. Nevertheless, Ó Héiligh believes that space was ideally located for people attending the Fleadh.

Figure 13.3: 'Music at the Gate'. Photograph: Robin Barnes (2018).

Figure 13.4: View of St Laurence's Gate. Photograph: Daithí Kearney.

This monument built in the twelfth century is a prominent emblem of Drogheda's heritage and provided a striking backdrop for musicians from Drogheda, other parts of Louth, Meath, Monaghan, Dublin and other areas of Ireland to share music in an open-air space on a Saturday morning. As a voluntary and family-friendly event, the website lists several aims including increasing the visibility and accessibility of traditional Irish music to everyone in Drogheda with emphasis on young families. Although not affiliated to CCÉ, there was significant representation from people also involved in the organisation of the Fleadh and members of the local branch.

'Music at the Gate' events were held every day during the Fleadh in 2018, but did not take place during the 2019 event due to difficulties complying with Health and Safety requirements set out by the Event Management company (Ó Héiligh 2020) and the location of spaces for televised recordings nearby (Drogheda Life 2019). While 'Music at the Gate' reflected a grassroots music desire to initiate change, it did so outside of the structures of the Fleadh and challenges relating to the use of public space, including issues of insurance and public safety, access to the tower for 'Visits to the Gate' and plans for filming in the area. While in many instances, efforts to 'professionalise' the Fleadh brought about benefits for performers and audiences, in this instance, it created challenges for those involved. This echoes the work of anthropologist Adam Kaul (2014) who has critiqued the tension between buskers and the local authority at the Cliffs of Moher. The politics of music festivals, including regulation and conflict, as well as identity construction in terms of authenticity, identity and performativity are key themes in Gibson and Connell's (2005) discussion of music festivals within the context of music tourism. Gibson and Connell note a shift in music festivals from a community orientation to commercial motives since the 1960s (2005, 211). However, it is notable that, at the Fleadh, many of the musicians, singers and dancers participate for the pleasure of the experience rather than for financial gain and the festival is also dependent on a very significant team of volunteers.

A statement from 'Music at the Gate' published in local newspapers prior to the 2019 Fleadh noted support for the initiative from Louth County Council, Drogheda Comhaltas, the Fleadh Executive Committee, Laurence Street residents and the commercial traders in Laurence Street and the surrounding area but acknowledged that 'Music at the Gate' was never a formal activity of the Fleadh programme in 2018. It states:

> There was an approach to the Fleadh Executive Committee early in 2019 to run 'Music at the Gate' during Fleadh 2019 on a more structured basis than it had been in 2018. The Fleadh Executive Committee (FEC) agreed that the event could be listed as a Fringe Event, but that the FEC, which is a small voluntary committee, did not have the resources to include it as a formal Fleadh event. (Drogheda Life, 2019, 1)

The FEC and their agents including Safe Events (the Fleadh Event Management Contractor) engaged with the organisers of 'Music at the Gate'. The ambitious plans for 'Music at the Gate' during Fleadh 2019 would have been accompanied by significant financial and production costs for the organisers that included stage and production management, sound, health and safety controls, security and medical cover to list a few. Despite the cancellation of some Fleadh activities, the efforts of Ó Héilligh and the 'Music at the Gate' team were otherwise recognised, including Ó Héiligh receiving a Local Hero award in August 2019 and Ó Héiligh and other regular contributors to 'Music at the Gate' engaged in other performances and music-making opportunities during the Fleadh.

It is arguable that unlike the Guggenheim in Bilbao (see Plaza, Tironi and Haarich 2009; Ockman 2004), St Laurence's Gate has not become a destination icon but, to some extent, it has developed a synecdochal role for Drogheda, being a part of the town but representing it as a whole (see also Smith 2005). The Council did do some minor works surrounding the Gate and, in conjunction with the Office of Public Works, the Gate was open for a small number of visits during the Fleadh. It was the backdrop for a lot of the television and video crews who wished to record artists playing in Drogheda and the success of it at the Fleadh has underlined the council's long-term plans is to improve that as a plaza area.

West Street and St Peter's Plaza

Drogheda retains aspects of the old medieval street layout. West Street provides a long but quite narrow street, which became the hub of the festival. The space in front of the church became an important space and was utilised for flash mobs and other broadcasts on Fleadh TV. Beyond the Fleadh, when the weather is fine the steps are a space that attracts people to sit and relax. St Peter's Parish Church is a Roman Catholic church in the French Gothic style built with local limestone ashlar in 1884. A popular tourist destination in the town, it contains the shrine of St. Oliver Plunkett, a local saint. The steps to the front of the building create a natural performance space that was popular during the Fleadh. Donnelly (2020) noted that when St Peter's Church was refurbished, it was agreed to take down the railings and create this open space in the centre of Drogheda that would be more inviting and more user friendly for people with access issues.

Like St Laurence's Gate, the church provided an iconic backdrop for some of the televised footage of the Fleadh. However, a large portion of this space remains the property of the church and there was close cooperation between the church authorities, the County Council, and CCÉ to ensure the safe use of this space, with agreements on issues such as insurance (Robinson 2020).[4]

One of the challenges for the FEC related to how the steps and plaza in front of St Peter's Church would be cleaned and how space would be managed. With the aid of the Garda Síochána, the steps were closed during the second year, with barriers each night from approximately 8.30 pm allowing capacity for them to be cleaned. It was a recognition that, beyond this time in the evening, the nature of the crowd and activities changed, affected by the consumption of alcohol. While there was never a significant issue, a changed approach was taken in the second year that was considered more successful.

It is clear from some of the printed material distributed by CCÉ that busking, the performance of music on the street in the expectation of receiving money from passers-by, is frowned upon. Nevertheless, there is a desire to have musicians play on the street and this has become a prominent feature of Fleadhanna Cheoil. Representatives of the County Council who were involved in the committee and who had visited the previous Fleadhanna in Clare and Cavan recognised the interest people had in artists performing on the street and sought to accommodate that, without engaging in a debate about the expectation of financial remuneration. Such a debate is beyond the remit of this chapter but it was noticeable that many musicians, particularly children and young people, performed with a receptacle, often an open instrument case, and received the money. Others, including some well-known older musicians, also performed on the street but with no visual means to collect money.

Opportunities and Challenges

The Fleadh seeks to promote a family-friendly atmosphere and many events facilitate inter-generational engagement. Activities such as Scoil Éigse, the weeklong workshops in Irish traditional music, song and dance, held in conjunction with the Fleadh, attracts large numbers of participants. However, the Fleadh has also been associated with the consumption of alcohol and has, since the 1950s, attracted a significant number of people who 'come for the craic' and engage in socialising without having a strong interest in the music or other involvement in CCÉ. The use and reconstitution of public spaces are critical to the success of the event.

Lefebvre (1991) acknowledges the constructed nature of the space, whilst also considering how it is simultaneously porous. The constructed and physical segregation of space at a Fleadh promotes, creates and changes the lived experience of festival attendees within it. The chapter identified how the Fleadh was spatially formed, segregating the contained spaces, before considering how they are being subverted and socially reconsidered. This division is important as it encourages a way of seeing space and conceptualising it. Space is segregated by using fencing, creating an inside and outside; these distinct areas have different production and consumption behaviours. For example at the Gig Rig, Bolton Square, the outside quickly becomes 'the real world', synonymous with everyday social, cultural norms and experiences of the normal production of labour, patterns and routines; while 'inside' becomes home with new forms of social and spatial phenomena and narratives, and where alternative production and consumption practices take place. The Gig Rig and 'Music at the Gate' have an almost invisible boundary between one socially controlled space and the emergence of a new form of space inside, one informed by a different set of norms and practices. The boundary of a Fleadh, the entry points and gates present a picture of social control. The gate and entry point between the two spaces is policed. This marshalling signifies how the authorities enforces social control – purposely making a statement about zero tolerance – which, within the fence, cannot and is not enforced to a successful degree.

Moving away from fencing there are other elements to the Fleadh that are unique in the space. Stages are erected to look out over the audience zone, and within the sites, there are designated areas for staff, performers, children, families, VIP campers and traders. 'Music at the Gate' utilised such space with different parameters– an elaborately constructed space, changing open streets into segmented spaces with their own sets of rules and regulations. As the space is segmented, objects take on new meanings, the lanyard takes on new importance by giving access to areas, allowing the owner freedom of movement or not. The ethnographic approach in the study identified a more porous construction of the Fleadh music festivals by their attendees and of what Lefebvre (1991) calls representational space, one that extends beyond the space and time of a festival. There is a longer-lasting effect and mentality that transcends the festival time and moves into attendee's everyday lives.

The success of the Fleadh in Drogheda can be measured on several levels but interviewees noted the engagement of the community as one aspect, in addition to the economic gains for business and the boost in marketing the town to a wider audience. The attendances at 'Music at the Gate' and the increased enrolment in Irish traditional music classes were also connected with the success of the Fleadh in promoting participation in Irish traditional arts.

Conclusion

The 'use and reconfiguration' of space in event contexts presents opportunities and challenges for stakeholders. Local authorities may make plans for these spaces and festival organisers may identify specific spaces for particular activities but it is critical to engage with other stakeholders for the event to be successful. Stakeholders may subvert or colonise spaces not intended as performance spaces, spaces for the consumption of alcohol or other activities that are engaged in during the Fleadh. Both the planned and unplanned activities highlight the potential of these spaces for future use and adaptation. There is an interrelationship between the social processes and the construction of space, with each influencing, shaping and transforming the other. Drawing on Lefebvre's (1991) classification of space, the chapter evaluated how the Fleadh context embodied the triad of space: conceived, perceived and representational space. The Fleadh attendees and performers appropriated and altered the space within the festival, producing space that allowed people to engage and play music in public spaces that were previously unused for such activities.

Drogheda demonstrated its success in terms of Fleadh attendance (750,000 people) and economic benefit (€50 million each year, Fáilte Ireland) but it is the reimagination of space in the town that may be the long-lasting legacy. The Fleadh was a flagship event that led to a reimagining of spaces in Drogheda and played an important role in the recognition of Drogheda as a 'Destination Town' by Fáilte Ireland. Joan Martin (2020) noted that a significant legacy for the town was the realisation that 'Drogheda can do festivals' and the enhanced confidence of local communities and businesses. Drogheda had the capacity both in terms of crowds and organisational resources and was well located to attract large crowds. The support and confidence of Fáilte Ireland, the National Tourist Development Authority in the town to deliver on future projects was also important. The successful use of public spaces highlighted how these spaces could be used differently, such as the part or temporary pedestrianisation of West Street for events – or in response to Covid-19 – as well as bringing Dominic's Park, the site of the Fleadh Dome, into public consciousness as a space that could be utilised more.

Notes

[1] At the time of the first Fleadh in 2018, Paddy Donnelly was Director of Services with Louth County Council with responsibility for operations and local services. He was seconded as a special project lead to facilitate the delivery of the Fleadh in 2018 and then subsequently reassigned again in 2019. He served as secretary to the Fleadh Executive Committee and was the Council liaison, providing an overarching awareness of council services as well as engaging with stakeholders on behalf of the Council around the Fleadh. He led a team that provided a secretariat to the Fleadh committee in Drogheda.

[2] While the word can refer to a social gathering in Irish or Scottish Gaelic, in this context it refers to a form of dancing, usually in sets of eight people.

[3] 'Cas Amhrán' involved primary school students learning six chosen Irish language songs in school before the Fleadh. The event was aimed at increasing children's awareness of Irish culture and tradition and encouraging them to immerse themselves in this year's Fleadh Cheoil na hÉireann.

[4] Concerns around security and a desire on the part of some to reinstate the railings were highlighted in local newspapers in July and December 2018, despite recognising the benefits of using the space during the Fleadh. (*Drogheda Independent* 2018; *Drogheda Life*, 2018).

References

Comhaltas, Ceoltóirí Éireann (CCE). 2018a. The Final Countdown to Fleadh Cheoil Na hÉireann. *Treoir*, 50(2), 2–7.

Comhaltas, Ceoltóirí Éireann (CCE). 2018b. Drogheda Welcomes Fleadh Cheoil Na hÉireann 2018. *Treoir*, 50(1), 4–5.

Comhaltas, Ceoltóirí Éireann (CCE). 2019a. Tuarascaáil Bliantúil. *Treoir*. Available at: https://treoir.comhaltas.ie

Comhaltas Ceoltóirí Éireann (CCÉ). 2019b. 750,000 Fans Share Fun and Fame at Friendship Fleadh. *Treoir*, 52(3), 4–5.

Drogheda Independent. 2018. Time to return the railings at the front of St Peter's Church, 8 December. Available at: https://www.independent.ie/regionals /droghedaindependent/localnotes/time-to-return-the-railings-at-the -front-of-st-peters-church-37590557.html

Drogheda Life. 2018. Violence and drunkenness on the streets of Drogheda condemned, 31 July. Available at: https://droghedalife.com/news/violence -and-drunkenness-on-the-streets-of-drogheda-condemned

Drogheda Life. 2019. No Music at the Gate during the Fleadh, 6 August. Available at: https://droghedalife.com/news/no-music-at-the-gate-during-the-fleadh (accessed 4 December 2021).

Gibson, Chris and John Connell. 2005. *Music and Tourism: On the Road Again*. Clevedon: Channel View Publications.

Kaul, Adam. 2014. Music on the Edge: Busking at the Cliffs of Moher and the Commodification of a Musical Landscape. *Tourist Studies*, 14(1): 30–47. https://doi.org/10.1177/1468797613511684

Kearney, Daithí. 2013. Regions, Regionality and Regionalization in Irish Traditional Music: The Role of Comhaltas Ceoltóirí Éireann. *Ethnomusicology Ireland*, 2/3, 72–94.

Lefebvre, Henri. 1991. *The Production of Space*. Oxford: Blackwell.

Louth County Council. 2013. *Urban Design Framework Plan for The Heritage Quarter, Drogheda*. Development Plan, Louth County Council. Louth: Louth Local Authorities. Available at: https://www.louthcoco.ie/en /publications/development-plans/drogheda-development-plan-/urban-design -framework-plan-drogheda-heritage-quarter.pdf

MacLeod, Nicola E. 2006. The Placeless Festival: Identity and Place in the Post-Modern Festival. In David Picard and Mike Robinson (Eds.) *Festivals, Tourism and Social Change: Remaking Worlds*, pp. 222–237. Clevedon: Channel View Publications.

Ockman, Joan. 2004. New Politics of the Spectacle: 'Bilbao' and the Global Imagination. In D. Medina Lasansky and Brian McLaren (Eds.) *Architecture and Tourism: Perception, Performance, and Place*, pp. 227–240. Oxford: Berg.

Plaza, Beatriz, Manuel Tironi and Silke Haarich. 2009. Bilbao's Art Scene and the 'Guggenheim Effect' Revisited. *European Planning Studies*, 17(11), 1711–29. https://doi.org/10.1080/09654310903230806

Reid, Sacha. 2007. Identifying Social Consequences of Rural Events. *Event Management*, 11(1–2), 89–98. https://doi.org/10.3727/152599508783943192

Smith, Andrew. 2005. Conceptualizing City Image Change: The 'Re-Imaging' of Barcelona. *Tourism Geographies*, 7(4), 398–423. https://doi.org/10.1080/14616680500291188

Smith, Andrew. 2007. Monumentality in 'Capital' Cities and Its Implications for Tourism Marketing: The Case of Barcelona. *Journal of Travel & Tourism Marketing*, 22(3–4), 79–93. https://doi.org/10.1300/J073v22n03_07

Smith, Andrew and Ingrid von Krogh Strand. 2011. Oslo's New Opera House: Cultural Flagship, Regeneration Tool or Destination Icon? *European Urban and Regional Studies*, 18(1), 93–110. https://doi.org/10.1177/0969776410382595

Interviews

Paddy Donnelly (2020), Louth County Council, 27 July.
Daragh Ó Héiligh (2020), Musician, 'Music at the Gate', 27 August.
Joan Martin (2020), Louth County Council, 5 August.
Lolo Robinson (2020), Drogheda CCÉ, 6 August.
Aideen Morrissey (2020), Louth County Council, 3 September.

CHAPTER 14

Public Value Outcomes of Festivals: Well-Being and Economic Perspectives

Niclas Hell and Gayle McPherson

Introduction

The values attributed to events and festivals are multifaceted and complex. The most commonly used concept of values presented in research and evaluations, as well as bids and prospects for events, is economic value (Brown et al. 2015). From a private organiser's viewpoint this is not surprising, being a primarily financial stakeholder. Public bodies (co-)organising events, however, tend to aim for wider notions of value rather than simply a positive bottom line figure. Despite this, Economic Impact Analysis (EIA) and methods for evaluating economic externalities such as multipliers, are the most common ways to present tangible value. This is complemented by an increasing trend of viewing events through the lenses of social and cultural perspectives, with a range of philosophical underpinnings, as described by Brown et al. (2015). These include human well-being and long-term cultural values, as well as triple bottom line perspectives (Fredline et al. 2005).

Due to the popularity of economic perspective approaches, alternatives have been expressed in open opposition to the economism of the status quo, both in terms of its limited scope and its inclination to be overly optimistic

How to cite this book chapter:
Hell, N. and McPherson, G. 2022. Public Value Outcomes of Festivals: Well-Being and Economic Perspectives. In: Smith, A., Osborn, G. and Quinn, B. (Eds.) *Festivals and the City: The Contested Geographies of Urban Events*. London: University of Westminster Press. Pp. 249–268. London: University of Westminster Press. DOI: https://doi.org/10.16997/book64.n. License: CC-BY-NC-ND 4.0

(Abelson 2011). Singular economic focus is not a constructive modus oper-andi for public bodies, and may limit their ability to produce good quality ser-vices for the public. However, retaining the economic perspective whilst also accounting for other values created in the hosting of public events and festivals gives additional opportunities for comparison, and deeper understanding of trade-offs. The dual perspective is present in some studies (Fredline et al. 2005), but there is no consensus on how to account for all that benefits the public's consumption of events. The Clifton, O'Sullivan and Pickernell (2012) Welsh study shows that although social and cultural *objectives* are common, these aspects are not evaluated. This chapter uses public value theory to explain the multitude of beneficial effects arising from events, and examines how this fits with the increasing need to tie to the neoliberal agenda of the marketplace and public bodies working in harmony. Using public value to assess events has been conducted in a small number of studies (Judd 1999; Foley, McGillivray and McPherson 2015), but none put this side-by-side with typical economic data such as willingness-to-pay and added value from local spending.

A public value perspective aids the understanding of festivals by assessing the effects of social change. Efforts to create change are almost invariably present in larger event initiatives hosted by public actors; positive economic externalities and providing beneficial social and cultural effects are prioritised by both local and national government event programmes. In the town of Paisley, Scotland, this dual focus was manifest in the bidding for UK City of Culture of the Year (UKCoC) 2021, ultimately losing to Coventry. Expected outcomes of investing heavily in culture were understood to be more than economic, including active efforts for equity and inclusion (Benington and Moore 2011). At the same time, the bid was created as a driving force in an urban regeneration scheme based on culture. The local authority's understanding of culture's potential to create many types of value, but with a need for economic regeneration, makes Paisley an interesting scene for assessment of public value.

Paisley Regenerated

Paisley is Scotland's largest town with some 77,000 inhabitants (NRS 2018). An old textile and automotive industry town, Paisley was hit hard by the deindustrialisation of the late twentieth century. Peaking at over 100,000 inhab-itants, Paisley shrunk in population, significance, reputation and economic output. During the second decade of the twenty-first century, a large-scale programme for cultural regeneration has been rolled out. Festivals and events have been placed at the core of the rebranding and regeneration strategy for Paisley. An ambitious events programme was a key tenet of City of Culture capabilities, and the local programme received increased funding and strategic development from the local authority during, and after, the bidding process. Bidding and legacy programmes have resulted in Paisley gaining ground as an event venue: the Halloween Festival was voted 'Best Cultural Event' of Western Scotland and gathered some 40,000 visitors (Visit Scotland 2019). Part of the bidding process enabled Renfrewshire Council to consult with a range of stakeholders, businesses and citizens around the use of space in the civic realm. Discussions about space being used for creative purposes, and a reimagining of the High Street and West End as a cultural quarter, gained a voice and commitment. Innovative uses of digital technology ensured that events were able to use light shows on the 800 year old Abbey creating both a spectacle and an increased basis for digital identity for Paisley, allowing Paisley to extend its digital reach through events. This is something that would not have been considered possible before the bidding process, as previously the focus was on keeping the image of the town associated with heritage and preservation.

With a plethora of urban renewal strategies to choose from, the defining features of a city's investment programmes will partially be shaped by the prevailing trends of urban planning, and sometimes include a review of scientific evidence for different strategies. During the first decade of the 2000s, the main urban planning trends included The Creative City, Event-Led Urban Regeneration, and the creation of Business Improvement Districts, all utilised to different extents in Paisley. Renfrewshire Council also adopted a policy for 'inclusive growth' through cultural regeneration aiming for growth through economic and social equity, not deeming all economic growth equally positive but prioritising weaker groups. Parts of Paisley are amongst the most deprived in Scotland, whilst others (especially in wider Renfrewshire) are affluent, suburban environments with very different demographics. The UKCoC bidding process created policy leverage for change; structural inequalities were to be challenged with cultural means. This aligns well with Bozeman and Johnson's (2015) addition to public value theory: 'progressive opportunity', where the former denotes active efforts to create equal opportunities as a public value in itself. Events may be leveraged as a progressive opportunity to be used to influence change in equity and social inclusion.

Cultural Regeneration as a Strategy for Public Value

The Creative City, popularised by Florida (2002) claimed that creative professionals in the service economy were the driving force of wealth and success rather than previous notions of industry and businesses. Specialised production and consumption by these 'creatives' was going to be even more important in the future (Florida 2002). This work inspired policymakers to increase the attractiveness of their urban environments for this so-called creative class, with cultural regeneration being one of the utilised methods. Culture-led regeneration is an urban planning approach for investing public money in culture and creativity, expecting economic, social, and aesthetic benefits (Miles and Paddison 2005).

The hopes for large-scale social effects may be high, expecting that the regeneration 'breathes life' into a rundown community (Evans and Shaw 2004). Some of the flagships of this method, including Glasgow and Barcelona, are associated with hosting mega-events (OECD 2018, Heeley 2011), or physical flagship developments such as Bilbao (Gonzalez 2011) but in turn have been criticised for putting tourist needs over the common good of citizens (Milano, Novelli and Cheer 2019). Bianchini and Parkinson (1994) mention three dilemmas: long- and short-term investments are both needed for culture, cultural production needs to match consumption and payment, and finally the periphery may suffer from investing in the city centre. These dilemmas form some of the basic problems of the method, and its subsequent scholarly interest (García 2004; Papanikolaou 2012). The approach is criticised for excessive place-making eroding local history, centre-periphery conflicts, and advantages only reaching those not in greatest need (Mooney and Fyfe 2006; MacLeod 2002). Proponents instead point towards the surges in tourism, people moving in instead of out, higher levels of investment, and broken negative trends in some cities employing the method (MacLeod 2002; Pike 2017). Yet again, the effect may become cyclical as with the benefits comes improved quality of life and thus attracting the above dilemmas again (Milano, Novelli and Cheer 2019).

In recent years, following the bid for UKCoC 2021, a shift was made towards *cultural regeneration* rather than *culture-led regeneration* with less focus on boosting new programmes (for typology, see Evans and Shaw 2004). The former is more focused on integrating culture as a long-term component of all public life and public value (Liu 2019; Ghilardi 2005). Extroverted cultural activities diminished, but the £100 million investment in culture and venues (such as the refurbishing of the Paisley Museum and Paisley Town Hall) remains, as well as an extended public events programme compared to before the bid.

Public Value and Events

Public value may tautologically be spoken of as something that is valued by the public, although it does not bring us much closer to a real understanding of the concept. Nabatchi (2012) speaks of a preferred, but ultimately impossible 'normative consensus' of what is valuable. In practice public value will be pluralist, with competing but partially overlapping notions of value. Jørgensen and Bozeman (2007) show that, in the literature, though centred in the public sector, 'public value is not governmental'. Rather, it may be underpinned by Jørgensen and Bozeman's perspective that common views on rights and obligations of citizens, as well as principles of governance and policy, are the public values of a society. Including different sets of ideals, these are as diverse as 'Democracy', 'Shareholder value', and 'Risk readiness'.

Public value as a guiding principle for public administration arose, not least, as an alternative to New Public Management (NPM) and its surge around the turn of the millennium. Where NPM held quantification, goal orientation, and market solutions in the public sector dear, Meynhardt (2009, 192) states that public value represented 'a view of the public sector that cannot be reduced to individual cost-benefit analysis, customer orientation- or rational choice-models'. Public value represented a virtuous rather than quantifiable perspective, which together with methodological critiques of CBA from happiness research and hedonic psychology posed some serious challenges to the economism of NPM reasoning. In the USA scholars such as Bryson et al. (2021), have taken a wider approach to examining the basis for creating public value. They argue that a shared understanding of leadership is key to create social transformations for the common good. In other words, if we truly believe we can use events as a progressive opportunity, something that Bozeman and Johnson (2015) suggest is possible, then shared leadership through public/private partnership is the key to success. Paisley may be on track for achieving the long-term goal of social transformation that Bryson, et al. (2021) attest to, with the ideological belief and practical approach to future Paisley partnerships in shaping the multifarious nature of public policy from a values driven approach.

Meyrick and Barnett (2021) highlight how cultural projects may face impossible demands of 'demonstrating value' due to the lack of common measurements and the low confidence in methods used for gauging cultural value (including qualitative data). This is exacerbated by the lack of a consensus on the method and variables to use in non-economic evaluation, though event evaluation researchers have called for it (Nordvall and Brown 2018). Using a well-documented approach such as 'public values' places the study of social values of events where it can more easily be compared to other policy areas. This partially bridges the gap of 'intangibles'; i.e. cost-benefit inputs that cannot be used to render the final sum of consumer surplus.

Meynhardt (2009) shows how the different parts of 'the public' may experience different things as 'value', with the public split into interest groups, consumers, represented (by legislative representatives), clients, and citizens respectively. Different types of public policy will allocate the scarce resources available in different ways, all producing public value to the different agents of 'the public'. Belonging and group identity, as well as increased self-worth, are important variables in most broad studies on social and cultural values of events (Foley et al. 2015). Meynhardt develops the thoughts of Jørgensen and Bozeman (2007) from a policy perspective to processes in individuals in addition to the relations between (public and possibly private) agents and the public. This addition makes several important non-economic values of events accessible for public value analysis. In addition to costs/benefits and positive/negative experiences, Meynhardt includes belongingness, group identity, and increased self-worth, extending to the well-being area with many of the same values demonstrated in the recent literature review on values of community events (Smith et al. 2021). Meynhardt also mentions 'equal opportunity', not unlike *progressive opportunity*. This develops the idea that an important aspect of value is having the tools to be able to achieve one's own goals, putting a value on achieving a more equal possibility to exploiting individual ability. A value concept taking into account community aspects and researching culture in a town with high levels of deprivation and, in some regards, limited opportunity, provides a strong addition to understanding the value of events.

Using a 'public service ethos' based on creation of public value was seen by Stoker (2006) as an important step in moving past NPM. In this model, well-being is one of the main targets of the ethics-based approach, in addition to performance, accountability, and individual rights. The rise of well-being as a central indicator of success, partially contesting the earlier CBA framework, has increasingly been subject to theoretical development as well as implemented in public policy, with adopters such as OECD (2020), New Zealand (NZ Treasury 2015), UK (Office for National Statistics 2019), and Germany (Die Bundesregierung 2020).

Festivals and Place

Public values associated with festivals are similar to other cultural activities, except for the importance of *place* and civic spaces' transformative capacities. Until recently, with the emergence of 'digital festivals', festivals were a matter of an effort designated in time and place. Though the classic understanding of a festival was as a predominantly religious community event (described in Foley, McGillivray and McPherson 2012), festivals can now be more broadly phrased as 'themed, public celebrations' (Getz 1998, 409). Despite the broadening of the concept, the ties to community values and the importance of 'place' remains. Festivals often embrace local community identity and engage local groups who come together for a common purpose, sometimes centred around shared values and beliefs: 'Festivals celebrate community values, ideologies, identity and continuity' (Getz, Andersson and Carlsen 2010). Even with festival themes far from localised community events, such as the Olympics, community actors are important stakeholders in the bidding, preparation, and organisation of an event (Glynn 2008). Several studies have shown the importance, and potential positive effects, of engaging the local community (Misener et. al. 2015; Higgins-Desbiolles 2017), and the negative effects of failing to do so (Yolal et al. 2016; Dredge and Whitford 2011). These and other studies show that positive effects of festivals include social cohesion, social capital, whilst negatives may include distrust, unrest, and rioting (Higgins-Desbiolles 2018; Talbot and Carter 2018).

Place identity is one of the forces driving event visitors and tourists to a place. Construction of place and related identities is not necessarily tied to traditional boundaries or designations, but can be created by adding new angles to old places, or create entirely novel identities tied to places which were not regarded as places, such as music or dance festivals, as suggested by Jaimangal-Jones, Pritchard and Jones (2010). However, to use existing traditions, places, buildings, and heritage is a strong incentive for developing a sense of place, and in the case of local government, to create stronger community ties in their area. The sense of a common good is often attributed to place and public value agreement. Festivals have a potent ability to shape and generate shared identities (George 2015) adding to a consensus of the value added to the community and town. Music festivals, for example, are often created around the name of the place: Leeds, Reading and Glastonbury are key examples of associating the festival with a place and space. There is often a contested role of the festival within the place and as Nabachti (2012) stresses, the need for normative consensus on public value attributed to the role of festivals and events is key here. This works for larger festivals but hosting events or festivals in smaller communities gives the role of maintaining and creating a common sense of community, an outsized role to play (Jaeger and Mykletun 2013).

Evaluating Festivals

Since the 1980s, festival and event hosts have increasingly focused not just on reputation and local culture or leisure, but also on local economic gains (del Barrio, Devesa and Herrero 2012). Events may have the positive effects of gathering interest, investment, and increased local economic momentum, and hopeful event organisers may want to turn the inevitable expenses of a large-scale event into a profit. Through standard economics evaluation techniques, such as EIA, the economic impact of festivals and events can be calculated in terms of effect on the Gross Regional (or, for mega-events, National) Product.

The EIA approach presents several problems, in particular generous applications in terms of spending and consumption estimates produce overly optimistic results. Also strict implementations use a limited range of variables with limited explanatory power and all spending by locals is subtracted; only economic influx to the region is positive (Abelson 2011). This is questionable in the Paisley case as the turn towards cultural spending is a goal in itself, and a large amount of spending on leisure is centred in neighbouring Glasgow. There are solutions, such as suggested by Snowball (2008), who suggests asking what respondents would have done with their resources and time instead. In this study, the local and non-local values are presented side by side.

The standard economic methods for evaluation consider primarily short-term effects (Misener et al. 2016). A major debate in this area is whether calculations of impact are overly optimistic, or indeed performed with adequate tools altogether. Overestimation of economic multipliers, the overshadowing focus on spending by non-locals, and ignoring community costs other than event-related transactions are all criticised but common features of cultural event effect presentation (Abelson 2011). Cost-benefit analysis has been suggested as an alternative, but does not necessarily solve the optimism of evaluations, and demands much more resources. Properly performed, EIA will provide some key figures on the economic success of a festival whilst remaining at a fraction of the cost of a CBA.

Scholtz, Viviers and Maputsoe (2019) calculate the social value to be 1.46 times that of the economic impact. In standard techniques, these values may be either simply omitted or considered intangible, unmeasurable. Measuring and planning for public value requires a longitudinal study of collective positive experiences, evaluating esteem, trust and well-being with a community. It often takes years before there is noticeable change. In this study, the public value framework was used to design questions on a broad scope of added value, and social value leading to a shared understanding of the common good, common benefit and social transformation. Additionally we conducted surveys on economic output and willingness to pay.

One of the downsides to a public value approach is the difficulty to quantify the effect in the short term, which in turn is a contributing reason for the popularity of CBA. The UK Green Book's thorough work with creating a softer approach to cultural value had the explicit goal of taking broad-spanning values into account whilst keeping it monetised in the last step (O'Brien 2010; Fujiwara, Kudrna and Dolan 2014). This means sticking to the principles of subjective well-being, foregoing some collective values which are clearly demonstrable, but with no agreed method for quantifying their extent. Well-being associated with culture is calculated at £90 per person per month in the UK (Fujiwara, Kudrna and Dolan 2014) so the possibility to use events and festivals as a progressive opportunity to bring a collective leadership together to effect change is one that is attractive in public value terms if one can secure consensus. Making use of sophisticated methods for calculating well-being of culture, most of the effects shown above remain partial or completely under evaluated. Though they may overlap with subjective well-being, important public values may be invisible for the individual respondent.

The Paisley Study

This study makes use of mixed methods to evaluate economic, social, and cultural impacts. Data collection comes from three main sources: an in-depth interview series, two on-site structured interview series at Paisley events, and the official Renfrewshire Council evaluations, the latter performed by external consultants.

Primary quantitative data was collected during 2019 with 140 structured attendee interviews partially based on the ATLAS event evaluation questionnaire were conducted at three events: Paisley Halloween Festival, Fireworks Extravaganza, and Christmas Lights Switch-on. In the days following two of these, semi-structured interviews were conducted with 60 representatives in shops around Paisley town centre. The interviews' partially open-ended questions gave respondents the possibility to express opinions relating to the events programme in their own words. Shop representatives were asked about both economic and other impacts to them and their peers. Local shops are regarded as important economic beneficiaries, which in turn is the main quantifiable effect of events. Their hitherto unheard perspective on Paisley events both economically, culturally and socially adds to the perspective of citizens-consumers, tourists, and public bodies.

One of the authors of this chapter was embedded in the Paisley 2021 bidding team, thus getting an inside perspective on the partnership approach and helping shape the process of developing cultural policy in Paisley around added public and social value. The other author was embedded in the regeneration team at Renfrewshire Council from early 2019 until lockdowns in March 2020. Both took observational notes of the processes involved and their participation in shaping the approach to evaluation. These form large informal pieces of knowledge on the subject matter of events in Paisley. In addition to the personal experiences gathered by being part of the teams, three in-depth interviews were conducted with local practitioners from different organisations in February 2019; a local arts project, a local community planning group, and a Renfrewshire Council officer. All three of these interviewees had been heavily involved in the bid, so these interviews were reflective discursive engagements, aiming to explore to what extent the vision and shifts in engagement, attitude and benefits from cultural engagement in the process, they and their communities they represented had felt came from the bidding process and beyond. They discuss the impacts and values of the bidding process, primarily in non-economic terms. These were used as a triangulation device for the researchers to check the results of the public and private sector survey against, the observations from the engagement of the community groups that both had witnessed and the testing of their understanding of how the bidding process had added to the cultural value and added public value for the town of Paisley.

In addition to the informal interviews with officers, a complementary interview was conducted with the events manager in Renfrewshire, in April 2020, to discuss the implications of Covid-19. The effects on the 2021 UKCoC would have been large (as seen in Coventry with reduced attendance and many additional precautions), and the programme envisioned by the Paisley 2021 group would not have been entirely possible during the Covid-19 pandemic. The respondent noted that even small-scale public events would likely not start until the pandemic was over, and that the type of large physical events with visitor numbers in the tens of thousands would possibly not be hosted for the foreseeable future. Paisley would likely not arrange these types of ambitious events in confined spaces until public trust has gone back to normal, but recognised that their approach to embedding and engaging more locally with communities on smaller scale outdoor festivals that promoted local identity would be of more benefit in the short term.

Secondary data was gathered on-site in Paisley. Evaluations were commissioned for the 2016 event season onward, and seven to nine major festivals and events are evaluated each year. Eight events spanning December 2017 to November 2018 are used in this study, soon after the 2021 bid was lost. The methodology, eventsIMPACT is an Impact Analysis tool, with EIA being the most prominent branch. Income is calculated as spending generated in the town centre due to events, including accommodation. Organiser expenditure, as well as local resident spending is subtracted. Evaluations consist of questionnaires conducted during event runtime, circa 400 per event. Relevant questions for this chapter were chosen from the evaluations: on local spending, on satisfaction and feelings about Paisley. These were chosen as they provide the best insight to Gross Value Added and our operationalisation of public value. The primary data interviews were designed with evaluations in mind: filling the gaps of the evaluations for the study's different purpose and using the strengths it provides in numbers.

Findings and Analysis

The findings were themed into key areas of importance and value as identified by local respondents and the bid team. We have presented the analysis under the different thematic areas below. These highlight the value areas that the community and policymakers deemed important in creating public value through events and festivals and were highlighted as part of the bidding process.

Sense of Community

Respondents showed a strong sense of altruism, and positive feelings towards the town, the local authority and population, sometimes all spoken of as the same thing. This is most notable amongst the shopkeepers. A majority of those affected negatively by traffic jams, re-routed buses, and the non-attendance of regular customers still supported the events programme and expressed positive values stretching beyond their own business. This was expressed as 'it's good for the town' — that events and regeneration helped the town into a better position than before was expressed by practitioners and attendees as well. More often than not this was expressed with more emphasis than other values such as personal gains or entertainment values. According to respondents, the common value of what is 'good for the town' was clearly a primary opinion about the program as a whole. There was a strong majority supporting the programme, and despite being gathered two years after losing, several primary on-site respondents still spoke unprompted about the 2021 bid.

These indicators of a functioning sense of community were partially the effect of cohesion created by the momentum from the bid. According to one practitioner, the events programme and the resources coming from the bid were intertwined: 'I think as those bigger events have continued to grow, they are very valued by the community. [...] I think it might have happened because of the smaller funds made available; communities in the town feel connected to the town centre and feel like the cultural events are part of the town's cultural landscape.' The attendees mirrored this, noting; 'It's nice to see the town come together', and also supported in the earlier evaluations. Several values associated with increasing community cohesion also show up in the data; evaluations show increasing perceived safety over time, strong community ties show in the focus on common goals, civic participation increases, and social capital is strengthened.

Local Pride

The experience of the physical events was overwhelmingly positive, partially due to the scheduled activities at the venue, but, to an even higher degree, due to the 'ambience' or 'atmosphere'. These words were used primarily by attendees but echoed by shop representatives and practitioners, one mentioning that the events' strategy created an attraction for grassroots movement due to the positive brand associated with Paisley events and community. All three in-depth interviewees mentioned a transition from a negative view of the town and its capabilities both based on cultural and social grounds before the bid, to an ambience of support and common good afterwards. Towards the end of the bid, if someone spoke negatively about Paisley in open channels on social media, they were very likely to be met with counter arguments, according to one respondent.

All data types also display how local respondents show pride in the town. In the 2017 event evaluations, at the height of the bid, only 4% stated they *didn't* feel more positive about Paisley than they used to, and a strong majority stated they were proud of Paisley's culture and heritage. The same was expressed by one practitioner arguing that the increase in cultural focus had not just given Paisley new things to be proud of, but noted how certain slogans had stuck in the public mind and were repeated by many, such as that Paisley had the second highest number of listed buildings in Scotland (after Edinburgh).

Progressive Opportunity

In the events programme overall, the public values were expressed by practitioners in terms of accessibility, community get-together, citizenship and a democratic process, key elements of Bozeman's model, and in some cases based upon the educational values found in Paisley's vibrant history. The Renfrewshire

Council officer noted that later steps in the investment plan for the bid were mainly goals of social equity: 'We have large programmes for tackling poverty and social deprivation, improvements in life chances and social outcomes for local people. [...] And then all of that manifested itself in terms of the vibrancy of our town centre. It's levels of occupancy and it's night time economy, all these sorts of things.' Again a key outcome of a public value approach is securing and alleviating some of the structural inequalities that exist. Given Paisley was deemed the most socially deprived area in the UK (Scottish Government 2016), this was a key strategic outcome for the Council and a lot of expectation for a cultural events based approach. Three years after the failed bid, but still believing and following their approach, the town has risen three places from the bottom in the multiple deprivation index, for the first time in 30 years. It is evident that the public value approach to embedding culture at the heart of policy decision making and developing approaches from a grass roots organic manner, led to the renewed common good approach from their festivals and events strategy.

The cohesive effects mentioned above were partially conscious designs by Renfrewshire Council to create 'inclusive growth'. Aiming at higher equity, explicitly in the form of more cultural participation by the outsized group of socially deprived living in Paisley (Scottish Government 2016). The analysis of postcodes in evaluations and primary interviews showed that attendees from all types of neighbourhoods were present, but there was a strong correlation between more deprived areas and more attendees at the events. This was not unexpected: evaluation data from the Spree music and performance festival revealed an inverse correlation, with less deprived people visiting ticketed events with well-known artists.

The practitioners spoke highly of how mobilisation had increased during the period of their interviews, including a strong influx of volunteers to social NGOs in Ferguslie, one of Scotland's most deprived localities, in Paisley, and a strongly increased visibility of social organisations, leading to more interactions with people in need of help. According to the social NGO practitioner, the public surge in interest and support for her organisation resulted in several prevented suicides and maintaining shelter, food, and paying the bills of several more, despite a positive socio-economic trend in the area.

Status and usage of public spaces were also echoed by practitioners and attendees as a valuable public asset. Comments on the 'town coming alive' was not exclusively denoting people in the streets, but also the creative use of space, including the light show on the Abbey and the festivalised (Harms 2021) utilisation of spaces which are usually empty. These include County Square outside the train station, the spacious civic areas around the Abbey and town hall, or the park at Dunn Square; all little used civic spaces amongst the most central addresses in Paisley. The transformation of some of these outdoor spaces are part of the bid's physical regeneration investment plan, which survived the unsuccessful bid, though the events programme also presented access to spaces to people otherwise unlikely to use them.

A key contributor to this outcome was the local authority officials making a conscious decision to plan with culture at the heart of their decision making, not necessarily planning for culture but changing the way they thought of culture, as public value. Culture was embedded in their approach to health, education and social justice as Foley, McGillivray and McPherson state: 'events can be used in public value terms as an instrumental means of the achievement of noncultural ends' (2012, 337). What Paisley succeeded in, where others have failed, is that they understood that using culture as a public value for the common good was a *process* and didn't need to be evaluated only as an outcome in the terms the way economic models present. The process and the use of the softer approach of engagement of local groups, citizens, even dissenting voices, enabled them to engage in a longer term process of re-engagement with communities on the periphery and brought them back in from the margins; adopting the approach of Meynhardt (2009) that public value creation is drawn from the experience of the public. Paisley's campaigns on social media of 'Paisley Is" and 'Why I love Paisley' and after the bid of 'Future Paisley' allowed the voices of cultural agents, citizens and producers to be heard as part of a collective voice and in securing the common good for Paisley; the key ingredients that Bozeman and Johnson (2015), stress are needed to demonstrate a progressive opportunity. Paisley leadership led the way and achieved the elusive normative consensus for their approach that Nabatchi (2012) suggests is needed in creating public value.

Use Values and Economics

The most striking similarity between the different types of data collected was respondents' expression of support for the Paisley cultural programme and the bidding process. In the official evaluations, this showed up as an increasing support for the bid over time, and ended up at very high levels. This was echoed by the policymakers and practitioners, who noted an initial scepticism about the bid based on locals' negative sentiments about Paisley, on the lines of; 'We couldn't be City of Culture'. During 2016 and 2017, the high degree of visibility, community mobilisation, funding, and the formal success of being shortlisted contributed to shifting opinions. Indeed, this was one of the main public values achieved according to several practitioners: the town appeared to rally behind a common goal; a common good. One noted that on social media, the few negative voices were met with many more arguing that the bid had brought positive change to Paisley; 94 % supported the bid in the late-2016 evaluations, and 98–99 % of evaluation respondents were 'satisfied' or 'very satisfied' with the events.

This was also true of both shopkeepers and festival attendees, two years after the bid was lost. The flagship events program and the general regeneration scheme had strong support. Several respondents noted how the current state was due to the 2021 bid, or that the state of the town and its culture had been improved for years: 'If they keep on improving like this, I have nothing negative to say'. The positive opinions were close to unanimous amongst respondents. Most traceable disagreements were found within data groups: where the majority of shopkeepers expressed a common narrative, stating that most businesses gained footfall and/or income from events. A small minority were convinced of a different version, where 'everyone knows' that events are bad for most businesses, except perhaps for a few bars next to the venues. It was clear that these different views were discussed amongst groups of apparently mutually exclusive business owners.

The positive effect on business, however, was corroborated by the evaluations. The Economic Impact Analysis showed a £5.4m increase in spending in the town centre per year (of which £2.2m from people from outside Renfrewshire); one Renfrewshire policymaker estimated that visits to Paisley had increased by at least 300% compared to before the regeneration scheme. Several pubs and restaurants answered that the events were the busiest days of the year, and that Halloween broke sales records, and attendees of the winter events did parts of their Christmas shopping in Paisley due to attending the Christmas lights switch-on or the Fireworks extravaganza.

Interestingly, the willingness to pay (WTP) was slightly below the actual cost for Renfrewshire Council (£6 compared to £6.80 per visitor). Many respondents reporting low WTP were still very happy with the experience, but were clearly uncomfortable with putting a price on it. Some mentioned that they had already paid for it (via taxes), and others protested the question altogether and did not want to give an answer. This is also complicated by the similar WTP from the ambitious Halloween festival and the comparatively limited Fireworks show; respondents thought that it may be worth 'a few pounds' but were hardly willing to develop it. The insincere £0 answers (so-called 'protest zeros') further shows the contrast between placing a value on an experience and expressing it in monetary terms. It is well known in the willingness-to-pay literature that different questions will produce very different answers (Snowball 2008).

The evaluations initially gauge volunteering activity with a monetary conversion coefficient (£14.09 per hour). This measure was dropped in later evaluations as the events did not attract or make use of many volunteers. In contrast to this practitioners spoke about the increased volunteering and civic organisation as a main effect of the cultural programmes, though not directly tied to the public events programme. Several groups reported surges in visits and volunteers, and that the small funds offered for community organisations were the key to a large increase in activity. In-depth interviews with policymakers revealed an increased third sector mobilisation, volunteering, local cooperation, and that policy leverage were at all-time highs during the bidding process.

Although this disappeared after the bid was lost in December 2017, the levels in February 2019 were much higher than before the bidding process started. Primarily, adding to the public value perspective rather than the economic, this clearly shows the need for qualitative methodology in event evaluation.

Conclusions

The public value of the Paisley festival programme does not lie exclusively, nor even primarily, in attending specific high impact events. This view was communicated by attendees, shopkeepers and interviewees. Values are expressed in terms of an increased sense of community, pride in the place, new usage of, and feelings for, urban spaces, and the willingness to work for social change or the common good. The values identified in this study have made a change in the internal and external reputation of Paisley; not because of advertising but because many in the community now get to associate Paisley with positive experiences.

The willingness to pay for Paisley's cultural programme was similar to the actual cost paid by Renfrewshire Council. Similarly, even with a cautious EIA, at least a million pounds (a conservative estimate from the EIA) are spent yearly in Paisley town centre by visitors driven by the festival programme, and several times more by locals. The economic influx is considerable, but respondents overwhelmingly put the softer public values first (Meyrick and Barnett 2021). This broad measurement of values shows the insufficiency of not just input-output style economic analysis, but also the softer well-being approach used by the UK Green Book, monetising subjective well-being variables created with a cost-benefit style calculation of surplus.

The bidding process opened up the opportunity for leveraging a wide array of reforms; investing in art, service sector jobs, creating a Paisley brand based on positive connotations, and the development of the civic realm in the form of a cultural district encompassing the 1000-yard walk between the east end Abbey and the Coats Memorial Church, the West End, via the High Street. This represented change which in several parts was needed anyway, but did not become possible until public and private actors in Paisley were onboard a reform ship already moving. Support for the town's cultural efforts came out of the bidding process but is retained by the commitment of the local authority to provide culture on what is largely perceived as the citizens' terms and for the common good.

Regeneration efforts such as the one in Paisley have the potential to change the access to civic spaces. In this case, the process had explicit focus on inclusion in the sense of equity. Cultural consumption increased in some under-represented groups, and the access to picturesque but under-utilised town areas increased. Sentiments about the physical surroundings in central Paisley were transformed by the bid and its most visible, and ever-growing part, the festivals.

This may be especially significant in a town such as Paisley with dilapidated areas and unique listed buildings both being major parts of the geography. Reigniting the pride in the latter and utilising events as a progressive opportunity to use civic spaces had a significant effect on what was seen as an increase in public values in policy and practice.

Whilst the neoliberal brand of culture-led regeneration guided some of the principles of the bid, with stated aims of achieving economic growth through culture, Renfrewshire Council and its partners partially outgrew that model. The willingness of local policymakers and businesses to remain in public-private partnerships remains strong, but the focus has shifted towards a model more permeated in public value thinking such as well-being and aligning to Scottish Government's strategy of the well-being economy and aligned to those of New Zealand's leadership model which is significant in policy terms of the level of ambition Paisley sees for itself.

The public values associated with engagement and community have become a selling point for Paisley, projecting a brand based on the idea of a town strongly engaged in their own community and history. Though a more low-key approach than the bombastic mega-event brand, it is used to promote Paisley nationally and internationally, not least in the form of the extensive festival programme and the historical buildings. The renovation of buildings has been the most costly part of the regeneration programmes, change largely impossible without the leverage created by the bidding process.

This study demonstrates the need for more effort to study the possibilities of public value created through events. Whilst subjective well-being is becoming common to study in relation to culture and events (Smith et al. 2021), the wide array of effects shown in this study would not be possible to monetise in the models used by UK Government, Economic Impact Analysis, and hardly even with an ambitious CBA. The equitable effects of progressive social opportunities, and the increased well-being in communities experiencing stronger coherence are key pieces in understanding what is possible to achieve with an ambitious community festival programme. This chapter adds significantly to the interdisciplinary understanding of using public value theory and economic theory as a process-led strategy rather than gauging success or failure of the use and re-use of public space on traditional economic impact terms only.

References

Abelson, Peter. 2011. Evaluating Major Events and Avoiding the Mercantilist Fallacy. *Economic Papers: A Journal of Applied Economics and Policy*, 30(1), 48–59.

Benington, John and Mark Moore (Eds.) 2011. *Public Value: Theory and Practice*. New York: Palgrave Macmillan.

Bianchini, Franco and Michael Parkinson (Eds.) 1994. *Cultural Policy and Urban Regeneration: The West European Experience*. Manchester: Manchester University Press.

Bozeman, Barry and Japera Johnson. 2015. The Political Economy of Public Values: A Case for the Public Sphere and Progressive Opportunity. *The American Review of Public Administration*, 45(1), 61–85.

Brown, Steve, Donald Getz, Robert Pettersson and Martin Wallstam. 2015. Event Evaluation: Definitions, Concepts and a State of the Art Review. *International Journal of Event and Festival Management*, 6(2), 135–157.

Bryson, John, Bill Barber, Barbara Crosby and Michael Quinn Patton. 2021. Leading Social Transformation: Creating Public Value and Advancing the Common Good. *Journal of Change Management*, 21(2), 180–202. https://doi.org/10.1080/14697017.2021.1917492

Clifton, Nick, Diane O'Sullivan and David Pickernell. 2012. Capacity Building and the Contribution of Public Festivals: Evaluating 'Cardiff 2005'. *Event Management*, 16(1), 77–91.

Die Bundesregierung. 2020. Gut Leben in Deutchland. 2020. Available at: https://www.gut-leben-in-deutschland.de/index.html

del Barrio, María José, María Devesa and Luis César Herrero. 2012. Evaluating Intangible Cultural Heritage: The Case of Cultural Festivals. *City, Culture and Society*, 3(4), 235–244.

Dredge, Diane and Michelle Whitford. 2011. Event Tourism Governance and the Public Sphere. *Journal of Sustainable Tourism*, 19(4–5), 479–499.

Evans, Graeme and Phyllida Shaw. 2004. *The Contribution of Culture to Regeneration in the UK: A Review of Evidence: A Report to the Department for Culture Media and Sport*. London: DCMS.

Florida, Richard. 2002. *The Rise of the Creative Class*. New York, NY: Basic Books.

Foley, Malcolm, David McGillivray and Gayle McPherson. 2012. *Event Policy: From Theory To Strategy*. Abingdon: Routledge.

Foley, Malcolm, David McGillivray and Gayle McPherson. 2015. Culturing Sports Mega Events: Leveraging Public Value. In David F. Suárez (Ed.) *Creating Public Value in Practice*, pp. 331–347. Abingdon: Routlege.

Fredline, Liz, Michael Raybould, Leo Jago and Margaret Deery. 2005. Triple Bottom Line Event Evaluation: A Proposed Framework for Holistic Event Evaluation. Paper presented at Johnny Allen (Ed.) *The Impacts of Events: Proceedings of International Event Research Conference*, pp. 2–15. Sydney: Australian Centre for Event Management University of Technology.

Fujiwara, Daniel, Laura Kudrna and Paul Dolan. 2014. *Quantifying and Valuing the Wellbeing Impacts of Culture and Sport*. Department for Culture Media and Sport Research Paper. London: CMS. Available at: https://assets.publishing.service.gov.uk/government/uploads/system/uploads/attachment_data/file/304899/Quantifying_and_valuing_the_wellbeing_impacts_of_sport_and_culture.pdf

García, Beatriz. 2004. Cultural Policy and Urban Regeneration in Western European Cities: Lessons from Experience, Prospects for the Future. *Local Economy*, 19(4), 312–326.

George, Jodie. 2015. Examining the Cultural Value of Festivals. *International Journal of Event and Festival Management*, 6(2), 122–134.

Getz, Donald. 1998. Event Tourism and the Authenticity Dilemma. In William F. Theobald (Ed.) *Global Tourism*, p. 24. Oxford: Butterworth-Heinemann.

Getz, Donald, Tommy Andersson and J. Carlsen. 2010. Festival Management Studies: Developing a Framework and Priorities for Comparative and Cross-Cultural Research. *International Journal of Event and Festival Management*, 1(1), 29–59. https://doi.org/10.1108/17852951011029298

Ghilardi, Lia. 2005. Culture at the Centre: Cultural Planning – A Strategic Approach to Successful and Sustainable Community-based Regeneration in Scotland. Edinburgh: National Cultural Planning Steering Group.

Glynn, Mary Ann. 2008. Configuring the Field of Play: How Hosting the Olympic Games Impacts Civic Community. *Journal of Management Studies*, 45(6), 1117–1146.

González, Sara. 2011. Bilbao and Barcelona 'In Motion': How Urban Regeneration 'Models' Travel and Mutate in the Global Flows of Policy Tourism. *Urban Studies*, 48(7), 1397–1418.

Harms, Angie. 2021. Festivalisation and the 'New Normal': Creating Multi-sensory Event Experiences Both Off and Online. Event Industry News, 13 January. Available at: https://www.eventindustrynews.com/news/festival isation-and-the-new-normal-creating-multi-sensory-event-experiences -both-off-and-online# (accessed 15 January 2022).

Heeley, John. 2011. *Inside City Tourism: A European Perspective*. Bristol: Channel View Publications.

Higgins-Desbiolles, Freya. 2017. A Pedagogy of Tourism Informed by Indigenous Approaches. In Pierre Benckendorff and Anita Zehrer (Eds.) *Handbook of Teaching and Learning in Tourism*. Cheltenham: Edward Elgar Publishing.

Higgins-Desbiolles, Freya. 2018. Event Tourism and Event Imposition: A Critical Case Study from Kangaroo Island, South Australia. *Tourism Management*, 64(C), 73–86.

Jaeger, Kari and Reidar Mykletun. 2013. Festivals, Identities and Belonging. *Event Management*, 17(3), 213–226.

Jaimangal-Jones, Deewi, Annette Pritchard and Nigel Morgan. 2010. Going the Distance: Locating Journey, Liminality and Rites of Passage in Dance Music Experiences. *Leisure Studies*, 29(3), 253–268.

Jørgensen, Torben Beck and Barry Bozeman. 2007. Public Values: An Inventory. *Administration & Society*, 39(3), 354–381.

Judd, Dennis and Susan Fainstein (Eds.) 1999. *The Tourist City*. New Haven, CT: Yale University Press.

Liu, Yi-De. 2019. Event and Sustainable Culture-Led Regeneration: Lessons from the 2008 European Capital of Culture, Liverpool. *Sustainability*, 11(7), 1869.

MacLeod, Gordon. 2002. From Urban Entrepreneurialism to a 'Revanchist City'? On the Spatial Injustices of Glasgow's Renaissance. *Antipode*, 34(3), 602–624.

Meynhardt, Timo. 2009. Public Value Inside: What is Public Value Creation? *International Journal of Public Administration*, 32(3–4), 192–219.

Meyrick, Julian and Tully Barnett. 2021. From Public Good to Public Value: Arts and Culture in a Time of Crisis, *Cultural Trends*, 30(1), 75–90.

Milano, Claudia, Marina Novelli and Joseph Cheer. 2019. Overtourism and Tourismphobia: A Journey through Four Decades of Tourism Development, Planning and Local Concerns. *Tourism Planning & Development*, 16(4), 353–357.

Miles, Steven and Ronan Paddison. 2005. Introduction: The Rise and Rise of Culture-Led Urban Regeneration. *Urban Studies*, 42(5–6), 833–839.

Misener, Laura, David McGillivray, Gayle McPherson and David Legg. 2015. Leveraging Parasport Events for Sustainable Community Participation: The Glasgow 2014 Commonwealth Games. *Annals of Leisure Research*, 18(4), 450–469.

Misener, Laura, David McGillivray, Gayle McPherson and David Legg. 2016. Examining Parasport Events Through the Lens of Critical Disability Studies. In Ian Lamond and Louise Platt (Eds.) *Critical Event Studies*, pp. 175–192. London: Palgrave Macmillan.

Mooney, Gerry and Nick Fyfe. 2006. New Labour and Community Protests: The Case of the Govanhill Swimming Pool Campaign, Glasgow. *Local Economy*, 21(2), 136–150.

Nabatchi, Tina. 2012. Putting the 'Public' Back in Public Values Research: Designing Participation to Identify and Respond to Values. *Public Administration Review*, 72(5), 699–708.

New Zealand Treasury. 2015. *Guide to Social Cost Benefit Analysis*. The Treasury, New Zealand Government. Available at: https://www.treasury.govt.nz/publications/guide/guide-social-cost-benefit-analysis

Nordvall, Anders and Steve Brown. 2018. Evaluating Publicly Supported Periodic Events: The Design of Credible, Usable and Effective Evaluation. *Journal of Policy Research in Tourism, Leisure and Events*, 12(2), 152–171.

National Records of Scotland. 2018. Available at: https://www.nrscotland.gov.uk/files//statistics/settlements-localities/set-loc-16/set-loc-2016-publication-updated.pdf

O'Brien, David. 2010. *Measuring the Value Of Culture: A Report to the Department for Culture Media and Sport*. London: Department for Culture Media and Sport.

OECD. 2018. Recommendation of the Council on Global Events and Local Development. Paris: OECD Publishing. Available at: https://legalinstruments.oecd.org/en/instruments/OECD-LEGAL-0444

OECD. 2020. *How's Life? 2020: Measuring Well-being.* Paris: OECD Publishing. https://doi.org/10.1787/9870c393-en

Office for National Statistics. 2019. Measures of National Well-being Dashboard, 23 October. Available at: https://www.ons.gov.uk/peoplepopulation andcommunity/wellbeing/articles/measuresofnationalwellbeingdash board/2018-04-25

Papanikolaou, Panagiota. 2012. The European Capital of Culture: The Challenge for Urban Regeneration and its Impact on the Cities. *International Journal of Humanities and Social Science*, 2(17), 268–273.

Pike, Andy. 2017. *Case Study Report–Glasgow.* Structural Transformation, Adaptability and City Economic Evaluations. Working Paper, 8.

Scholtz, Marco, Pierre-Andre Viviers and Limpo Maputsoe. 2019. Understanding the Residents' Social Impact Perceptions of an African Cultural Festival: The Case of Macufe. *Journal of Tourism and Cultural Change*, 17(2), 166–185.

Scottish Government. 2016. Scottish Index of Multiple Deprivation 2016. Available at: https://data.gov.uk/dataset/a448dd2a-9197-4ea0-8357-c2c9b3 c29591/scottish-index-of-multiple-deprivation-simd-2016 (accessed 7 July 2021).

Smith, Andrew, Bernadette Quinn, Sophie Mamattah, Niclas Hell, Gayle McPherson, David McGillivray and Tamsin Cox. 2021. *The Social Value of Community Events: A Literature Review.* Paisley: University of the West of Scotland.

Snowball, Jeanette. 2008. Using Willingness to Pay Studies to Value Cultural Goods. In Jeanette Snowball (Ed.) *Measuring the Value of Culture: Methods and Examples in Cultural Economics*, pp. 131–175. Berlin: Springer-Verlag.

Stoker, Gerry. 2006. Public Value Management: A New Narrative for Networked Governance? *The American Review of Public Administration*, 36(1), 41–57.

Talbot, Adam and Thomas Carter. 2018. Human Rights Abuses at the Rio 2016 Olympics: Activism and the Media, *Leisure Studies*, 37(1), 77–88.

Visit Scotland. 2019. Paisley Halloween Festival. Available at: https://www.visit scotland.com/info/events/paisley-halloween-festival-p1924351 (accessed 7 July 2021).

Yolal, Medet, Dogan Gursoy, Muzaffer Uysal, Hyelin Kim and Sila Karacaoglu. 2016. Impacts of Festivals and Events on Residents' Well-being. *Annals of Tourism Research*, 61, 1–18.

CHAPTER 15

Festival City Futures: Reflections and Conclusions

Bernadette Quinn, Andrew Smith and Guy Osborn

Introduction

The aim of this book was to explore urban festivity, particularly focusing upon how festivals and events affect urban places and spaces. Festivalisation processes are now well established in cities throughout Western Europe, their rise being closely associated with the prevalence of neoliberal, entrepreneurial city thinking. While these processes tend to be viewed as agents of exclusion and commercialisation, much remains to be understood about how festivals shape cities. To complement political economy perspectives, we need to know more about how festivals and events are produced and experienced on the ground in different kinds of spaces, by diverse cohorts of people (Fincher et al. 2014). This book has contributed to such analysis, in particular by examining the idea of inclusive urbanism and trying to establish the ways in which festivity affects this inclusivity.

Cities are currently under growing pressure to withstand the realities of exceptional political instability, climate change, and the need to address the challenge of building more inclusive, safe, resilient and sustainable cities in line with the UN Sustainable Development Goal #11. Mass migration has led to

How to cite this book chapter:
Quinn, B., Smith, A. and Osborn, G. 2022. Festival City Futures: Reflections and Conclusions. In: Smith, A., Osborn, G. and Quinn, B. (Eds.) *Festivals and the City: The Contested Geographies of Urban Events*. London: University of Westminster Press. Pp. 269–282. London: University of Westminster Press. DOI: https://doi.org /10.16997/book64.o. License: CC-BY-NC-ND 4.0

increased levels of cultural diversity in urban populations across Europe. Abascal and Baldassarri (2015, 726) argue that 'from the level of the neighbourhood to the nation, several studies have identified a negative association between ethnoracial diversity and measures of social capital', indicating the challenges that countries face both in assisting migrant communities but also in encouraging a sense of interculturalism where there is progressive dialogue and interaction between cultures. Accordingly, research interest in understanding how to manage cultural diversity and social relations in times of uncertainty is on the rise (Fraser, Crooke and Davidson 2021; Abascal and Baldassarri 2015). The Covid-19 pandemic, and its attendant economic crisis, has intensified these pressures even further, having radically disrupted the dynamics and budgets of cities everywhere. Municipal leaders are now considering policy interventions that hitherto had seemed highly unlikely (Low and Smart 2020), like the introduction of basic income (e.g. for artists in Ireland) and strict controls on car use. Organisations like the OECD are trying to encourage economic and societal recoveries that privilege 'inclusion' and 'transformation', whilst at the same time trying to manage 'just transitions' towards low carbon futures. These contexts lend a new impetus for interrogating festivals and the implications of using festivals to 'populate, animate, promote and subsidise' urban spaces (Smith, Osborn and Vodicka, Chapter 2) for inclusion, intercultural exchange and ultimately for social cohesion. This concluding chapter draws together some of the observations and findings from the studies covered in this collection, and, in light of the unforeseen disruptions caused by the Covid-19 pandemic, speculates as to how festivals are likely to affect urban places and city spaces in the years to come.

The Ongoing Quest for More Inclusive Space

Public space is produced through ongoing use and social practice, and festivals constitute an important example of this phenomenon. Festivals and events have long influenced the shape and character of urban public spaces, but today their multi-sensorial presence across cities and towns, as well as their symbolic presence in urban imaginaries, is pervasive. Festivals offer a means of correlating cities with the kind of excitement and spectacle that is tailor-made for urban branding; they energise and animate urban spaces, create attractive time-spaces that generate tourist and consumer footfall; and offer opportunities to regenerate city districts. Their contemporary omnipresence arises from the instrumentalisation of festivals in urban policy, and from associated processes of festivalisation, a term used in urban policy contexts as early as 1993 (Häussermann and Siebel 1993), and subsequently elucidated in detail by several authors including Ronström (2016), as well as in Chapter 1 of this book. One could argue that all of the chapters in this book relate to festivalisation in some shape or form, with Chapter 3 presenting Barcelona as a festivalised city *par excellence* and Chapter 2 explicitly reporting study findings that point to a festivalisation of London parks in the years up to 2019.

However, a well-established literature now critiques the contested geographies that typically ensue when event policy is driven by economic agendas (see Chapter 1). Accordingly, and for a variety of reasons including the establishment of Sustainable Development Goal 11, to 'make cities inclusive, safe, resilient and sustainable' (UN-Habitat 2016), cities are now showing a greater interest in using festivals to foster socio-cultural inclusion (Quinn et al. 2020). Hell and McPherson's analysis of the cultural regeneration efforts in Paisley, Scotland in Chapter 14, for example, underlines an important shift of policy thinking towards one that privileges public values like well-being, in addition to economic growth. The study of George Square, Glasgow, in Chapter 4 also notes a shift in thinking towards one that recognises the need for a more participatory approach to designing urban public space. The UN explicitly recognises public space as being key to achieving SDG 11, with profound implications for human health, well-being and the liveability of towns and cities. A recent study of festival related policies in five European cities found an important affinity between festivals and public space, with public space 'generally seen as vital in enabling festivals to meet the policy objectives they are expected to achieve' (Quinn et al. 2020, 14). Simultaneously, academic researchers are showing a growing interest in understanding the socio-cultural values associated with festivals (Kim et al. 2015; Wallstam, Ioannides and Pettersson 2020).

The role that festivals play in creating public spaces that foster inclusivity is therefore becoming more relevant in light of sustainability goals. Contemporary debates about social justice and inclusion, as well as social activism like the Black Lives Matter movement and the recent Reclaim the Streets vigils seen in the wake of violent attacks on women in the UK and Ireland, are building popular awareness that public space is not, in fact, equally and safely available to all. Space is socially produced in complex ways that are difficult for us to fully comprehend. Several chapters in this book take theoretical ideas about how space is produced and empirically interrogate whether festivals produce shared space (Lefebvre 1991). Importantly, several chapters do this by examining event portfolios or programmes for specific urban spaces, rather than examining the effects of individual events. This links to Mair and Smith's (2021: 1739) recent call for a greater focus on understanding how festivals and events can contribute to sustainable development, rather than merely exploring how individual events can be made more sustainable. Our book responds to this call by studying the topic through the particular lens of urban festivals. A key starting point is the belief that as with all kinds of public spaces, festivals can create opportunities for unexpected encounters (Madanipour, Knierbein and Degros, 2014), and constitute places where people are free to mingle in the company of strangers (Given and Leckie 2003). While public spaces, including the kinds of space created through festival activity, are grounded in the 'thin sociality' of fleeting encounters across societal divides, they hold the possibility that those encounters could grow into the thicker sociability of a community (Bodnar 2015). These spaces also offer opportunities to encounter what is going on in the world, and expose us to activities, practices and interests that we don't experience inside our domestic, private worlds. The social interactions generated through staging festivals in public space are an important 'building block of urban social order and cohesion' (Mehta 2019, 296).

Contested Spaces

The spectacular appeal of festivals has meant that cities across the world try to replicate festivals of all kinds, and to stage festivalised events like carnivals, Winter Lights and beer festivals. Cities have long used festivals to celebrate and mark momentous occasions, establish their international standing and construct 'destination brands' (see Gold and Gold, Chapter 9). The public facing nature of these festivals was always very important but how public were they in reality? A complicated aspect to this line of questioning is the highly debated nature of what actually constitutes public space (Carmona 2010). A strong feature of this edited collection is that individual chapters deal with many different kinds of public spaces. Some of these, like streets, parks, market and civic squares, are obviously identifiable as key public spaces and easily understood as event spaces; others like libraries and canals, are less frequently thought of in these terms. Several chapters, including Chapter 7, demonstrate how the social practice of engaging in festivals creates forms of public space and communities that ebb and flow, shift and change even within the confines of very specific boundaries. Festival spaces can come to feel more or less inclusive depending on factors like the composition of festivalgoers, the nature of the programme, the timing and location of the event and the kind of atmosphere created.

The perennial question of what constitutes public space has not been definitively resolved by this edited collection, but by closely analysing how festivals produce and affect public spaces, several chapters have elucidated and illustrated some related issues. With its methodological reliance on mapping, Chapter 3, for example, very graphically points to the uneven distribution of festival activities and resourcing in Barcelona, a city thought to exemplify festivalisation processes. Colombo et al.'s study found festival activity to be concentrated in the city centre, as well as in districts highly populated and well served by cultural facilities, although the situation varied depending on festival type. This highlights concerns not only about the potential exclusion of, or underprovision for, cohorts of people who don't circulate in the city centre, but also about potential tensions and conflicts between long-term residents, tourists and recent immigrants whose lives are city-centre based. This chapter demonstrates that while festivals constitute an important functional use and social practice creating public space in cities like Barcelona, the kind of publicness being generated may be conditional on a number of factors.

The publicness of particular spaces was debated in an entirely different context in Chapter 5. Turning its attention indoors, onto local public libraries, Quinn and Ryan found a clear awareness among festival attendees that the popular rhetoric of the library as a neutral, accessible space is not always borne out in reality. The uneven and contested geographies of the local libraries studied were found to be altered through the hosting of a festival, but only to a degree, in line with the fact that festivals staged here were conditioned by the same cultural norms that ordinarily condition library spaces. Again, a recurring theme is that festivals reproduce existing socio-cultural divides by default, and require conscious intent to challenge and unsettle the status quo, as recognised by the festival organisers in Rotterdam studied in Chapter 6. As Chapter 1 emphasises, festivals may be associated with alternative cultures and experimental practice, but they now tend to be more mainstream phenomena. Nevertheless, beyond 'official' strategies to counter social divides, the liminal qualities of festival time-space (St John 2001) open up possibilities for actors with varying kinds of involvement in the festival site to disrupt prevailing social norms, or to 'step outside their everyday mundane patterns of 'normalcy' (Howell 2013), and rework social ordering within the bounded time-space of the festival. Ballantyne et al. (2014) suggest that a festival atmosphere fosters a sense of escapism. In Chapter 7, Steadman and de Jong carefully explain that how festival time-spaces look, sound and feel is far from fixed, but actually is highly fluid and unstable. They do this by analysing festival atmospheres, showing how ambient power intersects with the spatialities and temporalities of festivals to influence how people feel a sense of belonging/non-belonging in festival sites. Clearly, festival organisers are important architects of festival sites. Their design decisions about physical and spatial arrangements influence atmosphere, the soundscape as well as attendee behaviours (Alves et al. 2021). However, the study of two craft beer festivals in Manchester presented in this chapter shows that while particular kinds of atmosphere may pervade festivals, attendees can actively construct micro conditions to counter dominant ambiences.

Analysing festival spaces can afford deep insight into the concept of urban space, and indeed space more generally. Much has been written about how festivals produce spatial transformations as they take over streets, quarters and sometimes entire cities, disrupting routine mobilities, appearances and patterns in how spaces are regularly used (Johansson and Kociatkiewicz 2011, Curtis 2011). Many researchers identify conflicts and tensions in this context, for example, in respect of the exclusions and omissions that characterise the commercialisation and privatisation of public space (Smith 2016). Several chapters in this book (e.g. Chapter 13) identify problems including the contests that come into play over space as a scarce and finite resource, and the difficulties agreeing marketing communications to festival and external stakeholders. Sometimes festivals are conceived as offering their host places a wealth of possibilities for positively reimagining their existence (Shields 2003, Pløger 2010). The theme of spatial transformation is taken up in this vein in Chapter 13, with Kearney and Burns discussing how spaces within Drogheda were deliberately transformed for the purposes of staging the Fleadh. Again, contestation of space was at issue in the process used to determine how the Fleadh's activities were allocated to particular sites within the town. More generally, urban spaces here were transformed in tangible operational ways, as when temporary infrastructures were erected; as well as in more subtle, fluid and unpredictable ways as people in various guises (e.g. buskers, dancers, drinkers and spectators) temporarily filled up space and used it in non-routine ways.

Some of the chapters provided useful reminders that time is an important consideration in these discussions. Gold and Gold's chapter, for instance, places their study of the Biennale in deep historical perspective, charting not only the historical origins of the event in a location that epitomises the idea of the festival city, but also projecting forward to question how the event can contribute to a sustainable future for the city (Chapter 9). The chapters dealing with the Scottish cities of Glasgow and Edinburgh also speak to the importance of temporality. In Chapter 4, McGillivray, Guillard and McPherson present Glasgow as an example of a city that, for several decades now, has strategically used events to regenerate the economy and reposition the city internationally. As elsewhere, festivalisation in the city has meant that the use of historically important civic spaces like George Square has intensified. However, civic spaces like this tend to be associated with powerful traditions and memories, some created through the historical staging of events, none of which are dislodged without opposition. In recent times, tensions have arisen over how the space is used for event purposes, leaving the authors to suggest that George Square is an exemplar of contested geographies in action. Todd introduces us to the Edinburgh festival city place-myth in Chapter 11. Built over time and multi-layered in meaning, Todd uses semiotics to deconstruct the place-myth and reveal fractures amongst management and community stakeholders, between core and peripheral location divides, and between idealised versions and those versions informed by the need for greater inclusion and accessibility.

In addition, there is the matter of festival imaginaries and festival futures: the visions and aspirations of stakeholders who understand that festivals have transformative potential. Several chapters deal with this, some within the 'time-bound' window of the festival as in Drogheda (Chapter 13) where 'renovation, repurposing and painting of derelict buildings' was central to event preparations and others within much longer future-oriented contexts as in the cultural repositioning of Paisley (Chapter 14). In Chapter 10, NicGhabhann, Ryan and Kinsella draw particular attention to how Capital of Culture events are premised on stakeholders imagining, and envisaging, new possibilities for cultural practices, cultural infrastructures and for cities overall. However, such imaginaries can emanate from stakeholders who are differentially positioned in the policy-practitioner-governance frameworks that encase the process of making these types of events. Emulating established initiatives like the European Capital of Culture programme, a range of countries and organisations are now running competitions where cities are nominated as 'cities of culture' or cities of specific cultural forms (film, literature, music etc). Chapter 10 highlights the tensions and negotiations that characterise the construction of these events, showing why some cohorts report disappointment with how the experienced reality of the event matches up to its promise, in line with other studies (Boland, Murtagh and Shirlow 2019).

Engaging Affectively with Space

Contestation, tensions and exclusions are uncovered in many of the discussions throughout these chapters, but sociality and communal interactivity is always a central feature of the festivals studied. Several chapters (e.g. Chapters 2, 7, 8) reinforce the realisation that participating in festivals is never one-dimensional. Rather, festivals create spaces where people engage affectively and multi-sensorially through embodied participation. The senses play a vital role in producing the transformations that festivals bring about and the sociability they enable, with Carter (2019: 201) arguing that 'affects infuse and circulate among bodies and across spaces, all the while constructing the social worlds through which they flow'. Several of the chapters report on festivals that create particular kinds of eventscapes that privilege engagement through taste (Chapters 7 and 12), sound (Chapters 7 and 13), as well those based on aesthetics and sight (Chapter 9). Others are more 'hands on' and celebrate the art of making, as in Chapter 8 which discusses festivals that involve boat building. All of these chapters help us realise that in order to fully understand how festivals and events are experienced as *lived* city spaces there is a need to consider their sensuous geographies. These geographies reveal the different dimensions of festival experiences (Lopez 2019), as the chapters referenced above make clear. Equally, when we speak about contested geographies, often the tensions or flashpoints of conflict at issue emerge as an affront to the senses, as identified in e.g. Chapter 5 with the noise levels in the library, and Chapter 7 with the amounts of alcohol being drunk at the craft beer festivals. An alertness to the senses leads, in turn, to the realisation that festival participation is not only sensuous but very embodied, another factor that deeply shapes how people encounter other social actors and experience festival performances and activities. Several chapters demonstrate how an alertness to embodiment yields insight into how inclusion/exclusion, belonging/non-belonging is experienced and becomes manifest in festival sites. Discussions in Chapter 12, for example, reveal how elderly and vulnerable residents in one of the study sites felt that the degree of crowding on the town's pavements during festival time meant they were occluded and excluded. Chapter 8 discusses how marginalised and transient communities achieved a greater sense of place-belonging by participating in water based festivals using boats they had made themselves. This reinforces the idea introduced in Chapter 1 that, in terms of producing positive, social legacies, participating in the *making* of the event might be as significant as participating in the event itself.

Methodology Matters

The research based work that features in this book also has methodological significance. Given the focus on inclusion, experiences and contested spaces, it is perhaps unsurprising that the chapters advance understanding of the ways qualitative methods can be used in festivals and events research. Contributions have highlighted the value of an array of qualitative research methods including mapping (Chapter 3), visual methods and semiotics (Chapter 11), social media analysis (Chapters 11, 7), qualitative surveys (Chapter 2), participatory workshops (Chapters 4 and 11), personal involvement in festivals (Chapters 7 and 13) as well as more conventional interviews and observations. Much of this book has tried to understand the relationship between festivals and city spaces from the perspective of audiences/participants (Chapters 5, 8), or the wider users of urban spaces (Chapters 3, 4, and 11), which helps the book to reach important conclusions about *experiencing* festive spaces. Some chapters also focus on the perspectives of festival organisers (e.g. Chapter 6) or local officials (e.g. Chapter 13). In trying to work out how urban policy and event policy intersect, it is important that future work also focuses on other significant stakeholders, in particular representatives of organisations tasked with managing urban spaces. In the contemporary era these include Business Improvement Districts; development corporations; neighbourhood associations, amenity groups, Community Interest Companies (CICs), trusts plus various other community partnerships and social enterprises, as well as City Councils. Whilst more work is needed to trial innovative ways of capturing festival experiences and atmospheres, perhaps the most significant methodological challenge is how best to capture the ongoing, longitudinal effects of festivals and events. Given the need to analyse programmes and portfolios, and the imperative to understand events in the plural, researchers need to think about how best to capture cumulative effects and legacies produced outwith the time-space of individual events. Only then will we be able to understand the wider effects of festivalisation.

Pandemic Disruptions and the Shift to Digital Space

As outlined in the preface, this edited collection emerged from the workings of the HERA funded FESTSPACE project which began in 2019. The specific genesis of many of the chapters in the book lie in a call for papers issued in early 2020 for a symposium sponsored by the Royal Geographical Society's (UK) Geographies of Leisure and Tourism Research Group (GLTRG). At this time, we had no idea that the world was about to be turned upside down by the Covid-19 pandemic. However, by March 2020 it was quickly becoming clear that festivals were under serious threat as governments issued public health guidelines that required social distancing and limited personal mobility. Shared space became something of an alien concept during the Covid-19 pandemic. Public health guidelines advised against sharing space, outside prescribed domestic units. Strict social distancing, 'contradict(s) everything that drives us as a social species' (Tonkin and Whitaker 2021, 2). For Courage (2021, 1) the pandemic has been at odds with 'the particularly urban design of collective occupation' and has 'taken from us our familiar collective social experiences'. It completely undermined the ethos of festivals and festivity, which is premised on communal interactivity (Falassi 1987). Having said that, the absence of festivity somewhat ironically fostered a new found appreciation of its importance in invigorating and enlivening the appearance, sounds and feel of city space, whether city-central or suburban, large or small scale, indoors or outdoors. City streets and squares unpopulated by social interactions and activities during the pandemic were vacant, empty and still.

As the pandemic passes and restrictions on using public space ease, it seems certain that festivals will return to parks, squares and arenas. Indications of this likely development emerged early on in the pandemic with numerous reports in cities and towns throughout Europe of spontaneous gatherings of people collectively creating and performing sociable public space, whether by dancing on balconies in Menorca (Villalonga-Olives, Kawachi, and Hernández-Aguado 2021) or by publicly displaying artwork on windows and garden railings in Dublin (Quinn 2021). Research during the pandemic pointed to a strong public appetite for the return of festivals (Peoples 2020). Undoubtedly, a desire for social connectivity is a key factor feeding this appetite. However, the effects of the pandemic will shape the return of festivals into the future, and while festivals and events will return to public space, there are unknowns and many unanswered questions.

Some of the chapters in this book raise concerns that prioritising inclusion might now become more problematic, given that the diversity of the festival populations in European towns and cities may have been depleted by the pandemic. In the UK, this is a particular concern given the demographic shifts associated with Brexit. Very obviously, the move to hybrid and online festival programming during the pandemic signalled the consolidation of virtual space as an additional important context for the inclusivity of festivals into the future. Florida, Rodriguez-Pose and Storpor (2021) argue that cities post-pandemic will experience a reconfiguring of urban space. In festival and event terms, this is likely to translate into investment in public spaces with, for example, the installation and upgrading of LED screens to enable events to function in hybrid form. Such investment is likely to be uneven, and highly dependent on the resources and political will existing at city, district and town levels, thus leading to new variations on the kinds of contested geographies already apparent throughout the interventions contained in this book. Undoubtedly, the rise of digitally enhanced festivals and events brings new opportunities in terms of expanding audiences, broadening the geographical breadth of programme inputs, extending the 'afterlife' of productions, and creating material for archives. However, somewhat counterintuitively, while digitisation makes it easier than ever for cities to create spectacles that animate spaces and create footfall, it does not inevitably foster inclusion. Simultaneously, another effect of the pandemic may have been to provide a space for reflection and a potential re-orientation of festival direction with inclusion in mind. Chapter 11, for example, suggests that the pandemic offers an opportunity for Edinburgh's festival managers and other city-based festivals stakeholders to 'shift focus towards stronger engagement with local communities', rather than prioritising external visitors and city centres. In focusing on more localised audiences and participants, it may be that festivals re-orient their activities to neighbourhoods and non-central areas. This has happened already in London. The Greenwich and Docklands International Festival received plaudits for taking performances into housing estates and suburban locations in 2020 with their 'On Your Doorstep' programme, introduced because of Covid-19. This was retained in 2021, notwithstanding the easing of restrictions. Another interpretation, however, is that for both festivals and an associated array of urban based stakeholders, more pressing financial imperatives may now take hold and strengthen the tendency to instrumentalise festivals to achieve financial returns and economic development in the years ahead. Irrespective of all these uncertainties, overall, the ongoing disruptive effects of the pandemic require, as Chapter 12 notes, that festivals and urban festival policymakers demonstrate a degree of 'adaptive capacity and resilience' (Wrigley and Dolega 2011, 2358).

Final Comments

This book has developed our understanding of cities as contested spaces by putting the interrelationships between festivals, urban public space and inclusion firmly on the research agenda. By foregrounding inclusion, this book has addressed an obvious gap in the literature and responded to calls for multiple actors – festival organisers, urban policymakers and academics alike – to conceive of festivals as potentially powerful tools to achieve social policy goals. In terms of future research priorities, there is a need to broaden enquiries to include different kinds of public space, including indoor sites. Public, cultural, institutional spaces such as libraries (as in Chapter 5), galleries, museums, and theatres are increasingly being festivalised too. Locating future studies here will advance our understanding of how festivals and events affect city spaces and the communities that use them. It will also prompt questions about the dynamic, yet under-acknowledged role, that festivals play in shaping urban cultural infrastructures. Equally, further work is needed on spaces like waterways, transport spaces, markets and religious buildings located in a variety of central and peripheral locations, to probe further into the kinds of geographical unevenness alluded to in Chapter 3. Various social and cultural groups have long standing associations with spaces like these and locating enquiries here would yield new insights into how, and by whom, urban spaces are constructed, controlled and experienced as festival and event spaces. As stated above, there is an obvious need for more research to be carried out on the enduring effects of staging festivals and events in urban spaces, in ways that move the focus beyond the time-bound staging of the actual event. Temporality arose as a key idea in several of the chapters in this book (e.g. 4, 9, 11) but it deserves to be prioritised so that we learn more about how the recurrent staging of events in particular spaces informs place associations and patterns of routine use, and shapes urban design decisions.

While these chapters were commissioned before the advent of Covid-19, there are indications throughout the book as to what the future might hold. The continued importance of festivals and events to the economies, societies and cultural lives of towns and cities is not in doubt. Indeed, it may well be that one of the effects of the pandemic is to further encourage festivalisation. The evidence presented in this book suggests that festivals and events will continue to (re)produce spaces and places in uneven and always contested ways. Hopefully further research can inform policies and practices that allow festive space to be 'democratic space where the performance of culture requires the interaction of artists, audience and locality' (Chalcraft and Magaudda 2011, 175).

References

Abascal, Maria and Delia Baldassarri. 2015. Love Thy Neighbor? Ethnoracial Diversity and Trust Reexamined. *American Journal of Sociology*, 121(3), 722–782.

Alves, Susana, Maria Di Gabriele, Saverio Carillo, Massimiliano Masullo and Luigi Maffei. 2021. Exploring the Soundscape and the Atmosphere of the Gigli di Nola Cultural Festival in Italy. *Emotions, Space and Society*, 41, 100848. https://doi.org/10.1016/j.emospa.2021.100848

Ballantyne, Julie, Roy Ballantyne and Jan Packer. 2014. Designing and Managing Music Festival Experiences to Enhance Attendees' Psychological and Social Benefits. *Musicae Scientiae*, 18(1), 65–83.

Bodnar, Judit. 2015. Reclaiming Public Space. *Urban Studies*, 52 (12), 2090–2104.

Boland, Philip, Brendan Murtagh and Peter Shirlow. 2019. Fashioning a City of Culture: 'Life and Place Changing' or '12 Month Party'? *International Journal of Cultural Policy*, 25(2), 246–265.

Carmona, Matthew. 2010. Contemporary Public Space: Critique and Classification, Part One: Critique. *Journal of Urban Design*, 15(1), 123–148.

Carter, Perry Labron. 2019. Looking for Something Real: Affective Encounters. *Annals of Tourism Research*, 76, 200–213.

Chalcraft, Jasper and Paolo Magaudda. 2011. Space in the Place. In Gerard Delanty, Liana Giorgi and Monica Sassatelli (Eds.) *Festivals and the Cultural Public Sphere*, pp. 173–189. Abingdon: Routledge.

Courage, Cara. 2021. What Really Matters: Moving Placemaking into a New Epoch. In Cara Courage (Ed.) *Routledge Handbook of Placemaking*, pp. 1–8. Abingdon: Routledge.

Curtis, Rebecca, 2011. What is Wangaratta to Jazz? The (Re)Creation of Place, Music and Community at the Wangaratta Jazz Festival. In Chris Gibson and John Connell (Eds.) *Festival Places: Revitalising Rural Australia*, pp. 280–293. Bristol: Channel View Publications.

Falassi, Alessandro. 1987. Festival: Definition and Morphology. In Alessandro Falassi (Ed.) *Time Out of Time*. Albuquerque, NM: University of New Mexico Press.

Fincher, Ruth, Kurt Iveson, Helga Leitner and Valerie Preston. 2014. Planning in the Multicultural City: Celebrating Diversity or Reinforcing Difference? *Progress in Planning*, 92, 1–55.

Florida, Richard, Andrés Rodriguez-Pose and Michael Storpor. 2021. Cities in a Post-COVID World. *Urban Studies*, 1–23. https://doi.org/10.1177/00420980211018072

Fraser, Trisnasari, Alexander H. D. Crooke and Jane W. Davidson. 2021. 'Music Has No Borders': An Exploratory Study of Audience Engagement with YouTube Music Broadcasts During COVID-19 Lockdown, 2020. *Frontiers in Psychology*, 12. https://doi.org/10.3389/fpsyg.2021.643893

Given, Lisa M. and Gloria J. Leckie. 2003. 'Sweeping' the Library: Mapping the Social Activity Space of the Public Library. *Library & Information Science Research*, 25(4), 365–385.

Häussermann, Hartmut and Walter Siebel. 1993. Die Politik der Festivalisierung und die Festivalisierung der Politik. In Hartmut Häussermann and Walter Siebel (Eds.) *Festivalisierung der Stadtpolitik. Stadtentwicklung durch große Projekte*, pp. 7–31. Opladen: Westdeutscher Verlag.

Healy, Ernest, Dharma Arunachalam and Tetsuo Mizukami. 2016. Social Cohesion and the Challenge of Globalization. In Ernest Healy, Dharma Arunachalam and Tetsuo Mizukami (Eds.) *Creating Social Cohesion in an Interdependent World*, pp. 3–31. New York: Palgrave Macmillan.

Howell, Francesca C. 2013. Sense of Place, Heterotopia, and Community: Performing Land and Folding Time in the Badalisc Festival of Northern Italy. *Folklore*, 124, 45–63.

Johansson, Marjana and Jerzy Kociatkiewicz. 2011. City Festivals: Creativity and Control in Staged Urban Experiences. *European Urban and Regional Studies*, 18, 392–405.

Kim, Wonyoung, Ho Mun Jun, Matthew Walker and Dan Drane. 2015. Evaluating the Perceived Social Impacts of Hosting Large-Scale Sport Tourism

Events: Scale Development and Validation. *Tourism Management,* 48, 21–32.

Lefebvre, Henri. 1991. *The Production of Space.* Trans. Donald Nicholson-Smith. Oxford: Basil Blackwell.

Lopez, Lucrezia. 2019. A Geo-Literary Analysis through Human Senses. Towards a Sensuous Camino Geography. *Emotion, Space and Society,* 30, 9–19.

Low, Setha and Alan Smart. 2020. Thoughts about Public Space During Covid-19 Pandemic. *City & Society,* 32(1). https://doi.org/10.1111/ciso.12260

Madanipour, Ali. 2010. *Whose Public Space? International Case Studies in Urban Design and Development.* Abingdon: Routledge.

Madanipour, Ali, Sabine Knierbein and Aglaee Degros. 2014. *Public Space and the Challenges of Urban Transformation in Europe.* New York: Routledge.

Mair, Judith and Andrew Smith. 2021. Events and Sustainability: Why Making Events More Sustainable is Not Enough. *Journal of Sustainable Tourism,* 29(11–12), 1739–1755.

Mehta, Vikas. 2019. The Street: A Fluid Place of Social Cohesion. In Patricia Aelbrecht and Quentin Stevens (Eds.) *Public Space Design and Social Cohesion: An International Comparison.* New York: Routledge.

Peoples, Glenn. 2020. Fans Are Ready for Concerts Once Pandemic Ends, Though Timing and a Vaccine Are Top of Mind: Survey. Billboard.com. Available at: https://www.billboard.com/pro/concerts-fans-return-corona virus-mrc-data-survey (accessed 21 February 2022).

Pløger, John. 2010. Presence-Experiences: The Eventalisation of City Space. *Environment and Planning D: Society and Space,* 28(5), 848–866.

Quinn, Bernadette. 2021. Digitally enhanced events in Dublin: Lighting up a future post-pandemic? Festspace.net. Available at: http://festspace.net /digitally-enhanced-events-in-dublin-lighting-up-a-future-post-pandemic (accessed 14 February 2022).

Quinn, Bernadette, Alba Colombo, Kristina Lindström, David McGillivray and Andrew Smith. 2020. Festivals, Public Space and Cultural Inclusion: Public Policy Insights. *Journal of Sustainable Tourism,* 29(12), 1875–1893.

Ronström, Owe. 2016. Four Facets of Festivalisation. *Puls – Journal for Ethnomusicology and Ethnochronology,* 1, 67–83.

Shields, Rob. 2003. *The Virtual.* London: Routledge.

Smith, Andrew. 2016. *Events in the City: Using Public Spaces as Event Venues.* Abingdon: Routledge.

St John, Graham P. 2001. Alternative Cultural Heterotopia and the Liminoid Body: Beyond Turner at ConFest. *Australian Journal of Anthropology,* 12(1), 47–66.

Tonkin, Alison and Julia Whitaker. 2021. Play and Playfulness for Health and Wellbeing: A Panacea for Mitigating the Impact of Coronavirus (COVID 19). *Social Sciences & Humanities Open,* 4(1), 2580–2911.

UN-HABITAT. 2016. Goal 11: Make Cities Inclusive, Safe, Resilient and Sustainable. United Nations un.org. Available at: http://www.un.org/sustain abledevelopment/cities (accessed 15 February 2022).

Villalonga-Olives, Ester, Ichiro Kawachi and Ildefonso Hernández-Aguado. 2021. Social Capital During the First Wave of the COVID-19 Outbreak: The Case of the Island of Menorca. *International Journal of Environmental Research and Public Health*, 18(23), 12720. https://doi.org/10.3390/ijer ph182312720

Wallstam, Martin, Dimitri Ioannides and Robert Pettersson. 2020. Evaluating the Social Impacts of Events: In Search of Unified Indicators for Effective Policy-Making. *Journal of Policy Research in Tourism, Leisure and Events*, 12(2), 122–141.

Wrigley, Neil and Les Dolega. 2011. Resilience, Fragility, and Adaptation: New Evidence on the Performance of UK High Streets During Global Economic Crisis and its Policy Implications. *Environment and Planning A*, 43(10), 2337–2363.

Editors and Contributors

Editors

Andrew Smith is Professor of Urban Experiences in the School of Architecture and Cities at the University of Westminster. His research addresses a key question: how do events affect the places and spaces that host them? Andrew's previous publications include two monographs on city events and two edited collections focused on the visitor economy. Alongside co-editing this book, he has co-authored a chapter that examines the festivalisation of London's parks, a subject he has researched as part of the FESTSPACE project.

Guy Osborn is Professor of Law at the University of Westminster and a Creative Director of the Soho Poly. He co-edits the Open Access *Entertainment and Sports Law Journal* and the Routledge monograph series *Studies in Law, Society and Popular Culture*. He is currently completing a book entitled *Olympic Laws* for Routledge. His contribution to this collection is as co-editor, and more specifically his contribution with Andrew Smith and Goran Vodicka focusing on London parks as part of the FESTSPACE project.

Bernadette Quinn is a Senior Lecturer at Technological University Dublin. She has a strong research interest in arts festivals and cultural events, having written extensively about the roles they play in transforming space, reproducing place and shaping identities. Her contribution to this volume is as co-editor, and as co-author with Theresa Ryan of the publicness of local libraries chapter. The material for this chapter came from research undertaken as part of the FEST-SPACE project.

Other Contributors

Pauwke Berkers is Professor Sociology of Popular Music in the Erasmus School of History, Culture, and Communication at Erasmus University Rotterdam, and Head of Department – Arts and Culture Studies. His research interests include inequalities in arts and culture. He is author of the monograph *Gender Inequality in Metal Music Production* as well as articles in *Gender & Society*, *Poetics*, *Cultural Sociology* and other journals on the sociology of music. His contribution to this collection – written with Britt Swartjes – is a chapter on how festivals organisers in Rotterdam deal with issues of diversity.

Kevin Burns is a Lecturer at Dundalk Institute of Technology, Ireland, and Director of the Institute's Tourism Research Group (TRg). His research focuses on the relationship between tourist behaviour and cultural festivals within destinations and places. Through these interests, Kevin's research has been published in a range of tourism journals, including *Journal of Travel Research* and *The European Journal of Tourism Research*. Collaborating with Daithí Kearney, here Kevin has written on locating an Irish traditional music festival in a city destination.

Alba Colombo is Associate Professor of Events and Sociology of Culture and currently she is Academic Director of the Culture and Events Management programs at Universitat Oberta de Catalunya. Her research focuses on the critical analysis of contemporary significance of cultural events, as social and cultural expressions, space of resistance and platform equity and rights. She is the principal investigator of the Barcelona FESTSPACE project team. Her contribution in this book focuses on the distribution of cultural events spaces in Barcelona.

Anna de Jong is a Senior Lecturer at the University of Glasgow. Her research interests focus on the relationship between tourism, events and place, guided by wider concerns of inequality and accessibility. Through these interests, Anna's research has been published in a range of tourism and geography journals, including *Annals of Tourism Research* and *Social & Cultural Geography*. Collaborating with Chloe Steadman, here Anna has written on atmospheres of belonging at Manchester's craft beer festivals.

John R. Gold is Honorary Senior Research Fellow at the Bartlett School of Architecture, University College London, and Professor Emeritus at Oxford Brookes University. He jointly edits *Planning Perspectives* and is author or editor of 23 books on urban-historical subjects. He is currently writing the final part of his trilogy on architectural modernism and, with Margaret Gold, a prequel to their book *Festival Cities* (Routledge 2020). Their contribution here examines the origins of the Venice Biennale and its historic and contemporary relationship to the city.

Margaret M. Gold is Senior Lecturer in Creative Industries at London Metropolitan University and also teaches at Goldsmiths, University of London. The joint editor of the journal *Planning Perspectives*, she has also published widely on urban cultural and historical issues, in particular examining the rationale and legacies of cities hosting mega-events. Her contribution here, written with John Gold, examines the origins of the Venice Biennale and its relationship to the host city.

Séverin Guillard is a Geographer and a Lecturer at the University Picardie Jules Verne. His research is mainly focused on cultural practices and power relations in cities, and he explores these issues through various topics (music, cultural policies, events) and countries (France, United Kingdom, United States). Séverin was a postdoctoral research fellow in the FESTSPACE project, and his contribution here, written with David McGillivray and Gayle McPherson, looks at the role of events in the design of squares, with a specific focus on the case of Glasgow.

Niclas Hell is a PhD candidate at the Centre for Culture, Sports and Events, University of the West of Scotland. His research focuses on evaluation of the social and economic values of cultural events and festivals. His contribution in this book looks at how public value analysis can be used to assess both the monetary and the social contributions of festivals.

Daithí Kearney is Co-Director of the Creative Arts Research Centre at Dundalk Institute of Technology. His research is primarily focused on Irish traditional music, dance and folk theatre, often with an emphasis on the expression of place and identity. His work has been published in a range of ethnomusicology, Irish Studies and Geography publications. Here, Daithí has collaborated with Kevin Burns to critically reflect on an Irish traditional music festival.

Katarzyna Kosmala is Chair in Culture, Media and Visual Arts at the School of Business and Creative Industries, the University of the West of Scotland, as well as a curator, and art writer. She researches heritage and identity, cultural labour and discourses of creativity and community in the context of a globalising network society, art production and enterprise, as well as gender and politics of representation.

Eleni Koumpouzi is a PhD candidate at the School of Business and Creative Industries at the University of the West of Scotland, and a curator and an artist.

Her research interests include engagement and inclusion in heritage environments. In this book her contribution is a study of participation in two community festivals, the integration and opportunities which they offered to transient communities, and the livescape as an emerging framework.

Stephen Kinsella is Professor of Economics at the University of Limerick, Head of Department, and Co-Director of the Bsc/Msc in Immersive Software Engineering. Stephen is a Senior Fellow at the Melbourne School of Government at the University of Melbourne and Fellow at the Rhodes Centre for International Finance at Brown University. His contribution here is as a co-author on a chapter on Limerick's bid to be European Capital of Culture.

Michael Luchtan is a PhD candidate at the Arts and Humanities Faculty of the Universitat Oberta de Catalunya in Barcelona. His research interests include the role that events and associations play in transmission of embodied rhythms across borders. His contribution to this book, a critical examination of events' usage of the public resources of space and time, is a result of his participation in the FESTSPACE research project.

David McGillivray is Professor of Event and Digital Cultures, and Deputy Director of the Centre for Culture, Sport and Events in the School of Business and Creative Industries at University of the West of Scotland. His research focuses on a critical reading of the contemporary significance of events and festivals (sporting and cultural) for the achievement of wider economic, social and cultural externalities. His contribution here focuses on the contemporary role of the urban square as a stage for events.

Gayle McPherson is a Professor in Events and Cultural Policy and Director of the Centre for Culture, Sport and Events in the School of Business and Creative Industries at the University of the West of Scotland. She researches and is interested in the societal impact from, and of, hosting events from a policy perspective. Her (two) contributions here focus on the public value analysis of events, and the use of public spaces for events as part of the FESTSPACE project.

Niamh NicGhabhann is Senior Lecturer in History at the University of Limerick. Her research focuses on histories of Irish art and architecture, and she has a particular interest in the dynamics of public space and the public sphere, in cultural institutions, and in festivals and festivity. She was the founding course director of the award-winning MA Festive Arts programme at the University of Limerick. Her contribution here is as a co-author on a chapter on bidding to be European Capital of Culture.

Esther Oliver-Grasiot is a researcher based at the Academy of Arts and Humanities, Universitat Oberta de Catalunya, Barcelona, Spain. She was a researcher and coordinator of the FESTSPACE project in Barcelona (January 2020–June 2021). Her contribution here, written with Alba Colombo and Michael Luchtan, analyses the locations and types of events staged in Barcelona.

Gareth Rice is a Human Geographer with interests in the development of cities, regions, and the sustainability of rural communities. His research has focused on how these places have sought to reinvent themselves to become more competitive in the context of globalisation; the social, political, economic, cultural, and environmental challenges they face; and the role of public policy in addressing the challenges. He is currently a Lecturer in Social Sciences at the University of the West of Scotland.

Elaine Rust is a Principal Lecturer in Marketing at the University of Portsmouth. Her research is mainly concerned with exploring social and economic impacts of small-scale cultural events, with a particular focus on how they support town centre vitality. Elaine's interests also include place branding through the medium of events and festivals. Her work has been published in the *Journal of Policy Research in Tourism, Leisure and Events* and her contribution to this book examines how local policymakers implement an events-focused policy, sometimes with unanticipated consequences.

Annmarie Ryan is Senior Lecturer in Marketing at the Kemmy Business School, University of Limerick. Her research is concerned with understanding the complexities of space and place (digital and analogue) in the shaping and reshaping of markets. Her work has appeared in *Human Relations, Marketing Theory*, and *Industrial Marketing Management.* She is currently co-editing a special issue in the *Journal of Business Ethics* on 'Place and Partnerships'. Her contribution here is as a co-author on a chapter on bidding for European Capital of Culture.

Theresa Ryan is a lecturer at the Technological University Dublin and is Programme Chair for the MSc Event Management programme. Her research interests include heritage interpretation, memory and identity, events and social inclusion, and she has a particular interest in commemoration and commemorative events. Collaborating with Quinn, her contribution here is a chapter which explores how functioning as a festival venue informs the publicness of local libraries. The material for the chapter came from research undertaken as part of the FESTSPACE project.

Chloe Steadman is a Lecturer in Marketing at Manchester Metropolitan University, and researcher at the Institute of Place Management. Her research interests concern consumer culture, the body, time, place, atmospheres and qualitative methods. Her work has been published in a range of journals, including *Marketing Theory, Social & Cultural Geography*, and *Consumption, Markets & Culture*. Collaborating with Anna de Jong, her contribution here explores ambient power and atmospheres of belonging at Manchester's craft beer festivals.

Britt Swartjes is a PhD candidate at the Erasmus School of History Culture and Communication at Erasmus University, Rotterdam. Her research engages with sociological approaches to music in the city, focusing on how music festivals can be public spaces where people from diverse backgrounds meet. Collaborating with Pauwke Berkers, her contribution to this book examines how music festival organisers deal with issues of diversity.

Louise Todd is an Associate Professor in Festivals and Events, based in Edinburgh Napier University's Tourism and Languages Group. Louise's research interests include arts and cultural tourism, and festivals. She is particularly interested in stakeholder engagement in these settings, alongside visual and art-based methods. Louise has published her research in journal articles, book chapters, and as exhibited artworks. Her contribution considers the place-myth and semiotics of Edinburgh as the festival city from community and management stakeholders' perspectives.

Goran Vodicka is Senior Lecturer in Architecture at Sheffield Hallam University. His research is mainly focused on diversity and inclusion in public space as well as socially-engaged spatial practice and pedagogy. Goran was a Research Fellow on the London based part of the FESTSPACE project and his contribution here, written with Andrew Smith and Guy Osborn, explores the festivalisation of London's parks.

Index

Lightning Source UK Ltd.
Milton Keynes UK
UKHW020611151022
410503UK00010B/128